"This is not your typical book that approaches Jesus' resurrection from an evidential or soteriological angle. Clifford and Johnson argue that, as crucial as it is, the Cross of Christ is not the center of Christianity. Rather, the authors go beyond evidential studies in order to relate Jesus' resurrection to a holistic, full-orbed approach to Christian theology, mission, and discipleship, as well as the daily life of the believer. Further, they find echoes of resurrection in many areas of popular culture, including religion, mythology, music, movies, and even comic books. The 'Spiritual Audit' questions after each chapter serve to challenge personal or group reflection. The authors' command of popular ideas serves to challenge modern culture, giving this volume a highly distinctive appeal."

Gary R. Habermas, Distinguished Research Professor,
Liberty University & Theological Seminary

"Have we lost seeing the significance of the resurrection for the Christian? *The Cross Is Not Enough* argues that we have and then fruitfully walks us through the ways we can think about resurrection. It correctly contends we need to regain an emphasis on the resurrection. Hopefully in doing so, we can see how the resurrection and the cross work together to form the core of Christian hope."

Darrell L. Bock, Research Professor of New Testament Studies,
Dallas Theological Seminary

"Christians say that they believe in the cross and the resurrection, but sadly many Christians focus almost exclusively on the cross and regard the resurrection as an appendix that God tacked on to prove that Jesus died for their sins. In this book, Ross Clifford and Philip Johnson show that many Christians are operating with a half-told Easter story. Contrary to popular notions, they explain how the Christian faith is a resurrection faith in the risen Lord. Without the resurrection, Jesus's death is martyrdom not an atonement, without resurrection Jesus is just another dead Jew not the Lord of Glory—the cross derives its meaning and power from the empty tomb. Clifford and Johnson describe what it means to have an authentic resurrection faith that drives theology, missions, spirituality, thinking about culture, and church life. If you want to know what to tell your church on Easter Sunday beyond the annual droning of 'well, there really is life after death, ain't that nice,' if you want to know how to be 'children of the resurrection' as Jesus said, then for the love of Martha, read this book!"

Dr. Michael F. Bird, author, *Are You the One Who Is to Come? The Historical Jesus and the Messianic Question*;
lecturer in Theological Studies, Crossway College

"Ross Clifford and Philip Johnson live in a land where Christians are a small minority. They have thought long and hard about what it means to bear witness to Jesus Christ when he is little known and less understood. Their reflections on the meaning of the resurrection will be exceedingly helpful to disciples who want to understand their own faith and relate it to a post-Christian culture."

Gerald R. McDermott, Jordan-Trexler Professor of Religion, Roanoke College; author, *God's Rivals: Why Has God Allowed Different Religions?* and *World Religions: An Indispensable Introduction*

"Arguing brilliantly for the resurrection to take back its place on center stage, this book carries readers on an exhilarating journey through wonderfully unexpected territory. Immensely practical, with its twelve zones of resurrection living and apologetic concern for skeptics, and grounded solidly in Scripture, it marshals astonishingly wide-ranging evidence for the resurrection in culture. Both skillful practitioners, the authors wear their scholarship lightly and pepper analysis with a wealth of personal stories and audit exercises. I completed this book with fresh conviction and excitement about living the resurrection. I know I shall preach differently now."

Michael Quicke, Charles Koller Professor of Preaching & Communications, Northern Baptist Theological Seminary, Chicago

"Without the resurrection, Jesus' death would scarcely have atoned for anyone. So why do treatments of the resurrection focus so little on its theological meaning and practical applications for life in this world? Clifford and Johnson rectify this problem, but they do much more, showing how the resurrection is the answer to the aspirations of proponents of most of the major religions of the world and of much of the current popularity of 'new spiritualities.' From movies to novels to near-death experiences, our authors show amazing command of an array of cultural developments about which all readers, Christians or otherwise, should be concerned. A must-read!"

Craig Blomberg, Distinguished Professor of New Testament, Denver Seminary, Colorado

"Inspired by faithfulness to the Bible, and informed by a sophisticated understanding of contemporary culture and the spiritual search of our generation, Ross Clifford and Philip Johnson have written a book that is both challenging and empowering for all who are concerned to communicate the heart of the Christian faith to today's people."

John Drane, author, *The McDonaldization of the Church* and *Introducing the New Testament*; fellow of St John's College, University of Durham

"While the title might turn some heads, this book should in fact transform our living. It is a call to responsible and transformational faith flowing out of the hope and reality of the resurrection. Knowing Jesus and believing in Jesus is not enough. The resurrection calls us to believe and live out the practices and values that Jesus and the resurrection point and empower us toward. A powerful addition to the call to discipleship and faithful living as followers of Jesus Christ."

Gary Nelson, president, Tyndale University College and Seminary, Toronto, Canada

"Clifford and Johnson are right to want to explore not only how the resurrection has been understood in the past, but why it can contribute to the care and growth of the whole person. A resurrection-centric worldview is concerned not only with proofs of an empty tomb but also with a distinctly Christian form of holism. The church today is ready for a book that sees the resurrection as central to the formulation of a holistic Christian worldview for post-Christendom today.

"Knowing Ross Clifford personally, I know that this subject is not merely an intellectual exercise for him. It is something that emerges from his own very holistic worldview. A book by him on this subject won't just be stimulating and ground-breaking, it will crackle with vitality and integrity."

Michael Frost, author, *Exiles: Living Missionally in a Post-Christian World*; coauthor, *The Shaping of Things to Come* and *ReJesus*; Morling College, Sydney

"Clifford and Johnson argue that the Good News of Christianity is not just the cross—that Jesus died for our sins. The Good News is the cross and the resurrection—Jesus died and he rose from the dead. They make a compelling case, one that influences every aspect of Christian living and thinking. A must-read."

Terry Muck, Dean of the E. Stanley Jones School of World Mission and Evangelism Professor of Missions and World Religions, Asbury Theological Seminary

THE CROSS
IS NOT ENOUGH

Living as Witnesses to the Resurrection

ROSS CLIFFORD AND PHILIP JOHNSON

BakerBooks

a division of Baker Publishing Group
Grand Rapids, Michigan

Published by Baker Books
a division of Baker Publishing Group
P.O. Box 6287, Grand Rapids, MI 49516-6287
www.bakerbooks.com

Printed in the United States of America

Library of Congress Cataloging-in-Publication Data
Clifford, Ross.
    The cross is not enough : living as witnesses to the Resurrection / Ross Clifford and Philip Johnson.
        p.   cm.
    Includes bibliographical references (p.   ).
    ISBN 978-0-8010-1461-1 (pbk.)
    1. Resurrection. I. Johnson, Philip, 1960– II. Title.
BT873.C65 2012
236'.8—dc23   2011025655

Unless otherwise indicated, Scripture quotations are from the New Revised Standard Version of the Bible, copyright © 1989, by the Division of Christian Education of the National Council of the Churches of Christ in the United States of America. Used by permission. All rights reserved.

Scripture quotations marked Message are from *The Message* by Eugene H. Peterson, copyright © 1993, 1994, 1995, 2000, 2001, 2002. Used by permission of NavPress Publishing Group. All rights reserved.

The internet addresses, email addresses, and phone numbers in this book are accurate at the time of publication. They are provided as a resource. Baker Publishing Group does not endorse them or vouch for their content or permanence.

12   13   14   15   16   17   18   7   6   5   4   3   2   1

Ross dedicates this book to Paris and Scarlett.
May the quest for life bring you to know the
awe of Christ's resurrection power.

Philip dedicates this book to Ruth, Christine, and Elwyn,
three women who live by Christ's resurrection power.

Contents

Abbreviations

ANF	Ante-Nicene Fathers		FemTh	Feminist Theology: The Journal of the Britain and Ireland School of Feminist Theology
AnthQ	Anthropological Quarterly			
AThR	Anglican Theological Review			
BibSac	Bibliotheca Sacra		GOTR	Greek Orthodox Theological Review
CBQ	Catholic Biblical Quarterly			
CH	Church History		Greg	Gregorianum
ChrLit	Christianity and Literature		HeyJ	Heythrop Journal
CoJ	Concordia Journal		HTR	Harvard Theological Review
Colloq	Colloquium		ICMR	Islam and Christian-Muslim Relations
CRJ	Christian Research Journal			
CSQ	Cistercian Studies Quarterly		IDB	The Interpreter's Dictionary of the Bible. Edited by G. A. Buttrick. 4 Vols. Nashville, 1962.
CSSRB	Council of Societies for the Study of Religion Bulletin			
CTJ	Calvin Theological Journal		IDBSup	Interpreter's Dictionary of the Bible: Supplementary Volume. Edited by K. Crim. Nashville, 1976.
CTQ	Concordia Theological Quarterly			
CTR	Criswell Theological Review		IJCS	International Journal of Children's Spirituality
CulRel	Culture and Religion			
CulSt	Cultural Studies		IJPsyRel	International Journal for the Psychology of Religion
CurTM	Currents in Theology and Mission			
			IJSCC	International Journal for the Study of the Christian Church
Di	Dialog: A Journal of Theology			
Did	Didaskalia		IJSysTh	International Journal of Systematic Theology
DiJMTh	Dialog: A Journal of Mormon Theology			
			IRM	International Review of Mission
EMQ	Evangelical Missions Quarterly			
			JAAR	Journal of the American Academy of Religion
EvQ	Evangelical Quarterly			
ERT	Evangelical Review of Theology		JAMusSoc	Journal of the American Musicological Society
			JBL	Journal of Biblical Literature
ExAud	Ex auditu		JBV	Journal of Beliefs and Values

JCA	Journal of Christian Apologetics	NPNF	Nicene and Post-Nicene Fathers
JCR	Journal of Contemporary Religion	Numen	Numen: International Review for the History of Religions
JET	Journal of Empirical Theology	PSCF	Perspectives on Science and Christian Faith: Journal of the American Scientific Affiliation
JETS	Journal of the Evangelical Theological Society		
JJRelStud	Japanese Journal of Religious Studies	RelArts	Religion and the Arts
		RelS	Religious Studies
JPara	Journal of Parapsychology	Ren	Renascence
JPTh	Journal of Pentecostal Theology	ResQ	Restoration Quarterly
		RTR	Reformed Theological Review
JRA	Journal of Religion in Africa	SBET	Scottish Bulletin of Evangelical Theology
JRCE	Journal of Research on Christian Education		
		SciCB	Science and Christian Belief
JRH	Journal of Religious History	SecCent	Second Century: A Journal of Early Christian Studies
JSHJ	Journal for the Study of the Historical Jesus		
JSNT	Journal for the Study of the New Testament	Spec	Speculum: A Journal of Medieval Studies
		SJT	Scottish Journal of Theology
JSSR	Journal for the Scientific Study of Religion	SR	Studies in Religion/Sciences Religieuses
JTS	Journal of Theological Studies	STJ	Sacred Tribes Journal
JTSA	Journal of Theology for Southern Africa	SVSQ	St. Vladimir's Seminary Quarterly
LitTh	Literature and Theology	Them	Themelios
LQ	Lutheran Quarterly	ThTo	Theology Today
LTJ	Lutheran Theological Journal	TOTC	Tyndale Old Testament Commentary
LW	Luther's Works		
Miss	Missiology: An International Review	TS	Theological Studies
		TynBul	Tyndale Bulletin
Mort	Mortality: Promoting the Interdisciplinary Study of Death and Dying	UUC	Unitarian Universalist Christian
		VC	Vigiliae Christianae
MusW	Muslim World	VT	Vetus Testamentum
NICNT	New International Commentary on the New Testament	WBC	Word Biblical Commentary
		WTJ	Westminster Theological Journal
NICOT	New International Commentary on the Old Testament		
		WW	Word and World
NRSV	New Revised Standard Version		

List of Figures

Prologue

Attention All Readers!

What's so special about our book as compared to other books about the resurrection? Unlike other books, ours is a one-stop-shop book that seeks to cover facets of the resurrection as it applies to daily life, mission, culture, discipleship, theology, and the church. It also uniquely challenges today's entrenched mindset that focuses exclusively on the cross as the lynchpin for Christian living. It is written for the followers of Jesus, whether they are church leaders, teachers, or those wondering if there is anything beyond the cross. Until we refocus on the resurrection all the chatter about a new day for the church is paralyzed. Here's an overview of some of the main ingredients to our book:

- We believe in both the death and physical resurrection of Jesus, but we believe that the church has seriously neglected the resurrection.
- Very few Christians realize that while the cross is vital, Jesus's resurrection is the theological lynchpin for every aspect of our living, thinking, and doing. We will offer fresh insights about the holistic effect of the resurrection. This new way of thinking involves a paradigm shift from the cross to the resurrection, and it asks what the appropriate symbol is for today's church.
- The resurrection can show us how to move beyond feeling like alienated nonpersons. We will offer an understanding of the resurrection that is about being empowered to live.
- The theology of resurrection is at the heart of Paul's worldview and the apostles' missionary messages in Acts. Resurrection theology is also present in the Old Testament, though scholars have traditionally underestimated it.

- The resurrection is important for our understanding of who Jesus is. It also affects ethics, creation, human rights, spiritual growth, pastoral care, and missions.
- We take you outside the safe walls of the church and examine numerous signs of the resurrection in pop and high culture, in the natural world, and in other religions and postmodern spirituality. We explore how these signs find fulfillment in the resurrected Jesus.
- This book is *not* just another apologetic defense of Jesus's resurrection. Yes, we will make a case for the resurrection in the context of missions, evangelism, and apologetics, but that is not the primary focus of the book.
- Unlike some books on the resurrection, we offer practical advice on how to talk to new spirituality seekers, atheists, and skeptics.

Each part of this book takes a different approach to understanding the resurrection and its implications for our lives, and we think you'll understand us best if you take the time to study this book in its entirety. We hope you find your reading both stimulating and enjoyable.

PART ONE

THE RESURRECTION GRID

If the Church had contemplated the Empty Tomb as much as the Cross of its Lord, its life would have been more exhilarating and its contribution to the world more positive than has been the case.

George Beasley-Murray[1]

1

The Resurrection Is the Lynchpin

Why do you keep filling gallery after gallery with endless pictures of the one ever-reiterated theme, of Christ in weakness, Christ upon the cross, Christ dying, most of all Christ hanging dead? Why do you concentrate upon that passing episode, as if that were the last word and the final scene, as if the curtain dropped upon that horror of disaster and defeat? Paint Christ not dead but risen, with His foot set in scorn on the split rock with which they sought to hold Him down! Paint Him the Conqueror of death! Paint Him the Lord of Life! Paint Him as what He is, the irresistible Victor who, tested to the uttermost, has proved Himself in very deed mighty to save!

Tommaso Campanella[1]

Is your view of the cross too big, and your understanding of resurrection too small? Do you see Jesus's atoning death as the "last word" about the gospel and salvation? Have you ever wondered what Paul meant when he said that Christ was raised for our justification (Rom. 4:25)?

These provocative questions flow from Tommaso Campanella's four-hundred-year-old complaint about a surfeit of paintings on the crucifixion. Campanella's complaint suggests that there may be forgotten truths about the resurrection that ought to be rediscovered. The shortage of resurrection-themed artwork is just the tip of the iceberg, but it indicates that the resurrection is often taken for granted. Worse than that, the beneficial effects of the way of the risen Jesus are neglected in many important aspects of Christian life and thought.

Out of Many, One Photograph

Philip was walking by a bus shelter one day that displayed a large advertisement for the environmental charity work of Oxfam. From the distance he could see a photo of a young guy, along with the slogan, "Who is really facing the impacts of climate change?" What was fascinating about the ad was that close-up the photo of the young guy faded and his silhouette was replaced by a jigsaw puzzle of smaller photos. Depending on your vantage point, you could see lots of micro photographs or one large one.

The church today, certainly in the West, is at the crossroads, and it is understandably picking at micro pieces of the puzzle: we must be missional, we must preach repentance, we must be moral, we must pray for revival, we must be kingdom-oriented, we must connect with post-Christendom spirituality, we must have multisensory worship, we must rediscover the fundamentals, we must challenge Islam. This book will argue, however, that the church needs to step away from the smaller pieces of the puzzle and take time to recognize and focus upon Christianity's lynchpin. We are convinced that there is a major theological picture that the rest of these little theological pictures hang from, and that this theological lynchpin is in fact the resurrection.

Jesus's world was also plagued with similar kinds of micro struggles, and the early faith community understood the small puzzle pieces. They had a different methodology for ministering to the Jews, as against the Greeks. They had to face religious challengers and discover the fundamentals of their faith. Yet the speeches and sermons in the book of Acts show that, even as they dealt with the micro questions, the early church did not lose sight of the larger picture.

FIGURE 1.1
The Centrality of the Resurrection in Acts[2]

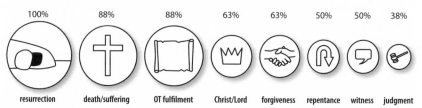

Figure 1.1 is reproduced by permission from Mark Barry, "The Centrality of the Resurrection in Acts," *SALT* magazine (Autumn 2009): 10.

Figure 1.1 shows us that the resurrection received the greatest emphasis in Acts and therefore should have the central place in our theology. *However, the central photo has instead become the cross.* The early church would not have agreed, as Walter Martin explains:

What was the central truth of the early apostles' preaching? What was the stimulus to the miraculous growth of the early church? What was the energizing force which spread the gospel across the face of the earth? The answer to all these questions is the Resurrection of Jesus Christ. "He is risen!" was the victorious cry of the early Christians, and they spread it to the ends of the earth.[3]

Martin's comments struck a chord with us recently, when, at a church-planting conference, we heard speaker after speaker argue that the key Christian message is the cross with the atonement. Not once was the resurrection mentioned.[4] We intend to demonstrate in this book how the micro pictures—morality, repentance, discipleship, apologetics, mission—although valid, only have full meaning when they have the resurrection as their fountainhead.

Hammering on the Door

When Martin Luther hammered up his ninety-five theses on the castle door at Wittenberg his catchcry was " 'The Cross, the Cross' and there is no cross."[5] Elsewhere he spoke of the cross as being the test of everything, and there are Christians today who also esteem that "test" as if it is the theological be-all and end-all.[6] Luther had numerous historical and theological reasons for his overriding concern about Christ's atoning death, and the Protestant Reformers who followed in his wake likewise emphasized the cross as *the* symbol of salvation, justification, and atonement. Many seem to have forgotten, though, that in his sermons and commentaries Luther also spoke about the centrality of Jesus's resurrection:

> When one wants to preach the Gospel, one must treat only of the resurrection of Christ. For this is the chief article of our faith. . . . The greatest power of faith is bound up in this article of faith. For if there were no resurrection, we would have no consolation or hope, and everything else Christ did or suffered would be futile.[7]

> It is not enough that we believe the historic fact of the resurrection of Christ. . . . But we must believe also the meaning—the spiritual significance of Christ's resurrection, realizing its fruits and benefits, that which we have received through it, namely, forgiveness and redemption from all sins.[8]

Those fascinating remarks point to a side of Luther's thinking that is not often emphasized. He certainly believed in both Jesus's death and physical resurrection. In theology such balances are called both/and, in contrast to either/or. However, Luther believed that the resurrection involved more than just an affirmation that Jesus rose from the dead on Easter Sunday. Luther saw the need for believers to embrace it and apply its "fruits and benefits."

The principal benefit he emphasized is the resurrection's importance for our salvation. Luther could hardly have missed this point because Paul himself said that Christ was raised for our justification (Rom. 4:25). *This is a forgotten truth we must rediscover: the cross is not enough because it is not the "last word"!*

We need to be both/and believers concerning the death and physical resurrection of Jesus. When the church separates the cross and the resurrection, its theology, mission, ethics, and pastoral ministry needlessly suffer from lopsidedness. That imbalance is just one reason—among several others—that compels the authors of this book to hammer up our statement on the castle door. Our catchcry is, " 'The Resurrection, the Resurrection' and there is no resurrection." In light of the past five hundred years of church history, maybe Luther—if he was walking around today—would even join us in our "protest."

An Unraveled Garment

Before you doubt what we have just said, please bear with us for the next few pages. We feel strongly that the church has lost its grip on the *centrality* of the resurrection. We are not saying that the resurrection has vanished from the church's confession; indeed, most Christians have believed in the physical resurrection of Jesus Christ. It is affirmed in church gatherings in creeds, liturgies, prayer-books, and catechisms, and in the lyrical content of hymns and choruses. The resurrection is affirmed in formal doctrinal statements of churches, parachurch ministries, and missionary agencies.

The resurrection is deeply embedded in the fabric of Christianity, but it is generally only talked about in isolated contexts and often in truncated form. Take a moment to consider three examples in which the resurrection surfaces in diverse but isolated church settings (and even there it is not as it should be):

- **Easter Sunday**: We all affirm Jesus's victory over death in the liturgical calendar. Actually, every Sunday is a symbolic reminder of the day of Christ's resurrection: the early church chose to worship on Sunday instead of the Sabbath or Friday (the day Jesus died). Each Sunday ought to be a time of celebratory renewal because of the resurrection. Easter is supposed to be a perpetual experience: "Sunday is not just a commemoration of a historical event but a realization (both the awareness and a making real) of union with the risen and reigning Christ by the power of the Holy Spirit."[9] That is why we see so much emphasis on the resurrection in the book of Acts. As part of our conversation with you we put this question: *Are church practices about the resurrection only about a past miraculous event that is, like Christmas, to be celebrated annually?*

- **Pastoral Comfort**: You probably have experienced resurrection talk in pastoral words of comfort at funeral services. One snag, though, is that most Christians tend to be very fuzzy about the general resurrection of humanity. N. T. Wright has recently highlighted that many do not really understand that the resurrection of the dead involves us on a new earth, but instead believe in an immortal soul or a disembodied spirit that floats on the clouds.[10] How many pastors comfort us by connecting our holistic resurrection to the "new earth" (Isa. 65:17; 2 Pet. 3:13; Rev. 21) and how that impacts us now? We put it to you: *Is the resurrection only concerned with comforting us in grief to bolster our hope for a spiritual life after death?*

- **Answering Skeptics**: Like us you have probably read books that stoutly defend the testimony and historical evidences for the resurrection. The discipline of apologetics involves giving reasons for faith, and the resurrection looms large in that genre. Apologetics texts play their part in encouraging faith, rebutting debunkers, and assisting in our witness to non-Christians. Apologists argue that the evidences show that Jesus has risen from the dead, and the resurrection is the sign that he is the Son of God (John 20:24–28; Rom. 1:4). Most apologists stop at this juncture, though, and do not explain the implications of a resurrection-based faith. We put it to you: *Why do apologists boldly declare that "you can believe" but then almost never bother to explain what practical difference the resurrection makes in the lives of those who follow Christ?*

Jesus's resurrection *should* be the focal point on Easter Sunday, as well as in pastoral comfort and answering skeptics, but those settings are still not enough! Like a woolen sweater, the resurrection consists of many threads that unite in a seamless garment. Unfortunately, individual threads are unraveled from parts of the Bible and then tailored to suit a given context: pastoral comfort for bereavement, and apologetic evidences for bolstering faith in the Easter event. Often the threads are disconnected when they should be referred back to the whole garment.

Our great worry is that the church has failed to understand the resurrection comprehensively and to apply it holistically to life. *The apostles understood the resurrection as the lynchpin of Christianity—integral to every aspect of life and thought—and therefore, so should we.*

Resurrection Eclipsed

All of us are familiar with a solar eclipse, during which the moon passes between the earth and sun. From our vantage point on the earth the moon's shadow completely obscures from vision the disk of the sun. During an eclipse only the sun's corona is visible around the moon's rim. Just as the moon's shadow obscures the sun, the cross often overshadows the resurrection. The resurrection has not been intentionally obliterated—after all even in a theological eclipse the corona is still present. It does, however, mean that a full view of the resurrection is obscured.

Solar eclipses have a short duration and then the sun reappears, but the resurrection has been eclipsed for a long time and remains stuck in the shadows. We are not satisfied with the corona of the resurrection peeping from behind the cross. We want to see the entire disk of the resurrection shining across the theological, missional, ethical, and pastoral sky! We will now briefly illustrate how the eclipse of the resurrection is unwittingly perpetuated.

John Stott: An Elder Statesman

We esteem John Stott as an elder statesman among Protestant and Anglican-Episcopalian evangelicals. One of the first books that we give to new seminary students is Stott's book *The Cross of Christ*.[11] Stott has many valuable things to say about the atonement and redemption that we affirm, and we want to emphasize that we are *not* calling for a reappraisal of the atonement.[12] Instead, we want everyone to think about what constitutes Christianity's lynchpin—is it the cross or the resurrection?

Nobody can doubt that Stott is a both/and believer in the death and physical resurrection of Jesus:

> The church was founded on the resurrection. Disprove the resurrection, and the church would have collapsed.[13]

However, Stott has always swayed towards making the cross preeminent by insisting that it is at the heart of the gospel:

> The cross is at the center of the evangelical faith. Indeed, as I argue in this book, it lies at the center of the historic, biblical faith, and the fact that this is not always everywhere acknowledged is in itself a sufficient justification for preserving a distinctive evangelical testimony.[14]

According to Stott the message of the cross is preeminent because it liberates and transforms us.[15] The way we understand ourselves before God and lead our lives under Jesus's lordship is shaped by the cross:

> It would be seriously unbalanced to proclaim either the cross without the resurrection (as I am afraid Anselm did) or the resurrection without the cross (as do those who present Jesus as a living Lord rather than as an atoning Savior). It is therefore healthy to maintain an indissoluble link between them. . . . [T]he gospel

includes both the death and resurrection of Jesus, since nothing would have been accomplished by his death if he had not been raised from it. Yet the gospel emphasizes the cross, since it was there that the victory was accomplished.[16]

Consider what Stott told the Southern Baptist Al Mohler shortly after *The Cross of Christ* was published:

> I think we need to get back to the fact that the cross is the center of biblical Christianity. We must not allow those on the one hand to put the incarnation as primary, nor can we allow those on the other hand to put the primary focus on the resurrection. Of course, the cross, the incarnation, and the resurrection belong together. There could have been no atonement without the incarnation or without the resurrection. The incarnation prepares for the atonement and the resurrection endorses the atonement, so they always belong together. Yet the New Testament is very clear that the cross stands at the center. Of course, we preach the whole of biblical religion, but with the cross as central.[17]

Nobody should be very surprised that the cross is paramount in Stott's theology. In *Evangelical Truth* he summarizes what others have had to say about the leading features of evangelicalism: "Each began with the supremacy of Scripture and the majesty of Christ, particularly of his cross."[18] In this regard Stott also relies on the earlier efforts of the Scottish theologian James Denny. Denny wrote the classic work *The Death of Christ* at a time when he felt that the cross and atonement needed to be defended and emphasized. Like Stott he valued the resurrection, but reading his text shows that his lynchpin is the cross. In fact he felt free to add the atonement to the primitive speeches in Acts:

> Even if the book of Acts were so preoccupied with the resurrection that it paid no attention to the independent significance of the death, it would be perfectly fair, on the ground of this explicit reference of St. Paul, to supplement its outline of primitive Christian doctrine with some definite teaching on atonement.[19]

Stott has consistently placed the message of the cross at the center so that we rejoice in Christ in both hope and suffering in this present life.

Resurrection and Justification

When it comes to justification Stott insists that the cross alone stands for Jesus's atonement for sin and the defeat of death.[20] He limits the resurrection to the vindication of the cross:

> What the resurrection did was to vindicate the Jesus whom men had rejected, to declare with power that he is the Son of God, and publicly to confirm that his sin-bearing death had been effective for the forgiveness of sins.[21]

Stott's explanation of the relationship between the cross and resurrection, in our view, is inadequate. As we explore in chapter 11, his suggestion that the resurrection endorses the atonement barely scratches the surface of its theological importance. Even though he believes there is an indissoluble unity between the cross and resurrection he fails to do justice to Paul's deeper thinking about it. Michael Bird implies that Stott's understanding of the resurrection in relation to justification is superficial and reductionist:

> In reading the Pauline epistles one is struck with the suspicion that the resurrection is far more intrinsic to justification than merely comprising an authentication that our justification has taken place at the cross.[22]

The Cross of Christ shows very clearly that Stott does not see Jesus's resurrection as the theological lynchpin, but instead views the cross as the center of biblical Christianity. We accept that the cross is an indispensable part of the gospel's message of reconciliation, and that it shows us the obedience, humility, and servanthood of Christ and forgiveness of sin in his atoning death. However, we see the effect of the resurrection as having a holistic and harmonious impact that the cross alone cannot deliver. The resurrected Jesus transforms us through both cross and resurrection. The cross alone is not enough, whereas the implications of the resurrection as the theological lynchpin are all-encompassing.

The Legacy

The Lausanne movement is a worldwide network of evangelicals whose founding fathers are Billy Graham, Leighton Ford, and John Stott. Its 1974 covenant is a well-rounded creedal statement adopted by many church and parachurch groups. While Lausanne papers have strongly affirmed the fact of the resurrection of Jesus, little appears to be said about its status as the holistic lynchpin of Christian belief. The cross-centered redemptive message eclipses the resurrection.

The *Evangelical Review of Theology* dedicated an edition to foreshadowing the 2010 Lausanne world forum in Cape Town, South Africa. The collected papers had the theme of the "whole gospel," which represented a project of Lausanne's theological working group. One paper placed the emphasis on "The Gospel and the Achievement of the Cross" and discussed in some detail various theories of the atonement. The author's clarion call was for both "Christians and churches to be thoroughly cruciform."[23] Other papers reflected on the gospel in biblical revelation, the gospel in the power of the Spirit, and the gospel and ethics, but surprisingly it is difficult to find any clear or explicit connection of these themes to the resurrection.[24] The resurrection is clearly not at the center in these papers, and the uncanny sense they convey is that the resurrection's sole purpose is to allow one to live out the sufferings of the cross.

So, the resurrection is present in various Lausanne documents but it has lacked any real theological grunt. In a separate publication released a few months prior to the Cape Town gathering, Christopher Wright made this telling statement that further reinforces the status of the cross as the centerpiece:

> And we must evangelically proclaim the glories of God's redemptive achievement in the Cross and resurrection of Jesus of Nazareth—as God's victory over evil in *all* its dimensions. There would be no gospel without the Cross. Indeed, all blessings of the gospel, from personal salvation through Christ's death in our place to the reconciliation of all creation flow from the Cross. The Cross stands at the heart of the Lausanne Movement; the key scriptural text for Cape Town 2010 is "God was in Christ reconciling the world to himself" (2 Cor. 5:19).[25]

Ross was one of four thousand delegates that went to Cape Town. He saw the cross-centered emphasis sustained in "The Cape Town Commitment," a paper prepared in advance by theologians worldwide. Our concerns had been raised before the conference. Then, at Cape Town and afterwards there was a small group that exchanged some healthy robust critique of the published paper. Chris Wright did hear the plea, and the confessional commitment was then changed from seeing the cross as the great saving act where God had the victory over Satan, death, and all evil powers to now include the resurrection in that saving act.[26] This stronger reference to the resurrection in the Lausanne paper is a small but vital step in the right direction, and it is heartening to witness the changing of strongly held views! So we encourage other theological gatekeepers to follow Lausanne's example and embrace the centrality of the resurrection that we are advocating in this book.

Darrell Bock's Tricky Challenge

By way of contrast to Stott, and Denny, we were delighted by observations that the New Testament scholar Darrell Bock made to us in a recent conversation. Darrell told one of us about a "trick" assignment he sets for one of his seminary classes. He tells the students he will give an A+ for an essay that sets out the theories of the atonement from the sermons in the book of Acts. He then laughed and indicated, "I then tell the class that no one has ever received the A+ because the Acts speeches do not unpack atonement theories."

Of course his aim is to shock these freshmen, who like most Christians, automatically assume the sermons of the early apostles were atonement-based. As we mentioned above, they are not, and the central theme of the speeches and sermons in the book of Acts is in fact the resurrection. Darrell also insists that evangelicals have a "lost gospel," as their teaching substantially stops at the cross and neglects our new life in Christ. The cross is a means to that glorious end but it is not an end in itself!

Chapel Sermon

Another curious example of cross-centered Christian belief occurred in a chapel service at our seminary. The preacher was talking on Romans 8:28–39 in order to pastorally address Paul's assurance that in Christ we are more than conquerors. His practical and inspiring sermon reminded us of Paul's words, "For I am convinced that neither death, nor life, nor angels, nor rulers, nor things present, nor things to come, nor powers, nor height, nor depth, nor anything else in all creation, will be able to separate us from the love of God in Christ Jesus our Lord" (vv. 38–39). Then there came the crunch: "How can we be sure of this truth?" he asked. His answer was, "The cross!" The cross is the justification, the warrant of our "victory" in Christ. His concluding illustration called us to the cross.

The interesting part of this anecdote is that this preacher "gets" the resurrection. In a friendly chat after chapel one of us asked him, "Why did you conclude with the cross?" He admitted that falling back on the cross is what we do instinctively, but on reflection he concurred that Paul's gate to his "high" Christology in Romans 8 begins with the cross (v. 32) but climaxes with the resurrection: "It is Christ Jesus, who died, yes, who was raised, who is at the right hand of God, who indeed intercedes for us" (v. 34). God is batting on humanity's side against the adversary—hardship, death, whatever—and the resurrection in this passage is our ultimate confidence for such a promise. An interesting conversation followed amongst some of the faculty as to how our beliefs have been so shaped that, without thinking, we go into autopilot and rest in the cross—even when Scripture demands otherwise.

Transatlantic Heritage

The emphasis on the cross as a defining feature of modern evangelical belief is something that has been observed by historians on both sides of the Atlantic. In Great Britain David Bebbington notes there is a pattern of four prominent convictions that consistently appear in history as distinguishing emphases among British evangelicals: the Bible, conversion, personal activism, and preaching of the cross ("crucicentrism").[27] The same emphases can be traced throughout the history of the British colonies of Canada, Australia, and New Zealand.[28]

A similar observation is found in George Marsden's discussions on how to define American evangelicals. Marsden indicates that it is possible to describe evangelicalism in two different ways. One understanding sees it as "a conceptual unity" of beliefs and practices, while another regards it as a dynamic movement inside modern Protestantism. Marsden lists its five principal unifying features: the authority of the Bible, the historical aspect of God's

Two Roman Catholic Scholars Speak[29]

Catholic Stations of the cross stop at the burial of Jesus and fail to include a station of the Resurrection. But there should be little need to pile up further evidence to establish the fact that Western Christianity has concentrated on Calvary and neglected to celebrate adequately the resurrection.

Gerald O'Collins

Our present hope in the face of all the challenges of life, suffering and death, is an effect of the resurrection. Unless *that* had happened, hope would at best be a repressive optimism, or an accommodation to routine despair. But the effect of the resurrection is to see the world and to live in it otherwise. . . . In fact it is so taken for granted that the originality of the resurrection's effect on the life of faith can be forgotten. What originally made all the difference gradually becomes a remote presupposition, only vaguely affecting the way we understand God, ourselves and the world itself.

Anthony Kelly

saving work in the Bible (the cross), salvation and conversion in Christ, the priority of evangelism and missions, and a spiritually changed life.[30] Neither Bebbington nor Marsden mentions the resurrection as a central belief of evangelicalism.

Continuing Eclipse

An overemphasis on the theology of the cross leads to a lack of a resurrection-based perspective in other areas of theology such as ethics, pastoral ministry, and spiritual growth. We focus on these matters more in chapter 2 but below are a few brief examples.

Theology and Spirit

When theologians overemphasize the outpouring of the Holy Spirit at Pentecost, we end up seeing only the "corona" of Jesus's resurrection. Both Jesus's resurrection and ascension took place prior to Pentecost, and these events are often presupposed by theologians who concentrate on the work of God's Spirit on the church. It is understood that the Spirit of the risen Jesus has been poured out on the church, but the centrality of the resurrection message in Acts is curiously bypassed.[31] Resurrection theology recedes as the gift of the Holy Spirit and the use of spiritual gifts take center stage. A lopsided emphasis on exuberant aspects of faith can obscure the holistic role of the resurrection in the pilgrimage of the church.

Missions

In the book of Acts Paul's missionary messages are grounded in declaring the risen Christ to both Jew and gentile. David Bosch observes:

> The most common summary of the early church's missionary message was that it was witnessing to the resurrection of Christ. It was a message of joy, hope, and victory, the first fruit of God's ultimate triumph over the enemy. And in this joy and victory believers may already share.[32]

Bosch believes that for our era "the central theme of our missionary message is that Christ is risen," so that as a consequence "the church is called to live the resurrection life in the here and now and to be a sign of contradiction against the forces of death and destruction."[33]

In the literature of today's missions, however, the resurrection is often *not* the central holistic theme. Models of modern missions typically present two polarized tasks: the imperative to make disciples by announcing salvation in the cross of Christ, and the imperative to pursue social justice. These twin tasks have been thought of as either/or imperatives rather than holistically as both/and. N. T. Wright says that "the split between saving souls and doing good in the world is a product not of the Bible or the gospel but of the cultural captivity of both within the Western world."[34] The missing link that justifies and sustains the both/and for the church's mission is the resurrection. Wright puts it in a nutshell by saying that the church's mission is "nothing more or less than the outworking, in the power of the Spirit, of Jesus' bodily resurrection."[35]

Interreligious Dialogue

The same problem ensues in the church's encounter with other religions. Timothy Tennant's imaginary evangelical roundtable dialogues with Hindus, Buddhists, and Muslims do not have the message of the resurrection at their center. He mentions the resurrection in one sentence in dialogue with Buddhists and in just a page in dialogue with Muslims. In the Islamic context Tennant is quite right to address disbelief about the crucifixion, which in turn has a bearing on the resurrection as an event. He echoes the common mantra about the death of Christ being the "central feature of the Christian message."[36]

A spectrum of views abounds in Roman Catholic literature on interfaith dialogue. William Thompson and Anthony Kelly stand out as Catholics who acknowledge the need to reshape interreligious dialogue based around the resurrection.[37] In the Anglican tradition Bishop Michael Nazir-Ali has said:

The cross may rightly be regarded as the climax to this work of atonement, reconciliation and sacrifice, but it cannot be separated from the rest of Christ's life. . . . The resurrection of Jesus Christ from the dead is part of the apparatus of the incarnation. I find it very difficult to believe people who claim to have a strong doctrine of the incarnation, but who have a weak doctrine of the resurrection.[38]

Nazir-Ali is probably pointing at theologians who reduce the resurrection to symbolic, existential, and nonmiraculous categories. Yet he is basically concerned about lopsidedness in mission and dialogue where the resurrection is eclipsed.

In summation, Jesus's resurrection is mentioned as a potential topic for dialogue with Buddhists, but it is taken for granted.[39] The evidence for Jesus's resurrection is sometimes debated between Muslims and Christians, but little else is said.[40] It is also debated with Jehovah's Witnesses, who deny Christ's deity and insist that Jesus was raised an incorporeal spirit.[41] Bearing witness to Jesus's resurrection occasionally occurs in response to popular alternative spiritualities that proclaim reincarnation.[42] Overall, though, the resurrection is not holistically emphasized in interreligious dialogue.

Ending the Eclipse

Not everyone is happy about the eclipse of the resurrection. A global movement seems to be stirring as scattered voices from diverse theological traditions protest. Here is a small sample of those voices.

Billy Graham's Grandson

Tullian Tchividjian, who is a grandson of Billy Graham and a church leader in his own right, calls for the connection to be made between the resurrection and the way of Jesus:

The gospel is both individual and communal. The gospel is not simply the story of Christ dying on the cross for sinners. It also involves Christ rising again as the first fruits that will eventually make all things new. There is a universal dimension to the gospel.[43]

Tchividjian astutely proclaims that it is wrong to displace the resurrection because doing so is not in continuity with the way of Jesus.

Voices from the Academy

Beth Felker Jones at Wheaton College emphasizes that the theology of bodily resurrection is crucial for discerning the fault lines of Western culture's distorted attitudes about the human body and gender. She asserts that "the doctrine of bodily resurrection is not peripheral to the Christian gospel" but rather is "determinative of any theological attempt to rightly conceive not only human bodies as created, but also human persons as redeemed."[44] She maintains that the resurrection stands as a significant bulwark against dualist cosmologies. It is holistic precisely because resurrection involves the entire human being, renewed and embodied. It affirms a fundamental point in the creation: that both females and males are equally made in the image and likeness of God. Jones uses the resurrection as the critical framework from which contemporary concerns of feminist thought on gender politics may be addressed.

Several British scholars have highlighted the centrality of the resurrection in specialized studies. In the "Bible Speaks Today" series Paul Beasley-Murray writes that "the resurrection is the first article of the Christian faith and the demonstration of all the rest."[45] Oxford University philosopher Richard Swinburne sees the evidences of Christ's resurrection as a crucial matter that must be faced in the philosophy of religion.[46] N. T. Wright has galvanized discussions on the historical and theological significance of Christ's resurrection in New Testament studies.[47] Wright also challenged a wider lay-Christian readership on how they understand the resurrection as it relates to life in God's kingdom in the here and now as well as life beyond the grave.[48] Scottish New Testament scholar I. Howard Marshall laments, "It is a remarkable fact that there are many monographs on the theology of the death of Christ but very few by comparison on the theology of his resurrection."[49] Marshall is one voice among several who highlight the centrality of the resurrection in redemption and justification.

American Reformed theologian Richard Gaffin sees the resurrection as integral to any understanding of redemption.[50] He maintains that the church has been so preoccupied with both the event and salvific meaning of Jesus's death that the saving "significance of his resurrection has been largely overlooked."[51] The Bible indicates that because Jesus was resurrected so we too will experience resurrection. Gaffin reminds us about the importance of Jesus being raised as the firstfruits from the dead: "The two resurrections, though separated in time, are not so much separate events as two episodes of the same event, the beginning and end of the one and the same harvest."[52] Gaffin argues that when we emphasize the resurrection there is no danger of the cross and atonement vanishing. Rather, the cross must be rightly understood (as Paul did) through the powerful lens of Jesus's resurrection.

We have already mentioned the Australian Roman Catholic theologian Anthony Kelly, who takes the view that Jesus's resurrection is "the focal event affecting all Christian faith and theology."[53] A decade before Kelly's book, two interdisciplinary symposiums convened in North America. One involved evangelical scholars concentrating on the resurrection in the New Testament.[54] The other brought Roman Catholic, mainline Protestant, and evangelical scholars together to examine the resurrection in biblical studies, theology, philosophy of religion, the history of preaching, and ethics.[55] Some fifty years ago the theological contributions of Roman Catholics such as François-Xavier Durrwell and Lutherans like Walter Künneth and Wolfhart Pannenberg preceded the current-day ferment.[56]

Voices from the Pulpit and Internet

Besides the voices in academia, some younger voices in the pulpit are joining in the protest against the eclipse of the resurrection. Sam Allberry's *Lifted* is a cursory outline for youthful readers of four life themes viewed through the resurrection: assurance, transformation, hope, and mission.[57]

Mark Driscoll and Gerry Breshears discuss Jesus's resurrection in both *Vintage Jesus* and *Doctrine*.[58] Neither book is exclusively devoted to the theology of resurrection but both contain chapters that concentrate on a traditional-style apologetic defense for the Easter event. In *Doctrine* there is also brief discussion about what a resurrection is, as distinguished from revivification of a corpse, soul sleep, and reincarnation.[59] Driscoll and Breshears point out that Jesus's resurrection "has put death to death."[60]

They have been joined by Adrian Warnock, who advocates a balanced understanding of the cross and resurrection. In *Raised with Christ* Warnock correctly sees the effect of the resurrection spilling over into various facets of life: prayer, confronting sin, calling others into discipleship, showing mercy and care for others, and our hope for the life-to-come. He feels that because of their neglect of the resurrection Christians have "meager" expectations about life, and he delivers this apt punchline: "The resurrection is far from being something we only benefit from in the future!"[61] We welcome these popular writers who seem to be arguing that the resurrection has both the apologetic and theological lynchpin status.[62]

Driscoll and Breshears and Warnock in their books quote John Stott as saying that:

> Christianity is in its very essence a resurrection religion. The concept of resurrection lies at its heart. If you remove it, Christianity is destroyed.[63]

This quote in turn has circulated among numerous blogs. The three authors just mentioned and the bloggers all fail to supply a bibliographical reference to the document where Stott originally made this statement.

On the surface this quote makes it look like Stott sees the resurrection as the theological lynchpin. But we hunted down the quote to try to understand its context and found that it comes from *Christ the Controversialist*, where Stott talks about skepticism on the resurrection. The Sadducees, like many modern-day skeptics, doubted Jesus on the resurrection. Upon closer examination, we found that Stott's quote about the resurrection fits within an apologetic context and not in a broader theological sense.[64] Our conversations with some close fans of Stott confirmed that we were not incorrect in our reading of him.

Driscoll, Breshears, and Warnock seem to assume that Stott ranks the resurrection as the theological center, but as we have shown, this is not so. Stott is not a chameleon and makes it very clear in *Christ the Controversialist* that in his theology the cross is preeminent:

> Although God's mercy is seen in the whole saving career of Jesus, and although in that saving career His birth, life, death, resurrection, ascension and gift of the Spirit belong inseparably together, yet the New Testament states that what He did to put away sin was to die. It was on the cross that He bore them in His own body, paying their penalty.[65]

Bloggers who rely on Driscoll and Warnock as trusted sources do not realize they are using a decontextualized quote that is at odds with Stott's larger theological position.

A Word from the Jewish Community

It is worth noting that the importance of the general resurrection of humanity is resurfacing as a matter for crisp debate outside the Christian community, in Jewish contexts. The Harvard University Jewish scholar Jon D. Levenson has challenged modern-day scholarly doubts about the importance of the doctrine of bodily resurrection in the Hebrew Bible. He has also questioned the diminution of belief in resurrection among contemporary Jews as belief in the immortality of the soul commands more loyalty in many quarters of today's Judaism.[66]

Back-to-Front Book

Over a decade ago we presented a popular and practical theology of the resurrection.[67] So we feel encouraged by the recent contributions of those who want the eclipse of the resurrection in popular Christian belief to end. Yet in most books we still see micro pictures, while the personal experiential effect of the resurrection is glaringly absent from most (but not all) discussions. Some books do address practical and personal matters but concentrate on the benefits of the resurrection for the individual.

Any discussion about the centrality of the resurrection must bridge the gap between Christians and the world beyond the church's walls. Christians need to be prodded out of their comfortable conformity to internal piety, their attraction-to-my-local-church models of revival, and the distortions that come from being captive to middle-class values. We intend for our journey of exploration in this book to partly bridge this gap by providing some practical illustrations and equipping skills to help us live and serve others.

We are not calling just for a refocus on the resurrection; we are calling for an understanding of the resurrection as the lynchpin of Christianity.

Our book is structured in four parts, with the material presented back-to-front. For the discerning eye there is a subtle "logic" embedded in the presentation so that it can be read cover-to-cover, and we recommend that approach to you. However, the linear format of books now competes with the nonlinear construction of the Internet. So those who love the hyper-real Internet can zigzag by choosing chapters of topical interest, such as those dealing with pop culture, myth, and selfhood, but you really must read everything.

Part 1 delivers our conclusions about Christianity's lynchpin. The present chapter has identified the contrast between a cross-centered position and a resurrection-based Christian theology. Chapter 2 provides a resurrection grid that demonstrates the shape of the resurrection and shows how it "works" as the lynchpin. There we outline twelve resurrection zones for living, which illustrate how the resurrection affects every aspect of life and thought. By using a combination of scriptural data and personal anecdotes we illustrate how the resurrection reshapes our consciousness and behavior at both the individual and communal level in the tasks of serving and ministering in the midst of massive cultural change. Our third chapter takes up both practical and theoretical concerns about the resurrection in apologetics. The chapter considers how different personality types in churches correlate to attitudes about apologetics. Readers will find some traditional apologetic material here, but we will also offer a fresh take on a resurrection-centered apologetic in conversations with post-Christendom searchers.

Part 2 involves working backwards from today into the past. We start by exploring signs of the resurrection in different facets of today's culture: art, music, film, TV, novels. Examining different beliefs about the afterlife helps us to better understand our society, so we illustrate afterlife beliefs through blockbuster movies, as well as outlining which major and new religions are open or closed to the idea of resurrection. We also look at the resurrection signs found in the creation and the idea of general revelation. New experiments with forms of selfhood characterize our era and so we outline them in light of the theology of resurrection. Then we examine how myths of dying-and-rising gods open up new conversations between Christians and their friends. In the last section of part 2 we take a peek at what Christians have thought about the resurrection in different epochs of church history.

In part 3 we continue the back-to-front theme as we turn to the Bible and climax the book with what is for us our ultimate authority. We start with the New Testament and then look at the resurrection in the Old Testament. The fourth and final part of the book is our symbolic gesture for renewal: our resurrection theses for the third millennium.

Resurrection and Worldview: A Way of Life

One of today's certainties is that when a group of friends gather at Starbucks for a serious chat there will be a "battle" about worldviews. A worldview is understood as a set of beliefs or a framework that refers to the way a person interprets the patterns of life. How someone sees their place in the world is expressed through their actions, aspirations, and convictions. These things give shape to the more formal beliefs that people have about the nature of reality, personhood, knowing and relating, values and purpose.[68] While the postmodern intelligentsia insists that there are no worldviews or that what passes for a worldview is just a power discourse, others are convinced that many incompatible worldviews are competing for primacy. For us this raises a big question: if there is any kind of legitimate worldview, what would be the shape of it?

Today's emerging, eclectic alternative spiritualities, perhaps surprisingly, offer a worldview focused on universal connecting myths. For example, Oprah partakes of a worldview that is eclectic but still involves drawing on common stories and symbols. It is possible, as we will show later on, that the idea of resurrection connects very well with the stories and symbols present in numerous religions and alternative spiritualities.

James Sire's fine primer, *The Universe Next Door*, illustrates the work still to be done with regard to worldviews. Sire admirably hones in on critical defects in non-Christian worldviews.[69] While he commendably draws attention to God's grandeur, the lynchpin of the resurrection is missing from his defense of theism and his rebuttal of other worldviews. We believe the Christian worldview involves much more than cognitive belief and affirmations. It is about our formation as followers of Jesus at both the individual and communal level. It is about who and what we love.[70] So in this book we will discuss worldview in a more holistic sense and seek to present the resurrection as not just a concept or doctrine, but as the paradigm by which we must live.

Don't Misunderstand Us

In light of what we have said so far, especially about concerns over the church's tendency toward lopsidedness with the cross, we do not want to be misunderstood: *We affirm that the death of Jesus on the cross is very important.* We are not belittling the agony and horror of the cross or downplaying the theological importance of atonement. In fact we want to underscore the point that Paul was right in saying that "the sufferings of Christ are abundant for us" (2 Cor. 1:5). Let us be very clear about what we are *not* doing in this book:

- We are not questioning the theological altercation over the cross that happened during the Reformation and Counter-Reformation.

- We are not dismissing or undermining the vital theological reflections that emerged from the Reformers about Jesus's suffering, the substitutionary atonement, and salvation.

- We are not entering into the contemporary debates about Paul's view of Jewish law and justification as found in the writings of James Dunn, E. P. Sanders, and N. T. Wright.[71]

Images of Renewal

If nothing else we want this book to be a transforming agent that offers a message for everyone. The holistic message of the resurrection overcomes our emphasis on the micro pictures, and we have found images of its message of empowerment in unexpected sources.

The first example comes from Tommaso Campanella, who gave us our opening quote. Campanella (1568–1639) was in many ways the provocative and edgy kind of guy many of us secretly admire and wish to be.[72] He was a maverick Dominican philosopher who bucked the system, participated in political conspiracies, fell afoul of the Inquisition but pretended to be insane and so escaped execution, spent much of his life in jail, protested about the sins of the institutional church, envisaged a Utopian society years before Thomas More, wrote poetry, dabbled in astrology, and defended Galileo's right to question cosmology.

As we discovered from the quote that opened this chapter, Campanella protested the lack of artistic representations of the resurrected Christ in his day. The matter must have bugged him greatly because he also composed a sonnet called "The Resurrection," in which he protested about our "blindness" to the power and joy of the resurrection:

> If Christ was only six hours crucified
> After years of toil and misery,
> Which for mankind He suffered willingly,
> While heaven was won for ever when He died;
> Why should He still be shown on every side,
> Painted and preached, in nought but agony,
> Whose pains were light matched with his victory,
> When the world's power to harm Him was defied?
> Why rather speak and write not of the realm
> He rules in heaven, and soon will bring below
> Unto the praise and glory of His name?
> Ah foolish crowd! This world's thick vapours whelm
> Your eyes unworthy of that glorious show,
> Blind to His splendour, bent upon His shame.[73]

Despite the deficit of artworks about the resurrection, it is possible to find some remarkable sculptures of the living risen Christ in unexpected places. Several years ago, we came across an alternative spirituality magazine produced in a small town on the edge of a rainforest. The magazine's editor, Mal, wrote about a visit to the Philippines in which he saw the thousands of people who live in shanties on a huge rubbish dump. He witnessed disease, death, and little hope there, but he also stumbled across a church with a healing center. Jesus's way was not central to Mal's own worldview but he nonetheless noticed something that made a deep impression: the chapel was adorned with the risen Christ with outstretched arms. He recognized that the resurrected Christ shows us God's concern for every aspect of human life.[74]

Can any of us conjure up a picture of Rio de Janeiro without immediately thinking of the image of Jesus on the mountain overlooking the city? This is probably the most obvious image of the welcoming embrace of the risen Jesus. It made an enormous impact on the vampire novelist Anne Rice in her spiritual journey from skepticism:

> Suddenly the clouds broke, revealing the giant figure of Jesus Christ above us, with His outstretched arms. The moment was beyond any rational description. . . . I had come thousands of miles to stand here. And here was the Lord. The clouds quickly closed over the statue; then broke and revealed the statue again. How many times this happened I don't remember. I do remember a kind of delirium. . . . I didn't acknowledge faith in these moments at the foot of the statue. But something greater than creedal formulation took hold of me, a sense that this Lord of Lords belonged to me in all his beauty and grandeur.[75]

We watched the telecast of the 2004 wedding ceremony of Frederik the Crown Prince of Denmark to Mary the Crown Princess in the Lutheran Cathedral at Copenhagen. As the cameras zoomed in on the happy couple and the minister our eyes were drawn to a magnificent statue of Christ with arms open wide. The pedestal is engraved with Matthew 11:28 (Message): "Are you tired? Worn out? Burned out on religion? Come to me. Get away with me and you'll recover your life. I'll show you how to take a real rest."

In each of these sculptures the figure of the embracing resurrected Jesus is depicted. Yet each one has a specific nuance. One is speaking of overcoming the evil of oppression and poverty. Another is cosmopolitan. The third is intimate. Each is an empowering symbol that incorporates the truth of the cross. It enhances the Easter Friday image of forgiveness and servant-hood, and signifies joy, hope, acceptance, and personal renewal. We need to deepen our repository of symbols and images so that death motifs do not marginalize the resurrection symbols that speak of new birth, new life, and new hope. It's the resurrection—a resurrection reformation—that the Spirit is stirring amongst us.

Spiritual Audit

1. Are the values you hold or the value statements of your group based on the resurrection?

2. Do your personal or group strategies connect to the various dimensions of the resurrection?

3. Does your own statement of faith or that of your group give prominence to the resurrection?

4. Do your prayers focus on the resurrection?

5. Do the devotional and spirituality books that you read give prominence to the resurrection?

6. Apart from theologically defending the resurrection, do you or your group live your life without its anchoring message?

2

The Resurrection Effect

Yours, Mine, and Ours

It is not sufficient merely to refer to the resurrection. It is the preacher's duty to change his hearers with the reality of the resurrection here and now.

Paul N. Tarazi[1]

As Easter approached, I began rehearsing the importance of Jesus' resurrection. I knew that for Paul and the other New Testament writers, there could be no Christianity without it. Yet one day as I was walking back to my dorm, it dawned on me that the gospel as I understood it had no need for Jesus to be raised from the dead. The story of salvation as I had learned it was, in its entirety, about the Cross. I would teach other students about the Romans Road to salvation and the Romans 6:23 bridge diagram. What each of these captured beautifully was that we had a sin problem that God overcame with the Cross of Christ. But each presentation also omitted the Resurrection entirely.

J. R. Daniel Kirk[2]

To his great shock Daniel Kirk realized one day that he was stuck in a very disturbed headspace. Before he became a New Testament scholar Kirk served in a parachurch campus ministry that sponsored evangelism and discipleship. Like many of us Kirk had rote-learned an evangelistic message about the gospel: God created us for a relationship, we sinned, in God's plan of redemption he sent Jesus who died on the cross, and we may receive forgiveness and salvation by repenting of sin and trusting in Jesus. It suddenly occurred to Kirk that this memorized message was so cross-centered that Jesus's resurrection had become irrelevant!

The Great Subversion

Kirk's personal story illustrates our great concern that Jesus's resurrection is being downplayed. Pick up a handful of different gospel tracts. While their titles and formats vary, they all look like they have been baked in the same oven. Lay them side by side and you will see that they point to the message of the cross, while the resurrection is often conspicuously missing.[3]

The problem, though, is not just found in tracts. Basic discipleship courses that are designed for new converts can also be a boon. We know many people have been wonderfully helped in such programs, but what worries us is that discipleship courses often give a lopsided view of the resurrection. Usually there is just one lesson using a few gospel passages to show that the disciples talked to the risen Jesus. Alternative explanations for the resurrection, like the swoon theory, the theft of Jesus's corpse, and mass hallucinations, are discredited. A popular trilemma argument to demonstrate Jesus's claims to divinity then follows. By a process of elimination Jesus is either a liar, a lunatic, or really is the Lord. With the liar and lunatic options eliminated the lesson concludes that the resurrection validates Jesus's claim to be the unique Son of God.

Even though those details are valuable, it is odd that basic discipleship courses do not teach any theology of the resurrection. New converts are not shown that Jesus's resurrection is connected to our justification (Rom. 4:25), and nothing further is said about it as the theological lynchpin. Instead, the way of discipleship is centered on the cross alone. The great subversion, then, is that the resurrection becomes an appendix to Easter. Its meaning and application to life, thought, and praxis are diminished. Recently a seminary graduate heard us outlining the problem of the great subversion. He had tears in his eyes and told us, "I've only ever seen the cross-side of the coin. Today I feel I've just been liberated by the resurrection-side of the coin."

Figure 1.1 showed that the resurrection has a 100 percent strike rate in the speeches in Acts. Today we tend to relegate the resurrection to the functional role of a postage stamp on an envelope. Unless you are into philately, you don't pay much attention to the stamp. What really matters is not the stamp (resurrection) but the letter (cross) that is inside the envelope. The stamp merely represents the official paid seal authorizing the letter's delivery. Gary Habermas, who has written more than a dozen apologetics books on the resurrection, is worried that not much else is being said about it:

> Christians should always be willing to investigate areas which potentially illuminate the glorious event of Jesus' resurrection. Many (if not most) evangelical studies on the resurrection appear to stress apologetic interests. . . . [E]vangelicals also need to explore other meaningful avenues of study with regard to the resurrection of Jesus. . . . [T]he interface between the resurrection of Jesus and the practical Christian life needs to be explored in much more detail.[4]

In this chapter we shift attention from the "postage stamp" mentality and concentrate on the deep interface between Jesus's resurrection and our way of life. We will explain the deep interface by exploring the resurrection in twelve zones of practical theology. We realize that some of the zones can be found in other areas of theology (e.g., creation and incarnation), but our key point is that *all twelve zones are only united and buttressed by the resurrection.*

Twelve Resurrection Zones for Living

What if Paul had been asked to jot down on a beer-coaster the essence of his message? We wonder if 1 Corinthians 15 is what Paul would write, because it is an incredibly significant part of his message. As scholars tell us, verses 3–5 represent one of the earliest confessional statements about the resurrection.[5] What would Paul think of our tendency to downplay the resurrection? He would not mind the liturgical procession that makes up the famous Stations of the Cross; however, he would be very puzzled that the fourteenth and final station leaves us with the burial of Jesus. He would be asking, "Okay, where is the 'station' of the resurrection?"

The resurrection opens us up to twelve practical zones for living that derive from Jesus's message of God's kingdom. These twelve zones, which could form the basis for a station of the resurrection, need to be integrated into the authentic way of discipleship that pursues wonder, joy, justice, and mercy. Dietrich Bonhoeffer said that Jesus calls us to die to our own self and values, but the call to discipleship is also about a new life.[6] The zones of discipleship that we are called into demonstrate a newness of life that can only be lived out by the power of the spirit of the risen Jesus. Figure 2.1 shows the twelve resurrection zones that we will explore in detail below.

FIGURE 2.1
Twelve Resurrection Zones for Living

- forgiveness
- whole person
- empowerment
- future hope
- eschatology
- Eden breaks in
- confidence
- face of God
- ethics
- judge/justice
- new community
- mission

Zone 1: Forgiveness

The starting point is zone 1, which centers on the resurrection assuring us of divine forgiveness. Most people have heard of Scott Peck (1936–2005), the psychiatrist and self-help guru. His book *The Road Less Travelled* was the book of the 1980s, but in the following decade his life changed. Peck came to our city as the headline speaker at a conference, and the place was packed to the rafters with people. What new pearls of wisdom would he offer? He spoke of how his journey in life had led him to an encounter with Christ, and he blew the audience away as he hit the nail on the head about the reality of sin:

> One of the reasons I very gradually gravitated toward Christianity is that I came to believe that Christian doctrine has the most correct understanding of the nature of sin. It is a paradoxical, multidimensional understanding, and the first side of the paradox is that Christianity holds that we are all sinners. We cannot not sin. There are a number of possible definitions of sin, but the most common is simply missing the mark, failing to hit the bull's-eye every time. And there's no way we can hit the bull's-eye every time.[7]

We discover from Paul in 1 Corinthians 15:15–17 that the resurrection is the divine *yes* to forgiveness. There is an undeniable unity to the cross and resurrection, but everything has to be read through the grid of the resurrection. Paul suggests that if Christ is not arisen then our faith is futile and we are still in our sins. We can build on this idea by dwelling on Romans 4:25 where Paul taught that Christ was raised from the dead for our justification. The resurrection shows us by moving beyond the Old Testament that there is a new day where no further sacrifices for sin are needed. As well, the resurrection shows that Jesus's death was big enough to cover all sin. We will look more at this passage in chapter 11.

The idea of the cross without the resurrection is very sobering. A caller once rang Ross's radio program and asked this provocative question: "Is there any sin too big that God cannot forgive?" There is always a deep story hiding behind such a question. Two weeks beforehand the caller and her son had had an almighty row over nothing in particular. Her son, who was dysfunctional in some ways, lived in his own apartment near her house. His father had left them years ago. She could not sleep all night, and the next day she visited the apartment and found that her son had taken his own life. She pleaded, "I'm asking for both my son and myself. Is there a sin too big that God cannot forgive?" Ross responded that through the resurrection we see God's confirmatory *yes* to forgiveness: we are not stuck in a moment that we cannot get out of—and the resurrection is what assures us that we can be forgiven.

Shortly afterwards at a Gideons' Convention Ross retold the above story. A woman at this convention came forward to say that her own story was not dissimilar. All her life she had rested on the cross. Now, she said, she was liberated. She understood the resurrection and for the first time in her life she could move beyond being "stuck in a moment." If Jesus is not resurrected but remains on the cross or in the tomb, then sin rules us. The resurrection is what gives us confidence that sin has indeed been forgiven. The resurrection shows that no sin is too big to forgive. Paul drives the point home in 1 Corinthians 15: unless Jesus arose, we are stuck in sin.

The resurrection's implications also extend into our forgiveness of others. We must emulate the risen Christ by forgiving. An archbishop recently told us in a radio interview that not only had he been hurt in his ecclesial role but he knew that he had hurt others. He had had to learn to forgive others and to seek forgiveness. Shortly afterwards a chaplain wrote to Ross and related that he knew a woman who had heard that interview. She had not spoken to her daughter in ten years because of a perceived wrong, but that night she rang her daughter. The chaplain attended the first family barbecue in ten years, and the family wanted to pass on the happy news.

Zone 2: *Whole Person*

Paul tells us in 1 Corinthians 15:20 that Christ is the firstfruits of the resurrection harvest, which means that he is like the first thing plucked at harvest time. He comes first, and the pattern is set for the end of time when we will be harvested—that is, raised from the dead like Christ as whole persons. This leads us to a valuable theological reflection. The resurrection of Jesus demonstrates that God cares for the whole person, and this holistic understanding of how God already sees us applies not just in the future, but also now. Jesus demonstrates this by treating people as whole persons. The New Testament indicates that this applies to all persons irrespective of our standing in society (Gal. 3:27–28).

Here is a challenging way of thinking about the immediate implications of the resurrection for the whole person: Last year Ross addressed a Christian parochial school at their commencement service, and many of the parents present were not churchgoers. During the speech he talked about his work conducting spiritual audits of Non-Government Organizations (NGOs) that are worried that they might be Christian in name only. In the audit process he measures the strength of the NGO to a large extent on the basis of the most vulnerable person. The provocative question for deep reflection is, is the most vulnerable person in the NGO treated as a whole person?

In his speech Ross said that parents should gauge this particular school in the same way—by its care for the whole student, irrespective of academic or sporting prowess. Is every student in the school treated as a whole person? Some friends later told him that a non-Christian couple who had a disabled child had attended the commencement service that day. What Ross said resonated in their hearts and gave them a great sense of confidence in the school. It opened up a new vista for them about the resurrected Jesus. They intuited that if the school could truly care for their "vulnerable" child, then there must be something about Jesus that is worth exploring.

After the school event some well-meaning Christians expressed their surprise about Ross's teaching on the wholeness of resurrected persons. They in effect said, "We haven't heard this in church before; is this real?"

Although in theory Christians have a theology that affirms the whole person, in practice we don't really talk about it or even grasp it. In our worship services we should be asking whether we have stimulated the intellect, touched the emotions, and expressed God's love for every aspect of our being. The same point applies in church and parachurch groups, and in mission and vision statements: Are we only speaking in reductionist terms, by counting numbers and dividing persons into programs and compartments? If we do, then we do not have a holistic view of God's love for the entire person. Also, we must cry out against the loss of wholeness and abuse that occurs in churches and places of employment by viewing people purely as numbers or objects. When the whole person is upheld, then many of the internecine debates about healing and the significance of spiritual gifts will recede. If one has a holistic grasp of the resurrection and hence of the whole person then it must be reflected in one's praxis, on both a personal and a communal level. We should live and pray for the whole person because God cares about everything.

Zone 3: Empowerment for Daily Living

In 1 Corinthians 15:19 Paul emphasizes the eternal nature of hope in Christ, but he takes it as a given that there is hope in this world too, and the rest of the New Testament agrees. In the risen Christ we have a comforter in the Holy Spirit who takes us through this life. Hebrews 4:14–16 makes it clear that we have confidence that Christ has walked this path before us. Kirk puts it this way:

> God has promised future embodied life on a new earth. The only way to take hold of this promise is to be joined to the resurrected Lord. Christian hope is more than wishful thinking, because the future on which we have set our hearts has already begun with Jesus' resurrection. . . . When we receive the Spirit of Sonship, we are receiving the Spirit of Jesus, the resurrected Son of God.[8]

The Baptist theologian G. H. Morling (1893–1973) provocatively remarks:

> The Spirit to be given was not the Spirit of a non-perfected Christ, but that of the God-man arrived at full stature. When we come and drink we receive the

Spirit who brings to us the Spirit of the Victor Christ, the glorified Christ of him who is alive forevermore.[9]

Morling is saying that though there are two different persons here—Christ and the Holy Spirit—the experience is identical. Is it the Christ on the cross or the risen Christ that lives in you? As Morling makes clear, it is the risen Christ.

Consider the case of the first martyr, Stephen, who is dragged out of the city for stoning (Acts 7). Stephen sees Christ the victor, the Son of Man standing at God's right hand, to whom he says, "Lord Jesus, receive my spirit" (7:59). He is full of the Holy Spirit and is radiant. The text notes that Saul of Tarsus approved of his martyrdom (Acts 8:1), leading us to wonder, what impact did Stephen's martyrdom have on Saul? Saul was fully aware of the cross but it did not move him. Indeed, he probably thought that Jesus had deserved to die. In the wake of Stephen's death, Saul went berserk, on a rampage against the church (Acts 8:1–3; 9:1–2). As a Pharisee he could believe in the general resurrection on the last day; therefore what peeved him was not an executed Jesus but that the Christians had the audacity to present a resurrection message of him as the firstfruits.

A dead Jesus does not confront us in quite the same way as does the risen Jesus. Stephen sees the living, risen Lord. The provocative question we face is, what kind of Christ do we have in us? Is it the risen glorified Christ? Stephen meets the one who comforts and forgives, and he is empowered to forgive those who are about to kill him. As a radical disciple Stephen has a both/and perspective. He has hope that Christ will empower him in the present turmoil and hope that as he expires he has the risen Christ with him. The same hope is ours when we answer the call to be a radical disciple today.

Paul later, after his conversion, expresses his deep yearning to combine the power of the resurrected life with Christ's example of suffering:

> I want to know Christ and the power of his resurrection and the sharing of his sufferings by becoming like him in his death, if somehow I may attain the resurrection from the dead. (Phil. 3:10–11)

Today, the quest for spiritual power is evident in the lives of people beyond the church walls. The church faces two great challenges in this area: first, that we may truly know the power of the risen Christ so that we may live and serve him; and second, that we demonstrate to others by our lives and our words that Christ alone is the source of real spiritual transformation. Our daily meditation and prayers should focus on Jesus's clear teaching, "I am the resurrection and the life" (John 11:25). Our prayers for strength, comfort, advocacy, understanding, and for our daily walk are enriched when we focus on the risen Christ. His resurrection from the dead confirms that he truly is able to empower us for daily living.

Zone 4: Future Hope of the General Resurrection

Paul teaches in 1 Corinthians 15:19–23 that the resurrection also gives us a future hope. As we have mentioned, those who belong to Christ are assured that just as he was resurrected from the dead so also will we be raised. Joni Eareckson Tada catches the drift of this as a future goal:

> I can scarcely believe it. I with shriveled, bent fingers, atrophied muscles, gnarled knees, and no feeling from the shoulders down, will one day have a new body, light, bright, and clothed in righteousness—powerful and dazzling. Can you imagine the hope this gives someone spinal cord-injured like me? Or someone who is cerebral palsied, brain-injured, or who has multiple sclerosis? Imagine the hope this gives someone who is manic depressive. No other religion, no other philosophy promises new bodies, hearts and minds. Only in the Gospel of Christ do hurting people find such incredible hope.[10]

Unfortunately, far too many Christians do not seem to have a clear understanding about the hope of the general resurrection. This is a major factor that goaded N. T. Wright into writing *Surprised by Hope*. Christians need a reality check. If we have really understood the implications of the resurrection, why is it that we still seem confused about it and have failed to impact our culture with it?[11] While most Christians do have a sense of eternal life as their hope, as we will see in later chapters there is so much confusion and vagueness about how the resurrection connects. By our lack of clarity and our failure to positively share the truth of the resurrection we actually help to create the cultural space into which alternative afterlife views now pour.

The church seems to have succumbed to the browbeating of skeptics about the resurrection. We slip back into a tangible bolt hole: we explain our faith and life by the cross and leave out the resurrection. We have fallen into the very trap that John Gerstner observed: once upon a time the church commended the faith by proclaiming miracles, but since the Enlightenment we have apologized for miracles, especially the resurrection.[12]

We need fresh encouragement about our future hope. Here is an incident that the non-Christian photojournalist George Gittoes witnessed. He was with a United Nations medical team providing emergency relief to people displaced by civil strife in Rwanda. He describes a memorable incident:

> It was horrific; we saw thousands of women and children killed before our eyes. We were going in and getting the wounded out as the people were macheting and shooting and killing. Suddenly, there was this guy standing in the middle of the people who were dying all around him. He just began giving this sermon in one of those beautiful melodious African voices, mingling English and French and Rwandan, quoting sections of the New Testament, those bits which give hope . . . passages to do with the resurrection.[13]

Gittoes took a photograph of this man dubbed "The Preacher," but he did not see the man again and has no idea if he survived. He goes on: " 'The Preacher' . . . represents what I think religion should do, raise people up, make people feel human and spiritually alive and give them courage and faith." The medical team could offer nothing despite all their skills and technology, but with the risen Christ there was hope for eternity.[14]

Zone 5: Eschatology

In 1 Corinthians 15:24–25, Paul speaks of the end with the coming of Christ that initiates his reign and then the Father's reign. God's reign is just and delivered with integrity (Isa. 11:5; Jer. 23:1–5); it is peaceful (Micah 4; Isa. 2:4); everlasting and not transient (Isa. 9:7); universally effective (Rev. 21:22–26; Isa. 25:6–7); causes rejoicing (Isa. 12; Rev. 4–5); and eliminates suffering (Rev. 21:4). The resurrection is the lynchpin that guarantees the return of Christ, and without it there cannot be eternal life for us or resurrection from the dead. Eternity is not a vaporous experience but it will bring a new world order and new creation.

A few years ago the winds of change swept over Russia as Marxism caved in. Suddenly the doors were open in university law schools and lawyers' associations. Ross's book on the resurrection had been translated into Russian, and the then-director of the Gorbachev Foundation had distributed it to one thousand lawyers and legal institutions. An invitation had been extended for him to talk to students and faculty at Moscow State University. The local Russian Christians were accustomed to preaching to these audiences rather than having dialogue, but Ross decided to take a different tack by opening the forum to questions.

After the initial tension of the first few questions, students began to line up at the microphone. The most repeated question was, "Will your Jesus bring in the Millennium that Marxism has failed to deliver?" The disillusioned students were looking for something more than just a hope. They wanted to know if the resurrection is about a new creation, a new world.

What is often missing from churches is a recognition that the resurrection and the new creation are inseparable things. The resurrection brings us to the realization that the world is to be re-created by transformed and renewed people. It shows us that the new creation is coming and has in fact already begun to break into this realm. In the book of Romans, Paul links the creation into the panoramic drama and describes it as suffering, poised, and waiting for release. Creation is in pain waiting for the final transformation and the rebirth that the resurrection heralds (Rom. 8:18–25). The resurrection promises us an eschatological hope for a transformed world.

Zone 6: Eden Breaks In

The resurrection of Jesus is not significant merely for pointing to the kingdom that is to come; it also signifies that through Jesus the kingdom has already begun breaking into our world and lives. The risen Jesus has authority and commissions both mission and a new way of things (Matt. 28:18–19). In 1 Corinthians 15:45 Jesus is identified as the second Adam and contrasted with the original Adam. The original Adam was placed in the garden as God's appointed steward and servant. Now, through the resurrection, Jesus has received the mantle as the second Adam and his reign has begun.

Though the Gospel of John does not directly refer to Jesus as the second Adam, it does emphasize a theme about creation. This is apparent in John's prologue as he opens with the words, "In the beginning." John records seven miracle signs:

1. Water into wine (2:1–11)
2. Healing the official's son (4:46–54)
3. Healing the man at the pool (5:1–9)
4. Feeding the five thousand (6:1–15)
5. Walking on water (6:16–21)
6. Healing the blind man (9:1–7)
7. Raising of Lazarus (11:1–44)

Some commentators regard these seven signs as acts of a new creation as the selection of *seven* signs deliberately echoes the *seven* days of creation (Gen. 1). The connections with Genesis continue as John announces that the resurrection story takes place on the first day of a new week (John 20:1). Jesus's resurrection is the start of a new day and a new creation.

Jeannine Brown highlights an easily overlooked detail that suggests that John is signifying Jesus as the new Adam. The climax of Jesus's life story begins, ends, and recommences in gardens. It starts when Jesus is betrayed by Judas in a garden (John 18:1–2). Then after Jesus dies on the cross John reports: "Now there was a garden in the place where he was crucified, and in the garden there was a new tomb in which no one had ever been laid" (John 19:41). Finally, Mary Magdalene meets a man in that garden on Easter Sunday morning and she thinks he is "the gardener" (John 20:15).

One of the literary techniques John uses is a play on words in which a person perceives meaning on one level, while Jesus reframes the meaning at a spiritual level. Think of the woman at the well (John 4). When Jesus offers her living water, she thinks he means an easy way to find drinking water. But Jesus means something deeper, and her perceptions change when she discovers this. In like manner, Mary mistakes the man she sees as the gardener, but when she has her eyes opened to the reality of the resurrection, she discovers it is in fact Jesus. But is she at first completely mistaken about the man in the garden? John's subtle writing signifies that the risen Jesus works in the garden unlike the original Adam who failed.[15]

The connection back to Genesis reminds us of the original family that was established to tend the garden. Now through the risen Jesus a new family is being created. We are adopted by the Father through the risen Christ, and through the work of Jesus in his death and resurrection we can be known as his sisters and brothers. The imprint of the second Adam is upon us, and Jesus's resurrection breaks in to transform who we are and how we are to live in the present.

The image of Jesus as the new Adam also draws our minds back to the point that originally we were created with the *imago Dei* and placed in Eden. Due to sin the image of God in us is damaged and harmed. Our transformation and renewal involves us being conformed to the image of the resurrected Christ (Rom. 8:29) as the Spirit regenerates us. The *imago Dei* is being renovated, restored, and reinvigorated through the power of the risen Jesus, so that we walk in his power. Our lives then must begin to manifest the signs of the future kingdom.

As we discover in both zones 1 and 11, we will manifest the signs of the kingdom in the way we treat each other and the rest of God's creation in the here and now. In the previous zone of eschatology we came to understand that there will be a new transformed world under God's reign. That eschatological resurrection-zone then casts a shadow backward from the end of time and reaches us. We have a foretaste of what is to come when we live in the power of the risen Jesus here and now. A full resurrection theology cannot coexist with a theology that does not take our responsibilities toward the creation seriously. A gospel that has been divorced from caring for the creation has no traction either with God or with the realities we face in a planet that is degraded and ruined by our sinful actions. When the resurrection is rediscovered the issue of our stewardship toward the creation comes into clear focus.

Beyond stewardship we are called to submit our attitudes, lives, and behavior to God's reign and to live by his principles right now. As Reformed theologian Anthony Hoekema teaches:

> There will be continuity as well as discontinuity between this age and the next, and between this earth and the new earth. This point is extremely important. As citizens of God's kingdom, we may not just write off the present earth as a total loss, or rejoice in its deterioration. We must indeed be working for a better world now. Our efforts to be bringing the kingdom of Christ into fuller manifestation are of eternal significance. Our Christian life today, our struggles against sin—both individual and institutional—our mission work . . . have value not only for this world but even for the world to come.[16]

Zone 7: Confidence

Christians are joined together by the belief that the resurrection is something true that happened to Jesus; it is the event that gives us confidence because the resurrection demonstrates that Christ is the Son of God, Lord and Victor (Rom. 1:1–4). Paul recites an early creedal statement of the church at the beginning of 1 Corinthians 15 that includes the list of witnesses to the event of Jesus's resurrection, and he is counted among their number. This creedal statement sums up the gospel in a nutshell: "For I handed on to you as of first importance what I in turn had received: that Christ died for our sins in accordance with the scriptures, and that he was buried, and that he was raised on the third day in accordance with the scriptures, and that he appeared to Cephas, then to the twelve" (1 Cor. 15:3–5).

Allison Trites, in his discussion of passages such as 1 Corinthians 15, says that the resurrection case involves the twofold evidence of fulfillment of prophecy and eyewitness testimony. This is the same twofold message throughout Luke-Acts and fulfills the Jewish expectation of twofold corroboration.[17] For example, the first Christian sermon attests to this:

> Fellow Israelites, I may say to you confidently of our ancestor David that he both died and was buried, and his tomb is with us to this day. Since he was a prophet, he knew that God had sworn with an oath to him that he would put one of his descendants on his throne. Foreseeing this, David spoke of the resurrection of the Messiah, saying, "He was not abandoned to Hades, nor did his flesh experience corruption." This Jesus God raised up, and of that all of us are witnesses. (Acts 2:29–32)

We also see in Paul's creedal statement in 1 Corinthians 15 and in sermons like Acts 2 that the resurrection took place in time and space; it is historical and fulfills prophecy. It might surprise many Christians but the certainty of faith rests not in our inner experiences but in the resurrection event. This confidence the resurrection gives us is not just intellectual certitude but can invigorate our attitudes about living.

A woman recently wrote to us seeking a copy of a small booklet we had written on the resurrection. She explained that her husband had dementia for a number of years and had not known who she was for some time. She visited him in his care facility three or four times per week, and it took a long time for her to commute. The medical staff had recently advised that her husband was so physically well that he could live for many years. She was at the end of her tether—emotionally, spiritually, and physically exhausted. She said her church is a very loving and caring community, but she needed something more than just hugs and friendly support. She needed assurance about the reality of the resurrection. She exclaimed, "They just don't understand. I need to know it's true. I'm just spiritually barren and I need to be able to cling onto something other than my feelings."

It is a tragedy of the modern church that the defenders of the faith seem to lack either pastoral sensitivity or apologetic rigor. The confidence Christians can have in the resurrection should be expressed by those pastors and caregivers who minister in believers' everyday lives.

Zone 8: Face of God

We wish we had a dollar for every time that we've been asked, what does God look like? Many Christians, it seems, have difficulty coming to grips with the incarnation and especially the resurrection. The nature and character of God is revealed through Jesus, and in him we are shown God's "face" of compassion, mercy, and love in his life, ministry, death, and resurrection. The resurrection makes clear that Jesus's kingship is over all and he is the messianic fulfillment of Old Testament expectations (Acts 2:29–32). Some Christians accept that God raised Jesus from the dead and believe he is the Son of God but struggle to see how the resurrection confirms his deity. We see the same sort of uncertainty in Thomas's thinking and behavior, but when he encountered the risen Jesus he cried out "my Lord and my God" (John 20:28).

In the last few years people became excited about Antony Flew's (1923–2010) intellectual shift from atheism to belief in God. His philosophical writings, like God and Philosophy, became classics, and he was arguably the most important atheist philosopher of the twentieth century.[18] Unlike the recent hostile posturing of the "New Atheists," Flew refrained from being vitriolic in his rejection of theism. He was courteous when debating Christian apologists like Gary Habermas, Terry Miethe, and William Lane Craig on the subjects of God's existence and the resurrection of Jesus.

In the last decade of his life Flew came to a theoretical understanding about God's existence. After reflecting on scientific findings about the complexity and order of human DNA, he realized that no naturalistic theory could explain its origins. The complexity of DNA, in his view, provided rational grounds for belief in an intelligent designer behind the cosmos.[19] He concluded that there is a Mind who is the first cause or Creator of the universe.

There has been a flurry of exuberant shop-talk about Flew's conversion, but the popular rhetoric tends to overlook the fact that he did not concede very much.[20] He saw no connection between the God of the Bible and the God who is the first cause of the universe. His position did not develop beyond a form of deism because he insisted that God is inactive and uninvolved in our lives, and so he retained a very nonsupernatural modernist mind-set.[21]

Even though he never converted to Christianity, Flew did say some interesting things about Jesus's resurrection. In a debate with Habermas he agreed that if it is a knowable fact that Jesus rose from the dead literally and physically it then constitutes "the best, if not the only, reason for accepting that Jesus is the God of Abraham, Isaac, and Israel."[22] In an appendix to Flew's book There Is a God there is a brief paper by N. T. Wright on Jesus's resurrection, followed by Flew's comments.[23] Although Flew still doubted that Jesus arose he acknowledged that Wright presented an excellent argument. If Jesus arose then he could accept that the Maker's voice has been heard.[24] If Jesus was resurrected, Flew understood that he would then have seen the face of God.

It is intriguing to observe the reaction of atheists to Flew's story. A month prior to Flew's death, Ross debated Dan Barker, who is an ex-Pentecostal pastor and former Christian songwriter. During the radio debate Ross mentioned Flew. Barker's response was very revealing: he dismissed it because in his view Flew must have become senile. Instead of coming to grips with the reasons why Flew found arguments for God's existence quite compelling, Barker shoots the messenger. It is a classic fallacy that philosophers call *ad hominem*—arguing against the person and failing to actually address the argument itself.

The resurrection is the sign that Jesus is truly God, indeed that he is "God with us" as his birth narrative tells us (Matt. 1:23). When challenged by the religious authorities he told them, "Destroy this temple [his body] and in three days I will raise it up" (John 2:19). When Jesus was raised from the dead, he demonstrated he was indeed Emmanuel, because anyone who could fulfill this prophecy of resurrection must indeed be worthy of worship. Even Thomas came to understand that point (John 20:28). In Jesus's resurrection we have his credentials as the Son of God confirmed, and when we look at Jesus we are looking at the face of God.

Zone 9: Ethics

A very strong theme in Peter's first epistle is our eschatological hope in Christ. Peter Davids remarks that in this epistle hope "is not divorced from behavior," but rather "it is the basis for Christian life-style."[25] The apostle calls us, as followers of the risen Christ, to pursue an ethical life that is lived in light of the resurrection: "he has given us a new birth into a living hope through the resurrection of Jesus Christ from the dead" (1 Pet. 1:3). In between other explicit reminders about the resurrection (1:21; 3:18, 21), Peter instructs that we are to lead a holy life (1:13–16). He outlines the manner in which we must conduct our relationships with each other and with unbelievers (2:12–17). We are to understand persecution in light of Jesus's sufferings (2:18–25), seek peace, shun evil, do what is good, have clear consciences, and from our ethical action we should expect people to ask us to give reasons for our hopeful faith (3:8–16). So, we must lead upright lives in light of Jesus's resurrection and our eschatological hope.

Peter's teaching leads us to the question, how does Jesus's resurrection relate to ethics? Across the centuries Christians have looked to the Scriptures for guidance, often drawing out the ethical implications of particular theological themes like covenant and revealed law, redemption, Jesus's kingdom message, and eschatology.[26] Some theologians believe that the resurrection ought to be in the foreground when we think about ethics. Let us briefly note what a few of them have said.

The *Second Letter of Clement* refers to the resurrection of the flesh and emphasizes that the continuity between our present and future body directly impinges on our moral behavior now.[27] John Chrysostom (ca. 344–407) also makes strong connections between the resurrection and ethics.[28] In modern times Edwyn Hoskyns and Francis Davey discern a pattern in New Testament ethics based around the crucifixion and resurrection.[29] Brian Johnstone explores the terrain for linking resurrection and moral theology within Roman Catholic thought.[30] Thorwald Lorenzen emphasizes the resurrection through the theme of discipleship and justice, and some of his Baptist colleagues relate the resurrection to the area of human rights.[31] Chris Sugden understands that the resurrection's effect ought to directly shape our preparedness to tackle social and moral injustices.[32] Some writers have also related ecological ethics to the eschatological significance of the resurrection.

We have distinguished three different layers that elucidate how the resurrection relates to ethical thinking. One emphasis is that the resurrection verifies Jesus's credentials and so confirms his ethical teachings. A second emphasis has been on how Jesus's resurrection can reshape our understanding of human ethics within the creation. The third emphasis is on the eschatological resurrection of humanity in which we start from the general resurrection and then look back at how we ought to treat not just humans but also the rest of the creation (ecology and animals). Let's briefly unpack each of these layers.

The need for a divine perspective on human ethics is something that the atheist analytical philosopher Ludwig Wittgenstein understood only too well. He noted that our human values are indeed relative to culture and cannot provide any ultimate or universal ethics. In his analysis Wittgenstein concluded that "Ethics is transcendental."[33] In some respects he was echoing an earlier intuition from Rousseau, who reasoned that "Gods would be needed to give men laws."[34] What Jesus's resurrection provides us with is the very solution that both Wittgenstein and Rousseau looked for but did not find. If the resurrection has taken place then Jesus's divinity is confirmed and whatever he said is ultimate truth. A transcendental perspective on ethics can be accessed through the resurrected Jesus.

Much valuable work about ethics has been produced on the basis of the cross. It opens up for us the model of servanthood as a framework from within which we may act. As the theological emphasis has been on the atonement through the cross, the themes of redemption and forgiveness have also come to the foreground as part of our ethical motivation. While we can indeed glean much that is important for our personal ethics from the cross, much more can be gained by turning attention to the resurrection as well. It is at this juncture that the second layer comes into focus.

Oliver O'Donovan's book *Resurrection and Moral Order* seeks to develop an ethical framework grounded in Jesus's resurrection.[35] In his book O'Donovan essentially discusses the resurrection as the structural influence for understanding the moral life of humans within the context of the theology of creation. Since humanity fell in sin, human relationships must be transformed, and the agency for that transformation comes through the risen Christ. It is from this understanding of transformed communities that ethical problems can then be sorted out. Some critics, while welcoming the pioneering aspect of O'Donovan's work, feel that he stops short in his ethical framework with human relationships. That is, O'Donovan has a human-centered agenda for ethics that does not properly address ethical responsibilities toward animals and the creation.[36]

Raymond van Leeuwen, Roger Olson, and Keith Innes emphasize the general resurrection, which shows us who we finally become and the destiny of the earth.[37] By considering the final goal they suggest we can then look back at current moral problems surrounding ecology and creation. If, as resurrected persons living in a resurrected community, we will one day inhabit a renewed and transformed world, then how does that relate to the way we should live in the present world? As the earth groans for our resurrection, our ethical behavior in the present matters greatly, especially as we seek to resolve problems besetting the degradation of the planet and its resources. It also has direct bearing on how we treat animals. We forget that animals are included in the new creation.[38]

The emergence of these outlooks is promising but still represents a piecemeal understanding of the relationship between the resurrection and ethics. We have yet to see a resurrection-based approach to ethics widen to encompass the whole gamut of ethics: medical ethics, human rights, and so on. The resurrection *can*, however, take us into these spheres of ethical concern. For example, the problem of human rights is one of the major issues of our time, and the resurrection of Jesus provides us with some important insights into how we approach abuses of human rights. The resurrection shows us that the whole person is important to God, allowing us to view human dignity through the lens of Jesus's resurrection.

Human rights have to do with respect in human relationships, and only a transcendent perspective can ultimately inform and assure us of how to properly view our neighbors. The resurrection offers us a transcendent outlook, reflective of Jesus's teachings and his divine approval of the duties and rights conferred in revealed law in Scripture. He confirms that human beings bear the image and likeness of God (*imago Dei*) and demonstrated it by his acceptance of even the most despised and marginal persons of his day: women, children, and sinners.

As we mentioned under zone 2, the resurrection puts a strong emphasis on the value of the whole person. At an ethical level, then, how we treat one another in the midst of moral dilemmas should be framed around how we view each other in light of the resurrection. Jesus answered the question, who is my neighbor? by recounting the parable of the Good Samaritan (Luke 10:25–37). A resurrection worldview sees people through Jesus's eyes in ministering to the whole person. Today the question, who is my neighbor? is relevant at a global level as we face the great human-rights challenge of providing clean water for all people. Lack of clean water is the major cause for twenty-five thousand children dying every day. Treating individuals as whole persons means that we must act decisively on behalf of those who are denied this basic human dignity. Individually, we can support groups like World Vision. Collectively, we must insist on global equity and push our Western governments to commit a larger percentageof their GNI (gross national income) to overseas aid.

Many Christians in their vocations as doctors, lawyers, and business leaders struggle to find avenues to express their faith beyond being in a prayer group in the workplace and giving of one's money to the church. When the resurrection becomes the grid through which our worldview is formed, the value of the person will stand out. The critical question in a spiritual audit for any workplace or NGO will be, how is the person valued? In the operations of the workplace is the whole person valued and treated with dignity? Are there moral compromises in the way human dignity is treated? This is where the resurrection of Jesus has enormous bearing on our ethics.

Zone 10: Judge/Justice

An element that Christians often overlook concerns how the resurrection connects with the messianic rule of God in Christ and the question of judgment. Paul before the Areopagus declared that God has "fixed a day on which he will have the world judged in righteousness by a man whom he has appointed, and of this he has given assurance to all by raising him from the dead" (Acts 17:31). This judgment is twofold: on one side is our eternal destiny of heaven/hell (Luke 12:8–9), and on the other are the faithful deeds of Jesus's followers (2 Cor. 5:10).

In the biblical worldview, for the justice of God to be carried out fairly the resurrection of both Jesus and us is required. Part of the messianic fulfillment in the first coming of Jesus was for salvation, while the fulfillment in the second coming is for judgment.

For most of us this is the aspect of resurrection theology that we least like, and not too many of us give "turn or burn" messages lightly. The Areopagus address shows us that the message of judgment for all is inextricably tied to resurrection and the justice of God. Perhaps we need to find a new boldness, for there are appropriate occasions where tough messages need to be proclaimed. The difficulty is we often do not connect the message of judgment to the web of resurrection theology.

Zone 11: New Community

Jesus's resurrection, which took place on the first day of the week, involves a new creation. One of its immediate effects is the creation of a new community of which he is Lord (Col. 1:18).

The church community should be a place of welcome and acceptance for all persons, but it is not always experienced as such. Ross knows what it is like to feel unwelcomed, because as a sixteen-year-old he lived on the streets of a city for a short time. He fled his home because of personal and family issues. He had no money and found himself in another city some thousand miles away. On the streets he had been offered all sorts of evil enticements. For safety reasons and for personal support he was looking for a church, and the minister of the first church he attended did not want to know him. In fact, when the service was over he was left standing alone, quite disheveled, at the church's doorstep. Fortunately he then went to a nearby park where some young women came up to him and invited him for dinner and church. This acceptance possibly saved him from the temptations most young street kids face. The first church he visited preached the gospel but in its actions reinforced his nonperson status and caused him to feel rejection.

Outside of our rejection of God the greatest sin of humanity is to treat others as nonpersons. In fact the biblical sign that we are right with God is that we love our neighbor as ourselves (Luke 10:25–37). The risen Christ calls us into a new community that dignifies and values every human being. This is what our world is looking for: affirmation and inclusion.

Nonperson status is rampant in Genesis. Genesis is not just a story of faithfulness and covenant, and scholars often fail to recognize that one of the themes in Genesis 12–50 is the actual outworking of the fall (Gen. 1–3). The central characters (Abraham, Isaac, and Sarah) at times protect themselves out of sheer self-interest and treat spouses, children, significant others, and other ethnic groups as nonpersons. Abraham, to protect himself, passes his wife Sarah off as his sister (Gen. 12:10–20). This exposes her to an adulterous situation with Pharaoh, and God and Pharaoh both become outraged. Isaac does the same to his wife later in Genesis (26:6–11). And Sarah follows suit by treating her maidservant Hagar disgracefully (Gen. 16; 21:8–21). Hagar, through no fault of her own, bears a child to Abraham, but when Sarah gives birth to her own son, she sends Hagar, with her son Ishmael, out into the desert to suffer an uncertain fate. All three of these key figures in Genesis treat others as nonpersons.

The pattern continues later in the book of Genesis. Laban treats his daughters Rachel and Leah shamefully and tricks Jacob into marrying Leah when he thinks he is marrying the one he loves, Rachel. Laban intensifies the problem by manipulating Jacob into working for another seven years with the promise that he can then have Rachel as his wife. The writer of Genesis does not moralize but simply tells the story, commenting simply that Jacob "loved

Rachel more than Leah" (Gen. 29:30).
Our world and churches are filled with
those who know the kind of rejection
and pain that Rachel and Leah most
likely felt. Laban played his daughters
off each other to achieve his own finan-
cial security.

Genesis finishes with the story
of Joseph, a blockbuster nonperson
drama (Gen. 37–50). What aggravates
Joseph's brothers is the favoritism their
father shows toward him. During his
youthful days Joseph was the only son
of Rachel, the one his father loved,
whereas the other brothers were chil-

> **Healing from Nonperson Status:**
> **Genesis 50:15–21**
>
> 1. Acknowledge the hurt—
>   weep (v. 17).
> 2. Leave the correcting of
>   wrongs to God (vv. 18–19).
> 3. See God's hand in the situ-
>   ation (v. 20; compare with
>   Rom. 8:28).
> 4. Practice forgiveness (v. 21).

dren of Leah or maidservants. Their jealousy eventually leads them to strip
Joseph of his coat, throw him into a pit, and then sell him to a group of traders
who take him to Egypt. Unbeknownst to Joseph, during his years in exile in
Egypt his younger brother Benjamin is born to Rachel. When Joseph's older
brothers finally come to Egypt, where he ends up in a place of authority, he
does not reveal his identity to them, but sends the brothers home with orders
to retrieve Benjamin from Canaan and return immediately to Egypt with him
(Gen. 42:15–24). Throughout the story when Joseph meets his brothers he
weeps uncontrollably (Gen. 42:24) as he is reminded of his nonperson treatment by his own family. Joseph's story concludes with how he handles his
nonperson status, as the sidebar shows.

These examples from Genesis illustrate what it looks like to treat others
as nonpersons, but the gospel reverses nonperson status, declaring that in
order to be right with God one must be right with one's neighbor. In Christ
there is no nonperson status. The apostle Paul states in Galatians 3:28 and
Colossians 3:11 that in Christ the three major forms of discrimination in his
day—race, economic, gender—are overturned. Peter is slower on the uptake
but finally gets the ramifications of the gospel when he meets the gentile
centurion Cornelius. Peter declares: "I truly understand that God shows no
partiality" (Acts 10:34).[39]

Few understand the centrality of Jesus's resurrection to the human worth
and dignity of all people. Before Paul's monumental statement in Galatians
3:28, "There is no longer Jew or Greek, there is no longer slave or free, there
is no longer male and female; for all of you are one in Christ Jesus," he sets
the foundation by stating, "As many of you as were baptized into Christ have
clothed yourselves with Christ" (3:27). Paul is declaring here that baptism
is the symbol that we have died to the old self and put on the new self. The
climactic act of baptism is our identification with the risen Christ as we come

out of the water. We were buried but are now raised in Christ. The way of the risen Christ is the path of human dignity and human worth for all people irrespective of race, economic status, or gender. First John affirms this idea, stating that to put on the garments of Christ is to love one's neighbor as oneself (4:7–21). The outworking of the fall in Genesis has been reversed. At the cross Jesus paid the price for our treatment of others as nonpersons and modeled true servanthood; but it is the resurrection, clothing ourselves in the risen Christ, that leads to a new day in human relationships. The resurrection is the lynchpin of God's new day for human dignity. The marks of the true church will clearly show that there is no racism, no sexism, and no socio-economic distinctions.

Are we individually and corporately, as the church, living as people did in Genesis, or are we living through the risen Christ? This is a crucial question in our day, as we are confronted by the hideous maltreatment of others in the form of sexual abuse within churches. The perpetrators of such violence make their victims into nonpersons, and our collective silence on these is-sues is a denial of the gospel of resurrection. Carol Penner urges the church to assist victims of sexual assault by approaching their emotional healing through the prism of a theology of the resurrection of the body.[40] Being right with God and right with other persons is the true mark of the new community.

Zone 12: Mission

The whole ethos of mission should be gripped by an understanding of resurrection. A Christian leader we respect told a story about how he encoun-tered two young guys who were medical graduates. They said that unless they heard otherwise they felt sure God was calling them to open up practices in mid-America. He responded by suggesting that unless they heard otherwise perhaps the real call of God would see them leaving America to serve in the poorest parts of the earth. Compare this to one of Oprah's favorite people, Catherine Hamlin. As committed Christians, she and her husband went to Ethiopia fifty years ago and dedicated their lives to establishing fistula hospi-tals there. This activity has liberated women from community rejection and stigmatization. Catherine's husband died in Ethiopia and in her eighties she remains an incredible example of grace and courage.

Clearly, being sent is at the heart of Christian mission and worship. Any paradigm of evangelism and church life should be hand-in-glove with mis-sion. The original impetus for Christian mission sprang directly out of the encounter with the risen Christ (Matt. 28:18–20). As Daniel Kirk has aptly said, "The resurrected Jesus is the one who has the authority to send us out to the ends of the earth with the assurance that we will not labor in vain."[41] If there is no resurrection, then there is no authentic mission.

Resurrection Culture

Over the last thirty years scattered voices have called for the integration of the resurrection into practical areas of theology and church life, such as in healing ministry, pastoral care, and spiritual development. In the following paragraphs we provide a sampling of these voices that advocate greater attention to the significance of the resurrection.

Cornelius Buller, a Salvation Army ethicist, emphasizes that physical healings are signs of the eschatological healing of creation and offers hope for the postmodern malaise.[42] Buller says that physical healings in the Bible signify something of the eschatological goal of the general resurrection, which will bring "the ultimate healing from all infirmities and all illnesses."[43] He argues that these healing miracles make sense only when placed firmly under the canopy of Christ's resurrection, which is a firstfruits of the resurrection harvest that is to come.

According to Robert Sorensen, many in the pastoral counseling movement have neglected theology. He argues that a theological understanding of the resurrection is essential for strengthening counseling ministries and enriching the processes of healing for those in distress.[44]

Daniel Louw in South Africa has expressed grave concerns over the stigmas attached to persons who have contracted HIV. Louw argues that a pastoral critique of the stigma is justified because of the whole person emphasis in the theology of resurrection.[45]

Glenn Weaver advocates a practical theology based on the resurrection in the pastoral care of persons suffering from senile dementia. He asserts that "the resurrection of Jesus Christ must be the centerpiece of our Christian faith."[46] He links the suffering of dementia patients to the sufferings of Christ but says that believers who suffer this malady will be victorious in the resurrection. Weaver argues that the church has a resurrectional responsibility to uphold the identities of those who progressively experience the loss of memory and physical functions.

Patricia Lull says that children's grief must be taken seriously and that there is an acute need for churches to reintroduce into local church life Easter pageants that involve the young: "The young learn much about the power of Christ's resurrection when we are bold enough to name that singular event as the source of our courage and the guide for our present living. . . . It is the same powerful God, who raised Jesus from the dead, who frees us to care about others."[47]

The Resurrection Grid

We can evaluate to what extent both as individuals and as a community we are following Jesus's way by examining ourselves through the mirror of a grid. In

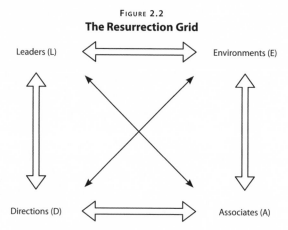

FIGURE 2.2
The Resurrection Grid

figure 2.2 we present a grid visually represented by four sectors that are linked by two-way directional arrows: leaders, environments, associates, and directions.

The grid asks the fundamental question, are we living by the values of the risen Jesus? In the first sector we reflect on leadership. Do we see Jesus's values embodied by leaders in their lifestyle and teaching? How does this flow from them into the environment in which they and fellow Christians operate? Are Jesus's values reflected in the community of faith's lifestyle and does this environment (the second sector) have a commitment to the twelve zones outlined above? For example, is there a genuine commitment to eliminating the nonperson-status treatment of others?

In the third sector are the associates. Do those who collaborate in the new community and assist the leaders by giving of their time by serving live by the values of the risen Jesus? Do they embody the power of the resurrected Christ in their lifestyle and words and deeds?

The last sector comprises the directions taken by leadership and the associates. To what extent are the values of the risen Jesus clearly manifested in the expressed or unexpressed strategies, mission, and vision of the individual and the environments in which they serve? We have found that groups large and small have found it a constructive process to consider their individual and collective life through the resurrection grid.

Resurrection theology today has to involve a total paradigm shift. It is not about adding a few new trick programs to duplicate as a recipe in local churches. It has to be an authentic, embodied way that humbly submits to the cross but lives the life of resurrection focus.

In speaking of hope Rob Moll calls the church to create a resurrection culture. In the case of the departed this could mean viewing the body, preserving the remains in church precincts, and acting as if the person is asleep waiting for the resurrection. The idea is to create a visible reminder of the culture of resurrection.[48] Our call is for the followers of Jesus in both teaching and practice to embody a culture of resurrection in every dimension of life. This will occur only if we embrace the twelve zones, and the resurrection grid is a practical tool for Christian communities to reflectively ask is it happening in every aspect of our journey together. The twelve zones highlight that the resurrection is holistic, and so there are negative implications for us when we overlook any of these zones. The zones weave together like a web. All the web's threads combine into a seamless reality through which our personal and collective spirituality must be embodied.

Spiritual Audit

1. Is your community of faith a culture of resurrection?

2. Do you live in complete reversal of what Genesis shows us about treating others as nonpersons?

3. Who are the discriminated-against groups in your community, and do they feel valued in your midst?

4. Who are the most vulnerable amongst you? Do they feel valued as whole persons?

5. Is forgiveness practiced?

6. In what tangible ways is the kingdom of God in-breaking in your mission?

7. Do you live your life in a sense of final accountability to Christ's judgment?

8. What are the visible signs that you are raised with Christ?

3

Cynics, Post-Christendom Seekers, and Resurrection

The Resurrection of Jesus stands fast as a fact, unaffected by the boastful waves of scepticism that ceaselessly through the ages beat themselves against it; retains its significance as a corner-stone in the edifice of human redemption; and holds within it the vastest hope for time and eternity that humanity can ever know.

James Orr[1]

The church has to turn to the pastoral and evangelistic message par excellence of the early church: "Christ is Risen!" To what extent is the paschal mystery of the crucified and glorified Christ evident in the style of life of the faithful, in the earthly ecclesiastical structures and decisions, and in the evangelistic witness of the church?

Ion Bria[2]

Different Ways of Knowing

An intriguing thing happened near our exhibitor's booth, known as the Community of Hope, at a Mind-Body-Spirit festival. It was located next to the performance stage. As the festival was drawing to an end, a crowd gathered to watch a group of women performing Polynesian massage. As the practical demonstration ended each masseuse addressed the audience, telling stories of their hurts and struggles in life. They then explained how Polynesian massage had transformed their lives and brought them purpose, renewed relationships, healing, and connection with the divine. The crowd was elated!

As the crowd dispersed Ross looked down at a little boy who was tugging at his trousers and crying, "Mister, I'm lost." Ross took him to the administration hub and they found his mother. As Ross walked back to our booth he thought about the boy's words, "Mister, I'm lost," and related them to the unspoken cries of thousands of attendees at the festival. We sometimes wonder, does the church ever hear this cry? The spiritual seekers we encounter at these festivals demonstrate an experiential search for healing and spiritual connection.

Not everyone identifies with an experiential spiritual quest, however. Some are seeking answers to their questions about the truth of Christianity and want to know whether Christian claims can be defended intellectually. Apologetics is something that can serve this latter purpose, in evangelism, in the marketplace, and even inside the church and seminary. We recall listening to an archbishop tell the story of his spiritual development. He had made an adolescent profession of faith, and then as a young adult he went to a theologically sound seminary. During his second year of studies he began having doubts about faith and teetered on the brink of apostasy. Fortunately for him, he found that the seminary actually provided a good environment for him to wrestle with his questions.

The archbishop's story is not an isolated one as we know others who can tell similar stories of struggling with doubt and wanting to find answers. These two stories above point to two different ways of knowing. The seekers at the Mind-Body-Spirit festival took a more postmodern approach, focusing on experience, while the archbishop was drawn to a more rational modernist style.

Our society is made up of many different kinds of people with different attitudes towards ultimate questions. Doubters and skeptics can be found within the walls of the church just as much as they might be found at an atheist conference listening to Richard Dawkins. The hard-nosed rationalist types prize reason, facts, and evidences before they are likely to commit to something, whereas postmodern seekers are likely to be found experimenting. The post-Christendom seeker is resolute and open to finding spiritual resources that will take them on a journey of reflection and growth.[3] They rarely visit a church but are more likely to be found at a meditation center, a spiritual retreat, or reclining on the couch watching Oprah. They are part of mainstream society looking for a workable spirituality. There are also many individuals today who do not fit neatly into one category or the other; they are both/and types who might dabble in both experiential and intellectual pursuits for truth and meaning.

Attitudes about Apologetics

Lots of Christians have heard about apologetics, and there are polarized feelings about its role, relevance, and application. Apologetics is concerned with commending and defending the theological and ethical claims of Christian faith in dialogue. It can provide a stepping-stone along the way to becoming a follower of Jesus. Apologetics has a long pedigree and has been used throughout the history of the church as missionaries, evangelists, and teachers have encountered non-Christian cultures and religions. It has also played a part inside the church in clarifying doctrine. The rise of heresy at various points in the history of the church compelled theologians to better explain doctrines like the Trinity, Christology, and the resurrection.

We want to take some time here to reflect on the importance of apologetics, since it is often used to defend Jesus's resurrection. Kenneth Boa and Robert Bowman identify four broad functions or goals of apologetics: vindication (positive case for faith), defense (showing the faith is credible), refutation (challenging arguments used to support other beliefs), and persuasion (that non-Christians will trust Christ in a committed way of living truth).[4] Each of those four functions can be tracked in Christian thinking about the resurrection throughout history.

From the apostles' time up to the present, apologists have attempted to speak into the culture of their day. As each era has faced new challenges, so apologists have adjusted their style and methods to address their contemporaries.[5] Whether we like or dislike the word *apologetics*, it is an integral part of Scripture, theology, missions, ethics, and pastoral care. At some point in our lives we have had conversations commending Christ to our friends and discussing questions about faith, lifestyle, teachings, and ethics. In those situations we have all been apologists whether we have realized it or not, even if we have never read a book about the subject. Those Christians who take a positive and enthusiastic view are persuaded that apologetics is indispensable to the mission and growth of the church. It helps to clear away misunderstandings that non-Christians have and instills a faith-building confidence in the lives of disciples.

Those who perceive apologetics in negative terms, however, have been appalled by the behavior of apologists who seem insensitive to a person's feelings and appear to be aggressive, obnoxious, and preoccupied with winning debates. The impression that apologetics is impersonal, and lacks empathy and spiritual depth, is easily reinforced by websites and textbooks that discuss abstract arguments. There is no doubt that the negative impressions have some substance to them, but we feel that an extreme overreaction has led many to dump the apologetic baby with the troublesome bathwater.

Horses for Different Courses

Why Christians have deeply polarized feelings about apologetics has rarely been addressed. These opposing attitudes actually reflect a much wider phenomenon: Christians tend to gather into clusters and networks of like-mindedness. Put another way, just as there are horses for different racing courses, so there are different sorts of people clustered into different networks or congregations.

Leslie Francis has, over the past twenty years, coordinated many empirical surveys into the subject of personality type and spiritual orientation.[6] He explores the attitudes of both adults and children on a range of questions concerning the church. He uses a variety of recognized psychological tools for testing personality-type and surveying religious attitudes, such as the Eysenck Personality Questionnaire, as well as his own tool, known as the Francis Psychological Type Scales. The latter builds on methods spearheaded by Carl Jung and further adapted by others into what is known as the Myers-Briggs Type Indicator. Francis and his colleagues have been able to obtain fairly consistent results in their wide-ranging surveys of many different churches in English-speaking countries.

Francis and his colleagues indicate from their research that "there is growing evidence that individual preferences for styles of prayer, spirituality and religious beliefs are related to psychological type."[7] It is possible to show that "psychological type theory can account for differences in attitude, belief, and behavior in the Christian context."[8] Some people are very sensate and introverted and avoid conflict, while others who are tough-minded are predisposed to entering into interpersonal and ecclesiastical situations where conflicts are resolved by a strong emphasis on logical rigor and facts. Personality types can be correlated to preferences in styles of learning and forms of social association. We should not be too surprised by the implications of what Francis has uncovered: that the formats for sermons and Bible studies, and the governance and operation of institutional structures, partly reflect the preferences of personality types that lead or dominate congregations.

Broadly speaking, there are specific personality types that tend to cluster together:

- The clergy of particular denominations.
- Students at seminaries, Bible colleges, and in university parachurch groups.
- Despite their theological differences, mainstream evangelicals and Roman Catholics tend to attract the same kinds of personality types into their respective churches.
- Charismatic and Pentecostal churches.
- Reimagined versions of Celtic Christian spirituality and Christian mysticism.
- Liberal Protestant churches.

Some personality types are underrepresented or marginalized within the broad constituencies of churches. For example, some congregations appear to be heavily populated by introverts who struggle to initiate conversations with visitors and newcomers.[9]

Beyond the church, other researchers have found that particular kinds of sensate and compulsive personality types are attracted to the Hare Krishna.[10] People who tend to be fantasy-prone find parapsychological beliefs appealing, while some maladjusted youth may gravitate to occult beliefs.[11] Personality profiles of teenage atheists also disclose particular dispositions.[12]

We caution you against leaping to reductionist explanations about this research or simplistically thinking that a congregation can be figured out just on the basis of personality types. While the data sharpens our understanding, it has to be correlated to both the social contexts and the theology proclaimed in local churches. We will be referring back to these findings on personality types throughout the remainder of our discussion.

It is not difficult to infer that particular styles of apologetics may attract and repel different personality types. Some who are artistically and mystically inclined within the church run from apologetics because they see it as an unspiritual activity. Other personalities that are tough-minded are drawn to it.

Alternative Apologetics

There are a few voices who are quite rightly calling the church to understand post-Christendom people, but who claim that we have reached the end of apologetics. Those who hold this view may not fully realize its implications in light of both the resurrection as Christianity's lynchpin and the possibility that unacknowledged personality-type issues are sidetracking the central issues.

One approach touted as being necessary for post-Christendom is an embodied apologetic, in which my life as a follower of Jesus *is* the apologetic. In this approach, instead of entering into discussions or debates, one must simply live a life that attracts non-Christians to Jesus. Objections will dissipate through loving friendships and by exposing non-Christians to the wonders of multisensory worship.[13] Some put it this way: "the only answer to others we have is our community."[14] This view stresses relationships based on trust, love, and mutual respect. Some Christians who are drawn to this position have personality types that are anything but tough-minded.

We agree that it is wise to create a friendly, noncoercive space that allows non-Christians the freedom to think, reflect, and pursue a journey with God. Integrity and authenticity in relationships are essential. We reject both boorish behavior and the manipulative attitude about conversion that treats people like they are an automobile being assembled on a conveyor belt. The apostolic call to give reasons for faith with gentleness and respect (1 Pet. 3:15–16) is directly linked to ethical living. Our lives and message must converge to truly reflect Christ. Jesus too rejected hypocrisy, particularly where one's beliefs were contradicted by one's lifestyle (Luke 11:42–44; 12:1–3). The Bible, though, does not restrict apologetics to lifestyle or friendly behavior and clearly includes cognitive discourse (Phil. 1:7, 16; Acts 24:10–21; 26:2–23; Jude 3).

While our lifestyle and behavior should be winsome, there is another side to post-Christendom that cannot be ignored. We live in a divisive society, and a lifestyle apologetic on its own is never going to be enough. Like Jesus and the apostles, we have to answer objections. The New Atheism movement is reactionary and propelled by rhetoric that scathingly typecasts religious people as gullible and unintelligent.[15] Some sneer that Christians believe in an invisible imaginary friend. Beneath that rhetoric lie persistent objections that, irrespective of our friendliness, will not evaporate.

Beyond the New Atheism, listen to Terry Muck's reality check about religious people:

> Most of the world's peoples are not just religious. They are religious with an attitude. Convinced of the truth of their religious traditions, of their ability to satisfactorily answer life's ultimate questions, people joyfully proclaim their good news to any and all.[16]

Most religious communities claim to embody loving truth and to show friendly hospitality to outsiders. In his poem "The Seven Spiritual Stages of Mrs. Marmaduke Moore" Ogden Nash highlights the spiritual confusion of someone who sampled seven different religions.[17] Ultimate truth and ultimate experiences of that truth require a reference point that goes beyond lifestyle and friendship: it is the person of Jesus. Hindu, Buddhist, Judaic, Islamic, Bahá'i, neo-pagan, and New Age apologists all commend their respective pathways while rejecting Christianity.

There is naïveté in the claim that "our community is our apologetic." Chismar and Brent remind us that "there is no conflict between relating interpersonally and dialoguing intellectually."[18] They point out that fruitful discussions can involve showing non-Christians that following Jesus gives us "a better way to interpret and face up to life."[19] The other serious point we must not bypass is that a community may not always be a positive apologetic for Jesus: well-intentioned gatherings do go off the rails, and many have been spiritually damaged or abused in churches.[20]

We know anecdotally that embodied, empathic love on its own is not enough. In alternative spirituality festivals many visitors commented on the genuine warmth, *communitas*, felt and the love shown by our volunteers at the Community of Hope stall. Yet, it was often these very same visitors who initiated contact not because of our friendly vibe but just so they could challenge our faith. The loving vibes made little difference to these individuals who had prejudged that any kind of Christianity—Catholic, Orthodox, Celtic, Liberal Protestant, Mystical, Charismatic, or evangelical spirituality—is passé.

Don't Dump the Baby with the Bathwater

The embodied apologetic model reflects an overreaction to individuals who lack humility and enjoy the adrenaline rush of debates. Peter Rollins has taken the idea of embodied apologetics to another level. He is well read by many of our colleagues in emerging church networks and has shaped the way a lot of people now think about apologetics and mission. He has declared the "end of apologetics."[21] Rollins sees traditional evidentiary arguments for the resurrection and appeals to logic—he calls them "word and wonder" apologetics—as comprising a modernist power discourse. Evidential apologetics relies on assembling historical and legal facts to support the Gospels, like in Lee Strobel's *The Case for Christ*. He goes on to say that this approach attempts to command people to believe and convert. An illustration he uses is where people are commanded to affirm Christ out of fear of hell. The result, as he sees it, is converts who lack any spiritual heart.

Rollins advocates a different approach where the church does not "provide an answer" but rather embraces "a type of communication that opens up thought by asking questions and celebrating complexity."[22] He is keen to present a powerless discourse—one that is not expressed as a top-down monologue emanating from an institutional power structure—that offers hints of the divine rather than explicit answers. He posits the emerging community as "a question rather than an answer."[23] This approach can appeal to individuals whose personality type inclines to mystical experience, poetry, and art rather than discursive verbal communication.

Three primary points must be considered. First, Rollins typecasts evidentialist apologetics as being out-of-step with both Jesus and with the uncertainties of emerging culture. His claim that apologetics commands conversions through argument ignores discussions on the role of the Holy Spirit in apologetics.[24] Rollins dislikes the legal flavor of modern apologetics but never considers the history behind this model or more importantly why the Bible uses legal imagery apologetically.[25] His analogy of manipulative and shallow sermons on hell has nothing to do with mainstream apologetics.

Second, he misuses Paul's remarks about worldly wisdom in 1 Corinthians 2:1–5 to claim (a) that the apostle was opposed to apologetics, and (b) that evidential apologetics reflects the worldly mind-set that Paul rejected.[26] Actually, Paul rebuked the Corinthians' obsession with impressive oratory, and the remainder of the epistle exposed their divisiveness, unethical behavior, abuse of charismatic gifts, and doubts about the resurrection. Rollins's rhetoric mirrors a common error made by other Christians who misapply this same passage to claim that Paul failed in Athens (Acts 17:16–32).[27] In reality Paul engaged in contextualized apologetics to both Jew and gentile in Athens.[28]

Apologists often emphasize miracles and eyewitness testimony. Although he does not completely reject "word and wonder," Rollins tries to reframe the place

of miracle beyond apologetics and speculates that Jesus's motive for performing miracles was out of love rather than for the purpose of compelling belief.[29]
There is no need, however, to infer an either/or motive because Jesus's healing
miracles were performed *both* out of loving compassion *and* to encourage
belief. John's Gospel sums up by saying the miraculous signs are recorded "so
that you may come to believe that Jesus is the Messiah" (John 20:31). Rollins
fails to acknowledge that apologists who have followed Paul's contextualized
model have constantly adapted as social and intellectual currents shift.[30]

Third, Rollins and his associates treasure apophatic spirituality but they
overlook a crucial matter. Gregory Palamas (1296–1359/60) was an apologist and
missionary who was a great proponent of Eastern Orthodox apophatic theology.
While the roots of apophatic theology derive from the fourth-century Cappado-
cian fathers Basil the Great, Gregory of Nyssa, and Gregory of Nazianzus—and
they were apologists too—it was Palamas who best elucidated it. This mystical
experiential theology emphasizes that God in his essence is unknowable because
no human words or thoughts are capable of grasping who God is. At the heart
of apophatic theology is the point that notions about God create idols of God.
Palamas said that what is known to us is what exists outside of God. We know
these things because of God's will or energy that is present and accessible to
us in creation. The analogy of the sun and its rays is often used to illustrate
the point: we cannot touch the sun but we do directly experience its rays. The
sun's rays are part of the sun but the rays are not identical to the sun. In like
manner the sun represents God's essence, which is beyond our comprehension,
while the sun's rays are the divine energies of God's grace that are accessible to
us. Knowledge of God's will and energy is experienced by Christians through
baptism and the Eucharist, both of which relate to the resurrection.[31]

Gregory Palamas: Monk, Mystic, Missionary

As enthusiasm grows for apophatic spirituality what is being forgotten is that
Palamas embodied *both* a breathtaking Christian mysticism *and* a heart for
apologetics. He did not set up an antinomy of *either* mysticism *or* cognitive
apologetics. John Meyendorff remarked that Palamas was "the greatest Greek
theologian of the Middle Ages."[32] His mystical theology developed partly from
an understanding of the resurrection. Emmanuel Cazabonne remarks that
"life according to the Gospel was for him the middle course between Baptism,
which is the beginning of the imitation of Christ, and its completion in the
Resurrection."[33] In his preaching Palamas "looked closely at all the Gospels
of Resurrection to determine who was the first to see the risen Christ."[34] He
harmonized the Gospel accounts concerning the first human witness to the resurrection. Notice that he did not drive an artificial wedge between his mystical
theology of experience and the apologetic task of harmonizing biblical texts.

In 1354 Palamas was taken captive in Turkey by Muslims. Over a period of sixteen months he took the opportunity to defend the Christian faith in a context where Islam was the dominant religion.[35] There are three surviving letters concerning this part of his life and ministry.[36] The letters disclose how Palamas dialogued with Muslims. He had his strengths and weaknesses. His polemical tone was harsh and he was ill-informed about Muhammad and the Qur'an. However, he did not hesitate, when Muslim officials challenged his beliefs, to "offer a sufficient defense."[37] When it was alleged that Muhammad had been mentioned in the Gospels but that later Christians had tampered with the texts, Palamas defended the integrity of the New Testament by stating that "nothing was ever cut out from it" nor was anything in the text altered.[38] Palamas also "talked about the resurrection and the ascension of the Lord and of the testimonies of the prophets which show that Christ is also God and that this God is the one who is witnessed to as having become man from the virgin and suffered for us and risen."[39]

Other Reflections

We want to make two further points. Some anti-apologetic arguments miss the point, while non-Christians—whether they are atheists or alternative spirituality seekers—"get it": if the resurrection is discredited à la Bishop Spong, Dan Brown's *The Da Vinci Code*, and Hollywood producer James Cameron's 2007 TV-documentary "The Jesus Family Tomb," then there is no lynchpin![40] If Jesus's corpse turned up then Paul was absolutely correct in saying that the game is up and the Christian worldview must cave in (1 Cor. 15:17). Discourses that delegitimate the reality of the risen Christ must be answered. It is erroneous to typecast resurrection apologetics as a power discourse. If someone is astute in posing a question then they deserve to receive an intelligent answer.

Finally, not everyone is mystically inclined or principally moved by art and poetry. In alternative spiritualities there are strong currents that prioritize myth, metaphor, intuition, and experiences. Yet at the same time, advocates of alternative spiritualities have not rejected cognition and human reasoning processes. Indeed, some advocates of alternative spiritualities end up posing very hard-nosed, evidentialist-style questions concerning the credibility of the Bible. We have found that holistic spirituality writers, such as Deepak Chopra, James Redfield, Wayne Dyer, and Gus diZerega, are not at all averse to cognition, facts, and evidence.

Resurrection Defense Is Not Passé

Unlike Rollins, some of his peers do acknowledge that "it is impossible to do any kind of mission without apologetics of some kind."[41] However, these commentators also regard evidential defenses of the Christ-event as passé: "We don't do Josh McDowell-style apologetics because it has little mileage in our culture."[42] It is easy to find fault with material that was written nearly forty years ago and then judge it a "failure" because it doesn't meet current expectations. Some imaginative sympathy is needed to understand the context in which McDowell's books were produced. They filled a heartfelt need, particularly among undergraduate students on university campuses, when the intelligentsia had its fair share of skeptics, particularly Western Marxists, Freudians, humanists, and existentialists. As we will now discuss, far from being marginal or irrelevant, there are different kinds of resurrection-based apologetic approaches that are eminently suited to the public square today.

Learning from the Areopagus

Our time is not that dissimilar from Jesus's and Paul's world. There were lots of religious movements to choose from then, and there were doubters among the philosophers. Athens was a religious and philosophical potpourri. In chapter 11 we will go into more detail about Paul's teaching in Athens in Acts 17:16–34. What we need to note for now is that Paul talked to different groups—those in the synagogue and those in the marketplace. He first visited the familiar turf of the synagogue where he had a shared culture and Holy Scripture. It was a relatively safe place because as a Jew Paul knew well how the order of service ran. He could read from the Hebrew Bible as a springboard to talking about the resurrected Jesus.

Similarly, today we see a lot of keen-hearted pulpit-based evangelism. The church is a great place for younger people to find acceptance, to be nurtured, and to develop in faith. Most Christians are very comfortable with attracting outsiders into the church to hear good news proclaimed. That kind of outreach is great if you happen to be talking to people who have some biblical framework—pull out the respected Bible and preach to a God-fearer!

Of course, as Luke tells the story, Paul did not stay within the synagogue. He could not sit idly by in a city renowned for its cultural achievements, religions, and philosophers, so he moved outside the comfort zone of the synagogue and entered the turf of the gentiles. The marketplace was the hottest scene for discussion about life's ultimate purpose, so there Paul had a ready-made audience of the curious and the cynical. The Stoic philosophers inclined toward a new spiritual ethos and had some sense of the divine permeating the earth. The Epicurean philosophers were the classic tough-minded skeptics. Paul presented the resurrected Christ in terms that each group could grasp.

We opened this chapter with two stories that reflect the same diversity of Paul's day, one representing the experientially inclined and one representing the rational thinker. The archbishop was inside the "synagogue" and in need of answers, while the masseuses were in the marketplace offering their experiences, but still groping for something more.

Being Alert to Post-Christendom

Paul Elie gives us a taste of what many feel about our era:

> We are all skeptics now, believer and unbeliever alike. There is no one faith, evident at all times and places. Every religion is one among many. The clear lines of orthodoxy are made crooked by our experience, and are complicated by our lives. Believer and unbeliever are in the same predicament, thrown back onto ourselves in complex circumstances, looking for a sign. As ever, religious belief makes its claim somewhere between revelation and projection, between holiness and human frailty, but the problem of proof, indeed the burden of belief, for so long upheld by society, is now back on the believer, where it should be.[43]

Elie's remarks reflect his North American experience of fragmentation and exposure to spiritual pluralism, along with his individual quest for a new kind of deinstitutionalized, boundless spirituality. The sign Elie seeks involves the convergence of life with the content of the message. Many Westerners today perceive the Christian view of God as untenable, so we should not be surprised to see a devolving into the self in popular metaphysics and spirituality. The collapse of belief in God's transcendence is apparent in the eighteenth-century Enlightenment and accelerated in the 1960s as youth turned to East Asian gurus. Many people in North America have personal experiences parallel to those of Elie, but clearly not everyone identifies with his experiences of fragmentation.

Resurrection Apologetic for Post-Christendom Seekers

For many years we have found ourselves among post-Christendom seekers in all kinds of places, from commercial radio and TV to Mind-Body-Spirit festivals. These experiences have taught us about what "works" in relating and communicating with seekers today. They want to know not only what works but also what is true. We have found that presenting the theology of the resurrection as well as an apologetic for the resurrection works very naturally in these contexts. Taking a look at some of the resurrection zones we set out in the previous chapter can provide a helpful starting point for conversation.

Post-Christendom seekers are keen to explore meaning through stories; therefore one of the most effective ways of entering their world is through stories connected to the mosaic of the resurrection. A combination of stories and scriptural passages works well in all kinds of contexts, be it one-to-one conversations, small groups, or from a podium/pulpit.

A conversation can creatively explore all twelve resurrection zones. Some zones like justice might surprise you as a place for conversation, but consider this: people now embrace the law of karma as an explanation for evil and suffering and as a tool for spiritual growth. Reflecting on justice can lead to an opportunity to converse about the resurrection providing a deeper and better understanding of fairness, or of good and evil.

Ethics likewise might initially seem an unusual place to start a conversation, but we need to recall that many seekers highly prize the quest for values to live by. The most amenable zones for starting conversations with seekers include: forgiveness, whole person, hope, empowerment, face of God, Eden breaking in, and new community.

Apologetics of Touch

We indicated earlier that different personality types link to different attitudes about spirituality both inside and outside the church, as well as to diverse gifts and abilities. Apologetics, to be effective, must involve empathy, the ability to understand and be sensitive to people's thoughts and feelings in a pluralist environment. But putting together gifts of empathy with the apologetic skills that enable understanding of questions and doubts isn't easy. In fact, these traits are not often found in the same person, and many churches tend to emphasize one over the other. Communities of faith can be great at emphasizing pastoral care and empathy *or* great at sharing the gospel or evangelizing. But effective communication of the gospel must involve these two elements working in tandem. We call this an apologetic of touch, and the next several paragraphs provide illustrations of this style.

Consider the "Play of Life," an interactive approach to positive change devised by Argentinean Christian Carlos Raimundo. It begins with a brief one-to-one chat about problems that a person may be experiencing. The person is then invited to create a sculpture of how they feel using small plastic figures that represent their relationships with friends, family, workmates, and God. During the time of figurine sculpture there is space for listening to the person. The Play of Life embodies the theology of the resurrection with forgiveness, wholeness, and new community flowing into the conversation. After further dialogue, the person is encouraged to create a positive sculpture of how they would prefer their situation to be. The boards constitute a "before" and "after" portrait, and a photograph of this is taken so they can be seen side-by-side. The person then moves over to a professional massage chair. During the massage they are encouraged to quietly reflect on how the risen Christ could make a difference. After the massage, the person moves to a third chair where a time of prayer occurs.

Another possibility for an apologetics of touch is interacting with the biblical images of the tarot card pack in one-to-one or group settings. As we discuss in chapter 4 the images on the cards are very explicit with reference to biblical stories/church art and are therefore very amenable to conversation and reflection as a person brings their story into contact with the bigger biblical story portrayed on the cards. Such encounters often lead to prayer and release from pain. It is also not uncommon for people to bring to the surface typical apologetics questions that relate to Jesus, the resurrection, and the Gospel accounts.[44]

Aromatherapy can likewise open up horizons for conversation, touch, and prayer. Essential oils are a product of God's good creation, and oil imagery is biblically associated with God's anointing of the Spirit. It is not difficult in a setting where personal integrity is shining through for conversations to flow around the zones of the resurrection grid. In one-to-one conversation accompanied by touch, a person feels comfortable about opening up over their life experiences and quest for meaning. It is a social context where a matrix of meanings can be explored in a gentle, noncoercive conversation.[45]

Neo-Pagan spirituality is earth-centered and includes a ritual calendar known as the Wheel of the Year. The Wheel of the Year includes an eight-episode story that coincides with changes in the seasons and equinoxes. The story begins with the goddess, who is also a queen, and she is carrying the child of promise (Samhain 31 October) and gives birth at Yuletide (Christmas). As the seasons progress the story involves the dark lord of the underworld clashing with the King of Light. The Wheel of the Year has a dying-and-rising god myth that teaches the annual cycle of the seasons is something that happens to both nature and the Divine because ultimately all of nature partakes of the Divine.[46]

There are some obvious points where the Neo-Pagan story is paralleled in the Gospels: the virgin Mary conceives the child who is born to be the savior of the world, and the savior is tempted by the Devil, and the savior dies and rises from the dead. What we point out is that the Neo-Pagan Wheel of the Year story's symbolism glimpses things that are only truly fulfilled by Jesus in the Easter-event.

It is feasible to develop an empathic apologetic that combines the tactile and visual, with story and meditative exercises. We have used artistic displays that bridge the gap between the Wheel of the Year and Jesus's story. We have displayed a painting of Mary carrying the Christ-child in her womb, rejoicing before God and nature. This painting is supplemented by eight visual slides illustrating Jesus's ministry that culminate in his death and resurrection. Next to the artwork are objects that can be touched—like a bird's feather, plant leaves, crystal rocks—that are symbolic emblems representing the good things that God has created. The visual and tactile items combine with some contemplative exercises about Christ as the one who truly fulfills the Wheel of the Year myth.[47]

Resurrection and the Tough-Minded

Not long after commencing seminary Ross was reading widely on the person of Jesus but then became a skeptic as to his divinity. The liberal texts blew his mind. He advised the president that he was leaving and returning to the practice of law when he happened to pass a sale of secondhand books in the administration center. His eye caught a book called *The Law above the Law* by John Warwick Montgomery, and he purchased it for twenty cents. In his reading he was drawn to historical and legal facts of Jesus's resurrection and reread the Gospels, which eventually led to him reentering the apostolic faith. For Ross, the truth of the resurrection was crucial, and he had to understand and believe in it in order to remain committed to the faith.

Post-Christendom seekers need not only empathy, but also intellectual answers and sound reasons to believe. Seekers like to explore how the resurrection "works," that is, how the implications of the resurrection apply to them and empower them for living; but after thinking through how it "works," they will often also ask, "But is it true?" They know of critics who confine Jesus to the grave and cast doubts on the New Testament.

We have set out a traditional resurrection historical-legal apologetics elsewhere, so we will not repeat it in full here.[48] What we propose to do, rather, is to set out two summaries of important points about the evidences for the resurrection from both sides of the Atlantic that have been tested in the best philosophical debates and one-to-one dialogue. These summations provide support for the historicity of the resurrection. They establish a strong case that Jesus rose from the dead that is difficult for skeptics to dodge. We will follow the two summaries with a section that presents a series of questions commonly asked in the marketplace about the historicity of the resurrection.

Commonly Agreed Facts

The first approach is what Gary Habermas calls commonly agreed facts about the narratives of Jesus's death and resurrection that can be gleaned from a wide range of texts from conservative and liberal scholars:

- Jesus's death by crucifixion.
- The earliest disciples' experiences of appearances of the risen Jesus.
- Their subsequent transformations to the point of even being willing to die for their faith.

- The resurrection as the very center of early apostolic preaching.
- The conversion and resulting transformation of Paul and James.[49]

Six Essential Details

The second approach is distilled from N. T. Wright, who responds to scholars whose conclusions reflect very negative and skeptical views. Wright counters the skepticism by emphasizing some essential details:

- Jews and Greeks understood that resurrection entailed physical embodiment.
- Paul believed in a physical embodied resurrection both in the case of Jesus and eschatologically for believers.
- Jesus was executed and did not lapse into unconsciousness. After burial Jesus's corpse subsequently came back to life and exited the tomb that was guarded by soldiers.
- The earliest Christians believed in Jesus's bodily resurrection and an empty tomb.
- The resurrection narratives are credible early sources deriving from witnesses who narrate events and claim tactile contact with the risen Jesus.
- The Gospel narratives do not support hallucinations or reductionist reinterpretations of the witnesses' experiences of the risen Jesus as mere spiritual visions.[50]

Top Four Questions

Here are the four questions that people most commonly ask about the historicity of the resurrection.

Can We Trust the NT Gospels?

At an interactive course for inquirers about the way of Jesus a woman who had actively participated asked Ross, "I love the things that Matthew, Mark, Luke, and John speak about, but how do I know the Gospels are actually the words of the writers and not some later embellishment?" Our response to that query is that there are three basic criteria or tests:

TRANSMISSION

Has the written document been carefully and reliably copied and recopied from one generation to the next? As we don't possess any of the original documents with respect to Jesus's life and journey, we must check the process of copying in the available manuscripts. In the case of the New

Testament books, there are more than five thousand Greek manuscripts that we can peruse to check on the copying process. When the copies are compared, they complement each other so that an original can be faithfully reconstructed and the pedigrees of different manuscripts can be established. Broadly speaking, there is every reason to have great confidence in the biblical texts. A survey of surviving manuscripts reveals that we have excellent manuscript copies.

Of course showing that the documents have been faithfully copied and recopied by hand does *not* establish that the actual contents of the New Testament are true. All this transmission test shows is that the books have been preserved and recopied with great accuracy.

INTERNAL

The second test addresses a more specific issue: Do the documents claim to be written by eyewitnesses or those closely associated with the original witnesses to the events recorded in them? In the case of the Gospels both Matthew and John were eyewitnesses to many events that they reported, while Mark's Gospel is believed to comprise the preaching of St. Peter. Luke's Gospel begins by acknowledging that he has carefully checked things out with the original eyewitnesses.

Of course even if the Gospel writers claim to be eyewitnesses, we still must scrutinize them. So the next critical step involves posing questions about the character and motives of these writers: Are they trustworthy? How transparent are they when recounting what they said and did in the company of Jesus? Do they falsify information?

That cluster of questions about the character and integrity of the eyewitnesses has been assessed by a variety of scholars. One approach is to consider what Simon Greenleaf, one of the greatest American lawyers on evidence from yesteryear, said. He insisted that we can test the Gospel witnesses to establish if they are telling the truth about what they experienced and observed. His tests apply common sense that most people would rely on in ordinary daily life:

> The credit due to the testimony of witnesses depends upon, firstly, their honesty; secondly, their ability; thirdly, their number and the consistency of their testimony; fourthly, the conformity of their testimony with experience; and fifthly, the coincidence of their testimony with collateral circumstances.[51]

The first three tests are straightforward. There is no compelling reason to doubt the honesty of any of the Gospel writers. In fact one is struck by their sincerity and confronted by their openness as they even deal with the issues of their own failures, the harshness of some of Jesus's teachings, and his own sense of despair and anguish at the thought of death. As John Warwick Montgomery says, "Their simple literalness and directness is almost painful."[52]

Besides the Gospel writers we have two more independent trustworthy witnesses in Paul and James. These two men offer independent and firsthand testimony of what they saw. In the discussions about the trustworthy witness to Jesus much attention focuses on what Paul and James wrote (1 Corinthians 15) because their material is devoid of any possible accusation of containing hearsay. James was one of Jesus's earthly brothers (Gal. 1:9; Matt. 13:55), and Jesus's brothers were very skeptical (John 7:3–5). James's words are the primary testimony of an eyewitness to the resurrection because the former skeptic has become Christ's servant and calls people to believe (James 1:1; 2:1). When we take Matthew, Mark, and Luke into consideration there is no doubt that they provide good historical material on the resurrection. However, apart from the Great Commission (Matt. 28:16–20), what they record of the resurrection appearances is other people's observations rather than their own. So in a technical legal sense they present "hearsay" evidence. Hearsay is not necessarily a bad thing, but Paul, James, and John are important here because they wrote down what they themselves saw and heard.

Greenleaf's second test, the witnesses' ability, depends on the accuracy of their powers to recall what they saw and heard. The original disciples were all either fishermen or, like Luke, had other professions. Unlike most laborers, fishermen in Jesus's time probably owned their means of production and belonged to a class of people who had the skills of a small businessman.[53] There is no reason to doubt their ability to provide reliable testimony to what they saw.

With respect to the third test—number and consistency of testimony—the disciples' accounts are all consistent on the basic details of the death and resurrection of Jesus, although they each tell the story in their own way. And the number of witnesses is never a matter of big debate, as there are plenty of people who tell the story of Jesus.

Perhaps the biggest issue concerns their testimony and its conformity to experience—Greenleaf's fourth criteria. We don't ordinarily see anyone returning alive from the grave, so our initial impression is that the resurrection looks like something beyond our normal experiences. However, as we indicate later in the book, there is a strong sense in which resurrection is not inconsistent with the phenomena of the natural world and the religious longings of most people expressing the hope for an embodied afterlife. The key point here is that if the way we view the world includes an acceptance of a God, then the possibility of resurrection and miracles is not inconsistent with our beliefs. Many people outside of Christianity are open to the possibility of the miraculous, and the skeptics and atheists who do not see the world this way are more the exception than the rule. Philosopher Richard Swinburne's observation is helpful here:

> I can only say that my own belief is that the historical evidence is quite strong, given the background evidence [God's existence], to make it considerably more probable than not that Christ rose from the dead on the first Easter day.[54]

Walter Chandler, who was an American lawyer, states that the coincidence of a testimony with collateral circumstances (Greenleaf's fifth test) is the key test of credibility when a witness is dead and his evidence has been reduced to writing. This is obviously the case for the Gospels.[55] The Gospel writers and witnesses do not avoid detail, and much of what they record and say has been shown to be consistent with external data. (This criteria, by the way, is one reason why secular scholars dismiss Joseph Smith's account of the origins of the American Indians in the Book of Mormon. The archaeological and anthropological evidence completely contradicts Smith's claims.)

Scott Peck, who had been immersed in the experiential approaches of alternative spiritualities, made these comments as he personally came to grips with reading the Gospels:

> But when I did finally come to read the Gospels, I did so with a dozen years of experience of trying in my own small way to be a teacher or a healer, so I knew a little something about teaching and healing and what it's like to be a teacher and healer. With this experiential knowledge under my belt, I was absolutely thunderstruck by the extraordinary reality of the man I found in the Gospels. . . . I discovered a man so incredibly real that no one could have made him up.
>
> It occurred to me then that if the Gospel writers had been into PR and embellishment, as I had assumed, they would have created the kind of Jesus three quarters of Christians still seem to be trying to create—what Lily refers to as "the wimpy Jesus." . . . So that's when I began to suspect that, rather than being public relations specialists, the Gospel writers were accurate reporters, generally going to great pains to record as accurately as possible the events and sayings in the life of a man they themselves hardly began to understand, but in whom they knew that Heaven and earth had met. And that's when I began to fall in love with Jesus.[56]

EXTERNAL

The third test addresses the question of corroborating details from sources that are external to the written Gospels. Some corroboration is available from archaeological inscriptions that mention the names of Roman officials (like Pilate). There are also Greco-Roman and Jewish writings—such as those of Tacitus, Suetonius, Pliny the Younger, and Josephus—that correlate to details in the Gospels. And finally, matters that were peculiar to the social, political, and legal background of Palestine at the time Jesus lived are reflected in the Gospels.

Did Jesus Really Die?

The question of Jesus's death is a critical issue for some (in particular, for Muslims, which you'll read about more in chapter 7), and there are those who attempt to explain the resurrection via the swoon theory—the idea that Jesus did not actually die but just lost consciousness and was mistaken for dead. In some respects the motion picture *The Passion of the Christ* graphically portrays how implausible the swoon theory is as a credible alternative explanation. Swoon theory advocate Barbara Thiering proposes that Jesus revived in the tomb as one of the thieves, who was a medic, used the aloes and myrrh. Even though they were respectively injured with broken legs and spear wounds they rolled the tombstone away and Jesus was declared to be resurrected.[57]

The great skeptic David F. Strauss makes a strong argument against the swoon theory:

> It is impossible that a being who had stolen half dead out of the sepulcher, who crept about weak and ill wanting medical treatment, who required bandaging, strengthening and indulgence, and who still at last yielded to his sufferings could have given the disciples the impression that he was a conqueror over death and the grave, the Prince of life: an impression which lay at the bottom of their future ministry.[58]

In addition to Strauss's points, we add four additional arguments that Jesus really did die:

- There is strong internal evidence in the Gospel accounts concerning Jesus's crucifixion, and it comes from writers who would have preferred to tell a very different story.
- There is also external evidence. For example, the Roman historian Tacitus in AD 112 recorded that Jesus was executed under Pilate's orders during the reign of Tiberius.
- The Gospels record that a number of women observed Jesus's execution and at least two of these women witnessed the actual burial. It is important to note the quality of their testimony. They alone give an unbroken chain of testimony from his death at point A and his burial to the resurrection at point B. They were certain he died and rose again. In the culture of Jesus's time, however, women were not considered reliable witnesses.[59] If the Gospel writers were inventing this part of the story, they would have ensured that *men* provided the important unbroken chain of testimony (Matt. 26:31–27:66; Mark 14:26–15:47; Luke 22:39–23:56; John 18–19).
- One of the key players in the death and resurrection events was Joseph of Arimathea (Luke 23:50–56). He was a member of the Sanhedrin, and his village of Arimathea has no symbolic or biblical value. It highlights the integrity of the writers that they mention such a trivial detail, since in effect one could have at the time looked him up.[60] Raymond Brown states, "That the burial was done by Joseph of Arimathea is very probable, since a Christian fictional creation . . . of a Jewish Sanhedrist who does what is right is almost inexplicable, granted the hostility in early Christian writings toward the Jewish authorities responsible for the death of Jesus."[61]

What Circumstantial Evidence Exists for the Resurrection?

Direct evidence in history or law consists of people who were present at the events and inscribe in accounts what they saw. Circumstantial evidence is evidence supporting these accounts. For example in a murder case, direct evidence is the testimony of who fired the gun. Circumstantial evidence would include that the accused had purchased a rifle, that his fingerprints were on it, and that the deadly bullet matched others fired from the rifle. The role of the historian, lawyer, or anyone involved in common-sense re-creation of an event is to build a strong chain of circumstantial evidence to help people deduce what took place. Here are five strong pieces of circumstantial evidence for the resurrection.[62]

- The empty tomb and the only hypothesis that fits the facts both indicate that Christ arose. It was not in the interest of Roman or Jewish authorities to inflame the legend of Jesus. They were about destroying Christianity, not enhancing its mystique. Why would the disciples steal the corpse when it is totally inconsistent with Jesus's teaching to be involved in such fraudulent behavior? Further it is absurd to suggest that they would suffer persecution, martyrdom, ridicule, and hardship for such a callous deception. Peter would hardly allow himself to be crucified upside down, nor would John accept exile on Patmos for what they both knew was a lie. Sir Norman Anderson, who was a prominent specialist on Islamic law, said, "The empty tomb, then, forms a veritable rock on which all rationalistic theories of the resurrection dash themselves in vain."[63]
- The fact that Christians worship on Sunday and not the Sabbath is another piece of circumstantial evidence. Only an event of deep significance could cause Jewish observers to make such a commitment.
- The fact that the tomb of Christ was not subject to early pilgrimages of worship also provides support for the resurrection.
- The existence of the church whose origins can be traced to the resurrection of its founder is another piece of evidence.
- Finally, we have an unbroken chain of testimony from the disciples' time to today of changed lives that find their new meaning in the resurrection.

Is There Any Evidence for the Theme of Resurrection outside of the Bible and Church Teachings?

Our universal human longing for an afterlife finds expression in resurrection symbols in pop culture and in the beliefs of some other religions. In later chapters we will explore the theme of resurrection as it is found within the natural realm as part of general revelation, and in myths about dying-and-rising deities.

Preaching and Teaching the Resurrection

When most Christians think about sharing about the resurrection they are immediately drawn to the truth question. A better entry point, however, is exploring what difference the resurrection makes in people's lives and showing that it really does work. In that regard we would structure a sermon, Bible study, or series around the zones of the resurrection, highlighting those that we felt were particularly significant for the occasion. For example, an expository sermon on 1 Corinthians 15:3–5, 17–25 would pick up the following zones:

- Forgiveness
- Whole person
- Empowerment
- Hope for now and future
- Confidence

Most people are both/and, and therefore want to grasp not just the practical implications of the resurrection but the truth question as well. Atheists and skeptics, on the other hand, will most likely want to start on the truth question. A traditional apologetic for the resurrection remains an essential part of our faith sharing today, and plenty of books are available that explore the subject. The Habermas-Wright criteria and the four questions discussed above are all useful steps in presenting an argument that the resurrection is the only plausible hypothesis to the question of whether Jesus rose from the dead.

The authors of this book have delivered expository sermons based on 1 Corinthians 15:3–10 that explain the following:

- The early nature of this account (around AD 55). The authorship of 1 Corinthians is not questioned by skeptics, and Paul clearly had an encounter with the risen Jesus.
- The fact that the resurrection was *predicted* in the Hebrew Scriptures (vv. 3–4) (see chapters 11 and 12 for details).
- That the resurrection *happened* and was witnessed by numerous people (vv. 5–8). Paul lists all of those Jesus appeared to, including James and himself (we mentioned above the significance of their testimony). This point allows us to address the reliability of the New Testament, the question of Jesus's death, and the unbroken chain of testimony.
- The significance of Paul's own personal *transformation* and the power of the *grace* of God (vv. 9–10). Even in a classical apologetic we would conclude by noting the difference that the resurrection makes.

A Few Stories

Philip had the privilege of being among several different people who bore witness to a man named Neil at university.[64] Neil came to faith in Jesus after he had devised his own worldview that combined New Age spirituality, meditation, and science. He saw the benefits of the traditional apologetic case for the resurrection as well as its impact on his own journey. A couple years elapsed after his faith commitment and he was part of a team that was going to undertake a short-term mission in a major New Age center. He caught up with Philip prior to his mission trip and heard that he was going to spend time investigating claims that Jesus went to India and Tibet. At the time Neil privately felt that this was probably not very significant. After his return from the mission trip he confessed that he had been staggered to find that among all the New Age people he met on the mission trip the single consistent problem raised concerned the "lost years" of Jesus between the ages of thirteen and twenty-nine.[65] The reminder here is that while many might think of New Agers as being more absorbed in experiential and mystical pursuits, they are very often both/and people who want to pursue the truth questions addressed in traditional apologetics.

The both/and issue comes out with crystal clarity in any alternative spirituality festival. Ross encountered Sharon at one such festival. Sharon was a woman who was fascinated by the tarot card imagery and what it might mean for her spiritual journey. The cards' images give us a picture book of biblical healing themes and powerful events that run from Genesis to Revelation. She was elated by the message that "it works": personal transformation and empowerment were on the horizon through the resurrection. Yet, after absorbing all these positive ideas Sharon asked a highly cognitive and fact-oriented question. She wanted to know about the reliability of the Gospels and the factuality of the empty tomb. We don't necessarily expect "postmodern" people to ask such questions;[66] but the real point that we all have to grasp is that in today's world one must not merely be flexible in dialogue but must also be ready to address traditional truth questions. We need to have greater sensitivity and openness toward those we have conversations with, acknowledging different personality types, ways of knowing, and the dynamics of people's current views with respect to Christianity. Do our personalities truly embody and express all the life-changing and empowering realities implied in Jesus's resurrection?

Spiritual Audit

1. Are you, or is your Christian community, entrenched in a specific approach to apologetics?

2. What personality type are you, and how does it impact your faith?

3. Are most of your Christian friends of a similar personality type and spiritual background?

4. Do you have a pastoral empathy towards your non-Christian friends and contacts?

5. Is it enough that you personally embody the way of Jesus as the answer to the questions about Jesus that non-Christians pose?

PART TWO

THUMBPRINTS OF THE RESURRECTION IN CULTURE

Whatever the wonder and whatever the questioning, Christ's rising from the dead is an irreplaceable "given" in the life of Christian faith. Without this event, there would be no New Testament; and the life, teaching and death of Jesus would have been lost in the fragile particularities of past history. But because the resurrection is central to faith's perception of the saving action of God, it provokes, from its very particularity, endless reflection on its universal significance.

Anthony J. Kelly[1]

4

The Resurrection in Popular and High Culture

The idea of the resurrection fills us with profound, deep, and for me at least, non-specific and extremely complicated emotions. Thus I do not want it represented in images that are otherwise. Above all, though, I do want it represented. That is, I want it, to paraphrase Luther, "spoken" but also "sung, painted and played." I also want it molded, sculpted, danced.

Linda Marie Delloff[1]

We who proclaim the resurrection for the world today need to ransack our imaginations for adequate images to express it.

Edgar Krentz[2]

Did you realize that there are analogies of Jesus's resurrection in novels, TV serials, and blockbuster movies? In this chapter we will identify some significant and popular examples of thumbprints of the resurrection in popular culture. A discerning Christian can talk about resurrected characters in movies and novels as stepping-stones to the story of the risen Jesus. Before we explore the cultural territory outside the church's walls, we will look at the production of church art and church music. As we discuss some creative examples of the resurrection in church art and music, we will also take note of how these things impact a wider non-Christian audience.

Taking a Risk

Looking for analogies of resurrections in culture is risky business because of the disturbing flak that comes from other Christians. Over twenty years ago we noticed that our friends and acquaintances were delving into astrology, complementary healing remedies, and tarot cards. They were on a personal journey of reflection and seeking transformation. They were open to exploring almost anything *except the church*.

We mused, how would they ever discover the rich transformation that Jesus offers? Like missionaries in far-flung cultures we felt that we were immigrants living in a new spiritually-oriented culture that had its own customs, rituals, special jargon, myths, and metanarratives. Like Paul's efforts to speak about an "unknown god" as a stepping-stone to the risen Christ (Acts 17:16–32), we looked for similar stepping-stones to speaking with our friends about Christianity.

We were surprised to find stepping-stones in tarot cards, including one depicting the resurrection of the dead. We were not naïve ignoramuses blithely ignoring the fact that tarot is used in fortune-telling. The occult use of tarot started around the time of the French Revolution, but tarot cards began as a game during the Renaissance. The earliest decks were lavishly decorated with explicit biblical images. When we examined several modern-day tarot decks we saw a pictorial panorama of biblical stories: creation, fall, crucifixion, and resurrection. Although the cards were not originally "Christian," the biblical imagery is unmistakable. We talked to hundreds of tarot fans who started to realize via the cards' images that a new beginning in life was available to them through the risen Jesus.

A few years rolled by and we had a visit from our friend and colleague the Scottish theologian John Drane, who regularly lectures at Fuller Seminary. He was excited when we showed him the biblical images in the tarot and the three of us agreed that a book must be written for today's non-Christian seekers.[3] We faced a challenge not only in finding a publisher brave enough to risk backing our book *Beyond Prediction*;[4] but after its release it was placed under an embargo by many Christian bookstores. Sometimes it was sold furtively in brown-paper bags from under the service counter! It was condemned and rejected by Christians but was having a positive impact on the lives of alternative-spiritualities seekers. There was great resistance and fear expressed about the "dangers" of tarot cards, but the actual point that we were making was not being properly heard. So be prepared for an inquisition if you hunt for analogies of the resurrection beyond the walls of the church!

Resurrection in Christian Art and Music

We are all familiar with paintings of Jesus as the Good Shepherd, the Nativity with Mary, his baptism, transfiguration, and the Last Supper. Europe's cathedrals have etched in their architecture, stained glass windows, and artwork visual expressions of the gospel drama. Eastern Orthodox churches are well renowned for their icons. Art galleries and museums exhibit many paintings and sculptures of Jesus. Every generation that embraces Jesus's story finds it helpful to relate to him through artistic works.

Both Christian and non-Christian artists (like Salvador Dali) have produced artworks depicting different facets of Jesus's life. Reluctantly, we must pass over many notable artists of the fifteenth, sixteenth, and seventeenth centuries who produced paintings, frescoes, or sculptures of the risen Christ such as Fra Angelico (1440), Donatello (1465), Giovanni Bellini (1475), Veit Stoss (1477–1489), Hans Memling (1490), Pieter Bruegel the Elder (1560), El Greco (1577), Rubens (1611 and 1616), and Rembrandt (1635).[5] We will restrict our survey here to earlier periods, but before we look at the resurrection in art we have some clarifying comments on crucifixion in church art.

Crucifixion and the Cross in Church Art

We began this book with Tommaso Campanella's protest about an excess of paintings on the crucifixion. Rita Nakashima Brock has much to say about the important place that the resurrection had in church art before the tenth century. However, she points out that from the tenth century onwards the resurrection was displaced in art by the crucifixion. In glancing back over the panorama of church history she makes this wry observation that virtually echoes Campanella's complaint:

> The crucifixion is one of the most recognizable images in all of Western art. Once he dies, that is all he seems to do. His death becomes the screen onto which is projected every imaginable human suffering. Jesus' death has become so characteristic of Christian imagery and theology, it is nearly impossible to imagine a time when his crucifixion did not claim the center of Christian art and piety.[6]

A technical distinction is made between the "empty" cross and the crucifix (which has the body of Jesus impaled). In art the empty cross preceded the crucifix and was a believer's sign of identification. Tertullian (ca. 160–220) noted that Christians routinely made the sign of the cross on their foreheads. The Roman Emperor Julian castigated Christians in the fourth century by saying that they adored the wood of the cross, drew it on their foreheads, and engraved their homes with the cross. The empty cross even became a lucky charm in medieval times for fending off demons. Jaroslav Pelikan indicates that the empty cross was once understood as a symbol of God's power over "the devil in the death and resurrection of Jesus Christ."[7] However in the passage of the centuries that understanding seems to have been lost in parishioners' consciousness. It has also been compounded by the association of the cross with triumphant colonial power.

Some evangelicals seem to be unaware that in church art the empty cross predates the Reformation:

> Although in some church buildings crosses have a statue of Jesus on them, since the Reformation many Christians prefer an empty cross. This underlines that the work of Jesus is complete. Christianity hinges not only on the empty cross but also an empty tomb. Surprisingly, little classical art, however, has focused on the resurrection of Jesus, as compared to the cross.[8]

Before the fifth century the death of Jesus on the cross was never illustrated in church art, although it was lampooned in pagan graffiti. An etching of a human body on a cross but with the head of an ass was found on the Palatine Hill in Rome that dates to AD 200. Underneath the etching is an inscription, "Alexamenos worships his God."[9] The first symbolic representation in church art of Christ suffering was via a sacrificial lamb. The earliest examples of a crucifix and its veneration come in the sixth century but surprisingly do not show Jesus suffering.[10] Instead Jesus is standing, clothed, crowned in victory on a cross. Other representations show him as alive, often praying and associated with heavenly images that point to paradise.

Very graphic representations of Jesus suffering coincide with the enforced conversion of the Saxons. An early surviving piece is a Saxon wooden sculpture known as the Gero Cross dated to AD 965 and now held in the Cologne Cathedral. That sculpture evoked Saxon grief about Jesus's death, but some interpreters of art believe that it may also have been a unifying symbol for their suffering under the Carolingian empire. When that empire flourished the celebration of the Eucharist was changed so that the figure of the resurrected Jesus was removed from the table and replaced by crucifixion imagery.[11]

A much stronger emphasis on crucifixion in art arose in the eleventh century around the time when theologians like St. Anselm (1033–1109) contemplated the meaning of atonement. Anselm's *Cur Deus Homo* made a great impact on Catholic medieval theologians, and on Protestant reformers such as Philip Melanchthon and John Calvin. Some feminist theologians such as Brock have been scathing in their reading of Anselm's theology of substitutionary atonement. Here we part company with those negative analyses. One thing that Brock does astutely observe is that artistic emphasis on the crucifixion increased with the Crusades. She further contends that by the fourteenth century crucifixion imagery had become "grotesque" to the point that "the resurrection fades in importance."[12]

Resurrection in Church Art

Images of the resurrection in church art stand in stark contrast to the grimness evoked by paintings of crucifixion. Until the tenth century the central

focus of Christian art was upon Jesus's incarnation, his miracles, and resurrection.[13] The resurrection was central in artistic images of baptism and
paradise. Baptism was obvious because it symbolized Christians dying and
rising to new life in Christ, while paradise depicted resurrected believers. In
the first four hundred years of church history Christ's bodily resurrection
was not shown visually. His triumph over death was symbolized by the Greek
alphabetical letters *Chi Rho* framed around a laurel wreath on top of the
cross. The laurel wreath was an important symbol of the Roman emperor's
military conquests, and this was transformed by Christians to symbolize
Christ's victory over death. The *Chi Rho* symbol and laurel wreath can be
found on some Christian sarcophagi and on Roman coins from the fourth
century.

Leslie Barnard has pointed out that in the pre-Constantinian era Christian art had the dual apologetic role of reassuring believers and of challenging pagan beliefs about life after death.[14] Catacomb paintings depicted
various biblical events but among the favorites was the raising of Lazarus.
The catacombs never show Jesus crucified, and even pictures of the Last
Supper focus on Jesus announcing his betrayal.[15] Frescoes show believers in heaven celebrating the Eucharist as the feast of the resurrection.[16]
Where paradise is depicted the images include the cities of Jerusalem and
Bethlehem, the rivers of Eden, various animals, saints and martyrs, and
the apostles, "while deer and doves symbolized souls of the risen dead"
and "a gold or jeweled cross stood for the resurrection."[17] Once we move
beyond the era of the catacombs, other representations of the resurrection emerge.

We feel sure that as individual tastes differ there will be many favorite
resurrection paintings from the Renaissance, Reformation, and modern era
that one could nominate as significant. For us there is one artwork that
really does the trick. The masterpiece in question is found in the historic
town of Colmar in the Alsace. There in the Musée d'Unterlinden is Matthias
Grünewald's magnificent Isenheim Altarpiece that includes the crucifixion
and resurrection of Jesus. It was originally commissioned for the monastery
church of St. Anthony's near Colmar (1511–1515), which was a place where
monks treated people with horrible skin ailments. The depiction of Christ
crucified shows his body pierced with thorns but also covered in horrible
rotting sores, while the body of the risen Christ is visually astonishing with
its promise of renewal and transformation from suffering. Those sick persons who first saw this work were offered a glimpse of their relationship to
Christ and the promise of wholeness and healing in the resurrection. This
sixteenth-century panorama is truly the watershed that changes a direction
in art from the supercilious to the graphic nature of Jesus's death and the
commanding triumphant power of his physical resurrection as the Roman
guards flee from the tomb.[18]

Resurrection in Pre-Reformation Art

- Fifth-century ivory carvings of the Passion show the empty tomb, followed by the risen Christ appearing to the disciples.
- The *Utrecht Psalter* from AD 830 has an illustration of Psalm 19 with two angels accompanying the risen Christ to heaven.
- From the eighth century onwards Eastern Orthodox icons portrayed the victorious Christ harrowing hell and resurrecting Adam and Eve.
- *The Evangeliary of Henry II* (AD 1020) shows St. Mark gazing on Christ, who is standing in an open sarcophagus.
- Meister Francke (AD 1424) showed Christ with his back to us climbing out of the tomb on an altar panel at St. Thomas's Church, Hamburg.

Resurrection and Church Music

Music reflects a range of human emotions and can briefly uplift us almost out of time. Peter Berger—about whom we will say more in chapter 5—has illustrated this point from what the citizens of Vienna did as the Russian army approached the city at the end of World War II:

> Just before the Soviet troops occupied Vienna in 1945, the Vienna Philharmonic gave one of its scheduled concerts. There was fighting in the immediate proximity of the city, and the concertgoers could hear the rumbling of the guns in the distance. . . . It was . . . an affirmation of the ultimate triumph of all human gestures of creative beauty over the gestures of destruction, and even over the ugliness of war and death.[19]

In like manner music connected to resurrection imagery may uplift people out of ordinary time to encounter the risen Christ.[20] When resurrection imagery is weak in church music the same weakness tends to be evident in theology and missions. Harold Taylor agrees, arguing that the theological depth of the church's music can be correlated to the strength of the church's missionary endeavors in history.[21]

Robert Hawkins remarks that over the centuries "a surprisingly close correlation can be charted between Christology, visual depictions of Christ, funeral rites, and the music of those rites."[22] Sadly this has not always led to an emphasis on the centrality, victory, or power of the resurrection. One such case is found in the medieval *Stabat Mater* which consisted of sixty lines but never once referred to the resurrection.

Charles Seeger, who is the father of folk singer Pete Seeger, pointed to an important aspect concerning music and lyrics. He said that when lyrics are sung and when an instrument is played there is a rise in the energy and tension as the pitch moves up to a higher note.[23] Mark Bangert, a Lutheran musicologist, builds on Seeger's observation by stating that "we perceive rising melodic lines as metaphors for energetic life and heightened emotion."[24] Bangert says that in music, images of the resurrection are reflected in the noises, tone, and pitch of musical notes.

Positive emphasis on resurrection themes came from early monastic communities composing hymns about Christ as the deliverer from death such as in *"Primo die, quo Trinitas."*[25] The defeat of death by Christ's resurrection was imaged in the lyrics and in the vocal intonation of the chants. Eastern Orthodoxy's chanted liturgies, particularly those centered on Christ's victorious resurrection, evoke a tremendous aural sense of exaltation. So at the Paschal midnight service come these exultant antiphonally sung words:

> Let none fear death, for the death of the Savior has set us free.
> Christ is risen and the demons have fallen.
> Christ is risen and the angels rejoice.[26]

Johann Sebastian Bach's Cantata BWV 51, "Make a Joyful Noise to God in All Lands" has been described as "a moment of musical resurrection."[27] The succession of chords together with the choral movement of the cantata is said to be "by its very performance a moment of resurrection, fully dependent on the life of God."[28]

Contemporary Christian and Non-Christian Music

Outside of church music, we find a variety of responses to the resurrection. The resurrection is noticeably absent from Tim Rice and Andrew Lloyd Webber's rock-opera *Jesus Christ Superstar*. But a curious allusion to the resurrection occurs in American bluegrass rocker Leon Russell's 1970 song "Roll Away the Stone." The lyrics concern a man who feels he is living in a strange world and laments being abandoned by the woman he loves. Both the song's title and chorus ambiguously evoke the burial and resurrection of Jesus. The man pleads in the chorus to be protected and resurrected, that he will not be left lying down alone, and muses about what people will think in two thousand years.[29]

The Stone Roses flourished in the early 1990s as a major alternative rock/indie music group.[30] On their debut album is an eight-minute-long track "I Am the Resurrection." The song conveys a strong anti-Christian tone in which the band's lead singer claims to be both "the resurrection" and "the light." In this song the resurrection has been hijacked to express rejection of the church. Perhaps we should ponder how this song symbolizes acute barriers existing between youth cultures and the church.

By way of contrast, American rock musician Lenny Kravitz has given glimpses of his faith in albums such as *Circus* (1995) and *Baptism* (2004). The final track on the *Circus* album is "The Resurrection." The lyrics do not mention Jesus by name but emphasize how Kravitz feels experiencing God's love. Kravitz senses the imminent return of the resurrected King, who will soon reclaim all those who belong to him. The resurrection sets us free because of the one who walked righteously. The message of resurrection is letting us know that the resurrected one is coming again.[31]

Evangelicals have not always conveyed a persuasive musical witness to the resurrection. Alfred H. Ackley's lyrics in "I Serve a Risen Savior" emphasize a personal, subjective, and experiential understanding, "You ask me how I know he lives, he lives within my heart." None of the three stanzas or the chorus ever mentions the empty tomb or the apostolic testimony as the basis for positively affirming that Christ is resurrected.[32] Ackley's deficient hymn stands in sharp contrast to Charles Wesley's theologically informed lyrics in "Christ the Lord Is Risen Today."[33]

The resurrection is upheld in some contemporary Christian songs. Ross once spoke at a conference about the resurrection, in which five songs were chosen to match the conference's theme, all composed by Reuben Morgan of Hillsong. Among his best known compositions are "For All You've Done," "Mighty to Save," and "What the Lord Has Done in Me." In the latter song Jesus's resurrection is triumphantly confessed: "My redeemer lives . . . my Lord has conquered the grave." Perhaps one reason for Hillsong's success is that the resurrection is celebrated in uplifting songs.

However, songwriters must ensure that their lyrics are theologically informed, as Hawkins reminds us: "The juxtaposition of the gospel and human response is crucial for a musician's understanding of death and resurrection, for it is the music of the church, most often the hymns, which tends to inculcate orthodox or heterodox belief."[34] They must be careful to avoid the error of emphasizing heaven as our resurrected destiny while ignoring God's promised reign over a "new earth."[35]

The melodic and lyrical depth of church music—regardless of its style (Gregorian, Baroque, Classical, modern)—must reflect a solid trinitarian focus (not simply a "me" focus) and be grounded in a holistic understanding of the resurrection life. These twin foci in music should inspire and exhort the church to worship God, to embody the resurrection life, and to encourage the proclamation of happy resurrection news. Luther went to the nub of the matter when discussing burial hymns:

> We do not want our churches to be houses of wailing and places of mourning. . . . Nor do we sing any dirges or doleful songs over our dead and at the grave, but comforting hymns of the resurrection of the departed so that our faith may be strengthened and the people be moved to true devotion.[36]

Images of Christ in Pop Culture

We now look at resurrection images of veiled Christlike characters in block-buster motion pictures, best-selling novels, comic books, and in cult TV series.[37] We believe that these resurrection images function in essentially the same way as the uncovering of redemptive analogies of Christ in non-Christian cultures that missiologists have spoken about.[38] Join us for a quick tour of some of our favorite resurrection analogies and images.

The Day the Earth Stood Still

In the classic sci-fi film *The Day the Earth Stood Still*, an extraterrestrial humanoid named Klaatu lands his spacecraft in Washington, DC. Klaatu has arrived on earth to warn of the dangers of atomic weapons and insists that humanity must choose to live in peace and harmony. Klaatu's message is treated with suspicion, and US military officials try to capture him. Klaatu evades capture and assumes the guise of Mr. Carpenter, an allusion to Jesus. He is befriended by Helen Benson, but soldiers shoot him dead. Before he dies Klaatu gives Mrs. Benson instructions on what has to be done in the event of his death. She summons Gort (Klaatu's robot). Gort places Klaatu's body in a resuscitation machine, which enables Klaatu's resurrection. Mrs. Benson then ponders if the robot has the power over life and death. Klaatu denies this and says, "No, that power is reserved to the Almighty Spirit."[39]

Superman

Most of us have seen the movies and TV series of Superman. We should not forget, though, that his story was originally told in comic books that are still being published. In 1992–1993 there was a trilogy of comic books in which Superman was killed, buried, and then resurrected from the dead. The first comic book tells the story of how a villain called Doomsday kills Superman. The next story has President Bill Clinton attending the funeral and shows the eruption of crime after Superman's death. In the final story Superman's adoptive human father Jonathan Kent suffers a fatal heart attack and has a near-death experience (NDE). In the NDE Kent talks to Superman's soul and urges him to return to life. Superman then resurrects himself from the dead.[40]

The Matrix

You may remember that near the end of the first film of *The Matrix* trilogy Neo is shot dead by Agent Smith.[41] To everyone's amazement (including his own) Neo rises from the dead, confirming what seems to be his messianic status.[42] Neo's resurrection was triggered by a kiss from his lover, Trinity. In the second film, *Matrix Reloaded*, Neo exhibits the power to resurrect Trinity from the dead after she is fatally wounded.[43] It must be noted that the plotline of the trilogy comprises an amalgam of religious and philosophical ideas that eventually coalesce in a Hindu-based cosmology in the final film.[44]

Doctor Who

One crucial source of inspiration for *The Matrix*—including both its name and the idea that humans could be plugged into a virtual world—was a 1977 story in the TV series *Doctor Who*.[45] The Doctor is a Time Lord from the planet Gallifrey who has saved the earth from multiple alien threats throughout its history. He is a much-beloved fictional character who even makes cameo appearances in three episodes of *The Simpsons* and is mentioned in character dialogue in *CSI: New York*.[46] Today the TV series is phenomenally sweeping the globe, attracting viewers from all age brackets.

Thomas Bertonneau and Kim Paffenroth have discussed the religious and mythic significance of *Doctor Who* through the lens of Christianity.[47] Barry Letts (1925–2009) served for many years as a producer for the show and shortly before his death said that we should expect to find religious parables in *Doctor Who*. Because the series deals with "the fight between good and evil," he noted that inevitably it "will have some Christian themes as a backdrop."[48] The idea of resurrection has been embedded in the series' overarching plotline since the mid-1960s. A recurrent thread concerns the bodily renewal of the Doctor: when he is mortally wounded he is "resurrected through Time Lord regeneration."[49] Every time it involves the Doctor undergoing a complete physical transformation. He is the same man but has a different appearance. From the TV-production side regeneration is a handy way of making explicable the visual transition from one actor to the next playing the Doctor.

Yet within the myth-making of the series the Doctor's "dying" and "rising" does echo some parts of Scripture. When Jesus arose he was the same but also manifestly different (the disciples on the Emmaus road did not immediately recognize him; he could appear/disappear in the upper room). Those who have known the Doctor but encounter him in later regenerations recognize that he is the same yet different.[50] In the joint US-UK television movie of 1996 the Doctor was shot dead and his body was placed in a hospital morgue. The visual representation of his resurrection shows him triumphantly emerging from the morgue robed in a white garment.[51] Since 2005, each time his resurrection is shown the Doctor stands in a crucifixion pose as his body dissolves and a new one emerges out of blinding light.

Two other heroic television characters have also experienced resurrection: Captain Jack Harkness and K9. Captain Jack Harkness appears in several *Doctor Who* stories. In "The Parting of the Ways" he is killed by the Daleks but the Doctor's assistant Rose Tyler accesses the power of the time vortex to resurrect him. In a later adventure, "Utopia," Captain Harkness acknowledges that he

Other Resurrected Heroes[52]

Sean Stewart's 1995 *Resurrection Man* novel is about Dante Ratkay who is an "angel" endowed with psychic powers including the ability to resurrect people from the dead. Dante grows up in a dysfunctional family with his aunt who is a witch and his rationalist-atheist father who sneers at religion and magic. Dante lives in an alternative modern world where China (not the Soviet Union) became the superpower nation after World War II.

In the comic book series *Resurrection Man* Mitch Shelly used to be a lawyer working for the Mafia. He was subjected to a nanotechnology test that gave him the power of self-resurrection. He fights various adversaries and whenever he is mortally injured he is resurrected with a new superpower every time that makes him invulnerable to previous methods of killing him.

is "the man who cannot die."[53] The Doctor says that Captain Harkness is a "fact"—a fixed point in a changing universe—implying that as a resurrected man he is the singular great unexplained "miraculous" anomaly. Captain Harkness is also the lead character in the adult spin-off series *Torchwood*, and within that series he also dies but always experiences resurrection. The Doctor's computer-dog K9 experiences a resurrection in the Australian-produced children's spin-off series called *K9*. In the opening story, "Regeneration," K9 sacrifices himself to save three humans in a battle with aliens but is then resurrected.[54]

Harry Potter and Captain Scarlet

We cannot overlook the resurrection analogy in the final Harry Potter novel. In an epic climax of biblical proportions young Harry Potter comes to understand that he must die in order to defeat the evil Voldemort. He does not raise a wand to defend himself. In *Harry Potter and the Deathly Hallows* everyone believes he has perished. Yet like the women at the empty tomb there comes the explanation, "he is alive": The "resurrected" Harry triumphs over his nemesis.[55] Greg Garrett sees in Harry Potter a Christ-type figure that is very much in line with Christlike characters found in the novels of J. R. R. Tolkien and C. S. Lewis.[56]

There is also the 1960s children's cult-classic marionette TV series *Captain Scarlet and the Mysterons*. Captain Scarlet is the quintessential hero who repeatedly dies saving the earth from the alien Mysteron invaders but he always rises again from the dead. He is identified in the show's theme song as being "indestructible."[57]

None of these characters' resurrections are exact counterparts to Christ's resurrection, as they remain mortal after they have arisen. Some characters, like the Doctor, Captain Harkness, and Captain Scarlet, undergo repeated deaths and resurrections. Neo dies a sacrificial death but it is framed in a Hindu cosmology. These resurrections are not once-for-all like Christ's, and the stories have their veiled ambiguities about the source of the resurrection (does the character possess the power to rise again or is there an external source?). Some of the ambiguities reflect the mixing together of various cosmologies and mythic ideas. So those characters that have many experiences of dying and rising again do so because of the lingering influence of pre-Christian ideas about a never-ending cycle of the emergence and recession of evil through time.[58] These cyclic resurrections have nothing to do with reincarnation. Instead, they reflect both the biblical concept of resurrection and those ancient religious myths where in a seasonal cycle a deity died and came back to life. In chapter 9 we examine ancient myths of dying-and-rising gods and discuss the impact of the resurrection of Aslan and Gandalf in the novels of C. S. Lewis and J. R. R. Tolkien.

Antichrist Resurrections in Pop Culture

The Bible indicates that the resurrection is not limited to Jesus or to anyone who becomes his disciple. In the apocalyptic symbolism found in the book of Revelation there is a many-headed "beast" that arises to deceive and to persecute Christ's followers. The beast is an antichrist figure who opposes the worship of God. This beast is mortally wounded but then recovers and performs counterfeit miracles (Rev. 13:3, 12–14). Besides the antichrist figure, the Bible indicates that those who rejected Christ will be called to account by rising back to life to face God at the last judgment (Rev. 20:5, 11–15). Popular culture has made room for "negative" resurrections that feature ethically doubtful decisions to revive the dead, malevolent characters, or individuals who return from the dead with horrific outcomes. Here are three prime examples:

Alien Resurrection

Sigourney Weaver first portrayed Ellen Ripley in the 1979 science fiction movie *Alien* and then reprised the role in three sequels. At the end of *Alien 3* Ripley commits suicide but comes back from the dead two hundred years later in *Alien Resurrection*. Although Ellen Ripley lives again—implying a resurrection—in the plotline she is the product of cloning of both human and alien cells, and so there is both continuity and discontinuity with the "original" character.[59] Her resurrected clone is the product of an ethically dubious genetic engineering experiment by scientists and military officials.

The Monkey's Paw

The occult-horror short story "The Monkey's Paw" by W. W. Jacobs features another disturbing example of the resurrection of an individual. In this story

Mr. and Mrs. White are given a magic talisman (lucky charm) in the shape of a monkey's paw that grants the owner the power to have three wishes fulfilled. Mr. White's first wish is for a specific sum of money. He obtains the exact sum in the form of insurance compensation for the death of his son Herbert, who was horribly mutilated by machinery. After Herbert is buried Mrs. White is so grief stricken that she begs her husband to use the talisman to bring their son back from the grave. Mr. White is very reluctant to attempt this "resurrection" but eventually agrees to make it his second wish. Soon there comes a knock at the door as Herbert has returned from the grave. While Mrs. White rushes to the door and fumbles with the lock and handle, Mr. White realizes what has happened. Herbert has indeed returned from the grave alive but is rotting, emaciated, and mutilated. Mr. White immediately exercises his third wish which is for Herbert to return to the grave. As Herbert disappears Mrs. White finally succeeds in opening the front door but discovers that nobody is there.[60] Here the power to raise the dead does not result in the holistic healing of Herbert as a new and immortal being. "The Monkey's Paw" is, of course, a parable about the Faustian pact of doing deals with the devil, and it is a commentary on the old adage: be careful what you wish for; you may receive it.

Doctor Who

Doctor Who also includes the resurrection of evil characters such as the renegade Time Lord known as the Master.[61] In the 1996 television movie the Master died when he was thrown into the eye of harmony but in recent stories has been resurrected from the dead and acts like an antichrist figure. In "The Sound of Drums" the Master subdues the earth and clashes with the Doctor. He explains to the Doctor that the other Time Lords were so desperate to defeat the Daleks in the Time War that they were prepared to resort to the dubious moral act of resurrecting an evil renegade. In the 2007 series finale, "Last of the Time Lords," the Master's antichrist-like reign is overthrown and the Doctor offers him the one thing he cannot face: being forgiven for his sins. The Master is shot dead by his earthly wife, who realizes that she has been deceived. The Doctor cremates the Master's body. However, in the 2009 series the story "The End of Time" begins with the Master rising from the dead. When the Doctor encounters the Master he tells him that it is a "resurrection" that has "gone wrong."[62]

Resurrection Images in High Culture

John Updike (1932–2009) was one of America's most significant novelists and poets of the past fifty years.[63] Updike said that "fiction holds the mirror up to the world," and his characters show that humans are "radically valuable and radically imperfect."[64] His remarks about humanity represent one of the best summations from a novelist about the essence of the gospel. In our speaking engagements with non-Christians we refer to Updike's comments, and they "get it" immediately.

It is very clear that Updike was gripped by the importance of both the incarnation of God in human flesh and the resurrection of Christ. His understanding of this underpins many of his poems, short stories, and novels. One of the strongest expressions of the centrality of the resurrection is found in his famous poem "Seven Stanzas at Easter" where he emphasized that unless Jesus experienced a literal bodily resurrection then the church will fall.[65]

In Updike's sexually explicit novel *Roger's Version* the narrator is a liberal theological seminary professor who is obsessed with Tertullian's writing on the bodily resurrection of both Jesus and of humanity. He is both fascinated and skeptical about the resurrection and is caught up in soulless sexual acts. His liberal theology leaves him with no reversal of the "cells dissolution" of Jesus, and he harbors doubts about the general resurrection. He ends up with his own ethic and a corresponding lifestyle that lacks a holistic approach to values and morality. Roger becomes the mirror of what it is to have a half-baked Jesus and no resurrection. Sadly Roger's protagonist is an evangelical scholar named Dale who gets something of Christ's resurrection but misses its centrality in his life and ends up in an adulterous affair. One commentator has observed that Updike's novel involves a diagnostic of the gnostic dimensions of American culture, particularly the dualism of flesh and spirit, and secular and sacred. The unanswered question of the novel is whether this dualism will ever be defeated.[66] Updike understood that the resurrection is the holistic fulcrum that moves and transforms lives.

Crime and Punishment

In some of the great prose classics, veiled Christlike figures appear in the guises of various characters.[67] Different facets from Jesus's life surface in the rejected and sacrificed Christ found in Herman Melville's *Billy Budd* and in the tragic redemptive hero in Joseph Conrad's *Lord Jim*.[68] Fyodor Dostoevsky's *Crime and Punishment* offers a great example of death and resurrection imagery. In this novel the central character, Raskolnikov, murders a woman and throughout the first half of the novel represents a spiritually dead man. All kinds of motives for the murder are mentioned including the "superman" concept that Friedrich Nietzsche would later on develop. Raskolnikov is plagued by guilt and oscillates between the desire to confess and the need to conceal his crime. He then encounters Sonia, who is forced by dreadful circumstances into prostitution. Sonia upholds her faith in God in Christ and reads to Raskolnikov the story of the raising of Lazarus. As Raskolnikov repeatedly visits Sonia she urges him to confess his crime to the police. Sonia acts as a forgiving Christlike figure. Over time Raskolnikov gradually comes to confront his need for spiritual renewal; he confesses to the police and in his interior life shifts from rejecting to accepting God. As Sonia remains steadfast and shares in Raskolnikov's exile to Siberia the novel draws to a close describing the new hope that is now etched in their faces, "bright with the dawn of a new future, of a full resurrection into a new life."[69] Dostoevsky's story stands in stark contrast to the novel *Resurrection* by his Russian counterpart Leo Tolstoy. Tolstoy reinterpreted the resurrection symbolically, which led to him clashing with the Russian Orthodox Church.[70]

A Tale of Two Cities

Andrew Sanders has dubbed Charles Dickens "the resurrectionist" because the motif of resurrection surfaces in several of his novels, particularly *A Tale of Two Cities*.[71] The story, which is set in the French Revolution, begins with Doctor Manette, who is apparently dead but recalled to life—a plot device signaling a resurrection theme. The main character, Sydney Carton, physically resembles another man, Charles Darnay. Both men love Doctor Manette's daughter Lucie but it is Darnay who marries her. Darnay is hunted by the Parisian mob. Carton in an act of self-sacrificial love takes Darnay's place and is executed by the guillotine at the same hour that Christ died. Kevin Rulo observes that in Carton we have an imitation of Christ that "extends beyond sacrifice, into resurrection."[72] On one level there is symbolic resurrection because Carton's name is immortalized through the Darnay family as they live on. However, there is much more to this because Carton calls to mind Jesus's words, "I am the resurrection and the life." As Carton gives up his life he receives the return gift of "the hope of redemption" found in the resurrection.[73]

Dickens admired Christ but understood faith as a philanthropic, neighbor-love morality. He disliked dogma and the sectarian spirit that led to theological squabbles over biblical interpretation. During his first sojourn in America he took an interest in Unitarian beliefs (Unitarians reject Jesus's divinity), which probably imparted to him a greater sense of esteeming Christ as a moral example.[74]

Gates Ajar and Shakespeare: Signs of a General Resurrection

During the late Victorian era life-expectancy was often low, so there was a cultural preoccupation with consoling people about life after death that was reflected in novels, in church hymns, and in the rise of alternative religious movements that emphasized contact with departed spirits. A classic case of seeking consolation was the best-selling post–American Civil War novel *The Gates Ajar*. It was written by the early feminist author Elizabeth Stuart Phelps and was of great comfort to millions of readers in North America and Europe.[75] The story's narrator is Mary Cabot, whose brother was a casualty of the Civil War. Mary is consoled by her aunt Winifred, who shares her understanding of the general resurrection. Winifred affirms the bodily resurrection of humanity by saying, "our bodies will be as real as these," but they will be beautifully transformed and will be reunited with loved ones and important people like the late President Lincoln and the poet Elizabeth Browning.[76]

In some of William Shakespeare's plays, characters who have been regarded as dead return among the living. Their absence throughout many scenes is often taken by other characters as evidence that they are dead. In later scenes the "dead" character reappears. Shakespeare here uses a theatrical artifice of "recognition scenes" for stage resurrections of characters like Cordelia in *King Lear*, Hermione in *The Winter's Tale*, and Prospero in *The Tempest*. The quasi-resurrection of these characters facilitates a reunion where forgiveness, redemption, and joy abound. Shakespeare uses these scenes of recognition to remind us of "the potential resurrection of the body and, with it, the life to come."[77] Sean Benson says that "the sense of a resurrection or quasi-resurrection having taken place is a recurrent motif" in Shakespeare's works.[78] Benson sums up that Shakespeare "delves into the resurrection of the dead with a seriousness that manifests his interest in the human desire to transcend death and live reunited and reconciled with others."[79]

Responding to the Stories and Images of Resurrection

We believe that these examples of resurrection in popular and high culture should be understood in their historical contexts. Some imaginative illustrations of resurrection, such as those from Dostoevsky and Updike, reflect their Christian beliefs. The creative works of Grünewald and Bach arose in the era of Christendom, while those of Dostoevsky and Updike were composed in the context of post-Christendom. Dickens hovered on the edges of nineteenth-century English Christianity. Resurrection images in popular works by non-Christians have positive images, as in the experiences of Klaatu, Superman, Harry Potter, Neo, the Doctor, Captain Harkness, and Captain Scarlet. Negative examples of resurrections are also apparent in Ellen Ripley, Herbert White, and the Master. These resurrection images function much like the uncovering of redemptive analogies of Christ in non-Christian cultures.

The Barriers: When Resurrection Analogies Are Not Recognized

We must be savvy about resurrection analogies in pop culture. Resurrection images are surfacing at a time when the Christian story has been exiled from the lives of many. Lots of young people doubt, disbelieve, or ignore the church. Skeptical attitudes about the supernatural coexist with wide interests in spiritual matters about death and the afterlife. Will Self's satirical novel *How the Dead Live* encapsulates irreverent cynical attitudes about death.[80]

Emma Thompson's role as Vivian Bearing in the film *Wit* also provides a bleak and skeptical outlook.[81] *Wit* tells the story of Dr. Bearing, who is a professor of English literature with a special fondness for John Donne's holy sonnets. She is stricken with cancer and in her deathbed scene recites Donne's sonnet "Death Be Not Proud," which avers "death shall be no more, death thou shalt die." However unlike Donne, who held to the resurrection, Dr. Bearing does not seek embodied immortality. The curtain-call happens around her deathbed with no prospects of an afterlife, other than being immortalized by culture.

Despite the current tendencies toward skepticism about the supernatural and life after death, today's culture offers plenty of imaginative room for resurrection motifs both of a miraculous and technological kind. Children's novels and comic books, cult TV series, and motion pictures clearly include resurrection motifs. (In chapter 8 we will discuss how youth are using elements of pop culture to form their own worldviews, and that includes using resurrection motifs.) There will always be deniers of Christ's resurrection, and there is always valid space to challenge skeptics. However, can the church reflect on why the resurrection is being transplanted into so many cultural stories? Dare we contemplate that maybe people desire the resurrection but without the baggage of Christianity?

When we spot resurrection analogies we should be aware that what seems obvious to us may not be so for others. How youth and adult non-Christians understand these analogies will vary. We have met some non-Christians who have positive intuitions about resurrection signs, others who lack any kind of background in Christianity and are biblically illiterate, and still others who are familiar with Christianity but have had negative experiences with institutional churches. We must be careful not to presuppose that biblical plotlines in cultural works are known and respected, let alone understood, by all consumers of culture. Moreover, we must be mindful that not everyone is excited by fantasy novels, TV shows, films, music, and art.

Barriers in Holistic Spirituality Contexts

We have met many people in alternative-spirituality festivals who have heard about *The Gospel of Thomas* and read books about Jesus's "lost years" living in India. Many are ignorant, though, about the canonical Gospels. Others are very skeptical about the resurrection after having read books by Bishop Spong and conspiracy books like *The Holy Blood and The Holy Grail*.[82] The actor, pop singer, and witch Fiona Horne expresses both admiration and reservation about Jesus:

> I have to say that I don't relate to Jesus as he's described in the Bible as well as I do to his presentation in alternative writings about him, like the book *Jesus the Man* by Barbara Thiering.[83]

Anatha Wolfkeepe understands Jesus as being a coven leader who was initiated in gnostic mysteries and whose death mirrored the dying-and-rising gods of the ancient Mediterranean world.[84] Then again, we have met other neo-pagans who agree with Timothy Freke and Peter Gandy in *The Jesus Mysteries*: Jesus never existed but was a mythical figure based on dying-and-rising gods in the mystery religions.[85]

It is our experience that non-Christians want to talk about these matters. We have found it is necessary to explain the empowerment of Christ's resurrection, to sketch the plotline of the Easter events, and to offer supporting reasons why the canonical Gospels can be trusted. Conversations naturally flow on to looking at the resurrection analogies we have talked about above. Seekers we have met are prepared to dialogue because we take their questions seriously. They want to know why we disagree with Spong and gnostic spirituality.

Misunderstanding Aslan and The Matrix

We chatted to some people after viewing the movie *The Lion, the Witch and the Wardrobe*. Even some lapsed churchgoers did not recognize that Aslan was a Christ-figure and that his death and resurrection mirrored the Easter event. Again, upon reading fan sites about *The Matrix*, it was clear that not everyone realized that Neo portrayed, amongst a pastiche of many parts, the role of a resurrected messiah. Non-Christian fans recognized postmodern, Hindu, Buddhist, and gnostic content but tended to miss the biblical material. Christian fans spotted biblical allusions but were often clueless in recognizing the Nietzschean superman idea and the gnostic, Hindu, and Buddhist material.[86] The latter point raises our eyebrows. It is easy to bemoan the biblical illiteracy of non-Christians but the flip side of the coin must be faced: To what extent are Christians really conversant with the spiritual pursuits of their peers in pop culture?

Anime Fans on Good versus Evil

Another mind-boggling example involves younger people who do not recognize an obvious major religious theme. Some young North American fans of anime (Japanese animation) claim to be spiritual seekers but do not see good-versus-evil plotlines as having anything to do with religion! Jin Kyu Park gathered together a small focus group of fans to view a ten-minute clip from the anime film *Doomed Megalopolis*. Park says that this film "includes many religious, supernatural images such as Shinto and Buddhist temples, demons, religious rituals, supernatural phenomena, religious signs and mythological symbols."[87] When he debriefed with the focus group they saw good versus evil as a "religious-free concept." One respondent understood it through the prism of capitalism opposing communism, while another said, "I didn't really see it in terms of religion either. I saw it as more *the struggle between good and evil, which is not really religious*. It's mostly just everywhere."[88]

Conclusion

The anecdotes we've outlined here about the poor response and lack of recognition of biblical themes by popular audiences, if they stand in isolation, might discourage you from looking for resurrection themes in pop culture. We can expect to encounter disenchanted people who will be resistant and even hostile toward Christianity, some who are utterly disinterested and indifferent, and others who are simply misinformed. Yet the negative groundswell has not cut them off from exposure to resurrection motifs. When Christians spot resurrection analogies we must be careful to make unambiguous links to the risen Christ. The analogies of resurrection in pop culture need to be correlated to the framework and context of Jesus's story and to his personal experience of resurrection. Conversations with non-Christians can provide opportunities to draw these connections and help those who are seeking to begin to understand the power of Jesus's resurrection.

Spiritual Audit

1. Do you and your local congregation celebrate the resurrection through the visual arts? If not, why not?

2. To what extent does the liturgy and music of your local congregation emphasize the resurrection of Christ and the general resurrection?

3. Non-Christian writers use analogies of the resurrection in pop cultural stories. Does your church gathering shun such stories or engage them?

4. If many people beyond the church desire the resurrection but without the baggage of Christianity, then what does that say about the spiritual vibrancy and witness of your local congregation in the community?

5

Cultural Expressions of Death-Refusing Hope

DNA has an emerging important function in individual and science worshipping societies where there is collective anxiety about what happens to personal identity after death. . . . One reason DNA has emerged as a pop cultural icon is because it in some sense has replaced the soul and become a sacred entity, a way to explore immortality. . . . Cryogenic labs deep freeze the bodies or heads of their once living clients with the hope of reanimating them in the future or cloning them through their DNA. In this sense, the corpses of scientific and forensic inquiry may also be operating as signs of faith, hope, and certainty, in an uncertain world, as we search for immortality.

Jacque Lynn Foltyn[1]

You have heard the adage that there are two inescapable certainties in this life—death and taxes. Death casts a shadow on us when those who are close to us die. The idea that we go through various emotional stages when a loved one is dying is widely accepted.[2] Our thoughts at such times may wander into contemplating our survival beyond the grave. People have all kinds of ideas about the afterlife. Some insist that death spells annihilation, and for skeptics and atheists it is inconceivable that we might continue to exist beyond the grave. However, others embrace the idea of eternity and the hope for a life beyond the grave.

What we believe about death and the afterlife has captivated the interest of sociologists. In general terms they analyze how societies are organized and develop, and study how social contexts shape our behavior and knowledge. Sociologists have looked at how traditional social groups, such as the family, communes, and religious bodies, have rites of passage for coping with dying. In high-tech societies death has become a taboo subject and traditional rites of passage have receded in the last hundred years. Sociologists have noticed that new social systems have developed for handling the taboo, such as the emergence of grief counseling and the social isolation of the dying in hospices.

Yet alongside the taboo there are signs that most people have convictions about an afterlife. Sociologists have observed that there is a widespread death-refusing hope that people manifest in daily life. In this chapter we will identify different types of death-refusing hope and look at how they are expressed culturally. Finding death-refusing hope in culture is not the same thing as finding analogies of the resurrection, but when we spot death-refusing hope we should understand that we can have good conversations about our resurrection hope.

Death-Refusing Hope and Sociological Theory

We quoted Sean Benson's remarks about "the human desire to transcend death" in connection with Shakespeare in the previous chapter. Benson's words neatly dovetail with an argument that the sociologist Peter Berger put forward about death-refusing hope. Berger believes that it is possible to identify social signposts that point to deep longings for surviving and overcoming death. In his book *A Rumor of Angels* Berger discusses our common hope for death-lessness as a signal of transcendence.

To fully appreciate what Berger says it is helpful to understand the context out of which he originally wrote. Although Berger believed in God, like most sociologists in the late 1960s Berger thought that the predictions of secularization theory were valid. This theory predicted that as secular institutions like government agencies assumed social roles previously controlled by churches, all religious beliefs and practices would swiftly decline. It was believed that theology had been completely undermined by scientific discoveries, the impact of industrialization, and the twin challenges of psychology and sociology concerning human behavior and beliefs.

By the late 1980s Berger completely changed his mind about both the predictions and assumptions of secularization theory. He accepts that various secularizing processes have affected the shape of modern life, but he argues that secularization does not spell the death of religion. Instead, both new and traditional religions represent influential counter-secular forces in society. He notes that the theory failed to predict both the collapse of Marxism (a worldview that influenced sociological thinking on secularization), and the astonishing rise of Pentecostal churches worldwide.[3]

When Berger wrote *A Rumor of Angels* (1969) he wanted to show that even though theology was collapsing in the midst of secularization, ordinary human experiences were still pointing to a transcendent reality. Berger was interested in sketching "an approach to theologizing that began with ordinary human experience, more specifically with elements of that experience that point toward a reality beyond the ordinary."[4] Unlike a lot of sociological texts Berger's study did not involve questionnaire surveys to poll beliefs but rather took a broad interpretive look at social behavior. He examined basic social experiences that take us "beyond the moment" and give us a greater awareness of that reality that is beyond the ordinary. He referred to these extraordinary moments as signals of transcendence—aspects of human experience that are in part signals of life beyond death. One important signal is the strong hope that humanity has in the face of death:

> Our "no!" to death—be it the frantic fear of our own annihilation, in moral outrage at the death of a loved other, or in death-defying acts of courage and self-sacrifice—appears to be an intrinsic constituent of our being. There seems to be a death-refusing hope at the very core of our humanitas. . . . In a world where we are surrounded by death on all sides, we continue to be a being who says "no!" to death—and through this "no!" is brought faith in another world.[5]

Survey of Beliefs on the Afterlife

Berger's argument reminds us that even in high-tech societies where death is taboo many people hope that it does not spell the end for us. Christopher Burris and Keehan Bailey have recently confirmed that death-refusing hope remains widespread, but they have reevaluated how sociologists measure afterlife beliefs in surveys.[6] They find flaws in questionnaires that merely ask, do you believe in an afterlife? and argue that the questions used in older surveys presupposed a particular form of afterlife and tended to strait-jacket the answers that respondents could make. Not everyone accepts heaven and hell, and there are other beliefs about an afterlife besides the resurrection of the dead.

To accurately measure what people believe new questions have to be asked, so Burris and Bailey devised a new survey that attempts to cover variations in belief. At the heart of the matter are what people think happens to human identity and consciousness, and the question of whether any physical form survives the grave. For example, in some beliefs identity and consciousness are preserved but exist without a physical form. So questions that refer to identity, consciousness, and physicality could produce more accurate results about what people believe.

Burris and Bailey argue that there are five categories of belief about the afterlife: annihilation, disembodied spirit, reincarnation, spiritual embodiment, and bodily resurrection. *Annihilation* typifies secular thinking and Burris and Bailey use this word to refer to death ending all of life (unlike the sense in which some sectarians and evangelicals use it—that is, that those who are outside of Christ cease to exist forever).[7] The *disembodied spirit* refers to a state in which consciousness is preserved but without retaining personal identity and the body. *Reincarnation* involves a cyclical path from this life to the next in which the spirit's consciousness is preserved but without one's current identity. In a cycle of many lifetimes the spirit inhabits new physical bodies, but when the cycle ends the body is discarded. *Spiritual embodiment* preserves personal identity and consciousness but dispenses with the physical body. And finally, *bodily resurrection* preserves all three elements: identity, consciousness, and physical embodiment.

Among the many intriguing results of their survey they find a "low level of endorsement of Bodily Resurrection among Protestants and Catholics."[8] The survey results should challenge Christians in two ways. First, it should goad the internal church community to refocus on the resurrection as the lynchpin of Christianity by providing clarity in teaching and in practical life applications. Second, it ought to challenge Christians to learn about what people beyond the churches believe about the afterlife and to discover ways to enter into dialogue with them.

Identity, Consciousness, and Physicality

The five categories of belief about the afterlife outlined by Burris and Bailey correlate to different understandings about how the human body and consciousness may continue in the afterlife. The skeptical annihilation view negates any afterlife and hence renders null and void any bodily or conscious survival. Christian conversations with those who deny an afterlife will center on questions about how we understand the way the cosmos works and on the reality of resurrection. Meanwhile, entirely different conversations will unfold with those who believe in an afterlife.

We can better understand people if we explore their ideas about the body and consciousness and seek to understand how these ideas fit into their beliefs about the afterlife. Until recent times the dominant attitudes in the Western world about us actually surviving the grave were shaped by three perspectives about the body and consciousness. The first perspective is the resurrection, which emphasizes *conscious embodiment for everlasting life*. The second perspective comes from ancient Greek philosophers who imagined human consciousness surviving in an immortal soul but *without bodily form*. The third perspective stems from philosophers like Descartes who have posited a mind/body duality, which holds that *our consciousness is not dependent on embodiment*. These three long-established perspectives have now come into contact with resurgent older beliefs about disembodied survival (think of ghosts) and with new emerging views about bodies and consciousness, such as:

- Feminist discourses, which place much emphasis on female experiences of broken physicality, embodiment, and gender identity. Feminists sharply criticize the "anti-body culture" that idealizes youthful beauty, hides the twin realities of aging and dying, and exploits animals and humans using biotechnology in the quest for the flawless and deathless body.[9]

- Medical-technological "denials" of death that suggest postmortem survival via cloning, cryogenics, and brain transplants. Another medical example which we will talk about shortly is where DNA becomes an icon that supplants religious understandings of the soul.

- Beliefs in reincarnation, near-death experiences (NDEs), and disembodied spiritual survival.

We will now take a closer look at views of the body, consciousness, and the afterlife that vie for acceptance today. While these beliefs have a very different meaning than the resurrection, they are nonetheless sociological pointers to death-refusing hope. We will start with bodily resurrection before moving onto the alternative views about the afterlife.

Bodily Resurrection Hope

It is good to be reminded that the hope for a bodily resurrection has been expressed in resurrection analogies in movies and novels, as we mentioned in the previous chapter. Caroline Walker Bynum refers to a resurrection template influencing Hollywood productions, pointing to a steady stream of stories that grapple with notions of human identity locked into some sort of conscious or bodily survival:

Movies such as Maxie, Chances Are, Robocop, Total Recall, Switch, Freejack, and Death Becomes Her gross millions; their drama lies in the suggestion that "I" am not "I" unless my body, with all it implies (sex and sexual orientation, race, temperament, etc.), survives.[10]

Bynum argues that bodily resurrection is one of the critical beliefs that influences Hollywood scriptwriters, and her assessment provides further evidence of the enduring grip of the idea of resurrection in our society. We need a wake-up call nonetheless, because human survival is currently being reimagined in ways that stand in tension with biblical eschatology. Contemporary films and TV series not only are influenced by the resurrection, but also partake of speculations about the soul, mind-body duality, human survival as disembodied entities, reincarnation, NDEs, and medical and technological answers to death. Another expression of the denial of death is embodied in the popular cultural idea of the "undead," in which humans become vampires, werewolves, and zombies and are quasi-immortal.[11] The quest for immortality reflected in many of these models does not have the goal of worshiping and glorifying God.

Surviving as Ghosts

Stories about ghosts stem from old folkloric beliefs about the afterlife. Within the idea of surviving as ghosts emerges a hope for some continuity between the present life and the next, since survival could still involve relationships between the living and the deceased. There is also discontinuity between the present and future life, however, in that although individual consciousness and identity endure, ghosts lack their physical body. Sometimes ghost stories evoke fear because the deceased "haunt" a familiar place by behaving impishly or malevolently. However, the "spooky" element of being afraid of the dead only represents one facet of folk beliefs about ghosts.[12]

In TV series and films featuring ghosts, death-refusing hope surfaces in different ways. Early TV series like the private detective show *Randall and Hopkirk (Deceased)* and the sitcom *The Ghost and Mrs. Muir* depicted the lead character's disembodied soul remaining on earth and continuing in relationships with the living.[13] In the 1940s, classic comedy films such as *Blithe Spirit*, *The Time of Their Lives*, and *Heaven Can Wait* depicted ghosts having a busy postmortem life wrapping up unfinished business on earth.[14]

In the last two decades we've seen a shift in emphasis that coincides with recent worldview trends. TV series like *The X-Files* and *Afterlife* portray the tensions arising between characters who "believe" in the paranormal and skeptics who look for reductionist explanations.[15] Both series offer open-ended stories where the lead characters' opposing views surface in investigations about ghosts and disembodied entities. The true believer characters exhibit a type of death-refusing hope. This tension between "believers" and skeptics exhibits the present clash between such worldviews in Western culture.

Some films and TV shows emphasize the need for ghosts and disembodied entities to "depart" from this world. In *The Sixth Sense* and *The Others* ghosts are so habituated to life on earth that they have not realized they are in fact deceased.[16] TV dramas like *Ghost Whisperer* and *Medium* center on emotionally strong female mediums who interact with the recently deceased.[17] The deceased souls must resolve unfinished business with the living—whether that entails experiencing forgiveness or providing clues to help solve murders—before passing permanently over to the "other side." The cosmology of these stories is consistent with Emanuel Swedenborg's late-eighteenth-century teachings about spirits, angels, heaven, and hell.[18]

While the deceased characters' souls have the semblance of a body on screen they are not really corporeal, and none of these stories include resurrection. Instead, there is death-refusing hope of souls being reunited with loved ones by surviving as ghosts. In older films (e.g., *The Time of Their Lives*) ghosts could eventually enter heaven where the voice of God and angelic choirs welcomed them. Apart from the short-lived TV comedy *Dead Like Me*, most recent productions have tended to be silent about encountering God, and each story falls short of a holistic outcome in which the entire person enjoys an embodied existence.[19]

Surviving via Reincarnation

Reincarnation revokes the ultimate importance of the body, which puts it at odds with the resurrection. In reincarnation one's soul is transferred from one body to the next until spiritual enlightenment is achieved and the soul ceases to incarnate on earth. Personal memory and identity in one life is replaced by a new identity in each successive time on earth. So reincarnation involves extensive periods of time in a transitional state of existence. When the cycle of life, death, and rebirth on earth is over, the disembodied soul enters a final and higher form of existence. That final state may be in relationship with a deity, or, as in Buddhist thought, may involve the cessation of the soul's existence.

At a sociological level, however, reincarnation still signifies death-refusing hope because it is yet another way of understanding that life continues after death. At least twenty motion pictures from the past fifty years have treated reincarnation in a favorable light, including *On a Clear Day You Can See Forever, Kundun, Reincarnation, Little Buddha,* and *Dead Again.*[20] In *The Matrix* the Oracle implies that Neo may have lived before, and as we have already noted Neo also dies and rises from the dead. The eclectic mix of beliefs about resurrection and reincarnation in *The Matrix* trilogy parallels the way in which people now assemble spiritual life-journey kits using diverse and contradictory sources.[21]

The romantic drama *What Dreams May Come*[22] examines several afterlife beliefs that are then reimagined. The lead male character, Chris, is bereaved by the death of his wife and children. He perishes in an automobile accident and arrives in heaven, where the landscapes resemble his wife's paintings. Chris has an afterlife mentor named Albert who suggests that he can script his own heavenly space using his consciousness. Chris is aware of Descartes's duality between mind and body, and Albert suggests that his consciousness is "trapped" in his head or brain. Until he learns how to harness his consciousness Chris flounders in navigating around heaven. Chris's wife Annie is absent from his idyllic heaven because she had committed suicide and her consciousness was transferred to an anti-fantasy realm of her own making in hell. The plotline alludes to both Dante's *Inferno* and ancient underworld mythology as Chris leaves heaven to retrieve Annie from hell. When he reaches her she is awakened by his words and they are briefly reunited in heaven until Chris suggests that they reexperience falling in love. The film closes with them being reincarnated on earth as lovers.

Medical-Technological Survival

Death-refusing hope is also expressed in nonreligious terms. The sovereignty of the individual (instead of God) is upheld in stories where humans survive through cryogenics, as replicated clones, or via brain transplants into cyborgs. Here secular anxieties about death and the fate of personal identity are handled by seeking technological solutions. The survival of human consciousness through technology is evident in stories like *Robocop*, where a mortally wounded police officer, Alex Murphy, is brought back to life as a cyborg.[23] Murphy as the cyborg resists perverted attempts to control his sovereignty. *Robocop*'s plotline presupposes medical definitions about brain-death as the cessation of life and reflects philosophical speculations about the body and soul, as well as the belief that consciousness is located in the brain.

Freejack illustrates the idea of the future storage of the human mind/consciousness for reinsertion into another human body.[24] Agents in the film can time-travel to the past and snatch a person moments before dying in accidents. Their bodies are harvested so that individuals in the future could survive with their mind/consciousness transferred into these replacement bodies. Though it does not point to resurrection, *Freejack* does emphasize the need for embodiment as part of surviving death. In both *Freejack* and *Robocop* death-refusing hope is expressed via reliance on technology rather than some spiritual or supernatural agency.

Vanilla Sky draws together questions about death, cryogenics, and altered states of consciousness via dreaming.[25] Like *Robocop* and *Freejack* the possibility of survival through technology is touted in this film. *Vanilla Sky* understands consciousness to be centered in the brain, and its plot focuses on an individual who is cut off from reality by cryogenic technology. The main character, David Aames, having committed suicide, is preserved cryogenically, but the storytelling leaves the audience wondering if the afterlife experience of Aames is real, if it occurs in a coma from which he is resuscitated, or if it is an illusory dream.[26]

These fictional visions of medical-technological solutions to dying relate to some broad cultural points about hope for continuing personal existence. To begin with, Christians' uncertainty about the general resurrection, the new heaven, and new earth has left a gap in the church's witness to society. We should not be surprised that our culture has acute trepidations about dying, is ambivalent about the idea of resurrection, and has some hope for technological answers to death.

Changes in cultural treatment of death and dying have also influenced ideas about medical-technological solutions to dying. In previous times family and pastoral care for the dying was centered in the household because most people died at home. During the Middle Ages European societies had the benefit of a resurrection-based worldview with meaningful social rites to rely on in coping with death—what was known as the *Ars moriendi*, the art of dying. The past century, however, has witnessed the segregation of the dying, and hospices represent the last vestige of the *Ars moriendi* in our time. Today, as our culture isolates the dying from domestic routines and as worldviews about the body-beautiful, soul, and afterlife are in flux, "managing" death has become much more difficult.[27] It is against this broad backdrop that a technological form of death-refusing hope is being expressed.

The future abuse of technology as it affects the body lurks in stories like *Freejack*, *Vanilla Sky*, and other stories about survival through genetic engineering and cloning (e.g., *Gattaca*, *Minority Report*, and *Alien Resurrection*).[28] Although people hope that death may be overcome via medicine and technology, these stories do not point to a utopian world. In fact, they often point to its opposite—dystopia—and are brimming with anxieties about individual postmortem survival. Such stories sharply contrast with the positive biblical hopes of the general resurrection.

These dystopian stories hint at some of the underlying worldview challenges that shape the attitudes of those who put their trust in cybernetic forms of immortality. Noreen Herzfeld identifies the underlying assumptions in this worldview about how humans are conceptualized and defined as our "thoughts, memories, feelings and action define the human person."[29] She says that the cybernetic (mind/technology) approach "assumes a dualistic understanding of the human person" and espouses "a hubristic faith in human power."[30] It is at loggerheads with biblical eschatology because "cybernetic immortality denies the importance of the body while at the same time tying immortality to the material world."[31] The theology of resurrection, in contrast, affirms the holistic transformation of people and the renewal of the *imago Dei*, as well as the liberation and transformation of the present creation.

DNA, Bioethics, Death Taboos, and Immortality

At the beginning of this chapter we quoted Jacque Foltyn's observations about the almost-sacred status accorded to DNA. The twin fields of genetics and forensic science offer a new vista for reimagining the body, death, and immortality in the midst of cultural change. The human genome project maps genetics by examining the proteins and chemical sequences that constitute the basis of our DNA. The scientific investigation of DNA opens all kinds of avenues for reimagining the human body, particularly at the developmental stages from conception to birth. DNA is understood as having the code to life that we can decode: it is biochemical information for us to access and process. The hope is that by testing every strand of DNA we may eventually control it and eliminate impurities.

In tandem with the scientific inquiry into DNA come a raft of questions and conjectures about the human body and who has control over it: What does it mean to be a human? Can we attain mastery over disease, aging, and dying? Does the state or individual decide our biological destiny? By refusing death via technology, what forms of human identity and consciousness will there be? These critical questions arise because technology has opened up new bioethical frontiers through in-vitro conception, animal and human organ transplants, genetic engineering, cloning, cryogenics, and nanotechnology.

As we have just seen, several pop cultural stories express doubts about what the future holds via technology, and yet attach death-refusing hope to technology. In classic gothic films the zombie is a former human being who becomes a feared "undead" creature. The symbol of the zombie is inverted in *The Matrix* where individual human selves begin life as genetic replicas in an unconscious zombielike existence. Human bodies are plugged into a simulated world controlled by artificial intelligence. The human body is hatched, programmed, and even harvested to serve as an energy source for artificial intelligence. Renegade humans who escape its technological clutches look to the Nietzschean superman, resurrection, and reincarnation as answers to death.

The feminist novelist Margaret Atwood describes a bleak bioethical dystopia in *Oryx and Crake*.[32] Atwood considers the implications of dubious practices currently used in secularized biotechnology that affect both humans and animals. In a future society hybrid creatures have been genetically produced such as rakunks (raccoon-skunks) and pigoons (pigs with balloon bodies containing organs for transplants). The socio-economic divide between rich and poor remains acute and people are entertained by playing trivia games such as Extinctathon (about extinct species) and watching voyeuristic televised broadcasts of frog squashing, live surgery, executions, child pornography, and naked females presenting the "Noodie News."

The plot of *Oryx and Crake* centers around two principal characters, Jimmy (also called Snowman) and his old school-friend Glenn, who is known as Crake, the genetic scientist. Jimmy studied literature and the humanities but in the future these marginalized fields are only useful as commodities for propaganda. Crake has pursued specialized studies in genetic engineering and xenotransplantation (harvesting animals for organ transplants into humans). Crake does not believe in the essence of nature or in God's existence. In his worldview humans must be corralled from notions of nature and God, because if one believes in nature one implicitly accepts there is a creator. Crake has developed a virus that is released as a pandemic to eliminate existing humankind, but before he exterminates humanity he genetically engineers new humans. He creates new gendered bodies that are freed from nature's control. They are herbivores, breed seasonally, have polyandrous relationships, and ostensibly will develop a peaceful harmonious society. In an ironic twist for the atheist scientist the new human species, called Crakers, come to regard Crake as their creator-god. Atwood's bleak dystopia maps out the terrain of bioethical topics that inform pop cultural discourses about DNA, the body, and conquest of death.

Several scholars have considered what these popular stories about overcoming death might mean. William Bogard is a sociologist who interprets cultural signs that he believes signal the demise of the modern paradigm of the individual self. The investigation of DNA comes with an emerging regime where humans are reimagined symbolically as "programmable, updatable, rewritable and renewable."[33] He interprets the screening of DNA as entailing a "quest for a new kind of immortality."[34]

The French Roman Catholic cultural theorist Paul Virilio interprets this new quest for immortality via purified DNA in terms of stunted development. Virilio does *not* see current efforts at uncovering the secrets of DNA as a Promethean attempt to be like God but thinks that the primary discourses in the contemporary project surrounding DNA render God irrelevant. DNA research is driven, he believes, by efforts to sculpt a new humanity where no one wants to be godlike but humans aim instead at a godless immortality. The goal of achieving control over DNA is to perpetuate youthfulness. Virilio locates in the cultural discourses an infantile utopian perspective in which the ageless human being can do what it likes, whenever it wishes, and never grow up.[35] In consideration of these bioethical trends, Christians must articulate and apply a resurrection-shaped theology and ethic in today's culture.

On the pop cultural canvas there is a threefold fascination with DNA, corpses, and the exalted status of forensic science. The hiding away of the dead has stimulated a new voyeurism associated with images of corpses. It may be understood as part of a widespread cultural quest to find meaning about death and hope for immortality. Foltyn notes that death is a cultural taboo in our time that parallels the earlier Victorian-era taboo about sex. He finds evidence for the new voyeurism in media spectacles associated with the deaths and funerals of famous persons such as sex icon Anna Nicole Smith, rhythm-and-blues godfather James Brown, the eccentric wildlife warrior Steve Irwin, actor Heath Ledger, ex-Beatle John Lennon, Princess Diana, and Pope John Paul II, and in YouTube video clips of executions, such as the hanging of the deposed Iraqi dictator Saddam Hussein. American medical-crime documentaries such as *Actual Autopsy* and *Forensics Files* further fuel the fascination because they feature the dissection of actual corpses.

Foltyn describes how the legitimate investigative tools of forensic science have metamorphosed in pop consciousness. DNA evidence has been exalted "as a miraculous crime-solving substance" in TV fiction series such as *Bones, Cold Case, CSI, CSI: Miami, CSI: New York, NCIS,* and *Silent Witness.*[36] Foltyn refers to "the CSI Effect" in public consciousness, in which DNA is "regarded as more definitive than it actually is."[37] These fictional TV series reflect current uncertainties "about what happens after we die" because "traditional religious convictions about the afterlife" have shifted.[38] Foltyn sees the emphasis on DNA, corpses, and forensic science "as signs of faith, hope, and certainty, in an uncertain world, as we search for immortality."[39]

Near-Death Experiences (NDEs)

Death-refusing hope also comes in tales of near-death experiences (NDEs) like the movie *Flatliners* and in the TV series *The Simpsons* and *The Sopranos.* In all three cases stories contain negative or horrifying experiences of life beyond death that indirectly point to a wider, more positive hope.

Flatliners is a thriller movie about five medical students who deliberately undergo medically induced clinical death. After being revived each one eventually tells their experiences of what they saw when they died.[40] The term *flatline*—technically known in medicine as asystole—refers to the absence of any cardiac electrical activity as measured on an electrocardiograph machine. Each student undergoes a flatline and then in death reexperiences life by revisiting a hidden and traumatic episode from their past. After resuscitation all five students find themselves being eerily confronted in the here and now by their past deeds or experiences. All of them try to find ways of being reconciled with the dreadful consequences of their personal deeds.

The long-running comedy animation series *The Simpsons* provides a typically sardonic and humorous case of an NDE. Mr. Burns is driving his car and knocks Bart Simpson off his skateboard. The unconscious Bart has an out-of-body experience and commences his ascent toward heaven. As he rides the escalator to heaven a voice tells him to hold on to the rail and not to spit over the side. Bart glimpses the departed souls of deceased relatives and the family cat but then promptly disobeys by spitting. The escalator steps flatten into a slide and Bart rushes downwards. The earth opens up and he cascades into hell where the devil checks his database concerning Bart. As Bart has arrived prematurely in hell the devil expels him back to the earth where he awakens in a hospital.[41] Unlike the characters in *Flatliners*, Bart continues to be anarchic and dysfunctional.

In *The Sopranos* Christopher Moltisanti is a nephew of the mafia boss Tony Soprano.[42] Moltisanti is shot and while being treated in the hospital has a cardiac arrest. He then has an NDE in which he finds himself in an Irish bar where he encounters deceased mafia criminals. Among them is his father, who repeatedly experiences the reenactment of being shot dead. When Moltisanti recovers from his coma he tells Tony that he has been to hell.[43] During the final season of the series Tony Soprano has his own brush with death. In back-to-back episodes he is in a coma from gunshot wounds and in an NDE assumes the identity of a guest in a hotel who has unpleasant encounters. He subsequently recovers and later in the series divulges that in his NDE he went to a place that he never wants to see ever again. Both characters are disturbed by what awaits them in the next life.[44]

Making Sense of NDEs

In the above NDE stories the common element is some kind of life beyond death. Each story reflects the revenant (an astral body or spirit-like body that survives) or quasi-resurrection understandings of life beyond death. These stories do not, however, permit a simplistic reduction of NDEs that suggests everyone will experience positive survival. New Age books about NDEs often retell positive stories where all is happy in the afterlife, but this is not always the case, and a small body of mostly Christian literature highlights evidences concerning negative NDEs.[45] What NDEs implicitly express is a *desire* to find a holistic positive experience of life beyond death. This human hope and yearning is one that can truly be fulfilled in Christ's resurrection.

What is the sociological and cultural significance of the NDE phenomena? Carol Zaleski made a detailed cultural study of NDEs and found that these kinds of stories are found in most cultures.[46] Death-refusing hope has a near-universal form of expression across culture as expressed in NDE stories. Zaleski finds affinities between NDE phenomena and the Christian hope of resurrection. In *Life of the World to Come* she notes that the season of Easter simultaneously draws us into reflections on both death and resurrection. Zaleski has urged Christians to appreciate NDEs as a way in which human beings can come to a greater awareness about life and the realities of experiencing death. In a creative set of meditations she has interrelated images and accounts of NDEs with meditations on the hope of resurrection from the church fathers. She uses the liturgical observances of Lauds, Vespers, and Compline to fold into one day a series of spiritual meditations about the mystery of the resurrection and hope for an afterlife.[47]

We find the NDE phenomena interesting for many reasons, but ultimately these cultural expressions of death-refusing hope are mere shadows in light of Jesus's resurrection. Those who long for a holistic life on earth and beyond need something far greater than the tantalizing hints found in NDE stories. Let us not forget that people need to encounter the risen Lord Jesus. In dialogue with people who gravitate to NDE stories we have found it helpful to suggest that the near-death traveler has only glimpsed at things beyond the grave. As Jesus has had the decisive experience in death and resurrection he is the trustworthy guide on the afterlife.

Celebrities and Death-Refusing Hope

We noted above Foltyn's observations about pop voyeurism connected to celebrity deaths. Death-refusing hope also coalesces around celebrities. It is easy to find examples of major public outpourings of collective grief in ancient and modern contexts. In living memory the world has stood still over the assassination of President John F. Kennedy (1963) and the deaths of Elvis Presley (1977), Princess Diana (1997), and Michael Jackson (2009). Deceased celebrities function in post-Christendom as role-model substitutes for what the Christian saints represented in the Middle Ages.

For many individuals collective bereavement for celebrities has opened up expressions of death-refusing hope. This is evident in the informal folk spirituality expressed in the wake of these famous deaths. J. Gordon Melton, a specialist scholar on new religions in North America, notes the emergence of the "Kennedy Worshippers." After President Kennedy's assassination various individuals claimed to have contact with his spirit and credited him with performing postmortem healing miracles.[48]

John Drane points to the popular spiritual symbolism, rituals, and storytelling that emerged in the week following the death of Princess Diana.[49] Both the grief and sentiments of admiration expressed about Diana were focused for many people in nonecclesiastical symbols and rites. Diana was a significant cultural icon, and people insist on the hope that she lives on beyond the grave. Fan reactions to Michael Jackson's death likewise reflect that death-refusing hope.

Madeleine Rigby comments on what has transpired since Elvis died:

> Since his death in 1977 at Graceland, at the age of forty-two, there has developed, apparently spontaneously through his fans, a quasi-religious mythology about Elvis Presley. This ranges from concepts such as Elvis the martyr, sacrificed to the lifestyle of fame, to the myths, rumours and sightings which suggest that he is still alive and will return one day. There would appear, however, to be quite a lot of quasi-religious symbolism and imagery associated with Elvis Presley and Graceland since his death. Most of this symbolism would appear to be based upon Christian symbols and myths and would seem to be generated both by fans and by journalists. Some people see a cult arising from the worship of Elvis, with the fans as disciples and Elvis impersonators as the priests. To others, it would appear that devotion to Elvis goes along with and finds a place within their more orthodox religious beliefs.[50]

John Updike captures death-refusing hope in a poem called "Jesus and Elvis."[51] In the poem Updike notes both the similarities and considerable differences between Jesus and Elvis as kings with devoted followers. The closing line of the poem reads: "He lives. We live. He lives." John McTavish points out what Updike means here: (a) "that Jesus lives and that because he lives, we are able to live"; (b) as a part of pop culture Elvis continues to live through his music; (c) some have the death-refusing hope that Elvis continues to live beyond the grave; and (d) all of this "means, in the end, 'Jesus lives. We live. Elvis lives.'"[52]

Conclusion

Alongside the resurrection analogies we discussed in chapter 4, we see abundant evidence of what Berger identified in the sociology of human experiences. Both resurrection analogies and the phenomena of death-refusing hope cry out for Christians to creatively bear witness to the fulfillment of the analogies and hopes in Jesus's resurrection. Resurrection motifs can serve as redemptive analogies that speak meaningfully into the life experiences of people. These analogies in turn serve as stepping-stones to exploring both the Christ-event and the holistic understanding of resurrection charted throughout this book.

Although some people do not immediately recognize or understand Christ-like motifs in culture, there remain those who intuitively grasp resurrection imagery alongside death-refusing hope. They intuit that there is a life-empowering way of living behind the resurrection imagery and want to see how that is all unpacked.[53] We need to be alert to what is signified by today's different forms of death-refusing hope. The near universality of death-refusing hope indicates sociologically that, aside from skeptics who reject notions of an afterlife, almost everyone hopes for an enriched life *before* death and for one that continues positively *after* death. The more sharply honed sociological signals associated with the "no" to death scream at Christians to embody and declare a holistic resurrection-based way of living.

We have noted various examples about surviving death as told through film and TV, all of which remind Christians that people are seeking a tangible, experiential, and workable spirituality that delivers on the death-refusing hope. Although people have varied understandings of life after death—ranging from bodily resurrection to survival as ghosts to reincarnation to medical-technological survival—this chapter's survey has shown a popular insistence on the hope for some form of existence beyond death. As Christians, we must ensure that our proclamation and our embodiment of faith prepare people for life on earth as well as for life in the new earth and new heaven. Christ's resurrection is like Cinderella's slipper: it is the costume piece that people have lost and in which all their hopes are concretely fulfilled. Christ, the Prince of peace, invites us to wear the resurrection slipper.

Spiritual Audit

1. Why is the preservation of our identity, consciousness, and physical body important in the doctrine of the resurrection?

2. Genetic engineering and cryogenics appear to exclude belief in the resurrection of the body. Are these medical-technological trends irretrievably opposed to the resurrection? How would you introduce the resurrection into public dialogues on these bioethical developments?

3. In what practical ways does your church minister to the dying? Do you personally play any active part in ministering to people in hospices (and if not, why)?

4. What is the sociological makeup of your local church gathering? What would be the strongest understanding of life after death in relation to the five views discussed in this chapter?

6

Signs of the Resurrection in General Revelation

What inclines even me to believe in Christ's Resurrection? . . . If he did not rise from the dead, then he decomposed in the grave like another man . . . but if I am to be REALLY saved—what I need is certainty—not wisdom, dreams or speculation—and this certainty is faith. And faith is faith in what is needed by my *heart*, my *soul*, not my speculative intelligence. For it is my soul with its passions, as it were with its flesh and blood, that has to be saved, not my abstract mind. Perhaps we can say: only *love* can believe in the Resurrection. Or: it is *love* that believes the Resurrection . . . what combats doubt is, as it were, *redemption* . . . so this can come about only if you no longer rest your weight on the earth but suspend yourself from heaven. Then *everything* will be different and it will be "no wonder" if you can do things you cannot do now.

Ludwig Wittgenstein[1]

Major forest fires are a summertime hazard in many countries. One recent fire devastated substantial national parkland on the fringes of our home city. After the disaster the plants and bushes began regenerating and the park rangers erected signs saying "the park lives again!" Witnessing this reminded us that in nature's way rebirth comes through death.

We feel that some Christians today have unwittingly put a barrier between the signs of the creation and the biblical signs of the resurrection. Bishop Joseph Butler in the eighteenth century was keenly aware of this tendency. Taking his cue from ideas that were first raised by Clement of Rome, Butler's way out of the muddle was to reveal analogies to the resurrection in nature.[2] Butler says that to exist hereafter, in a different state from our present, is but according to the analogy of nature. Considering how different our state of life in the womb and infancy is from that in maturity and old age, we shouldn't find the

---

General and Special Revelation

What is "general revelation"? This refers to what can be known about God in the creation and through history. It is generally available (Ps. 8; Rom. 1:19-20; 2:1-16; 10:14-18). Romans 2:1–16 explains how God's judgment on all people is fair because even those who have not heard the gospel nonetheless have God's moral law written in their hearts.

What is "special revelation"? This refers to God's revelation in the person of Jesus and in Scripture. It is "special" because this oral/verbal revelation comes directly from God and is not immediately available to all people. Romans 10:14–18 provides a slice of both general revelation and special revelation by pointing to the importance of gospel proclamation (vv.15–17) but also explains (v. 18 quotes Ps.19:4) that those who have not heard a preacher nevertheless are exposed to truth in general revelation.

---

claim that we will be resurrected in another state of life so remarkable. It is not unusual in nature, Butler argues, to see transformations from one stage to another—like worms turning into flies, or caterpillars into butterflies.[3]

In light of Butler's argument from nature, this chapter will explore the creation signs concerning the resurrection. We begin by looking at some iconic people who have thought outside of the box in exploring the connection between nature and the resurrection. They have not minded being "out of step" with conventional religiosity, and they offer a challenge for Christians not accustomed to interpreting signs within the creation.

Resurrection Motifs in Creation

C. S. Lewis

C. S. Lewis's books are easy to read, and many Christians have been helped by his thoughts in *Mere Christianity* and *The Problem of Pain*, and have enjoyed his fictional stories like the *Chronicles of Narnia*. There are two avenues to his thinking that are relevant to our discussion of nature and the resurrection. The first comes from his book *Miracles* where he looks at some of Jesus's miracles as signs of the new creation. Referring to the feeding of the five thousand, Lewis points out that in the ordinary course of nature it takes time for grain to be sown, grown, and harvested before loaves can be baked. What Jesus has done is a miracle that speeds up some natural processes. Lewis understands Jesus's miracle as extraordinary, but also encourages us to understand miracles occurring within the sphere of nature. The divide between nature and miracles need not necessarily be exaggerated.[4] Lewis echoes ideas here that originated from St. Augustine of Hippo and Irish medieval theologians.[5]

The second avenue comes from Lewis's thinking about mythology, which we discuss in further detail in chapter 9. Lewis felt very strongly about the importance of mythic thinking as a way of understanding the world. Like the nineteenth-century romanticists, he had a nostalgic view of the past and believed that myths could point us to intangible and spiritual things that were beyond the capacity of rationalist and scientific thought. Central to his thinking are his beliefs that myths can prefigure the good news of Christ and that myth can be a genre through which the Christian story is retold.[6] His Narnia stories and science-fiction novels are examples.

Lewis argues in his writings that elements of the Christian good news were prefigured in pagan myths; for example, the old pagan stories of dying-and-rising gods prefigured the actual entrance into human history of Jesus Christ. We should not be surprised or embarrassed to discover "pagan Christs," he insists, since the good news of Jesus's story contains elements of both the joy of myth and the facts of history. Ancient stories of dying-and-rising gods are grounded in the structures and rhythms of nature—fertility gods dying and rising in conjunction with the annual seasons. For Lewis, the Christ-story offers much more because it happened in history and fulfilled what pagans had imagined in their myths.[7]

Leon McKenzie

Leon McKenzie is an American Roman Catholic scholar who wrote *Pagan Resurrection Myths and the Resurrection of Jesus*.[8] In a framework that parallels some of Lewis's ideas McKenzie argues that God has put resurrection analogies into the very structures of the world. He points to the ancient pagan myths about the sun dying and rising, both daily and seasonally. He also speaks of our experiences of sleep and wakefulness as analogies of death and resurrection. McKenzie's main point is that these revelatory signs and analogies point to the historical reality of the resurrection of Jesus. When Jesus died and rose again the ancient world had already been prepared to understand resurrection.

E. W. Bullinger

Evangelicals love preaching on Romans 10, particularly verse 15, "How beautiful are the feet of those who bring good news!" The theme of this passage is the need to preach the gospel. As verse 17 says, faith comes from hearing the message, and the message is heard through the word of Christ. Some teaching on this passage, however, fails to note verse 18 where Paul says that the people have already heard the "message" found in general revelation. He reminds them of Psalm 19:1–2: "The heavens are telling the glory of God . . . day to day [they pour] forth speech."

E. W. Bullinger (1837–1914), who was an Anglican priest, refers to this idea as the "gospel in the stars" and believes that the stars and constellations symbolize key biblical themes and truths.[9] In an attempt to bridge the gap between Christians and followers of astrology, Bullinger and others who rely on the work of Frances Rolleston offer an alternative understanding of the zodiac. These writers argue that the names of the stars and constellations relate to biblical images of creation, fall, redemption, judgment, and resurrection. This leads Bullinger to claim that Romans 10 refers to the gospel drama being embedded in the stars. In effect, the stuff of the creation points to the gospel.

In *The Witness of the Stars* Bullinger discusses what he believes is a resurrection symbol in the sign of Capricorn. He indicates that there is within the constellation a cluster of eighteen stars known in ancient times as Delphinus or the Dolphin. The shape of the cluster can be seen as a "fish full of life, and always with the head upwards." Bullinger says, "The great peculiar characteristic of the dolphin is its rising up, leaping, and springing out of the sea."[10]

Joseph Seiss, a Lutheran contemporary of Bullinger, points out that as Capricorn symbolizes the sacrificial goat, the sign of the dolphin in this constellation takes on added importance: "Our great Sin-bearer not only died for our sins, but He also rose again, thereby becoming 'the first-fruits of them that slept.' . . . We thus have the vivid symbol of both the resurrection of the slain Savior as the Head of the Church, and the included new creation of His people, who rise to their new life through His death and resurrection."[11]

Some early church frescoes that depicted paradise had dolphins and other creatures alongside the resurrected believers.[12] It is impossible to say if the frescoes signified that dolphins are a symbol of resurrection. In today's context where dolphins feature in alternative spiritualities we might consider reemphasizing the resurrection symbolism associated with these marvelous sea-mammals.

Ancient Indigenous Art

Recently, we gave some thought to the relevance of general revelation and its possible link to the wider search for signposts about ultimate meaning. The TV documentary *Prehistoric Astronomers* features the research of the astronomer-ethnologist Chantal Jegues-Wolkiewiez, who has spent twenty years examining the famous Stone Age paintings and engravings in the caves at Lascaux, France.[13] She has a persuasive theory about the animals featured in the cave paintings; in her opinion they represent a kind of map of the night sky. The imaginary animal images that ancient peoples sketched between the stars in the night sky are the graphic basis for the classic images of the signs of the zodiac in astrology.

After measuring the paintings and engravings in 130 caves Jegues-Wolkiewiez discovered that when sunlight enters the caves at the seasonal equinoxes the light shines on the night-sky map of the animals. The animal imagery—like Taurus the Bull—found on the cave walls is similar to the zodiacal imagery found later on in Egypt and Babylon. Using a night-sky map of the Stone Age prepared by a planetarium she has been able to match the position of the paintings and their images to those of the constellations at the time of the solstices. The only constellations missing from the cave walls are Aquarius and part of Pisces. Jegues-Wolkiewiez suggests that Stone Age culture was not as "primitive" as we might imagine, as the link she discovered indicates that they recognized the position of the stars, the sun, and moon phases. The academic jury is still deliberating on aspects of her theory, but her peers have not dismissed her case.

After watching the documentary, it occurred to us that maybe we need to reflect more on how oral and preliterate cultures could have understood general revelation. The "pagan" and "astrological" spirituality of ancient oral cultures interests anthropologists and contemporary devotees of astrology and nature-centered spirituality. Christians usually emphasize discernment about false gods when these topics arise; however, we should leave some room for reflection on the value of general revelation both in antiquity and today. Jegues-Wolkiewiez's theory does not necessarily "confirm" any aspect of Bullinger's "gospel in the stars," but her theory about Stone Age "astronomy" should goad us into appreciating how such cultures observed the natural realm, lived within it, and looked for signs and meaning. In our day, the same kind of quest is taking place. Are we awake to the possibilities of making connections from the signs of resurrection in nature to general revelation, and can we correlate that as a meeting-ground with our peers who are questing for fulfillment and meaning in nature?

Flood and Analogy of Resurrection

Whether he is admired or reviled the Romanian academic Mircea Eliade stands out as a figure of enormous influence in modern discussions about the importance of religion, symbol, and myth.[14] His ideas have influenced the way our generation thinks about the study of religion, the role of myth and ritual, and the enduring impact of myth even in modern scientific times.[15] Eliade was noted for finding patterns in religious rituals and myths concerning the sacred in antiquity and its relevance in today's world. He maintained that even when one allowed for those aspects of religious ritual and myth that were peculiar to a given cultural context, it was still possible to identify similar or common themes cross-culturally in various religious myths about the quest for ultimate meaning.[16]

One recurrent mythic theme is the prevalence of flood stories in many different cultures. While the recurrence of some myths might be explained by cross-cultural borrowing, it is not possible to account for the presence of all flood myths in this manner. Flood stories can be found on all inhabited continents, and cultural borrowings cannot explain the diffusion of these tales: Polynesian, Melanesian, and Australian Aboriginal cultures did not enter into trade with the ancient Near Eastern world. The archaeologist William F. Albright remarked:

It is very difficult to separate a myth found all over the world even as far away as pre-Columbian South America, from the tremendous floods which must have accompanied successive retreats of the glaciers in the closing phases of the Pleistocene Age. In other words, the Flood story presumably goes back, in one form or another, at least ten or twelve thousand years.[17]

The story of Noah and the flood looms large as part of the "story arc" of universal narratives that make up the first eleven chapters of Genesis. The flood story offers a tantalizing hint about resurrection. In this story the plants, animals, and earth itself experience forms of dying and rising again. This story is certainly not identical to Jesus's resurrection, but it does provide imperfect, analogous hints. The consummation of the natural world's yearning for a complete resurrection is centered in Jesus's death and resurrection (Rom. 8:22–23). The earth has borne witness to its own death and resurrection in the flood. The flood story also hints at something else that is integral to Jesus's story: it is resurrection to new life (and not death).

We believe that in this motif of resurrection the creation "speaks" to us: resurrection is an integral part of the natural order. It is an analogy, of course, because nature "dies" and "rises again," and dying-and-rising in nature is not identical to the bodily resurrection of human beings; however, what we need to bring back into focus is that nature itself reveals a resurrection motif, and this motif should be appreciated as being part of general revelation.

Why Not Reincarnation in Nature?

Ross was chatting to a couple about being their marriage celebrant. They were a fun, connected couple who were agnostics but also believed in reincarnation! His encounter with them reconfirmed our finding that many young adults seem open to reincarnation but are otherwise vague or fluid about what they believe. Even some who are "soft" agnostics hold to reincarnation from their observation of the world and the cycles of nature. It is important to simply note that reincarnation is a widespread belief held not just in traditional cultures across Asia; it is probably the major global competing view about life after death.

In reincarnation the spirit is either transmitted to another human life or transmigrates into another species. Reincarnation offers a continuous cycle of life, death, and rebirth. Resurrection is about continuity of the same being; reincarnation offers a continuous cycle of rebirth in other forms.

The analogies and stories from nature that we have already referred to, such as the caterpillar's metamorphosis into the butterfly and the flood, point in the direction of resurrection rather than to a circular pattern or cycle of continuous reincarnation. The resurrection framework emphasizes continuity of the thing that dies and rises again. The caterpillar's DNA includes the "program" to change into the butterfly. The analogies of the bushfire and of humans in the state of sleep/wakefulness likewise point to the continuity of the form of life.

Assessing Claims of Resurrection Signs in Creation

When we talk about the relationship between nature and resurrection in light of Bishop Butler, C. S. Lewis, Leon McKenzie, E. W. Bullinger, and the flood, we are often asked if we are pushing the envelope too far. Some feel that we should stick with the Bible because the message of salvation is clearly revealed, and it is a big diversion looking for signs of the resurrection in creation. Others are not convinced that the signs in creation can really withstand critical scrutiny. In the case of Bishop Butler, C. S. Lewis, and Leon McKenzie, our answer is no. Sure they have their foibles; for example, Joseph Butler was a creature of his day in understanding nature. Our understanding of science has moved on, but Butler's premise about the wonderful transformations in nature still stands.[18]

Bullinger's "gospel in the stars," though, does generate some real controversy. His claims ignite conversations among Christians in churches and seminaries, and also among non-Christians who visit alternative holistic spiritualities festivals where we have operated exhibitor's stalls. On occasions we have operated visual displays that reflected his claims relating zodiac signs to the message of Jesus.

Christians have opposing opinions about Bullinger. Some agree with him, and some think he went too far and his entire case has no credibility. Although we recognize the problems inherent in accepting Bullinger at face value, we are not convinced that one can just summarily dismiss him. Many New Spirituality people are able to meet us in the middle ground—they "get it" about Bullinger.

Those who have a New Spirituality mind-set are attracted by the Gospels' references to a star-sign heralding the birth of Christ. Contemporary believers who follow that heralded Messiah perhaps ought to rethink things. First, the Magi who came to the infant Christ were astrologers, and there is no escaping the fact they were guided by it. Second, Bullinger tries to be faithful to what is found in both nature and in Scripture. He takes the cue from Genesis about stars being signs and seeks to decode the biblical meaning in the zodiac. He reminds us of a point that the church in the Reformation era was happy to uphold, the two-sided coin of reality: the macrocosm and the microcosm. The individual (microcosm) is interconnected with the macrocosm (the universe) in a seamless reality. The gospel in the stars is not about predictive astrology.

The weakness in Bullinger's approach is that he is caught up in a bit of a circle. It is fair to ask if he ended up "reading into" the stars what he had already taken from Scripture. Bullinger thought he had found the content of God's special revelation in Jesus already mapped out in the zodiac. Most theologians have said that natural or general revelation is incomplete because if it was enough then the incarnation of Jesus would not have been needed. So in this respect Bullinger's work has an Achilles' heel.[19] Still, as we have suggested elsewhere, there is a legitimate need to overhaul and rehabilitate the idea of the gospel in the stars.[20]

Fresh thought about the "gulf" between general and special revelation is much needed today. We should remember that quite a few apologists like Lee Strobel and Josh McDowell have argued a case for Christianity from history. The realm of history is also the realm of general revelation. Some historians and New Testament scholars have started with the work of God in history, particularly starting with the life of Jesus. The stories of Jesus have been examined like other historical artifacts. In those records we discover that Jesus died and rose again, and it is from that cluster of events that apologists have made the link from the realm of general revelation over to special revelation.[21]

We offer here another level of understanding about the links between the creation and God, and specifically about signs of resurrection in nature that can lead us on to the sign of Christ's resurrection. We are building on what Lewis and McKenzie have done in drawing attention back to the signs found in the cosmos, earth, and human culture.

Signs and Symbols Pointing to Resurrection

All of us are familiar with the signs, symbols, and company logos that surround us in advertisements. Our awareness of symbols, though, transcends advertising.

In pop culture one hero of the moment is the character portrayed by Tom Hanks in the films *Angels and Demons* and *The Da Vinci Code*. The Tom Hanks character (Robert Langdon) is enmeshed in conspiratorial, suspenseful, and mysterious plots that amuse us. We had an "aha" moment while viewing the film *Angels and Demons*: we realized that a shift in heroic figures has suddenly happened. The symbologist is now assuming the popular mantle of the hero. Robert Langdon has clearly displaced the romantic adventurer-archaeologist Indiana Jones.

Semiotics is concerned generally with the study of patterns in communication but also involves the study of signs and symbology. What we find striking about the emergence of the symbologist as a heroic character in fiction is that the symbologist is someone who decodes and interprets the hidden messages of signs—signs and symbols that can carry spiritual messages.

There is a fascination today with signs and symbols, which is a curious problem for Christians to try to come to terms with. Many have been dismissive of signs and symbols in contemporary culture. Sometimes this dismissive attitude can be explained by the difficulty that some Christians have in appreciating religious symbols, icons, and classical religious art. Evangelicals seem to cope quite well in retaining the symbol of the cross yet paradoxically cannot show much sympathy for, or appreciation of, other church symbols.

Their dismissiveness of signs and symbols might on some occasions reflect an anti-Catholic attitude or be rooted in the mistaken linking of signs to the biblical prohibition on "graven images" or to anti-Christian and occult symbology.

Types of Divination

Casting Lots	Inspecting Livers
Visions	Predetermined Signs
Oracles	Astrology
Prophecy	Dream Interpretation
Palmistry	

Another unacknowledged "control" mechanism that affects our thinking about signs and symbols stems from the curious influence of the radical German biblical scholar Julius Wellhausen (1844–1918). Wellhausen was one of many scholars who suggested that in the ancient Near East there were two broad kinds of religion: prophets and divination.[22] Divination has a lot to do with interpreting signs or symbols when seeking guidance, direction, and control over immediate circumstances (like finding a cure for an affliction). Across time and cultures divination has been a constant grassroots religious practice. It is the familiar "way" for many people to deal with life's mundane matters and is sometimes practiced despite official religious teachings.[23]

Wellhausen regarded prophecy in ancient Israel as being a completely different phenomenon than divination. His way of understanding prophecy and divination has been misleading, though. It tells us a lot about the mindset of his era in its attempts to classify ancient Israelite and Mesopotamian religions. The actions of the biblical prophets often involved pointing to signs and symbols or using "props," just like their Mesopotamian rivals. In the Old Testament the patriarchs, judges, and prophets did things that were a form of divination (like interpreting dreams and night visions, casting lots, and following predetermined signs). Two major features made them stand apart from their Canaanite neighbors. The first was the big question, which God stands behind the signs—Yahweh or Baal? The second was the prophets' emphasis on ethical duties and speaking out on matters of social justice.[24]

The church needs to find its prophetic voice so it can do what the biblical prophets did: (a) point to the signs and symbols, and (b) be a voice on social justice issues. We need to be adept at pointing to the resurrection signs in nature, as well as the sign of the resurrection in Scripture. We must become the Robert Langdon of our culture and encourage our peers to join us in reading, understanding, and acting on the signs.

Ben Witherington reminds us that if we want to better appreciate Jesus in his day then we need to discern the signs he offered.[25] Witherington wants us to realize that while it is important to see Jesus's uniqueness as Lord and Savior we must also not divorce him from his time. In Jesus's day there were seers, sages, and diviners offering signs and symbols too, and Jesus sometimes acted in ways that were not dissimilar from contemporary seers and diviners. When his peers asked him to give a sign, he replied with some irony, because they could discern the signs of changing weather but were blind to The Sign. Jesus made it clear he offered to Israel the sign of Jonah, a sign that leads us directly to the resurrection (Matt. 16:1–4; 12:39–41). John's Gospel is often referred to as the "Gospel of signs." The Greek word *semeia* is used by John to refer to the various signs that Jesus gave, the first of which was turning water into wine. All these signs signified who Jesus was and showed that God vindicated his mission. The supreme sign given of course was the resurrection.

Traditional Proofs

Many of us have had experiences of meeting people who inquire about God and faith, and those casual conversations can prompt us into talking about proofs for God's existence. This is quite common in formal debates between contestants of rival views, and many of us have attended such debates to observe "classical" apologists like William Lane Craig argue for God's existence.[26] The kinds of "proofs" for God's existence that are commonly used have their own "history" or "pedigree" in philosophy and theology. Some of the earliest arguments can be found in the writings of Aristotle, and many of his points were later refined by the medieval Roman Catholic theologian Thomas Aquinas.

The traditional or classical proofs for the existence of God involve claiming that the design of the creation points to the existence of God as the designer of all life. The cosmological proof asserts that everything in the universe must have an external cause, and since the universe by itself does not explain its own existence, one can reason that God is the external cause. The proofs affirm the existence of a God, but they do not on their own show us the God who is revealed in Scripture and in the person of Jesus.

It is more surprising that the nature-resurrection link has not been made by apologists when using the traditional proofs. The link from nature to analogies of the resurrection seems to move us from general to special revelation. The analogies seem to cry out at us to reflect: Has there been one who has indeed gone before all of us to die and rise again? Is there one who could be called the firstfruits (1 Cor. 15:23)? Paul uses the illustration of the harvest of the first-fruits to show that Jesus has gone before us and is the promise of what is yet to come. Paul in his famous Areopagus speech also shows something of this (Acts 17:16–32) when he sets out a biblical framework through general revelation to remind us of God's provision and then shifts directly to the resurrection of Jesus.

These days there are many different attitudes about spiritual realities ranging from hard-nosed skepticism and atheism, to softer agnosticism, and to many more experimental practices. The classical apologetic plays its part in suggesting ways for tough-minded skeptics to contemplate God. The strategy consists of two steps: The first centers on demonstrating that God exists as the Creator by using philosophical proofs from design and explaining the origin of the universe from a "first cause." It then moves on to claiming that the Creator has revealed truth via the person of Jesus. In this second step the case about Jesus centers on the historical evidence and the philosophical challenge about miracles.

Our alternative approach to classical apologetics takes up analogies of resurrection in the creation. For people who perceive a deeper connection to the mysteries of life and are open to the possibility of finding God in the natural world, resurrection analogies can offer an "aha" moment of personal discovery. Some people who are highly intuitive are very responsive to encountering God in the world and feel a heightened sense of the divine in geophysical spots of transition—such as the borders where land and sea meet, where open fields become a forest, where mountaintops touch the sky. Such places of transition are often called "thin places" simply because the geophysical zones are wafer-thin and can be portals to spiritual encounters. So for people who are hardwired for the creative and intuitive and experiential, the resurrection analogies in nature can be connected to other kinds of thresholds or "thin places."

The following figure illustrates the differences between these contrasting apologetic styles.

FIGURE 6.1

Approaches to Sharing Faith from Nature

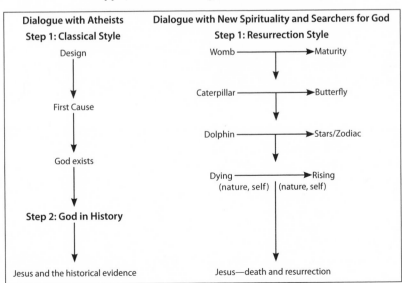

Conclusion: Nature and Scripture in Harmony

Most of us live in a world of big cities. Our intensive urbanization tends to isolate us from feeling and living in the natural world. We may regard nature as scenery that we look at in a framed picture on the wall. We tour parts of nature on vacation at the beach, forest, and mountain retreats. Our disconnection from general revelation seems to parallel our limited connection to the natural world.

There is a movement toward the natural world that is obvious among people wanting to escape the urban rat race for a simpler lifestyle. Even postmodern alternate spirituality is strongly connected to the environment, finding meaning or spirit or God in the natural world. Our habits of living divorce us from a sense of belonging among rivers, trees, and animals, and we cling to binary or dualist ideas that undervalue our own bodies, which are a part of the creation too.

Christians have tended to divide general and special revelation into separate categories. Perhaps because of the kind of urban setting we live in, and also for theological reasons, Christians have often been reluctant to place much emphasis on general revelation. Can God speak to us in the natural world or only through a written word? Part of the reluctance centers on how much we can really know about God from nature. A lot of theologians in the twentieth century were divided over this question. Those who have appealed to the positive role of general revelation have tended to center on using the traditional proofs for God's existence.

FIGURE 6.2

Does the Natural World Speak of God?

Yes	No	Yes . . . But![27]
John Calvin[28]	Immanuel Kant	Carl F. H. Henry
Alister McGrath	Karl Barth	Cornelius Van Til
Lee Strobel	Donald Bloesch	Lesslie Newbigin

Have we made a mountain out of a molehill? If we would connect the resurrection to general revelation, a lot of the hassles for people would fall away.[29] We have seen that signs in nature can point us to resurrection. The resurrection is the bridge that interconnects nature and Scripture, and isn't that the link a lot of people are searching for today? Linking general revelation with the resurrection is surely a way for us to connect with those who are looking for some connection to personal and ultimate meaning in nature retreats and spiritual writings.

This chapter has aimed at documenting a paradigm shift that has been percolating away since Bishop Butler's time. It is time to move beyond in-house debates over the limits of general revelation. Ross once had a lawyer-mentor who used to say to clients and legal foes alike, "You annoy me when you confuse yourself!" We need to desist from confusing ourselves and reconnect the exploration for meaning to resurrection signs. It's time to catch up with searchers in contemporary spirituality. The church has an answer but it has yet to hear the question.

Spiritual Audit

1. What emphasis does your church gathering place on God's creation in liturgy, music, and celebration of the Lord's Supper?

2. How often do the signs of the resurrection in creation surface in your gathering's discussions of the Bible?

3. Do you incorporate the signs of resurrection in the creation in your prayer life?

7

Other Religions, the Undead, and Resurrection

If God's power which was active in Elisha is great enough to resuscitate even a dead person who was thrown into the tomb of the prophet (2 Kings 13:20ff), then the bodily resurrection of a crucified Jew also would not be inconceivable.

Pinchas Lapide[1]

When we think of religions what usually springs to mind are the Jewish, Muslim, Hindu, and Buddhist faiths. However, folk religions, alternative spiritualities, and new religious movements also shape the lives and worldview of many people today. We are going to look at beliefs about resurrection and the afterlife in: *the* major western folk religion, major world religions, new religious movements, and alternative spiritualities.

Folk Religions and the Undead

Over the centuries, folk religions have represented a grass roots way of approaching life that relies on rituals or divinatory tools (astrology, magic, fortune telling) to find guidance, healing, and personal power over circumstances. Folk religions have sometimes come into existence alongside the major religions. Those who use folk religious practices often relate them back to the culturally dominant religion (e.g., folk religious practices in many parts of India are related back to Hindu faith).[2]

141

In recent decades new kinds of folk religions have emerged. These newer kinds of folk religion still include aspects of divination but also leave room for the development of complex rituals and thought. As time goes on some folk religions may end up developing into "mainstream" religions.

Vampire spirituality is *the* new emerging folk religion in North America, Europe, and Australia.[3] For example, we have found by talking about Vampire spirituality in public forums that lots of young women tell us how they have been exposed to and influenced by it. Most Christians freak out over vampires. We wave the garlic and thrust a stake at them because we think they are demonic. It is easy to condemn what we do not understand. There are both serious aspirants and dabblers. Aspirants see themselves as "real vampires" and claim they are spiritually empowered by absorbing the life-essence from consenting "donors". The life essence may be imaginatively drawn from a donor in a psychic rite, or more literally in sado-masochistic blood-sucking rituals. When a person is initiated as a vampire they are "reborn" and believe that they have experienced a "spiritual resurrection."[4]

Aspirants of Vampire spirituality create their beliefs by referring to esoteric groups that existed centuries ago, as well as today's neo-pagan groups. They also draw inspiration from both Gothic literature and pop culture. Vampire spirituality is practiced in formal contexts where spiritual groups have been established such as House Sahjaza, House Kheperu, Order of the Vampyre, and Clan of Lilith. Informal contexts include Internet-based vampire websites and in Goth dance clubs where vampires socialize, role-play, or perform blood rituals.

Cultural Mix of Beliefs about the Undead

You have probably heard the words "life imitates art," and in some ways this captures what happens in Vampire spirituality. For example, a study in Wales has shown that the more time adolescents spend watching TV shows about vampires the more they are likely to believe they exist.[5] Adult aspirants in Goth dance clubs role-play as fictional characters like Morticia Addams and Count Dracula. Adolescents seem to use TV series like *Buffy the Vampire Slayer* and *True Blood* as springboards for creating their own spirituality.

What important ideas are explorers of Vampire spirituality exposed to? Classic tales about vampires and other undead creatures have thrived for centuries in the misty borderland where folklore, folk religion, and traditional religious pathways meet. The undead characters include vampires, werewolves, zombies, the Wandering Jew, Frankenstein's monster, the mariners on the ship the *Flying Dutchman*, the Golem, and the Homunculus. In Gothic literature and folktales the "living dead" or "undead" characters use magic to cheat death or are under a curse to live until the world's end. Vampires and werewolves feed on the blood of the living in a way that parodies both the death of Christ and the blood motifs connected to atonement. They are classic embodiments of evil or loathing, and the older undead tales usually warn about the dangers of trying to cheat death.

What many Christians fail to recognize is that these tales convey a moral lesson: the undead are flouting God's will by seeking immortality in the flesh apart from God's grace and plan for the resurrection.[6] The message is, do not seek immortality in this flesh or you will be cursed.

These stories reflect cultural trends about morals and ways of being. Classic stories like *The Vampyre, Frankenstein, Carmilla, Dracula,* and *The Island of Dr Moreau* picked up the angst of the Industrial Revolution, during which humanity's *imago Dei* was believed to have been discredited by Darwin. The horrors of multiple revolutions in Europe during the mid-nineteenth century highlighted humanity's darkness, and moral decadence was celebrated by social elites.[7]

Newer vampire stories include some "good" vampires such as Angel and Blade. Edward Cullen in *Twilight* has achieved iconic status as a dashing romantic vampire, although he was foreshadowed by the suave English nobleman-vampire Lord Ruthven in John Polidori's 1819 story *The Vampyre*. One major idea that is apparent in the newer stories concerns the redemption of vampires. Several new stories hold forth the possibility that some vampires are seeking redemption, love humanity, and will "save" us from the threat of the undead, perhaps heralding a portal to the resurrection.[8] As Vampire spirituality is partly influenced by newer stories it is possible that some aspirants are subliminally prepared to think about redemption. Many practitioners believe that they have already experienced a spiritual resurrection. So Christians could easily have dialogue about both redemption and the meaning of Christ's bodily resurrection.

Recent Gothic novels and films have explored themes of blood, eroticism, heroines, prejudice, and meaninglessness. This new genre of vampire stories coincides with experiments in DNA and cloning, and implicitly poses questions about the wisdom of tampering with human biology. So, some of the questions that we saw in chapter 5 about an embodied identity in this life and the afterlife are paralleled in the stories that are influencing Vampire spirituality.

Stephenie Meyer's *Twilight* series has captivated many female readers because of the strong romantic Romeo-and-Juliet theme. Some female readers may be drawn to the series because of the appeal to "redeem" bad boys: the vampire is the ultimate "bad boy." Meyer's novels involve a bit more than just Mills-and-Boon-meets-Dracula because she opens up the literary horizon for vampire *redemption*. The intrusion of a redemptive theme is not too surprising given that she is a member of the Church of Jesus Christ of Latter-Day Saints (Mormons). Her fiction exhibits both moral strengths and theological pitfalls related to her church's unorthodox cosmology (see our later section about the Mormons).[9] Meyer's novels can be theologically contrasted with those by Tracey Bateman and Eric Wilson, who as evangelical novelists have not shied away from the Gothic genre.[10]

Undoubtedly Anne Rice's *Interview with the Vampire* stands out as a highly imaginative work about vampires.[11] The novel expresses the perspective of a vampire who seems to express bleak despair, and other characters who begin to question the tediousness of an unending life. We may ask, if we keep God out of the picture will we become the hideous undead?[12] Rice wrote her first novel about the undead partly in reaction to her experience of personal tragedy with the death of a child. Like many of her contemporaries she was unable to find succor in the Roman Catholic beliefs of her childhood. She rejected Christianity as she knew it, drifted into atheism, and became a voice for many who share similar tragedies and disenchantment with faith. She wrote many vampire novels that became best-sellers and enjoyed strong appeal among people committed to neo-pagan pathways. Her life story eventually brought her to a point of deep reflection and she reinvestigated the story of Jesus, which included reading books by Ben Witherington and N. T. Wright. She has returned to Christian faith and has, to the amazement of many, set aside writing any further vampire novels.[13] As the fascination with the *Twilight* series intensified Rice was asked to comment, and she said:

> Since the vampire starts out as a human being it's quite natural to explore the idea of his wanting redemption or to put an end to his cursed existence of drinking human blood. In other words, the myth is very compatible with Christian ideas and can obviously be developed well in that direction.[14]

Vampire spirituality is emerging as the West's new folk religion. We have concentrated on it because of its focus on the undead and immortality, and its pick-and-mix of ideas drawn from (a) the classic stories that uphold a human-based resurrection without God, and (b) the new writings that focus on grappling with meaninglessness, the search for redemption, and finding a spiritual kind of resurrection. We see a new vista opening up for Christians to talk to aspirants of Vampire spirituality about the practical application to life of Christ's resurrection. We call the church to reflect on these questions: Does the undead genre seek one who can conquer death? Is emerging Vampire spirituality groping for signs of the resurrected Jesus?[15]

Conversations about Life After Death

We leave Vampire spirituality behind us. In the next few pages we will briefly unpack Zoroastrian, Muslim, Bahá'i, Jewish, Hindu, Buddhist, Taoist, and Shamanist understandings of life after death. This is followed by a similar overview of diverse understandings in new religions and alternative spiritual pathways. The aim is to discover what these worldviews say about the resurrection of Jesus and the destiny of humanity—be it resurrection or some other form.

It's fascinating to see the wide-ranging interests that many people have in what the world's religions teach about resurrection and the afterlife. This became crystal clear to us at a Mind-Body-Spirit festival when two women talked to us about the meaning of the tarot card for judgment. It portrays humans answering the angel's trumpet blast and rising from the dead based on Revelation 20. This tarot card opts for resurrection and not reincarnation. Our newfound friends loved the smorgasbord choices of spirituality on offer. They were interested in exploring how the various pathways understand life after death. Our conversation led us into a short tour of what the smorgasbord is saying.

Pilgrims' Tour of Traditional Pathways

Zoroastrianism

It was long ago in ancient Persia that the teacher Zoroaster (or Zarathushtra) lived.[16] His followers flourished in Persia until the coming of Islam and then scattered to India because of persecution. They are known in India as Parsees because of their Persian ethnicity. Zoroastrians teach that everyone will be resurrected to face judgment. In the past one hundred years there has been a big debate as to when the Zoroastrians started teaching resurrection. It partly carries over into hotly contested claims that the exiled Jews in Babylon borrowed the idea from the Zoroastrians. Others insist there are Zoroastrian influences on the New Testament.[17] The earliest Zoroastrian holy texts are not that explicit about our resurrection. Zoroastrian belief in the resurrection of humanity possibly emerged no earlier than the fourth century BC. It is very clearly found in texts dating from the ninth century AD.[18] Zoroastrians do not seem to have written much about Jesus's resurrection, although some have converted and become followers of the risen Christ.[19]

Islam

Muslims have a very clear understanding that everyone will be resurrected and judged. The Qur'an teaches that those who are rewarded by God enter paradise while others are lost forever in hell.[20] Belief in resurrection contributed to early thinking about martyrdom in the early history of Shi'ite Islam. In the last thirty years traditional Islamic views of martyrdom have been altered by extremists taking the political-military action of suicide bombers. Muslims have different opinions about the fate of Jesus. Most Muslims feel that God would not have permitted Jesus (whom they esteem as a major prophet) to have suffered a humiliating death at the cross.[21] So there are those who insist that he was never crucified, while others (like the Ahmadiyya sect) appear to hold to a swoon theory where Jesus survived the cross and relocated to

Kashmir where he later died.[22] Some Muslims believe that Jesus was translated into heaven, and there are popular traditions that he will return at the world's end to convert everyone to Islam.[23] From the earliest history of Islam up to today Muslim apologists have debated Christians about the historical fact of Jesus's death and resurrection.[24]

Bahá'i

The Bahá'i faith began as an offshoot of the Shi'ite branch of Islam in what is now the modern state of Iran. According to the Bahá'is God has, so far, sent nine different religious messengers into the world: Moses, Lao Tzu, Jesus, Muhammad, Krishna, Buddha, Confucius, the Bab, and Bahá'u'lláh. The latter two men are foundational characters in the Bahá'i movement. Each messenger was just "right" for the time and place in which they lived. The Bahá'i explain references to the day of resurrection (in both the Bible and Qur'an) as meaning that God will send another prophet. The New Testament was pointing to Muhammad's coming, and the Qur'an was pointing to the Bab. So, in Bahá'i thought the day of resurrection is not referring to a literal bodily resurrection. Jesus's resurrection was instead purely symbolic and spiritual.

There are two reasons why a literal bodily resurrection is difficult for the Bahá'is to accept. One is that they make an important distinction between the spiritual and material worlds. The material world, in which our physical existence occurs, is a training ground where we prepare ourselves for an advanced spiritual life. In the spiritual world we are not resurrected with our physical body. The material or physical human form belongs only to the present world. In the present life the capabilities of our soul—the mind, will, and heart—are expressed through the physical body. After physical death the soul exists apart from the body. So the second reason why the physical resurrection of Jesus and of the rest of humankind is rejected is because Bahá'i teaching upholds the immortality of the soul. It is the soul that survives physical death and exists forever in the spiritual world.[25]

Judaism

Jewish religion has its various schools of thought and traditions.[26] Among them there is a tradition of mysticism known as the Kabbalah (not identical with "occult cabala," which emerged in modern times). Kabbalah has its roots in the Jewish community that lived in Alexandria in pre-Christian times. The Jews of Alexandria encountered Greek philosophy, and much of that Greek thought was concerned with the immortality of the soul and not positive about the survival of the body after death.

Those Jews became familiar with the mystical view of mathematics held by Pythagoras. The Greek alphabetical letters were also used as numbers, and Pythagoras held that numbers are an expression of ultimate reality that can be measured and predicted in patterns or cycles. Pythagoras also believed in a form of reincarnation. So the early Kabbalists began to speculate about discovering divinely inspired numerical patterns in Scripture and looked for hidden meanings in the biblical text about God's attributes.

The central Kabbalist text, called the Zohar (Book of Splendor), seems to convey the idea of reincarnation. It is possible that Pythagoras's view of reincarnation may have influenced some Kabbalists. However, there is a division of opinion between the Judaic Kabbalist historian Gershom Scholem (1897–1982) on one side, and a variety of contemporary orthodox rabbis on the other side, over the dating of the Zohar. Scholem's analysis, which is widely acknowledged by many religious studies scholars, holds that the Zohar was created by the thirteenth-century Spanish Jew Moses de Leon. While Scholem does allow for the presence of earlier source material in the Zohar he argues that it is principally a late medieval text.[27] Those rabbis who reject Scholem's position believe the Zohar was produced by Rabbi Shimon bar Yohai sometime after the Romans destroyed Jerusalem in AD 70. No matter what date is ascribed to the Zohar, the flowering of a Jewish belief in reincarnation came in the sixteenth century through the Kabbalist writer Isaac Luria.[28]

Orthodox Jews have traditionally believed in the general resurrection at the end of time. They have accepted belief in the corporate resurrection of Israel as a community and in individual bodily resurrection based on passages in the Hebrew Bible. It is further elaborated on in rabbinic teaching found in different parts of the Mishnah and Talmud. Jewish prayers for the dead and burial customs reflect belief in bodily resurrection, and for this reason cremation is not a favored practice. However, since the Enlightenment, and especially after Auschwitz, some Jews—particularly those in the school of Reform Judaism—have shifted away from any notion of the resurrection and replaced it with the idea of the immortality of the human soul.[29] In chapter 12 we will discuss the resurrection in the Hebrew Scriptures.

During Jesus's earthly ministry different Jewish schools or sects existed. The Pharisees believed in the general resurrection of humankind, but the Sadducees were skeptics on that point.[30] Our opening quote from the Jewish scholar Pinchas Lapide (1922–1997) indicates that acknowledging the miracle of Jesus's resurrection is not inconsistent with Judaic thinking: "Why should the resurrection of a personal ego after passing through death be more miraculous than the gradual awakening of a human being out of the lifeless matter of a fertilized ovum?"[31]

Classically Jews from apostolic times onwards have disputed whether Jesus was the firstfruits of the resurrection from the dead. Perhaps Lapide charted a new trajectory for dialogue. The emphasis ought to be more on what Jesus's resurrection means rather than debating the empty tomb. Lapide of course did not accept the deity of Jesus but was happy to say that Jesus is the gentile Messiah for Christians.

Karma

The concept of karma originates from the religious traditions of India. Karma involves a chain of cause and effect of good and bad deeds. It encompasses time, nature, consciousness, the will and soul, the living and dead, past and present. Karma stops us from totally controlling our lives. It operates in a cyclical view of reality because we are spiritually evolving. The focal point is finding release from the chain of cause and effect and avoiding rebirth in this world. Terminating rebirth is essential to achieving the ultimate goal in the transcendent realm.

Hinduism

One contemporary sect of Hindu spirituality is the International Society for Krishna Consciousness (ISKCON), which is known for its devotion to the god Krishna. One of its teachers, Srila Bhaktipada, has remarked, "This gross body, which is composed of earth, water, fire, air, and ether, is born of an earthly father and mother. But the subtle body, composed of mind, intelligence, and false ego is different. . . . The soul is superior to the gross and subtle bodies."[32]

Bhaktipada's view is consistent with the position taken by many (but not all) Hindu teachers in other traditions and sects. We should be careful to not make the mistake of thinking that all Hindus think alike. Hindus are considerably diverse in their understanding about God, sacred texts, and what sacred practices are most beneficial. Perhaps the distinct feature is that Hindu thought supports the idea of the transmigration of the soul: at death the soul passes from one life form to another. The soul may experience rebirth in human form (popularly called reincarnation) or it may pass to a nonhuman form of life as an animal. The return of the soul to life on earth is causally linked to the concept of karma.[33] In traditional Hindu experience one does not seek to "return" to any life on earth because existence here is not ultimate and can be hellish. The ultimate aim for the soul is some form of reunion with Brahma.

India is often known as the land of signs and wonders, and marvelous or miraculous events are "normal" for a holy guru (teacher). So with respect to the resurrection of Jesus some Hindus won't stumble over the possibility of a miracle. Some ancient Hindu myths allowed room for the reassembling of dismembered bodies, but this did not prefigure resurrection. What Hindus are unlikely to accept is that Jesus's resurrection represents the firstfruits for humans beyond the grave. Hindus might accept that Jesus is divine in much the same way that everyone else is understood to have the divine within them. The way in which Jesus is then understood is framed in a Hindu-based grid.[34] It is worth noting that in Hindu thought the concept of a god taking on human flesh (an incarnation) is perfectly understandable: Krishna is recognized as an incarnation of Vishnu.

Buddhism

Just like the Hindus, Buddhists are very diverse in their beliefs, practices, and sects, so it is unhelpful to regard Buddhism as a uniform religion or philosophy.[35] Perhaps the best known contemporary Buddhist teacher is the Tibetan leader the Dalai Lama. He is well known in the West for emphasizing happiness while in East Asia his message comes in more stringent traditional forms.

A few years ago the Dalai Lama chatted with the Benedictine Father Laurence Freeman before a packed auditorium in London about the teachings and ministry of Jesus. The Dalai Lama finds many wise and admirable insights in Jesus's teaching that he feels are paralleled in the Buddha's words. In the dialogue he summarized various Buddhist understandings about spiritual insight and the concept of rebirth.[36] He admitted he was unsure about what the resurrection entails and asked Father Laurence for clarification. The dialogue shows that the Dalai Lama understands that the resurrection is not at all identical to reincarnation.

Unlike the Hindu view of human beings, every Buddhist pathway upholds:

a. There is no soul (anatta).
b. There is no permanent self (anicca).

For Buddhists it is an illusion to suppose that there is a soul or self. Instead at death the illusory self that is shaped by karma reincarnates, in the same way that one candle may be lit by another candle. Resurrection does not fit into the Dalai Lama's understanding of the afterlife. Father Laurence remarks, "The Resurrection of Jesus is the basis of Christian faith. . . . [A]t a doctrinal and philosophical level of dialogue, the importance of the Resurrection is that it shows the *uniqueness* of Jesus. . . . The Resurrection is also important . . . because it shows that the greatest human fear, of death, is based on illusion."[37]

In *Living Buddha, Living Christ* the Vietnamese Zen Buddhist monk Thich Nhat Hanh propounds the view that reincarnation is part of Christian belief:

> Most Christian leaders say the idea of reincarnation does not fit with Christianity. . . . Elements of reincarnation are certainly present in the teachings of Christianity.[38]

The stance taken by Thich Nhat Hanh is one that is echoed by many alternative spiritualities advocates. We will explore this specific claim later in the chapter. By way of contrast, Tucker Callaway was a personal friend of the popular Japanese Zen writer D. T. Suzuki. Callaway was also one of the first Southern Baptist missionaries to enter Japan after the end of World War II. After thirty years of careful study of Zen Callaway wrote:

> In sharp contrast to the Zen Way of no birth and no death, the Jesus Way takes both individual life and individual death with utter seriousness. Jesus offers

deliverance from fear of death not by denying its objective existence, but by his own victory over death through Resurrection.[39]

Lastly, an Australian Buddhist monk Dhammika (born as Paul Boston) has a book that is going gangbusters on the Internet with a very scathing polemic against the Bible and Protestant fundamentalism. Using the pseudonym A. L. De Silva he has written *Beyond Belief* and argues that "the four accounts of the supposed Resurrection differ in nearly every detail."[40] He rejects the Gospel accounts as implausible because they vary in naming the women who visited the empty tomb; because of the failure of three Gospels to mention Matthew's "earthquake"; and because of the different number of angels that appeared at the tomb. He concludes sarcastically, "and it is on this garbled 'evidence' that Christianity rests."[41] De Silva's polemic is very poor in tone, charity, and depth of understanding as compared to some other contemporary Buddhist responses to Christianity.[42]

Taoist/Daoist Way

The Taoist (pronounced Dowist) traditions of China trace back to their fountainhead teacher Lao Tzu. Taoist beliefs of an afterlife have tended to mix together concepts of survival as ancestral spirits with reincarnation. Belief in resurrection is evident in some Taoist funerary texts found in excavated burial sites.[43]

The idea of a resurrection occurs in texts dated to what is known in China's history as the Warring States Period (ca. 475–221 BC) and into the first few centuries of the Christian era. A resurrection back to life on earth required someone living who knew the deceased to negotiate with an underworld bureaucratic figure known as the Director of the Life-mandate. One account dated to 297 BC concerns a man named Dan. He killed someone but then committed suicide. Xi Wu was Dan's patron and he put forward a legal suit pleading that Dan's death was untimely and requesting the underworld authorities to release him from the grave. Three years after his suicide Dan was released from the grave bearing the suicide scars on his body with four useless limbs.[44] It was not ideal given his useless limbs but does indicate that in ancient China some believed in the possibility that the dead could be resurrected to life on earth.

Shamanism

A shaman is a man or woman who mediates between this world and the unseen world of deities and spirits. Shamans typically are healers who have divinatory powers and visionary experiences. They are found in many cultures: African, Chinese, Korean, Siberian, American Indian, Inuit, Maori, Melanesian, and Australian Aboriginal.[45] Different attitudes concerning the fate of the dead are held across shamanic traditions. Many emphasize the journey of the soul of the dead into an unseen world. Some believe in both reincarnation and the resurrection of the soul. In Eastern Siberia the Nivkhi people "believe that the dead go to the village of the dead (*miy-vo*), then after a new death the soul goes down to another *miy-vo* where they either disappear or are reincarnated, but a woman's soul dies four times and is then resurrected."[46] Eliade observed that when the shaman is first ritually initiated he or she metaphorically "dies" and is then "resurrected" as a new person to the tribe.[47] While shamanism continues to flourish in many traditional cultures aspects of its general rites and cosmology have been incorporated into neo-pagan spiritualities.[48]

Pilgrims' Tour of Popular Pathways

It was a hot Sunday afternoon in a public hall where over a thousand people had turned up. There was a debate over whether Jesus is coequal with the Father. Ross's team was opposing a **Christadelphian** team. A key issue of discussion was Jesus's resurrection. The Christadelphians accept the literal bodily resurrection of Jesus as the firstfruits and that his followers will be resurrected. However this belief in resurrection actually undermines the idea of Jesus's divinity. Christadelphians do not believe that there is any existence between our death and resurrection at the last judgment, so when Jesus died he ceased to exist until his own resurrection. Since God cannot cease to exist Christadelphians argue that Jesus is not divine. Ross defended an intermediate state of existence by pointing to the thief on the cross who was promised that he would be alive with Jesus in paradise (Luke 23:43). He also directed attention to Thomas's confession of the resurrected Jesus's deity (John 20:28). So the Christadelphians accept the bodily resurrection of Jesus but reject his deity because they do not accept that God is triune. Among the Christadelphians there are partisan views as to whether all humans or only faithful believers are resurrected.[49]

"The Door-Knockers"

Unless you are living like St. Antony did, perched on a pillar in an Egyptian desert, then the chances are strong that you have met a **Jehovah's Witness** at your front door. Jehovah's Witnesses have a mixed bag of beliefs. On the one hand they hope that after the battle of Armageddon they will be physically resurrected and live on a new earth. Those who do not belong to Jehovah's kingdom are annihilated forever. On the other hand, they hold that Jesus was resurrected not in bodily form but as an invisible spirit. They also hold that 144,000 believers in a special class will be raised like Jesus as invisible spirits to reign in heaven. Jehovah's Witnesses view Jesus as the first being created by God; he was originally Michael the Archangel. When Jesus lived on the earth he was only a human, but after his resurrection he returned to an exalted angelic state as God's adopted son.[50] Jehovah's Witnesses have been at loggerheads with Christians about the resurrection since the 1870s.

The **Mormons** (Church of Jesus Christ of Latter-Day Saints) accept the literal bodily resurrection of Jesus. They also hold that everyone will be resurrected from the dead. In their teaching Jesus Christ is revered as Savior and is also divine. However, Jesus is not the only deity to exist. The Mormons hold that there are many gods that exist and the ultimate goal of the faithful is to be resurrected as a god. For human beings there are different resurrection bodies and different states of reward depending on whether one was a baptized Mormon, belonged to a non-Mormon church, or was a completely unrepentant person.[51]

These three movements differ from mainstream Christianity in various ways. The above sketches indicate that it is possible to affirm that Jesus rose from the dead without necessarily knowing him in his unique relationship to the Father and the Holy Spirit. One of the theological issues that these groups must face is the biblical witness that Jesus's resurrection is truly a sign of his deity (John 20:28; Rom. 1:4).

Unpaid Bills of the Resurrection

The missionary community has recently acknowledged that frontier mission work involves reaching modern-day sects, cults, and new religions. These groups, which have traditionally been treated as heresies, are now being identified as unreached subcultures.[52] Several of these subcultures have disputed the resurrection. The Unity School of Christianity opts for reincarnation.[53] Mary Baker Eddy teaches in Christian Science that Jesus did not really die on the cross.[54] The Unitarian Church (now known in the US as the Unitarian Universalist Association) traces its nontrinitarian theology back to Faustus Socinus (1539–1604) and William Ellery Channing (1780–1842). In its earliest phases Unitarian theology was open to biblical miracles while rejecting the divinity of Christ; later on it rejected miracles and reinterpreted the resurrection symbolically.[55] Today it is universalist about all religions being metaphysically valid.[56]

These movements hold up a mirror to the church over its deficiencies. Our failure to properly teach and embody the effect of resurrection theology in our lives is mirrored in the teachings of new religions that claim to be the custodians of true apostolic faith. J. K. Van Baalen picks up a slogan from the 1930s and bluntly puts it to the church that these sects, cults, and new religious groups represent "the unpaid bills of the church."[57] We refine his point and ask: What are the unpaid bills of the resurrection?

Postmodern Spiritualities

Many people now approach the spiritual search independently of any organized religious community; they construct a do-it-yourself religion, in which they can mix-and-match and test out practices rather than starting a quest for "the truth." People look for self-enhancement as summed up in the line, "How can I be the best person I can possibly be?" We will now consider postmodern spiritualities as regards their understandings of the afterlife.

Deepak Chopra has recently rebranded as "The Shift" what was previously known as New Age. **New Age spirituality** rocketed to prominence in the 1980s and 1990s. It is an eclectic consumer form of spirituality in which aspirants are very open to trying different spiritual tools to achieve personal recovery and growth, and to reconnect with the earth, the cosmos, and the divine. New Agers strive to fit everything together in a holistic understanding of life and reality. The individual consumerist flavor of New Age means that diversity is the name of the game. No two individuals are necessarily going to agree on what spiritual tools are best or what beliefs are "logical."

We have found that a lot of people who identify with the self-spirituality quest of New Age opt for reincarnation. The New Age view of reincarnation differs from that of traditional Indian religions by emphasizing that in each successive incarnation one is constantly evolving toward a positive goal of finally leaving the world for a higher spiritual state. James Redfield best expressed the essence of this view:

> Such growth will move humans into ever higher energy states, ultimately transforming our bodies into spiritual form and uniting this dimension of existence with the after-life dimension, ending the cycle of birth and death.[58]

Others see the afterlife through the NDE paradigm. Unlike the negative cases of NDEs noted in chapter 5, in this pathway NDEs are always positive. People tell us how they have had brushes with death in accidents, surgery, and other life-threatening situations. They sense that their spirit has exited the body and travels into the spiritual realm where deceased relatives or people of notoriety are met. During these NDEs, the traveler has conversations that center on the purpose of life on earth and usually encounters a being of light identified as God or the Source. The NDE experience for the New Age seeker is always euphoric.[59]

These stories underscore a sense of continuity from life on earth to life beyond the grave. Each individual's spirit survives as a knowable and tangible entity. The survival of the individual as a distinct spiritlike entity seems to be very different from the higher energy state of being that Redfield spoke of from the reincarnation paradigm. Some NDE accounts have great affinity with the afterlife beliefs of occult writers like Emanuel Swedenborg (discussed in detail below), and from the Spiritualist churches that emerged in the nineteenth century.[60] In the **Spiritualist** churches a distinction is made between the physical body and the spiritual body, the latter of which can survive in different invisible planes of existence. Spiritualists have different opinions about Christ's resurrection. The resurrection of the body may be interpreted as surviving death in a noncorporeal body (sometimes called a light or astral body), but what Spiritualists commonly hold is that Jesus's resurrection proves that we survive physical death.[61]

Other NDE accounts reflect beliefs that have developed in a tradition of Western magical thought called **Theosophy**.[62] This tradition, which has been another fountainhead for New Age, holds that humans have both a physical body and an astral body. Theosophists use the term *astral body* differently from the way Spiritualists use it. In Theosophy the astral body takes the NDE journey through the tunnel of light and encounters dead loved ones before returning to life on earth. The astral body is the conduit through which desires and emotions are transmitted to the physical body in this earthly realm. While the physical body is alive, the astral body is capable of out-of-body experiences associated with sleep, trances, and other altered states of consciousness. In death the astral body is a replica of the now deceased person and may journey through another invisible layer of existence called the astral world. According to Theosophical thought there are seven worlds: Our physical or corporeal existence is the first and lowest, while the astral world is the second realm. There are five other higher worlds or planes of existence in which life may endure. It is not uncommon to find pop New Age writers confusing astral bodies and reincarnation with the biblical understanding of bodily resurrection.

Sampling New Movements

There are three other relatively young worldviews that are worth a quick mention in our discussion of perspectives on the resurrection. **Neo-pagans** embrace an earth-centered spirituality focused on different expressions of divinity in the world, which may include gods and goddesses. Some neo-pagans hold that at death one's spirit sojourns in a place called the Summerland, and it may subsequently reincarnate on earth. Other practitioners sense the presence of spirits and entities in this world and the unseen world, and use a variety of shamanic tools and techniques to interact with these beings. Neo-pagans uphold sacred ritual observances that are grounded in the seasonal equinoxes and phases of the moon. There is an annual cycle of eight major sacral observances known as sabbats that form what is called the Wheel of the Year. The Wheel of the Year involves the ceremonial rites observed at each of the eight sabbats, and each sabbat comprises an episode in an eight-part myth. Within the myth is a cyclical symbolic death and resurrection of a deity.[63]

The Raëlians constitute a new UFO-based movement that claims that immortality is available through cloning. In their worldview humans were cloned by beings from an advanced interplanetary society known as the elohim some twenty-five thousand years ago. Through biotechnology we too can attain everlasting life as "resurrected clones."[64] This is an "atheist" religion that espouses a spiritual message grounded in bioethical technology and dovetails with the sociological trend we noted in chapter 5 concerning the sacred status of DNA.

Finally, the Japanese new religion Mahikari has brought to the rest of the world a Shinto-influenced understanding of the afterlife. In Mahikari the earth interacts with ancestral spirits who may bless or afflict our lives. So the afterlife does not involve resurrection but survival as an invisible spirit entity. Mahikari adepts claim that Jesus studied in Japan prior to his ministry in Palestine. Jesus escaped crucifixion and returned to Japan where he died at the age of 106 years old.[65]

Earlier in the chapter we mentioned speaking with two women at a Mind-Body-Spirit festival about the smorgasbord of spiritual choices on offer. As our conversation wound down we realized we had looked at three basic paradigms for how spiritual groups understand life after death:

1. *Resurrection*: Humans will be resurrected (usually physical in form or, in case of some Jehovah's Witnesses, merely spiritual in form).
2. *Reincarnation*: Humans enter a cycle of reincarnation/rebirth before reaching ultimate reality.
3. *Revenant*: Humans become a revenant, meaning that their spirits survive as embodied entities or as disembodied apparitions.

These women could see that resurrection is holistic and quite different from reincarnation and spirit apparitions. They asked us if anyone else apart from Jesus has been resurrected, and we informed them that in the Bible there were various individuals such as Lazarus who were revivified, but those cases were not resurrections. We noted Gary Habermas's study of resurrection claims of individuals in other religions. Habermas indicates that there are two categories of claims. One category concerns the ascension into the heavens of Julius Caesar, Augustus Caesar, and the philosopher Apollonius of Tyana, which turn out not to involve resurrection. The second category concerns five cases of claimed resurrections for historical persons. Two of them were Jewish teachers: Rabbi Judah I and Sabbatai Sevi; while the other three were teachers from the Indian subcontinent: Kabir, Lahiri Mahasaya, and Sri Yukteswar. Habermas concluded that not one of the accounts offered any substantial evidence or testimony that could pass muster.[66] We are really left then with the specific case of Jesus, the evidences for his resurrection, and the holistic implications of it for the empowerment and growth of our own lives.

FIGURE 7.1

Who Believes What on the Afterlife

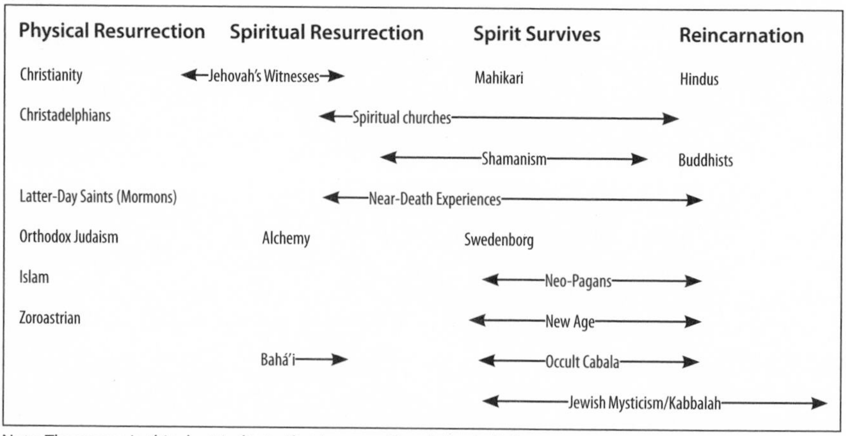

Physical Resurrection	Spiritual Resurrection	Spirit Survives	Reincarnation
Christianity	◄—Jehovah's Witnesses—►	Mahikari	Hindus
Christadelphians	◄———Spiritual churches——————►		
	◄———————Shamanism————►		Buddhists
Latter-Day Saints (Mormons)	◄———Near-Death Experiences———————►		
Orthodox Judaism	Alchemy	Swedenborg	
Islam		◄———Neo-Pagans———►	
Zoroastrian		◄———New Age———►	
	Bahá'í—►	◄———Occult Cabala———►	
		◄———————Jewish Mysticism/Kabbalah———————►	

Note: The arrows in this chart indicate that in a specific religion beliefs may cross over one or more categories of the afterlife. Diversity of opinion often exists among fellow believers.

Christianity and Reincarnation

We want to address one matter mentioned briefly above. Zen Buddhists, postmodern spiritual pilgrims, and others make the claim that reincarnation is found in the Bible and in the traditions of the early church. These groups claim that traces of belief in reincarnation are evident in the Gospels. The principal example touted concerns the possibility that Elijah the prophet was reincarnated as John the Baptist. In Israel at the time of Christ there was an expectation that Elijah would return: "I will send you the prophet Elijah before the great and terrible day of the LORD comes" (Mal. 4:5). The Gospels note the expectation that Elijah would prefigure Messiah's coming:

> "Why, then, do the scribes say that Elijah must come first?" He replied, "Elijah is indeed coming and will restore all things; but I tell you that Elijah has already come, and they did not recognize him, but they did to him whatever they pleased. So also the Son of Man is about to suffer at their hands." Then the disciples understood that he was speaking to them about John the Baptist. (Matt. 17:10–13)

Elsewhere when Jesus referred to John the Baptist he said: "and if you are willing to accept it, he is Elijah who is to come" (Matt. 11:14). Edgar Cayce, the American trance medium, claimed that Jesus was teaching that Elijah had reincarnated as John the Baptist:

> What logical thought process induced the disciples to draw such a conclusion so promptly, unless Jesus had made them thoroughly familiar with the laws of reincarnation?[67]

Three Key Words

Metempsychosis: Used by ancient philosophers such as Pythagoras, Plotinus, and Plato. It signifies that at death the soul passes from one body to the next body.

Rebirth: For Hindus "rebirth" refers to the soul passing at death (transmigrating) to another body which may be human or animal.

Reincarnation: Literally means to come again in the flesh. Among contemporary Hindus this is a synonym for the transmigration of the soul. For Buddhists, who deny the soul's existence, an illusory "self" reincarnates in any life-form. In the West, it generally refers to coming back as another human.

Cayce's inference ignores the fact that Elijah was bodily translated into heaven (2 Kings 2:11–12) and did not die. Also, if Elijah was reincarnated as John the Baptist then one must explain the accounts of Jesus's transfiguration. In Matthew 17 Elijah and Moses appear. By that time John the Baptist had been beheaded. In reincarnation, the latest incarnation emerges in human life. If John the Baptist was truly Elijah reincarnated, then John ought to have appeared. Another point is that John the Baptist was asked about this matter too, and he denied that he was literally Elijah: "And they asked him, 'What then? Are you Elijah?' He said, 'I am not'" (John 1:21). Other Gospel passages refer to John the Baptist as ministering in a manner just like Elijah (Mark 1:2–3; Matt. 11:10; Luke 1:17; 7:27). So, when Jesus spoke about John and Elijah, he was not teaching reincarnation but confirming the similarities in their ministries.

Besides the claim that Jesus taught reincarnation, there is the parallel claim that some leading figures taught it in the early church. The central allegation is that the church father Origen taught reincarnation and that at the Council of Constantinople (AD 553) the teaching was declared a heresy and the Bible was censored. Origen never taught reincarnation and in fact expressed his opposition to the Greek idea of the transmigration of soul (metempsychosis). Origen's last book was a commentary on Matthew's Gospel. In commenting on the passage concerning the appearance of Elijah at the transfiguration he said that the "dogma of transmigration [reincarnation] . . . is foreign to the church of God and not handed down by the Apostles, nor anywhere set forth in the Scriptures."[68] The peculiar teaching that Origen did believe in and that we discuss further in chapter 10 was the preexistence of the soul in heaven prior to our physical conception.[69] This particular dogma was rejected by the Council of Constantinople, and the council did not tamper with the contents of the Bible.

Visions of the Risen Christ

As we have seen, the idea of resurrection is found in several but not all religions, and the Christian worldview will continue to encounter those who emphasize reincarnation or the revenant. Another startling phenomenon related to resurrection views is the rising prevalence of people encountering the risen Jesus in dreams and trances inside other religions. It is a lifelike, not ghostly, figure that they claim appears to them. Quite a number of stories are emerging from Islamic contexts where individuals or even large groups claim to have seen the risen Jesus (and these encounters result in conversions). We are not privy to the firsthand data for these conversion stories of Muslims but we do have direct knowledge of other accounts.

Jesus Appears to Buddhist Monk

The first story concerns one of our graduates involved in an incarnational ministry among Buddhist monks in southeast Asia.[70] He spent some years building relationships and dialoguing with monks on their own turf. A major breakthrough occurred recently when one of the monks came to him and said he had a dream in which he encountered the risen Christ. He just knew it was Jesus and knelt down and worshiped him. Just before Jesus could speak to him the dream finished. So the monk went to our friend and asked him, "What was Jesus going to say to me?" He had the opportunity of sharing the full gospel with this man with whom he had been sharing his life, and his conversion has led to other monks becoming followers of the way of Jesus. They are continuing to live in their monastic world and seeking to connect others with Christ.

Astral Traveler

A few years ago in the city of Adelaide Ross was presenting a seminar on New Age and the local mayor had invited church leaders to a special forum on the topic. All the ministers attended, apart from one Anglican minister who brusquely advised the mayor that he did not need to be there because New Age was not part of his congregation's world. After the seminar, one of the ministers shared that only a few years ago he had been a compulsive astral traveler (where one's spirit travels in a spiritual realm while the person is in a trance or other altered state of consciousness). Astral travel had taken such control of him and had taken him to so many dark spaces that he decided to end his life. He had a shotgun by his side, and his intention was to use the gun during his next astral travel. As he was traveling he came upon a bright light and heard a voice that he recognized from the age of eight, a voice that had brought him comfort in a time of illness. The voice said, "I am the Holy Spirit, you have come upon the risen Christ, you cannot go any further. Go back into your body and read John's Gospel." He did and he said he was born again. He went to a number of churches to find guidance, and they basically sniggered at his story. So he realized he could tell no one his story until now. He went to theological college. He laughed and said, "I am the associate minister of the Anglican priest who declined to attend this forum."

Yogic Devotee/New Age Guru

An extraordinary story concerns Michael Graham, who spent twenty-eight years as a serious adept of Siddha Yoga as well as in the human potential movement within New Age. Michael reached a point in his spiritual journey where he was determined to distill all of the insights he gathered from his studies and experiences. He went into personal isolation for a fortnight to meditate and make the final spiritual breakthrough. One morning as he sat on a sofa he had an encounter with the risen Christ who appeared to him in his chest cavity. Michael knew in an instant that it was Jesus. He felt an overwhelming sense of relief and of an inexpressible love and welcome. He sensed that Jesus was speaking to him to surrender his whole life and telling him that all would be well.[71]

Lessons about Sadhu Sundar Singh

In the remarkable stories recounted above, each person claims to have met the resurrected Christ in either a dream or some other altered state of consciousness. As a result of these encounters each one has been transformed. However, Christians seem to have divided opinions concerning these stories. Some are highly skeptical and assume that such phenomena cannot really happen, while others accept at face value any story told. When one hears these remarkable accounts it is a good idea to seek a balanced understanding. Each story deserves to be heard; yet, at the same time, there is also a need for careful discernment about them. A middle way needs to be found between skepticism and naïveté.

Evangelicals love the story of Sadhu Sundar Singh (1889–1929?), whose date of death is an unsolved mystery.[72] He was born in a Sikh-Hindu family and after having a vision of Christ converted to Christianity as a young teenager. The risen Christ showed him the scars of his crucifixion and told him, "I gave my life on the cross, so that you and the world might win salvation."[73] There are several slightly contradictory versions of his visionary encounter with the risen Christ, but there is no denying he had a genuine faith.[74]

Visionary experiences were central to Sundar Singh's spiritual life as a Christian. He did not just encounter Christ. Evangelical biographies never mention it, but he had several encounters with the spirit of Emanuel Swedenborg (1688–1772) as well. In the final thirty years of his life Swedenborg became renowned as a clairvoyant and wrote prolifically about his conversations with the spirits of the dead. His influence has been considerable among people who are attracted to the Western magical mystery religions, New Age channeling, and spiritualist mediums, but he also may have influenced Joseph Smith, the founder of Mormonism.[75]

From 1920 until his death Sundar Singh read several books by Swedenborg and corresponded with Swedenborgian followers in India, America, and Europe. He indicated in various letters that "I have seen the venerable Swedenborg in my visions several times."[76] Again he related: "I often speak with him in my visions. He occupies a high place in the spiritual world . . . having read his books and having come in contact with him in the spiritual world, I can thoroughly recommend him as a great seer."[77]

John Wesley (1703–1791), who exchanged letters with Swedenborg, regarded his teachings as heretical, and most evangelicals agree.[78] We need to exercise discernment regarding Sundar Singh's visionary encounters with Swedenborg and his endorsement of his books. One lesson is that not all visionary experiences are spiritually edifying. When people claim to have encountered the risen Christ we should not be automatically dismissive but neither should we naïvely take at face value all visionary stories.

Conclusion

This chapter's survey on beliefs about life after death in other religions makes clear that the *idea* of resurrection is found in several religions. Many understandings of the afterlife in alternative spiritualities do not, however, offer a holistic destiny for humans. The resurrection of Christ is what points to our holistic future resurrection. Today's challenge is bearing witness about Jesus's resurrection to our neighbors and friends in other religions.

Spiritual Audit

1. Does your church group shun vampire stories on the grounds that they are demonic?

2. Does your church group actively dialogue about the resurrection with Jehovah's Witnesses, Mormons, and Muslims?

3. Does your understanding of the afterlife include or reject reincarnation?

8

Understandings of Selfhood and the Resurrection

> The doctrine of the bodily resurrection points us to a way of conceiving our whole selves, body and soul, as ordered toward God. It points to the need to understand the signs of our created difference not as unimportant physical superfluities but as central to our theological anthropology and ethics, as inseparable from a politics that hopes to embody peace in any meaningful way.
>
> Beth Felker Jones[1]

People like exploring different roles that take them beyond the predictable routines of their work. Work routines can stultify the imagination and make people feel like they are operating on autopilot, shuffling papers from in-tray to out-tray. Not surprisingly the routines of life often make people feel that they must "escape." The "caged in" feeling can lead to moments of self-absorption where office time "stands still" and attention is diverted to checking personal emails, blogging, and updating Twitter. Some people seem to use their Blackberry or "text" on their cell phone like a digital substitute for rosary beads!

No wonder then that many people want to become another kind of "self." We meet people who freely swap modes of self in spiritual and nonspiritual ways. The urge to explore forms of selfhood is very much about filling needs. It stems partly from the experience of personal isolation in large urban centers and the transient mobile nature of settling in neighborhoods for short periods of time. Forms of selfhood are not identical with personality types. Thomas Streeter explains that forms of self comprise "discursive patterns" that are "embedded in institutions and historical processes that become available to individuals as ways of making sense of who they are in given contexts."[2]

We can better understand each other if we consider what forms of selfhood people are exploring. In this chapter we will look at experiments in selfhood that appeal to non-Christians and connect them to the new sense of self that is found in the resurrection. The church should be concerned with articulating a theology of resurrection that palpably manifests changes to selfhood, our identity, and our personalities.

Rigidity and Openness

How would you feel if you were in a public arena talking to some non-Christians about Jesus only to have a complete stranger interrupt you by saying "this is inappropriate evangelism"? We know what that is like! Christian "pests" routinely intruded on our Jesus-centered conversations at Mind-Body-Spirit festivals. These "pests" never came to bear witness to Christ but seemed to be there just to reconfirm their prejudices about the weirdness of alternative spiritualities. It never dawned on them how inappropriate it is to argue about evangelistic techniques within earshot of people who are being invited to follow Christ. None of them ever said, "What you are doing bothers me. Could we discuss this somewhere private?" Our uncanny impression is that these "pests" share a similar personality trait of rigidity.

At one festival our booth was packed to the rafters and two young guys from Kentucky approached us. They heard us proclaiming good news about the risen Jesus but they told us that our message was incomplete. These guys said that we were failing to obey what is found in Mark's Gospel: "these signs will accompany those who believe . . . they will pick up snakes in their hands" (Mark 16:17–18). They seriously wanted us to handle serpents in our booth to provide the accompanying signs to the gospel! As you might have guessed these guys were members of a fringe snake-handling Pentecostal church.[3] They were confident that this biblical verse would "sink in" and our testimony would be visibly true by taking up serpents. Once again, we noticed some common personality traits including dogmatism and rigidity.

Some of our hunches about churchgoers have been validated by Leslie Francis's research, which we discussed in chapter 3. However, we have discovered that there are wider issues than just personality types. People who are sampling alternative spiritualities tend to have less dogmatic attitudes about the smorgasbord of tools and techniques that they were prepared to "taste and see." Aspirants seem to share similar traits of intuition and creativity, including many who write with their left hand! They are sampling new forms of selfhood framed by a holistic spirituality.

Boundless Selves and Holistic Empowerment

In chapter 5 we looked at different ideas about the afterlife, and in the present chapter we are looking at different views about selfhood. We want to encourage Christians to cultivate reflective thinking about how the resurrection addresses selfhood, and how we might relate the resurrection to the ways in which people now explore selfhood.

Some scholars have noticed that people are sampling different kinds of self. A few years ago, the theologian-sociologist Linda Woodhead got the ball rolling by describing four strands of generalized forms of self. She saw two strands being very evident in church contexts, while the other strands she described help us to understand those who are exploring holistic spirituality.[4]

- Authoritative strand: the Bestowed Self
- Liberal humanistic strand: the Rational Self
- Expressive strand: the Boundless Self
- Utilitarian strand: the Effective Self

Bestowed Self

In traditional religions, including Christianity, we discover who we really are from God and/or a holy text.[5] The bestowed self belongs to the authoritative strand because a divinely revealed text or an important social institution tells us who we are. In the Bible we discover that our true self is bestowed redemptively through Christ. We were originally created in God's image and likeness (*imago Dei*) but have fallen through sin. God's bestowal of new personhood (a renovated *imago Dei*) comes upon us through Christ's resurrection and by the Holy Spirit's regenerative work. It is symbolized in rites like baptism (signifying we are a new creature) and is anchored in the doctrines of sin, redemption, and resurrection. The effects of Christ's resurrection are to be manifested in our thoughts, attitudes, and ethical behavior, and the bestowed self finds completion in the general resurrection.

The Bible shows us the horizons for the growth and destiny of the bestowed self; however it does not equate the bestowed self with a single personality type. We are created with diverse personalities, but we are corporately united in Christ and released to serve and to creatively express ourselves. While the bestowed self provides the primary framework for our spiritual development, we are not prohibited from expressing ourselves in other modes of selfhood. When exploring other forms of self we must constantly refer back to Jesus and the Bible for guidance and inspiration, as well as to the collective wisdom of the church.

Woodhead mentions that there is also a secular form of bestowed self that emerges in nonreligious communitarianism. This is where one's identity is received in a social institution like the family or from a cultural authority that acts as a substitute for God.[6]

Rational Self

Those who see the epitome of humanity tied up in the cognitive capacities of the mind esteem the rational self. In this model freedom of thought is highly prized. The rational self is autonomous and primarily expressed sociologically in the strand that Woodhead calls liberal humanistic.[7] The rational self acknowledges that there are some limits to human capacities and some boundaries to personality. In some forms of liberal theology the rational self is emphasized as constituting the *imago Dei*. In secular-humanist contexts Woodhead notes that the human being is defined by having rationality. As regards the resurrection, the rational self will tend to consider it as symbolic or hold to a mythological and reductionist view of the miraculous.[8]

Although Woodhead offers various illustrations one clear case that she does not refer to is the rationalist mind-control theory about conversions to new religious movements. Many advocates of the mind-control theory claim that people are not converted of their own volition but rather have been subjected to subtle forms of control of information and of emotions. In what must be regarded as a reductionist attitude, it is assumed that a rational person is meant to be autonomous and free and so no one would willingly convert to a new religion or cult![9]

Boundless Self

The boundless self refers to those who tend to be very intuitive and inclined to sampling from a mosaic of spiritual possibilities. The boundless self belongs to the "expressive" strand of Woodhead's paradigm. She says that the concept of the boundless self has its roots in the Romantic movement that rejected the hard-nosed rationalism of the Enlightenment in favor of exalting feelings and intuition. The boundless self does not see rationality as the hallmark of humanity, nor does it accept the notion of a bestowed self from an external authority. It refuses to distinguish between the self, God, nature, and other human persons because ultimately we are all of the same essence and substance. Most individuals who identify as the boundless self are unlikely to have any idea that what they are seeking by way of personal fulfillment is ultimately available through the holistic empowerment that Christ's resurrection brings.

Woodhead notes that the boundless self is expressed in "self-referential notions of authenticity" where the individual is basically good, is immersed in the divine, creates its own meaning, and is the ultimate source of values and morality.[10] People who identify with the boundless self gravitate to self-help literature and eclectic forms of self-spirituality. Paul Heelas sees New

Age spirituality as the epitome of this because it celebrates the divinity of self.[11] Self-spirituality also has affinities with the shamanic experiences of neo-pagan and Wiccan pathways. The boundless self is characterized by being experiential—hands-on in sampling and experiencing spirituality. Prepackaged religious messages that begin by asserting "this is what you must believe" are unappealing.[12] Those who identify themselves as "Cultural Creatives" generally have affinity with self-spirituality.[13]

At an anecdotal level we have found that many (but not all) individuals who work in Information Technology tend to embrace the boundless self and explore non-Christian holistic spiritualities. Theodor Nelson, an influential figure in the rise of computer culture, played a role in romantically idealizing notions of self-transformation. Nelson saw himself like the romantic hero Lord Byron leading a personal revolution where autonomous individuals would be positively changed by computer technology. His ideas about creating computer networks were woven around the global vision and spiritualities expressed in the 1970s counterculture.[14] We should keep in mind that countercultural beliefs that inspired Nelson comprise some of the spiritual DNA for today's holistic spiritualities.

Any non-Christian who embraces the boundless self will feel uncomfortable in both conservative and liberal churches because their messages about the resurrection are usually cognitive and lack practical application to a holistic way of life. The boundless self needs to discover first of all how the resurrection makes a difference here and now. Woodhead remarks that a modified form of the boundless self can be detected in the "deeply experiential focus" of Charismatic and Pentecostal churches;[15] yet in their authoritarian leadership and administrative sides these churches reflect the bestowed self.

Effective Self

A younger colleague found his life falling apart in family relationships and at work. A friend of his suggested that he sign up for a life-changing seminar called the Forum. He attended a weekend intensive program and walked out a changed man. He got the message to take control of his life and to quit making excuses for failure. His relationships bounced back and he was on track with work priorities. It all began with controlling his mind to control his destiny.

This story provides an example of the fourth kind of selfhood, known as the effective self. People in this model are chiefly concerned with achieving maximum individual satisfaction in this life, and often have a minimal concern with spiritual matters. This model of self is in Woodhead's fourth strand, dubbed "utilitarian." Woodhead does note that the self-help human potential writer Anthony Robbins tends to epitomize the ideals of the effective self. His books appeal among those who fit into this latter group.[16] To the effective self, human potential is basically limitless as one's mind has the power to rescript one's life from victimization over to growth and success.[17] The pragmatic priorities of life will disincline the effective self from listening to a resurrection-based message that addresses the bestowed self and rational self. To such a person the blunt point is: What use is it speculating about a remote event in history that has nothing to do with life in the here and now and is just about life beyond death?

In this section we have shown that each of the four kinds of self has different sets of questions about the resurrection. For the bestowed self the crucial question is, what is your authority for accepting the resurrection? For the rational self the crucial question is how to reinterpret it to suit a mind-set that is skeptical about miracles. For the boundless self the crucial point is discovering that the resurrection is truly holistic. For the effective self there is a pragmatic emphasis: What difference does the resurrection make in my life? Throughout this book we have discussed themes about the resurrection that clearly relate to the bestowed, rational, and effective selves. The church has concentrated a lot of energy in generally catering to the bestowed and rational selves, and to a lesser extent effective selves. Unfortunately, not many recent works in resurrection theology interact with the boundless self. In the remainder of this chapter we are going to concentrate on the boundless self and to also examine its "cousin"—the expressive self.

Expressive (Feminine) Self and Holistic Spiritualities

Linda Woodhead has collaborated with Eeva Sointu in a study that examines the relationship between holistic forms of spirituality, gender, and another kind of self known as the "expressive self."[18] The expressive self has affinities with the boundless self but they are not identical.

In two different surveys about women's spirituality Sointu and Woodhead analyze their data using Charles Taylor's model of the "expressive self."[19] According to Taylor, much of contemporary Western social life—including the religious sphere—is infused with an "ethic of authenticity" and a "principle of originality."[20] These two items blend for individuals who want to be true to themselves by being true to their own originality. Only the individual can discover what is authentic and original to their life. This authenticity is accessed within by staying in touch with one's inner wisdom, which resides in the "soul" or "core self." So, expressive individuals want to choose a path that is experientially meaningful, results in personal growth, and is socially relational but not handed to them via religious tradition. Taylor characterizes this attitude as "soft relativism" concerning "practices that link spirituality and therapy."[21] This attitude is trendsetting in both social practices and emerging concepts of selfhood.

All this points to a big overlap between the "expressive self" and "boundless self," although Sointu and Woodhead's conclusions imply that there are some subtle yet important differences. Before we come to the nuanced differences we must briefly sketch their findings. Sointu and Woodhead's studies map the social terrain where the expressive self looks at life as being interconnected. One major connection is in complementary healing modalities (acupuncture, aromatherapy, reflexology, therapeutic touch, etc.). Other areas include these industries: beauty, hotel and leisure, marketing, advertising, retail, and publishing. Holistic concepts of self are also present in public and private education, health care, and the workplace.[22]

Although both women and men explore these paths, Sointu and Woodhead indicate that many females are attracted to it. They have noted how holistic spiritualities specifically relate to changing roles for women that are not often mirrored in churches.

Three Distinguishing Factors

There are three broad factors that characterize the expressive feminine self in its search for a fulfilling holistic spirituality:

- Bodily Emotional Practice
- Self-Worth and Holistic Well-Being
- Intimate Relationships

BODILY EMOTIONAL PRACTICE

Sointu and Woodhead note that the holistic spiritualities embraced by their interviewees all begin with physical embodiment. In complementary therapies the body provides an entry point into the individual's emotions and spiritual state. "The body offers a means of working on a wide range of emotional issues emerging from the authentic and inherently benign inner core of the person . . . the goal of holistic practices is 'to find your own truth' by 'feeling what's right for *you*.' "[23] This aspect of a holistic embodied self could be reframed through the prism of resurrection. A future task for theological reflection is to cross-pollinate holistic embodied practices with Beth Felker Jones's work on bodily resurrection and feminist politics.[24]

SELF-WORTH AND HOLISTIC WELL-BEING

As the body, mind, and spirit are interconnected the goals focus on "health, wholeness and self-worth."[25] This involves a strong awareness of self-determination and freedom that revolves around self-acceptance and creativity. So self-worth and well-being are strongly emphasized in the expressive feminine self. In contrast, Christians understand through the creation and resurrection that God shows us what authentic self-worth comprises.

INTIMATE RELATIONSHIPS

The third factor is that these kinds of holistic spiritualities have a strong sense of fulfillment in personal relationships. The top-rated TV show *The View* is a good example. It presents a panel of women, chosen for their differences in worldview, who nonetheless share relationally with each other. The relational element among women is a strong defining component in holistic spiritualities. This emphasis on the relational element differentiates holistic spiritualities from what characterized some cultural forerunners to the New Age like the Theosophical Society and Romantic movement where the boundless self merges with the universe and God. Instead, for the expressive self holistic "spirituality is more accurately described as relational, rather than monistic, pantheistic, or idealist."[26] For the expressive self daily life consists of a web of relationships and there is no major interest in the self being merged into one divine consciousness. The self is physically embodied and socially oriented for intimate relationships. There is freedom and autonomy but no sense of being divorced from quality relationships. This spirituality does not leave it to the individual to just "do your own thing" but also is cautious of subordinating autonomy to a social group:

> Thus projects of selfhood and self-worth are carried out in the context of one-to-one consultations or small groups that lay particular emphasis on the authenticity and empowerment of all.[27]

The relational emphasis for the expressive self could easily lend itself to a resurrection-based understanding of self, which we saw in chapter 2 embraces the formation of community. The challenge for Christians is figuring out how to form networks of personal relationships in a gathered community so that the expressive self belongs theologically.

New Vistas of Femininity

Holistic spiritualities celebrate being relational and caring and involve much emotional self-disclosure. While there is a strong emphasis on self-fulfillment, expressive selfhood is not necessarily narcissistic in its moral tone. It is not "lacking in moral horizons" but rather involves a practical commitment to the "care for all the forms of life that the self encounters" by affirming the unique worth of everyone.[28]

Traditional feminine modes of being relational are being reframed in ways that women find appealing. Relational care and care for self are both emphasized. Self-fulfillment is enhanced through spiritual practices that emphasize being interconnected in relationships. As Sointu and Woodhead sum up, holistic spiritualities appeal to the feminine expressive self because they "offer a practical setting for the construction and performance of forms of selfhood traditionally demarcated from respectable femininity—such as self-fulfillment, bodily pleasure, inner authenticity, freedom and self-expression."[29] We want to reiterate that the twelve zones of the resurrection discussed in chapter 2 show there is a practical spirituality of the resurrection. What Christians must now do is to relate the zones to the quest of expressive selves.

Other Kinds of Selves

Besides the five different kinds of selfhood we sketched above, there are several other models on the social and spiritual horizons. In the next section we will look specifically at various other examples about the boundless and expressive selves. Before we do that it is worth being reminded that in our postmodern context the topic of selfhood has many more facets to it. While we lack the space for any detailed discussion we want to briefly refer to other kinds of selves that should not be overlooked.

Terry Muck observes the dilemma facing the self in our post-Christian, fragmented, complex Western culture[30] and reminds us that in biblical times there was the corporate understanding of self as a collective people or tribe or nation that responded to God. The corporate self in Israel involved family, tribe, and nation and was even transgenerational.[31] Ancient societies were shaped by cultural hierarchies, and these social structures mirrored what was understood to be the hierarchy found in the heavenly realm.

Since the Renaissance a strongly formed individual self has emerged, and this shift represents a major break with the classical biblical world and ancient cultural hierarchies. Today we seem incapable of relating to a corporate responding self and our societies have discarded ancient hierarchical structures. The images of a divine hierarchy and of a corporate responding self belong to a world long gone.[32] We have also lost any corporate understanding of the resurrection of the dead. If we take up the twelve zones of resurrection from chapter 2, perhaps we can regain a corporate understanding of selfhood.

Muck points out that in the modern era there emerged in Western culture the idea of an autonomous transcendental self. Unlike the responding or bestowed self who is chosen for a pattern of living by God, the transcendental self stands apart from God. It is grounded in the rationality and self-sufficiency of the individual. This mind-set understands God either as a remote being (as in seventeenth-century deism) or as nonexistent (as in secular rationalist ideology). Two different and broad kinds of transcendental self have developed: one grounded in the certainties of rationality, and the other grounded in the certainties of evidence. The emphases on rationality and evidence certainly characterize secular attitudes and, in a modified form, have shaped the church in modern times, especially where logical and rational doctrine have become the sole priority.

While secular and theistic notions of the transcendental or rational self still endure today, Muck indicates that they are gradually being undermined. The illusionary "No Self" that has emerged in secular postmodernist thought, and through the diffusion of Buddhist thought, has debunked the accepted framework for the transcendental self. The "No Self" outlook, notes Muck, does not offer much in a positive way but merely succeeds in stripping away the foundations for the various kinds of modern-day selfhood.

Other Kinds of Boundless and Expressive Selves

Earlier we outlined the broad contours of the boundless and expressive selves. We feel that for purposes of enabling Christians to undertake effective missions, some nuanced examples of the boundless and expressive selves should be illustrated. So, in the remainder of this chapter we will explore a few examples of subcultural networks where different understandings of the boundless spiritual self and expressive self are found.

Eclectic Self

The eclectic self represents a particular version of the boundless self, and is best seen in a particular youth subculture. Since the 1960s anime—the Japanese form of animation—has found a niche among youth worldwide. While it "has gained a great deal of popular status within the US Culture" its "cross-cultural popularity is not limited to North America but it has been widespread on a global level, inside and outside of Europe and Asia."[33] It began with animating Japanese comic books in television shows like *Manga Calendar* but is best known worldwide through trading card and video games like Pokémon and Digimon.[34]

Anime is "filled with images and symbols that are related to religious motifs, spirituality, the supernatural, and mythology."[35] The paranormal characters in anime stories are drawn from many religious and mythological traditions. Although anime originates from Japan it has a repertoire of ideas borrowed from the world's religions. Anime also draws on the world's mythology for purposes of plot or character development and uses symbols from the Western magical tradition like pentagrams.

Jin Kyu Park's study of young North American anime fans has uncovered some surprising countercultural attitudes. As we noted in chapter 4 some anime fans do not see the concept of good versus evil in religious terms. Park's study indicates that the fans acknowledge the significance of spirituality in their lives but they reject organized religion. Park accounts for this attitude by noting that among many North American youth "religion is often equated with morality" in the public square.[36] These young Americans create their own spiritual kits by looking to the eclectic integrative style of the Japanese. They do not embrace Shinto or Buddhist ways, and they distance themselves from organized traditional religion. These youth resemble Woodhead's boundless self but they are not necessarily following their parents' spiritual preferences.

Park also points out that anime fans tend to be cynical about US pop culture. "The participants' feelings towards US pop culture in general, the entertainment media in particular, were articulated in languages such as 'boring,' 'recycled,' 'simple,' 'easy,' 'always the same thing,' 'brainless stuff,' and 'too commercialized.' "[37] For these fans anime offered a more enriching and imaginative alternative to mainstream pop culture.

Park observes that "anime's distinctive quality in its description of religious and spiritual realms—integrating symbols, themes, doctrines, and mythologies from various religious traditions—is a cultural manifestation of the Japanese integrative spirituality, which would provide a valuable explanation why some American young people, who are characterized as spiritual seekers, are fascinated by the cultural artefacts."[38] Most users do not see anime as a religion or a religious practice, but it joins together youth who are tired of America's mainstream religious and pop culture. They prefer the eclectic yet integrative style of the Japanese approach to spirituality, which serves as a model for creating and expressing their own spiritual path.

Some Christians are fearful about anime and react defensively to its popularity.[39] A shallow exegesis of Scripture and a poor grasp of God's missional work in the creation can easily produce an us-versus-them mentality and degenerate into a distorted gnostic view of both culture and of human personality.[40] Were the church to examine itself, however, it would find that its theology and praxis lack the integrative power of the resurrection. Such an inadequate understanding of the resurrection can prompt Christians to typecast Pokémon (or the Harry Potter novels) as a monstrous threat to social stability.[41] The social consequences of this are disastrous because it misrepresents the Christian life to non-Christians.

A holistic Christian response to anime must involve careful theological reflection. Here are some questions that call for positive pastoral, apologetic, missional, and ethical action: Does the biblical understanding of the bestowed self necessarily prohibit us from enjoying the full range of human creativity in culture? How does an understanding of the resurrection liberate us to respond with great gusto to those who enjoy anime? What theology should the church draw on to develop an understanding of the blessings of play and imagination? How does anime reflect the use/misuse of God's gift of creativity to humans? Is our negative understanding of anime consistent with a deep, balanced reading of Scripture? Are we "cursing" an aspect of culture that ought to be "blessed"? Are we verging on an unbiblical, simplistic dualism that distorts our Christian worldview by dividing the creation up into good versus bad? How are we relating to people attracted to anime? Are we conveying to them the impression that a particular sort of personality type is synonymous with biblical selfhood?

Hyper-Real Self

Lots of spiritual groups use the Internet to promote their beliefs.[42] Some neo-pagan believers rely almost exclusively on using websites.[43] Each type of self—bestowed, rational, boundless, effective, and expressive—uses the Internet for religious purposes. Earlier we mentioned that the boundless self originated in the Romantic movement. We will see below how attitudes about using computer gadgets are influenced by people whose ideas reflect both the Romantic movement and alternative spiritualities. Another emerging form of the boundless and expressive spiritual selves is what the sociologist Adam Possamai refers to as "hyper-real" identity.[44] By hyper-real Possamai is referring to the Internet. A hyper-real identity may be created by using the Internet to simulate various pop cultural ideas about self-transformation.

HUMAN POTENTIAL

Possamai maintains that the hyper-real identity mirrors the goals of the human potential movement that arose in the 1970s. The spirit of the human potential movement has been popularized in some streams of New Age spirituality, and by TV guests on *Oprah*.[45] One of its fundamental assumptions is that humans possess latent abilities or powers that can be tapped. A similar idea of latent abilities exists in superhero comic books. Several comic-strip superheroes appeared decades before the human potential movement emerged in the 1970s (e.g., *Superman*, *Wonder Woman*, *Batman*, *Spiderman*, and the *Fantastic Four*).[46] According to Possamai the comic-book superheroes and the human potential movement have coexisted as important cultural influences that have jointly shaped current hyper-real attitudes about humans possessing latent powers.

Most superheroes do not have their powers bestowed on them by a god. Spiderman and the Fantastic Four experience self-transformation due to accidents. Batman undergoes long arduous training and inner reflection as he learns to tap into his full potential.[47] The source of Superman's powers comes from living under the rays of our yellow sun.[48] Wonder Woman is slightly different in that the storyline about the source of her powers has changed over the years. Originally her powers were bestowed by the Goddess Aphrodite, and as an Amazonian tribes-woman she had the attributes of both Greek and Roman goddesses. Later she renounced her Amazonian powers so that she could remain permanently in our world. She then transformed herself and regained her powers by studying the martial arts and the Chinese divinatory text *I Ching*.[49]

The idea that we can develop latent powers appeals to people who tend to believe in paranormal and mystical phenomena. J. E. Kennedy surveyed the profiles of people who believe in the paranormal and found that they are very intuitive, immerse themselves in fantasies, and are prone to self-absorption.[50] The iconic spiritual figure of the paranormal and occult is the Magus, who is a master of divination and of hidden knowledge about ultimate reality.[51] While Christians need to discern the pitfalls of replacing God with paranormal power, the challenge remains to positively articulate and embody a holistic understanding of selfhood rooted in the resurrected Christ.

JEDIISM AND MATRIXISM

Through the Internet new forms of religiosity and myth-making are emerging that center on acquiring latent abilities for self-transformation. According to Possamai the hyper-real self involves the construction of a new spiritual self. It is inspired by diverse sources such as fantasy literature, science-fiction, stories of personal and global reenchantment, human potential ideas, and the examples of contemporary comic book superhero characters. What is remarkably different is that the hyper-real self is expressed primarily through the Internet.

Some hyper-real religious identities are expressed in new myths inspired by science-fiction motion pictures such as *Star Wars* and *The Matrix*. Jediism, which was created in 2001 and propagated through the Internet, appears to involve diverse social actors. Some with their tongue-in-cheek mischievously claimed it as their religion when various national census surveys were taken. It clearly appealed to people who find the idea of inventing a religion quite hilarious. In many ways this electronic form of satire mirrors what has occurred in earlier decades through underground forms of publishing, especially the satirical lampooning of "sacred cows" that college and university students find amusing. Before Jediism other wise-cracking artists parodied established religions by the creation of Discordianism, the Church of the Sub-Genius, and the Church of the Flying Spaghetti Monster.[52]

For some participants, however, this invented religion is not a joke or hoax. Jediism offers them the opportunity to ignore organized religion and to reimagine themselves as Jedi Knights who can draw on untapped latent abilities to achieve self-transformation. Possamai points out, "Jediism is not a fan community discussing issues from the *Star Wars* movies, but is a global movement expressing itself via the Internet."[53] In a similar vein, Matrixism emerged in 2004 as a hyper-real religion. Its advocates also look for self-transformation and draw inspiration from some aspects of the Bahá'i faith, from various metaphysical beliefs, and from key ideas in the film *The Matrix*.[54] Jediism and Matrixism are only two examples of a broader cultural phenomenon concerning the hyper-real self.

Romanticizing Geeks

Computer technology is sometimes regarded as if it will deliver personal and global transformation. Thomas Streeter indicates that the current vision surrounding computers and their social usage is "bound up with competing constructions of self, motivation and social relations."[55] Programmers have come to computer culture with preexisting ideas about selfhood, and those ideas have in turn shaped how the technology has been designed and used. Although the prehistory of computers is rooted in the inventions of some notable Christian apologists, Streeter argues that many computer programmers reflect romantic forms of selfhood.[56] We have already seen how romantic notions of selfhood shape the boundless self and aspects of alternative spiritualities. According to Streeter, computer culture has been shaped by "a naïve abstract individualism" and "a view of selves as naturally and preferentially isolated and autonomous."[57] He observes:

> Playing with a computer in fact has come to *feel* like an escape into another, more autonomous world, into a kind of freedom. But it is probably not coincidental that this feeling happens to mostly white, mostly male, mostly educated and middle- and upper-middle class people in the USA.[58]

Earlier we mentioned Theodor Nelson as a pivotal figure because he coined the word *hypertext* and was an early advocate of graphic-based personal computers. Nelson is "a self-described radical" who seems to have begun his career shaped by romantic individualist forms of selfhood. Streeter points to an important link between the famous countercultural annual publication *Whole Earth Catalog* (1968–1972) and Nelson's major book on computers:

> His magnum opus, the 1974 self-published *Computer Lib*, presciently promoted all these ideas by essentially transposing the style, format, and counter-cultural iconoclasm of the *Whole Earth Catalog* into the world of computers. It is apparently not unusual to encounter computer professionals who say that "*Computer Lib* changed my life."[59]

Some technicians who have shaped the Internet hold to the romantic view of self. Many consumers of computer culture take a further step by creating a hyper-real boundless self. Both kinds of selves often glamorize Web 2.0—the emergence of blogging, YouTube, social network sites—as heralding a new inclusive global era. The world is no longer controlled by elite "experts" but is open, democratic, and inclusive because everybody can contribute to "open-source projects" (like Wikipedia). However, naïveté abounds when everyone is regarded as a potential expert.

Similar claims are echoed in some blogging conversations about contextual ecclesiology. An open-source approach to theology and mission has been touted as a transformative tool.[60] Yet this sort of inclusive participation has led to some muddy thinking, and old Christological heresies have been unnecessarily rehashed. The pot has also been chaotically stirred by Mormon, Unitarian, neo-gnostic, and neo-pagan participants in these forums looking for theological validation while simultaneously denying Jesus's kingdom message.

Web guru Andrew Keen is disturbed by a pervasive attitude in computer culture that seems to devalue the skills and knowledge of experts. Keen is alarmed by the erosion of professional standards concerning truth and that these standards are being replaced by self-proclaimed experts who blog and self-broadcast on YouTube. His worries extend to open-source projects like Wikipedia:

> For the real consequence of the Web 2.0 revolution is less culture, less reliable news, and a chaos of useless information. One chilling reality in this brave new digital epoch is the blurring, obfuscation, and even disappearance of truth.[61]

A holistic understanding of the resurrection reminds us that human sinfulness is a constant factor in history. It is the risen Christ—not computers—who can transform us from the curse of sin. Some bloggers who represent the "boundless self" need a reality check: it is a naïve, romanticized idea to think that "everyone" is globally linked. The world's poor are excluded since they cannot pay for Internet services and do not own laptops. Inside North Korea the Internet barely exists.[62] The Internet social networking site Facebook did assist in agitating for the removal of political leaders in Tunisia and Egypt. However, the romantic idea that Facebook revolutions will inevitably transform the world is contradicted by the events in Libya in 2011 when Gaddafi's government refused to budge and civil war erupted. Even if six billion people had computer access this would not produce a cyber-utopia.

Reflections about the Hyper-Real

In Christian thought about the hyper-real, it is easy to correlate the hyper-real self's impulses for latent power with the fallen state of humanity. The autonomous individual set apart from God longs for power in order to be spiritually self-sufficient. This can develop into serious forms of self-deception in which the individual worships anything other than God. The quest for latent power may be interpreted and understood through the Johannine formula of the world, the flesh, and the devil, or money, sex, and power.

However, we need much deeper theological reflection. God did create human beings with the capacity to exercise their imagination. The Internet provides an outlet for creativity that was previously catered to by the printing press. People are reimagining themselves in those spaces of living not dominated by the demands of domestic and corporate life. The systems and processes of daily living, such as the routines imposed by one's employment, may stultify the imagination; so it is understandable that people need to find other outlets to give expression to certain aspects of their humanity. A resurrection-based way of living can speak positively into these contexts because creativity and the imagination are God-blessed capacities.

The chaotic heart-cry for acquiring latent power makes the hyper-real self susceptible not just to idolatry and narcissism. It also influences how people try to reimagine themselves by yearning for a better way of being. This can surely be cultivated theologically as a sign of our unconscious longings for the *imago Dei* to be healed. The hope for latent power also echoes humanity's paradoxical and collective self-doubts about attaining perfection unaided. Christian proclamation of the cross indicates a recognition of the need for spiritual renewal; however, the holistic resurrection message is often lost. It is because of Christ's resurrection that we are enabled by the Spirit of Christ to have the *imago Dei* restored. Christians must embody the joy and power of the risen Christ in our lives so that our dialogue with hyper-real selves is not perceived as hollow rhetoric. The hyper-real self has yet to hear what kind of exciting life comes through the risen Christ.

Virtual World Avatar

Many individuals look for a renewed sense of self in Internet-based virtual worlds. It is estimated that some 130 to 150 million people worldwide exercise their imaginations in virtual worlds like *Habbo, Gaia Online, Second Life, Warcraft, YoVille*, and many more.[63] The most popular is *Second Life*, which reputedly has had some nineteen million people register since its inception. *Second Life* was featured in an episode of *CSI: New York*.[64]

Philip Rosedale is the entrepreneur-creator of *Second Life*, which was officially launched on the Internet on June 23, 2003.[65] Rosedale, who was born in 1968, attended a Baptist school. He says, "I went to a born-again Baptist school . . . and it was just so interesting because they just . . . preached fire and brimstone, and it was crazy, and it scared the crap out of me."[66] He became disenchanted with Christianity and contemplated his reason for living: "Why am I here, and how am I different from everybody else? What am I here to do? What is my purpose here? But I don't think I thought it in a real religious sense. . . . I want to change the world somehow."[67]

Several influences compelled Rosedale's creation of *Second Life*. He had a long-held ambition to create a digital space where people could co-create a new world, an interest that was spurred on after viewing the film *The Matrix*. Another catalyst was his experiences at the famous annual countercultural festival held in the Nevada desert called Burning Man (which we will discuss below). He modeled the structures of his company and employee duties directly on the temporary form of governance that Burning Man uses.[68]

Second Life users create a three-dimensional digital self called an "avatar" and have text-based or audio conversations. The word *avatar* has been common in computer-user parlance since the 1980s and originally derives from the Sanskrit term referring to a Hindu deity stepping down or incarnating into the world. The word has reached a cultural saturation point through the motion-picture *Avatar*.

While *Second Life* has generated media commentary about online sexual relationships, a wide range of other activities can be found, including universities using the simulated world for teaching purposes.[69] *Second Life* carries with it various implied meanings: one may have a recreational second life alongside one's nondigital life; one may lead a double-life of deception by pretending to be someone else; one may hope that perhaps a new life can be found in a digital existence rather than in the external world. *Second Life* provides a creative outlet for the imagination. People with physical disabilities that are socially isolated have a digital arena for friendship and can reimagine themselves. In a time when urban living makes us feel alienated from our neighbors, virtual worlds offer introverted people a sense of community that may be otherwise absent from their lives.[70]

In virtual worlds all kinds of spiritualities are expressed: Buddhist, Jewish, Muslim, Mormon, neo-pagan, New Age, Unitarian, and Vampire. Christian congregations have also been set up in these virtual world arenas as points of contact with searchers, but how astute Christian participants are in dialoguing with people of other pathways remains questionable. Is a holistic understanding of the resurrection connected to these efforts at digital outreach? Another challenge for the church is generating dialogue with those who co-create and celebrate inside *Second Life* the annual "Burning Life" festival. "Burning Life" is an intentional digital simulation of the real-world event known as Burning Man,[71] which as we mentioned above inspired Philip Rosedale's creation of *Second Life*.

Rave and Burning Man

There are many activists who express themselves in anti-globalization rallies, road-protests, and in underground subcultural rave dance events. These arenas appeal to the boundless and expressive selves because they are outlets for visionary, artistic self-expression and provide a context in which self-transformation may be experienced. The rave dance culture owes a great debt to alternative holistic spiritualities and gives voice to yearnings for self-transformation and healing, as well as for global renewal.[72]

A parallel avenue that attracts boundless and expressive selves and that brings together activists, anarchists, artists, and alternative spirituality devotees is the annual Burning Man festival. The festival gathers for a week in the Nevada desert where a temporary community is created, experienced, and then disbanded. Participants bring their own supplies and offer their creative talents and gifts for others to enjoy. The festival celebrates the possibilities that humans can reimagine themselves and the world. Like the underground rave culture this festival also offers an outlet for those who yearn for spiritual transformation and healing and who want to see the world renewed. It is growing in patronage as some fifty thousand people from different parts of the world gather each year.[73]

Burning Man offers non-Christians a temporary sense of community and belonging in the framework of festivity.[74] It caters to people's intuitive and creative sides, which is something the church used to offer the community. For many Christians today the notion of festivity is a forgotten truth, but in church history feasts and festivals played an important part in village and town life. In the past the church had liturgies that centered on reenacting major Bible stories as well as regular festivities where the death and resurrection of Jesus was "performed" as a liturgical drama.[75]

It is exciting that some Christians have a missionary-passion to reach into the rave culture. To do so, it helps to be conversant with non-Christian holistic spiritualities and aware that many participants have intuitive personalities that are drawn to boundless and expressive modes of selfhood. Every missionary venture requires that a team has the critical capacity for reflection and the theological maturity to apply a resurrection-based form of cross-cultural mission.

A highly creative mission team has made commendable efforts to inculturate Jesus's way at rave events in Ibiza. However, cross-cultural outreach can misfire despite good intentions. Stella Lau spent time observing and interviewing the mission team and attended their Christian rave event in Ibiza. Then she interviewed non-Christians who participated and found that they had no awareness that the event had any Christian message to it at all.[76] Lau's sobering field report indicates that the message about Jesus was not even recognized by the intended audience. We wonder how that mission team might have fared had they (a) had a grip on understanding the boundless and expressive selves in the rave culture and (b) been grounded in a holistic understanding of the resurrection.

Conclusion

Woodhead's typologies of forms of self are best understood as a broad generalization concerning the religious and spiritual orientation of many people in European and North American cultural contexts. As with all generalizations, one must guard against making reductionist conclusions. Human beings are complex in their identities and personalities, and our societies encompass diverse and complex ways of living. Streeter remarks:

> Most of us find it necessary or useful to adopt roles, to think and speak of ourselves in various established ways, at various moments in our lives. We often

have to think of ourselves, for example, as alternately passionate and as administrators, one moment as caring individuals, and the next as self-interested rational actors in a marketplace and after that as competent professionals with resumes. . . . [T]here are typically several forms available to any given individual in any given context, and it is possible, and probably sometimes necessary, to move between them.[77]

Although the problem of sin cannot be downplayed, Christians need to wake up to the sociological and psychological barriers that deter people from joining churches. We suspect that in theologically conservative churches both the dominant style of proclamation and the message's content are only speaking to a particular kind of personality type that has accepted a narrow and limited understanding of the bestowed self. But we are concerned that today the bestowed self is less grounded in the resurrection and more a reflection of particular personality types that we discussed in chapter 3—particularly, the constricted yet dominant types who share similar attitudes about how gatherings should be structured, governed, and operated; what controlled, predictable worship-styles are preferable; what cognitive styles of preaching are accepted; and where the boundaries between the church and external world should be.

Christian assemblies that emphasize the rational self also attract participants who share similar attitudes about ecclesial structures, what forms of teaching and preaching are preferred, and how the external world is understood. Conservative and liberal churchgoers broadly speaking hold to two different models of understanding selfhood—the bestowed and the rational, respectively. Perhaps it is not surprising then that the two groups hold different attitudes concerning the resurrection. Arguments from actors on both sides about the resurrection reach different conclusions: historical-literal versus spiritual-symbolic. Often the debates legitimately center on questions of facts, history, mythology, logic, and cognitive approaches to textual hermeneutics. These debates about the miracle of resurrection and its accompanying theology raise valid questions.

Broadly speaking, assemblies that cater to either the bestowed self or the rational self fail to enter the wider world where the boundless self, effective self, and expressive self are found. Both forms of assembly tend to adopt positions that are self-reinforcing. The very ethos in which they organize, administer, foster relationships, devise their missions, and proclaim messages is a reflection of these differing models of self, and more bluntly of personality types. Some slight exception to this can be found in the Pentecostal churches. Pentecostals have inherited the bestowed self because of the role of scriptural authority, and this sense of the bestowed self is evident in their forms of governance and structures, yet in many experiential aspects Pentecostals have given space to modifying the boundless self within a Christian context.

As this book repeatedly argues, the church is in danger of holding to a limited, truncated, and pea-sized understanding of the resurrection. We must understand and embody in our lives and our assemblies a resurrection message that is holistic. Instead of just debating the evidence for God and the truth question, a holistic understanding will require us to explore the practical applications of the resurrection in the present—an approach that will be much more effective in our dialogue with the boundless self, expressive self, and effective self. Many seekers who start journeys of reflection begin with questions about meaning long before they will ponder the truthfulness of Jesus's resurrection.

Spiritual Audit

1. Does your group in its teaching, worship, and structure emphasize any particular kind of "self"?

2. How would your group respond to individuals who were expressing themselves as a "boundless self"?

3. In what ways does your group or gathering encourage the use of the imagination?

4. Do you ever find yourself seeking an "escape" from life by exploring a virtual world? Do you bring into the virtual world any sense of empowerment or creativity based on the resurrected Christ?

5. What passages in the Gospels give you an indication that Jesus met individuals at their own level of understanding of self?

9

Myth, Resurrection, and the Human Psyche

The heart of Christianity is a myth which is also a fact. . . . We must not be ashamed of the mythical radiance resting on our theology. We must not be nervous about "parallels" and "Pagan Christs": they *ought* to be there—it would be a stumbling block if they weren't. We must not, in false spirituality, withhold our imaginative welcome. If God chooses to be mythopoeic—and is not the sky itself a myth?—shall we refuse to be *mythopathic*? For this is the marriage of heaven and earth: Perfect Myth and Perfect Fact: claiming not only our love and our obedience, but also our wonder and delight.

C. S. Lewis[1]

The story of Jesus is proverbially the greatest story ever told or performed. The drama of Jesus's arrest and execution grips us as he interacts with a cast of sly and perfidious characters who betray, scheme, and dish out injustice. We are outraged as Jesus is subjected to kangaroo court trials, humiliation, abuse, excruciating pain, and sorrow, and we lament at the agonizing climax when Jesus utters his final words, "It is finished" (John 19:30).

At the tomb we feel it is over, finished, kaput. We are inconsolable as Jesus is buried. All the excitement generated by what he said and did, the miracles, and astounding teaching about God's kingdom dissipate like air let out of a balloon. This story brimmed with hope but its ending is bleak and tragic. We call to mind the words of Ecclesiastes: "All is vanity and a chasing after wind" (Eccles. 1:14).

We might try to move beyond the despair and theologize about his death: perhaps like the blameless animals sacrificed in ancient Israel, Jesus's death signifies atonement for sin. If the story ends at the tomb then at best we might want to emulate Jesus's compassion and try to abide by his kingdom message. The somber end, though, would remain: Jesus died and we too will die. A savior's corpse permanently occupying a tomb is not likely to become a world-shaking story that transforms lives.

Unlike the biographies of other marvelous individuals, this story's sorrow gives way to a surprising, joyful, and triumphant conclusion. Jesus's resurrection is the denouement to the entire drama. The resurrection gives us the most satisfying conclusion, and without it all we are left with is a gigantic tragedy.

J. R. R. Tolkien intuitively understood the power of the story of Jesus's resurrection, as his discussion of the impact of happy events in fairy stories shows. Readers are captivated when an imperiled character is rescued or triumphs and the tensions of the plot are resolved by a wondrous event or happy ending. Tolkien called these happy events "eucatastrophes," situations so wonderful that we would want the experience repeated forever:

> The gospels contain . . . a story of a larger kind which embraces all the essence of fairy stories. . . . The birth of Christ is the eucatastrophe of man's history. The resurrection is the eucatastrophe of the story of the incarnation. This story begins and ends in joy. It has pre-eminently the "inner consistency of reality." There is no tale ever told that men would rather find was true, and none which so many skeptical men have accepted as true on its own merits. For the art of it has the supremely convincing tone of primary art, that is, of creation. To reject it leads either to sadness or to wrath.[2]

Tolkien's reflection on the power of the resurrection in Jesus's story forms the basis of our journey into myth in this chapter. We will explore the significance of myths about dying-and-rising characters and heroes, as well as how resurrection images in these stories affect the human psyche. We will analyze some theories about myth that skeptics use to undermine belief in the resurrection. And finally, we will discuss the positive connections between myths and the resurrection of Jesus and their relevance today.

A World Saturated with Stories

Storytelling saturates our digital age. The excitement among children about reading the Harry Potter stories (well before Hollywood began adapting them into films) provides a good indicator of this cultural enthusiasm. Margery Hourihan comments about the enduring importance of stories:

> Stories are important in all cultures. People have always used stories . . . to explain the behaviour of the physical universe and to describe human nature and society.

They are the most potent means by which perceptions, values and attitudes are transmitted from one generation to the next. All teachers know the power of stories as educational tools. They are vivid, enjoyable, easily understood, memorable and compelling. They appeal to people of all ages, but for children who have not yet achieved the ability to reason abstractly they provide images to think with.[3]

Myths are stories that carry symbolic meaning.[4] They assist us in reimagining ways of being: envisaging a nation's character; exploring questions of emotional growth and well-being; and shaping the way new religions emerge. Myths appear in our culture in numerous expressions: In the corporate arena motivational seminars often use myths to illustrate lessons about self-discovery and achievement. The plotlines in fantasy literature (e.g., *The Lord of the Rings*) and TV series (e.g., *Star Trek*, *Doctor Who*, *The X-Files*) are mythic. Hollywood film scripts (e.g., *Indiana Jones*, *Star Wars*, *Mad Max*) have drawn on elements of the psychoanalytic thought of Joseph Campbell and Carl Jung concerning hero myths.[5] The veteran journalist Bill Moyers noticed these trends about myth in culture and interviewed Campbell about it in the TV series *The Power of Myth*.[6]

Defining Myth

We have all probably used the word *myth* to mean different things at different times. A negative sense predominates our usage. For example, we sometimes cavalierly dismiss something as a "myth" when we mean that it is not factual. This negative nuance has a long pedigree extending back to pre-Socratic philosophers like Xenophanes (570–475 BC) who were among the earliest scathing critics of mythology. The New Testament declares that the gospel is not a fabrication based on "cleverly devised myths" (2 Pet. 1:16). Of course that negative sense of the word is not the sole meaning of *myth*.

Mythological—or mythopoeic—thought comes into its own when the outer limits of logical categories of thought are reached. So *myth* can refer to narratives that express our intuitive experiences about reality. We are being mythic when we use picturesque and symbolic expressions in stories about ultimate meaning. Our mythic understandings about existence may be expressed in religious or nonreligious contexts.

Irving Hexham and Karla Poewe provide this helpful definition:

Myth is *a story with culturally formative power*. This definition emphasizes that a myth is essentially a story—any story—that affects the way people live. Contrary to many writers, we do not believe that a myth is necessarily unhistorical. In itself a story that becomes a myth can be true or false, historical or unhistorical, fact or fiction. What is important is not the story itself but the *function* it serves in the life of an individual, a group, or a whole society.[7]

They maintain that today's new religious movements have formed global cultures that crisscross national boundaries by way of a shared view of reality. Each movement has developed its own understanding of the world through a collection of beliefs created out of various disjointed myths. Hexham and Poewe discern both personal and cosmic mythological fragments percolating in today's religious world: pseudoscientific myths, myths of fate and prophecy, healing myths, myths of decline, other civilization myths, and myths of transformation.[8]

Epic stories involving heroic characters have influenced our era to such an extent that Mark Levon Byrne asserts that "the hero has been the central mythic figure in Western culture."[9] We will explore the significance of hero myths a little later, but first let's look at what people thought about myths in earlier times.

Ancient Mind-sets

Western civilization has been influenced by both hero myths and myths of dying-and-rising gods that sprang from the Greeks and ancient Near Eastern world. Myths from Northern Europe about gods and heroes have also contributed to Western thought, though to a lesser extent.

Mythopoeic Thought

Mythopoeic thought flourished alongside reflective and logical forms of thinking in the ancient Near East. In Canaanite, Egyptian, Mesopotamian, and Persian civilizations mythopoeic thought involved imaginative ways of depicting ultimate reality. What was understood and intuited about ultimate reality was narrated in poems, songs, and stories using symbols to refer to gods and goddesses and to the relationships these deities had with each other and with the created world. Mythic narratives expressed the mystical awareness of those who perceived divine things in the world. What we today regard as inanimate objects (sky, moon, mountains) or the forces of nature (volcanoes, wind, river currents) were imaginatively perceived as being animated by divine powers. These powers or forces were described as personal and real, existing in the form of divine beings. Broadly speaking, mythopoeic thought in these ancient Near Eastern cultures was polytheistic and connected the natural world with ultimate reality.[10]

Greek Mythology

When ancient Greek culture flourished it carried forward from earlier times its native religious traditions, including myths about gods and goddesses (Zeus and his children), monsters (Cyclops, Minotaur), and heroic figures. The original Greek myths predated those pre-Socratic philosophers who questioned sacred beliefs. Unlike the corpus of ancient Near Eastern mythology, Greek myths as we now know them aimed to amuse as well as to instruct. Homer's epic stories *The Iliad* and *The Odyssey* poked fun at the gods, and many Greek plays also satirized the deities. Plato rejected the traditional mythical world of the gods as handed on from his cultural forebears, but he nonetheless reworked mythic material to use for teaching philosophy and offered allegorical interpretations of myth. As Greek literary myths in their current form come from a time long after the myths were originally composed, their sacred content has been reworked to reflect the ambivalent thoughts of Greeks living in a later period when satirical and skeptical attitudes held sway.[11]

Myths of Dying-and-Rising Gods

Pre-Christian myths about dying-and-rising gods are found in Greece, Egypt, and the ancient Near East. Modern scholars ask the big question, did the biblical writers borrow from these myths when writing about the resurrection? As you might expect scholars have reached all kinds of conclusions. The debate is echoed by both skeptics and adepts of alternative spiritualities.[12] Skeptics sometimes say that the resurrection is just a rip-off from the stories of dying-and-rising gods, and a few neo-pagans dismiss it as a retold myth; yet many covens ritually celebrate a dying-and-rising deity in their Wheel of the Year myth. We cannot afford to ignore this important topic if we expect to have informed and fruitful conversations with people beyond the church.

Pioneering Thinkers

Over the last 180 years scholars have wondered whether we can better understand the ancient world if we imagine a culturally shared or universal category of myth about dying-and-rising deities. Similarities have been noted between what the ancient mystery religions taught about these myths and the theological images used in the New Testament to refer to Jesus's resurrection. Some argue that the biblical writers borrowed from these myths when writing about Jesus's resurrection. Understandably, Christians worry that the uniqueness of Jesus's resurrection is being undermined.

We can better grasp what this all means for us if we first take a backwards glance at what some influential thinkers have said about myths of dying-and-rising gods and their connections to the Bible. We should keep in mind that theories come and go, and the social sciences are littered with discarded thoughts about dying-and-rising god myths.[13] A similar rubbish dump exists in modern biblical studies.[14]

Today's interest in myths of dying-and-rising gods was largely kick-started by two German-born scholars: Johann Wilhelm Mannhardt (1831–1880) and

Friedrich Max Müller (1823–1900).[15] They influenced two famous scholars in the study of myth: Carl Jung and James Frazer. Even though Mannhardt and Müller were not collaborators they both presented the same grand theory about dying-and-rising gods. Where they differed was in their methodology.[16]

In the back of their minds was a fashionable notion, namely, that myths personify elements of nature. They thought that sun worship as the source of life was the key to understanding myths about dying-and-rising gods. After comparing myths they devised the "solar theory" of dying-and-rising gods to explain what looked to them like a discernible pattern. In this theory all the dying-and-rising deities—Attis, Adonis, Osiris—were just local manifestations of the same deity—the solar Good God of Light. Every year at the winter solstice the solar Good God of Light "died" as sunlight retreated, and then at the spring equinox when nature bloomed he was "resurrected." So these myths were allegories about the cycle of the seasons. Carl Jung adapted the solar theory in his work about universal myths, while Nazi intellectuals used it in their occult Aryan-race myth.[17]

James Frazer's Golden Bough

Sir James Frazer (1854–1951) spent his academic life working on a multi-volume work in anthropology called *The Golden Bough*.[18] While he personally held to a liberal religious worldview he did not write *The Golden Bough* to debunk Christian faith.[19] Frazer felt that similar myths meant that people in different cultures believed in similar things. He partly relied on Mannhardt's work but collected more myths, made much wider cross-cultural comparisons, and canvassed more theories than either Mannhardt or Müller. He conjectured about the psychological meaning behind myths about dying-and-rising gods and solidified the argument that they formed a universal category of myth. He equated the dying-and-rising gods to a universal mythic theme about nature's fertility and the seasons. His comparative work suggested that the writers of the Gospels may have modified myths of dying-and-rising gods.

Bible and Myth

The hypothesis that Jesus's resurrection story was influenced by pre-Christian myths has prompted endless speculation. Here we will summarize criticisms of Frazer's views on dying-and-rising gods and then briefly refer to what a few others have said about the Bible, resurrection, and myth.

Pros and Cons of Frazer

Today scholars reject Frazer's claim there is a universal category of dying-and-rising gods that equates with fertility. Some dying-and-rising god myths from Greece and Northern European countries *do* make sense when connected to nature and fertility themes. However, it is very speculative to interpret *all* myths of dying-and-rising gods along this line.

Some of Frazer's examples of dying-and-rising gods are problematic. The ancient Mesopotamian myth of Tammuz has him slain, and Frazer thought the goddess Ishtar resurrected him. He saw the story as a prototype for Jesus's resurrection. He conjectured that the myths of Tammuz and Adonis were variant versions of the same story, but this is now deemed unlikely. Edwin Yamauchi points out that Ishtar sent Tammuz to the underworld to take her place there and she abandoned him. Tammuz was never resurrected.[20]

Three other myths that Frazer discussed actually contradict his theory. Mithras, who was a mystery religion deity known in Persia and later favored by Roman soldiers, died but was never resurrected.[21] When Osiris, the Egyptian god of the dead, was killed, his vengeful brother Set dismembered him but Isis reassembled his body in the underworld. Osiris lived again but only in the realm of the dead and never returned to the earth.[22] The myth of Adonis involves him being mortally wounded by a boar and emasculated. Adonis is laid to rest in a patch of lettuce leaves, which was popularly thought of in ancient Greece as a sign of impotence.[23] None of the early versions of the myth state that he was revived or resurrected. While these four examples cast doubt on specific cases, overall Frazer's work cannot be completely dismissed.

There is a new debate about Frazer's work that follows after decades of scathing criticism by anthropologists. Frazer was a man of his times, and today it is easy to see that his theory involved oversimplification.[24] John Parrish says that present-day scholarship is clawing its way out from underneath Frazer's discredited universal category of myth. He says Frazer's category is flawed as a tool for the comparative description of all dying-and-rising god stories.[25] So scholars now wonder how extensive the myths of dying-and-rising gods in pre-Christian times were. There clearly are myths about dying-and-rising gods, but do they all fit into one neat category? The other big question is, what influence did these myths have on the New Testament writers?

On one end of the spectrum are those scholars who argue that Frazer's universal category must be rejected. Mark Smith accepts that there are dying-and-rising god myths but is not persuaded that there is sufficient evidence to show a universal theme in ancient Near Eastern mythology. He does not believe that Baal, the Canaanite fertility deity, was a dying-and-rising god.[26]

Another critical voice is Jonathan Z. Smith. He argues that Frazer made too many conjectures using flimsy evidence. In some myths the gods die but do not undergo resurrection, while in others gods vanish but do not die. Smith says there has to be agreement on what myths are genuine stories of gods that die and are resurrected before a new technical category of dying-and-rising gods can be devised. He insists that the relationship between the dying-and-rising gods in the mystery religions and the New Testament needs a fresh look and raises critical questions that apologists must not dodge.[27]

At the opposite end of the spectrum is an erudite Scandinavian scholar, Tryggve Mettinger. He agrees that Frazer's work was seriously flawed and interacts with the critical views of Mark Smith and Jonathan Smith, but also puts forward a fresh case favoring a broad category for dying-and-rising gods that differs from Frazer's theory. He disagrees with Mark Smith about Baal and offers evidence from recently discovered texts to sustain his point. Unlike Frazer, Mettinger does not argue for any common origin of belief in deities that died and were resurrected. He also sees a contrast between the historical witnesses to Jesus's resurrection and the seasonal myths of dying-and-rising deities.[28] The jury is still deliberating over what Mettinger has argued, while Jonathan Smith's methods are under scrutiny.[29]

Problems for Skeptics

Skeptics outside the academy tend to be unaware of drawbacks in Frazer's work and have used it to debunk Christian apologetics for the resurrection. Their rhetorical agenda often stops them from thinking about the contexts in which these myths arose. By quoting material out of context they miss the critical point: the religions that produced these myths had their own inner systems of thought that tell us what these stories are about.

Another difficulty emerges about claims of parallels. Lay skeptics tend to isolate material from myths that appear parallel to things in the New Testament and then infer it is evidence of borrowing. In the early 1960s the Jewish scholar Samuel Sandmel highlighted many fallacies of "parallelomania" in the study of religion.[30] Based on Sandmel's advice it is easy to see how simple mistakes occur in pointing to isolated parallels. Both Osiris and Jesus die and are revived after death, but that is not tantamount to proof of borrowing. The manner of their respective deaths differs: Osiris is dismembered by another deity while Jesus is crucified. The religious meaning behind their deaths is radically different. Osiris revives and stays in the underworld, while Jesus appears to his disciples on earth *before* he begins reigning in heaven.

The genres of myth and Gospel are wrongly conflated. Myths belong to a recognizable form of literary text that is not intended to be read as history. The Gospels do have a clear rhetorical and theological aim of persuading readers, and at times they make use of poetic and figurative language, symbols, imagery, and discursive discourses to convey theological truth. Nevertheless the Gospels do not fit in the genre of myth. If the Gospel writers wanted to tell the story of Jesus's resurrection as a myth then they were using the wrong genre to get that message across.[31]

Skeptics need a reality check about key discontinuities: None of the pagan gods died on behalf of humanity, whereas Jesus died voluntarily for the sin of the world. The vegetation deities symbolically died and rose again every year, whereas Jesus's death and resurrection are tied to an unrepeated specific event in history. The myths of dying-and-rising gods are not tied into historical narratives.

Old Testament

Some of Frazer's scholarly contemporaries—Jane Harrison, Gilbert Murray, Francis Macdonald Cornford—spearheaded an approach known as the Myth and Ritual school that examined the relation of myth to religious rituals in Greco-Roman cultures.[32] Sidney Hooke then explored myth and ritual in the world of the Old Testament. He argued there was a common pattern to myths and rituals in Near Eastern contexts that influenced Israel's beliefs. He examined Canaanite and Babylonian New Year Festival myths that involved the symbolic death and resurrection of gods.[33] He believed that ancient Israel's Feast of Tabernacles had parallels to these New Year Festivals and went on to conjecture from passages in the Psalms that Israel observed an annual ritual ceremony that enthroned Yahweh as king. Later scholarship has found the whole Myth and Ritual school's position too speculative, and Hooke's theory has been judged to be based on flimsy evidence.[34]

Many other scholars have argued that the idea of resurrection entered the Hebrew Bible via Canaanite myths or Zoroastrian beliefs. We will take up this question in chapter 12.

New Testament

In New Testament studies the names of David Strauss (1808–1874) and Rudolf Bultmann (1884–1976) loom large. Strauss argued that the Gospels comprised elements of myths and legends, with a small amount of historical material. In his view the story of Jesus's death and resurrection was largely mythical with no connections to any actual events.[35]

Rudolf Bultmann argued that the New Testament contained mythological ideas and language, and that meant we could not know much about the Jesus of history. He emphasized that theologians must demythologize the Bible because a mind bathed in the modern discoveries of science cannot embrace miracles. He believed that Jesus's atoning death and resurrection is integral to proclaiming the word of God but is nonetheless purely mythological. Bultmann was deeply influenced by the existentialist philosopher Martin Heidegger, and so he read the Bible through that philosophical lens.[36]

In the case of both Strauss and Bultmann we face reductionist interpretations that presuppose miracles are impossible or can only be understood symbolically. In chapters 3 and 11 we make it clear that the Gospels describe events where witnesses personally encounter the risen Jesus. Whatever one thinks about the witnesses' credibility, they did not explain Jesus's resurrection as just a symbol.

A Funny Thing Happened on the Way to the Movies

Other learned voices insist that evangelicals are evading the evidence about these myths. Robert Price, who is a Jesus Seminar scholar and an ex-fundamentalist Christian, bristles at theologians and apologists who "have never been at ease even recognizing the existence of the dying-and-rising-god motif in non-Christian Mystery Religions."[37] Doubtless there are evangelicals who fit Price's portrait. Price has a polemical agenda to show that Jesus's resurrection story is *not* unique: "it is very hard not to see extensive and basic similarities" between Christianity and the mystery religions.[38] He argues that since the mystery religions preceded Christianity with ideas of resurrection, arguments about Jesus's uniqueness evaporate.

It is curious that Price does not discuss the works of evangelical historians Edwin Yamauchi and Ronald Nash, both of whom grapple with questions about Christian origins in light of gnostic myths and mystery religion myths of dying-and-rising gods.[39] These historians make it clear that the Christian story is unique in its focus on historical events and that Jesus is shown in a role that the dying-rising gods never assume, which is dealing with the curse of sin. Since Price's book was published one could add Nicholas Perrin's recent analysis of the claim that Paul's resurrection motifs of seeds and the body in 1 Corinthians 15 derived from the myth of Osiris—a claim Perrin finds unconvincing.[40]

Jesus's story did not occur in a cultural vacuum. In the wider matrix of the ancient Near East and Mediterranean world there certainly were various *ideas* about resurrection, but enormous problems arise by claiming there was a mono-myth of dying-and-rising gods from which many myths sprang, including the Gospel narratives about resurrection. John Drane says that against this broad cultural backdrop we can see that the story of Jesus's resurrection represents "the culmination of a long history of thought," but unlike the non-Israelite stories "the distinctive mark of the Christian view of resurrection is the survival of the totality of the human personality."[41]

What upsets Price's apple cart, though, is the widespread evangelical interest in C. S. Lewis and J. R. R. Tolkien. Both Lewis and Tolkien emphasized the unique historical character of the gospel narratives. They also had a very positive view about the Bible fulfilling pagan mythology and from an apologetics standpoint saw legend and history being fused. We have already glimpsed this in our chapter's introductory quote from Lewis and from Tolkien's remarks about fairy stories. Towards the end of this chapter we will point out the role that myths played in Lewis's conversion from atheism to theism.

Given Lewis and Tolkein's understanding of general revelation, one would expect them to see the figure of Christ surfacing, albeit in imperfect guises, in the world's mythology. They supposed that myths of dying-and-rising gods obliquely foreshadowed what would be fulfilled in the historical details of Jesus's life. Leon McKenzie's point that resurrection motifs preexist in nature also hints at where the idea of resurrection originated.[42]

Christlike resurrection parallels are found in the fictional characters of Aslan and Gandalf. Aslan the lion dies a substitutionary death on behalf of the sin of Edmund Pevensie and rises again from the dead in Lewis's *The Lion, the Witch and the Wardrobe*. In *The Last Battle* all the inhabitants of Narnia are resurrected and they meet the resurrected Aslan in a day of judgment. Gandalf the grey wizard dies in mortal combat with a fearsome Balrog to save his companions and then rises again as a victorious white wizard in Tolkien's *The Lord of the Rings*. Aslan and Gandalf evidence immortality through their resurrection experiences.

Both Lewis and Tolkien were colleagues at Oxford and drinking buddies at the Eagle and Child pub. Out of their friendship came the formation of an informal literary club called The Inklings where Lewis, Tolkien, and others read aloud their works-in-progress. Lewis's sheer enthusiasm for *The Lord of the Rings* helped motivate Tolkien to finish writing the story.[43] Tolkien's novel was mythical and not an allegory.

As professing Christians their worldview was integral to what they wrote. Lewis's *Chronicles of Narnia* have sold over a hundred million copies since their release in the 1950s. The series of seven novels contains some obvious allegorical elements but is woven together as a grand mythic tale. One commentator has remarked that "Aslan is a conscious attempt at Christian education *within* and *for* a society that knew about Jesus Christ's atoning sacrifice but which Lewis believed had lost the plot" and that the Narnia stories "point towards something of the reality of the Incarnation-Resurrection narrative."[44] What unified their stories in their resurrection events was the conviction that Lewis and Tolkien shared about the world's fairy tales.

The influence of resurrection analogies in both *The Lord of the Rings* and *Chronicles of Narnia* is reflected in book sales worldwide. *The Lord of the Rings* has been repeatedly voted the "book of the century" across the English-speaking world. Both the novel and film adaptations have captured the imaginations of audiences worldwide. Similarly, the *Chronicles of Narnia* have entered that illustrious niche reserved for children's classics, and the film adaptations of the stories so far have witnessed considerable box-office success.

Hero Myth and the Collective Unconscious

The resurrection triggers embedded in both Lewis's and Tolkien's stories can illuminate aspects of the works of Carl Jung and Joseph Campbell. Jung, Campbell, and their followers have taken the iconic figure of the hero and woven together a contemporary understanding of personal psychological transformation. Life is recast as a hero's quest so that to achieve individual well-being one must take a challenging interior journey to healing. We will discuss a few details about their respective theories in what follows.

Jung and Archetypes

Jung presented a psychoanalytic theory about human beings based on his personal dream-life, his clinical work with the dreams of his patients, and his research into religious symbols and myths.[45] Jung encountered a common fund of symbols that he understood as expressing deep yearnings from within the human psyche crying out for healing and wholeness. Symbols of the hero, the deceiver/trickster, and the old father figure were apparent in the dreams of his patients but could also be detected in myths and religious rituals. Jung inferred that since this symbolism could be encountered across time and civilizations there must be a common psychic or interior life that humanity shares. He hypothesized that there is a collective unconscious to humanity that is expressed symbolically. Jung described the universality of these symbols as the archetypes of the collective unconscious. For Jung ancient mythology was a prototype of psychoanalysis, and he felt that the best counterpart to psychoanalysis was found in ancient gnostic myths.[46]

Campbell's Monomyth

Campbell started with Jung's work but developed his own theory about a universal hero myth. He noted that the figure of the hero popped up in various myths cross-culturally. He inferred that behind all the world's religions and folktales there stands a single myth: the hero who undertakes an epic journey to self-transformation. He saw this universal myth as a way of teaching men in midlife that they must go through three steps in their psychological development: symbolically dying, separating from their mother, and coming to terms with their father.

He also took up the archetype of the dying-and-rising god as he saw it in the tarot deck and in relationship to the world's mythology. Campbell pinpointed "The Fool" card as highly significant. He understood the imagery of this tarot card as symbolizing the dying and resurrected sun god.[47]

Campbell's monomyth has critical drawbacks.[48] One weakness is that Campbell's theory involves overstatement. It is reductionistic to interpret the essence of the world's religions and mythology as revolving around the monomyth of the hero. A second problem is that Campbell ignores myths where heroes fail, bad characters win, and not everyone succeeds in living happily ever after. In the collective psyche of a few Western nations there are strong antiheroic attitudes that constitute important exceptions to Campbell's sweeping generalization about the universal hero.[49]

Various responses to Campbell's hero myth express the problems implied in its treatment of gender. Feminist writers point out that the hero myth is male-centered, patriarchal, and misogynist.[50] It enshrines a male-warrior mentality and relegates females to the role of a mother.[51] The hero is neither sensitive nor suitable as an image for the development of female psyches.[52] George Miller, the maker of the *Mad Max* movies, upholds the Jungian-Campbell theories about myth in his filmmaking.[53] However in an ironic twist the theme song for *Mad Max Beyond Thunderdome* that Tina Turner sang was "We Don't Need Another Hero."

Not all men like warrior imagery or admire action figures like Rocky Balboa, John McClane, or Luke Skywalker.[54] Many men shun both macho heroics and aggressive competitiveness in corporate, political, and sports contexts. Byrne observes that "a strongly heroic culture is one in perpetual adolescence."[55] Harold Schechter and Jonna Semeiks see Campbell's monomyth trivialized in action films like *Star Wars* where Luke Skywalker is a clichéd prepubescent hero.[56]

A popular Christian understanding of Campbell's work involves seeing Jesus as the universal hero who faces death and rescues us. The New Testament presents the risen Jesus as the triumphant king or as a conquering warrior (Col. 2:9–15; Rev. 1:12–18; 19:11–16), and early church fathers used the *Christus Victor* motif because he defeats the powers of sin, death, and the devil through his resurrection from the dead. Some Christians feel that the imagery of Jesus as a warrior needs to be emphasized today because "it is an image that a man can relate to."[57] We will talk more about the divine warrior images of the Bible in chapter 12.

Although this Christian view has become popular some sober discernment is needed. As churches wrestle with gender roles, we must not create a distorted Christology where Jesus as *Christus Victor* is symbolized like a macho warrior hero. The *Christus Victor* motif, when it is properly understood along the lines that the early church taught, stands as a healthy corrective to Hollywood myths that glorify the lawless macho hero. The church does not need to perpetuate negative impressions that it is a male-dominated institution that worships a God of violence and marginalizes women.

Further criticisms of the hero myth that Byrne notes relate to our digital era. He indicates that as cyberspace dominates our lives and is premised on nonlinear movement, the idea of a hero on a linear journey to self-transformation is becoming less relevant. Byrne also says that in postmodern times a plurality of roles typifies the normative experiences of many people today. In other words, the idea that everyone must take the hero's quest in order to develop and grow does not fit in with the exploration of the multiplicity of models of selfhood we surveyed in the previous chapter. Byrne notes that "the postmodern West is already moving away from its earlier captivation by the hero."[58]

Resurrection Triggers in the Human Psyche

While the weaknesses and limitations in the stances taken by Jung and Campbell must not be ignored, it is also true that their ideas are seminal. Hollywood is clearly gripped by the influence of the hero myth. One does not have to agree with Jung and Campbell in order to make an apologetic point about resurrection triggers. F. F. Bruce says that in his speech in Athens (Acts 17) Paul had no difficulty in using material that "could corroborate his argument," so he quoted the Stoics' words, "giving them a biblical sense as he did so."[59] In like manner, we use Campbell and Jung's ideas here but do not endorse everything that they believed.[60]

Archetypes and Scripture

If there are universal symbolic archetypes of the resurrection that are expressed through ancient myths about heroes and dying-and-rising gods, how do they relate to the Bible? Can symbols of the resurrection in pop culture and in myth reflect the truth of "eternity in our hearts" (see Eccles. 3:11)? We find theological support in answering these questions from:

- The theology of the creation.[61]
- The theological meaning of humans bearing the image of God (*imago Dei*).[62]
- The theology of the Spirit of God at work within the creation.[63]

Let's briefly explain these points. We look to creation theology because of the unity of the creation and fall. Humans have solidarity because we are made in God's image and likeness. We are made to have relationships with God, each other, and the rest of the created order. In chapter 6 we discussed via general revelation that the creation has embedded in it analogies of resurrection. A sensitive psyche may feel deep affinities with these analogies in creation that form patterns (like sunrise/sunset, waking/sleeping), and they may trigger within us receptive desires to embrace the larger reality found in Jesus's resurrection.

In the Old Testament God's Spirit is constantly moving throughout the creation. We see that God's Spirit not only sustains all life but prepared the way for Jesus's life, ministry, and resurrection. In the New Testament the Holy Spirit guides the church to proclaim the resurrection. The Holy Spirit bids us to live in the power of Christ's resurrection as light to others and to serve God in the creation. When we reflect on general and special revelation the Holy Spirit can prompt us to see that resurrection archetypes in creation and culture should meet and kiss the risen Jesus. In light of what we learn from creation theology and the work of God's Spirit, we should not be surprised that across time and cultures humans share similar aspirations and have common needs. We should likewise not be surprised that resurrection triggers will be found across the creation and across human cultures.

In Romans 1:18–23 Paul argues that the human condition comprises our sinful state before God and that we suppress the natural knowledge of God and substitute it for idolatry. R. C. Sproul has offered a tantalizing psycho-logical profile of humanity based on this passage.[64] Sproul suggests that our response to the knowledge of God in nature has three basic phases, which may be described as trauma, repression, and substitution. By trauma Sproul means that our encounter with God's self-revelation is shocking and threatens our propensity for autonomy. God's holy presence is too traumatic for us to bear. This leads to the second phase of repression. The conscious knowledge of God's holiness is so unbearable that we repress it. This knowledge is buried deep down in the subconscious, where we strive to conceal it. However, this process does not fully succeed, nor does it obliterate or destroy the knowledge as it lurks within us subconsciously. The final phase is to exchange or sub-stitute this knowledge about God by reverting to idols. This repression and substitution also plays out over Jesus's resurrection. It is easy to turn away from his resurrection and substitute for it belief in myths of dying-and-rising gods who do not call us to repentance.

We can deepen what we have just outlined with reference to Christology. At the start of the chapter we quoted Tolkien on fairy stories and the eucata-strophe. Royce Gruenler has applied Tolkien's thoughts in a study of the Christology of the Gospels.[65] The person of Jesus is the only one who can meet our spiritual needs. Through his death and resurrection Jesus shatters the forces of sin, death, and the devil. Since we share solidarity in both creation and fall, we subjectively and intuitively sense that our lives are overwhelmed by those forces that Jesus opposed and defeated. So we should not be surprised by deep stirrings within us when we encounter stories and cultural images that foreshadow Jesus's resurrection.

If archetypes symbolically refer to deep encoded truths that are part of our inner being, it should not be surprising that such symbols percolate to the surface in our consciousness and are expressed in culture in different guises. The challenge for Christians is to invite people to move beyond exploring archetypes of resurrection found in the creation and in the myths of dying-and-rising gods and to embrace the fullness of them in Jesus.[66]

Tying It All Together

C. S. Lewis's life and thought is helpful here in enabling us to understand everything we have been talking about concerning myth and resurrection im-ages. There are three phases to his life's story that are highly relevant. Lewis had a lifelong interest in mythology that began in his childhood reading and continued on in his career as a scholar of English literature. He maintained a lifelong friendship with his Belfast childhood neighbor Arthur Greeves (1895–1968), and they shared a common love for reading myths. At an emotional level Lewis was often deeply moved in his childhood and teenage years reading Norse and Greek myths about dying-and-rising gods.[67]

During his adolescent and early adult life Lewis was an avowed atheist, while Greeves was a regular churchgoer. Lewis corresponded with Greeves about their differences in worldview. At that time *The Golden Bough* had been recently published and Lewis found Frazer's theory about dying-and-rising gods very plausible. He also liked some of Frazer's other theories about the origins of religion because, he believed, they seemed to support atheism. Lewis castigated Greeves for believing in a religion that simply retold the age-old myth of a dying-and-rising god. Frazer had outlined a theory about myth and religion that originated with ancient Greek skeptic Euhemerus (330–260 BC), who wrote a novel *Hiera anagraphé* (*The Sacred Inscription*).[68] In that story Euhemerus found in Zeus's temple a story that explained that the gods had originally been men and women of high social distinction who were then worshiped and deified. Lewis loved this theory and told Greeves that Jesus was just an obscure Hebrew prophet who after his death was deified by his followers. The Gospel writers just imitated other dying-and-rising god myths when telling the story of his crucifixion and resurrection.[69]

At Oxford University Lewis became friends with two English literature scholars: Tolkien and Hugo Dyson, both of whom were professing Christians. One evening in 1931 the three of them shared a meal and then strolled around the college quadrangle discussing religion, paganism, and myth. Lewis indicated that while he enjoyed immensely tales of dying-and-rising gods he could not fathom how the life of Jesus could help us much today except possibly as a moral example. Tolkien and Dyson honed in on his enjoyment of pagan myths involving both sacrifices and dying-and-rising gods. They explored with Lewis how the pagan myths contained poetic hints of what God was going to ultimately do in history in the person of Jesus. The story of Christ then is the fulfillment of those myths. That long night of discussion about myths helped Lewis in his second phase to shift from atheism into believing that God existed.[70] A little later in his journey he professed faith in Christ as Savior.

The final phase in Lewis's life involved his role as an apologist for faith, using myth to convey Christian truth. Lewis turned the atheist interpretation of Frazer's theory on its head. Instead of dying-and-rising god myths being viewed as a threat to the Christian message, Lewis now had a new way of looking at those same myths. Like Tolkien, Lewis was conversant with Jung's ideas about archetypes in myth.[71] In his new apologetic understanding, the pagan myths represent in general revelation both pointers and echoes of greater truths that would come in the life of Jesus. So he argued that the dying-and-rising god myths imperfectly foreshadow things that Jesus concretely fulfilled. Even though Frazer's theory has now been critiqued, Lewis blazed a trail for informed apologists today to critically and prudently follow about pre-Christian myths of dying-and-rising gods.

Lewis wrote about theories of myth not just as an apologist but also as a literary scholar. In *An Experiment in Criticism* he held that scholarly theories about myth such as the Myth and Ritual school, psychoanalysis, and nature allegories are limited as all-encompassing explanations.[72] Lewis argued that "myth continues to evoke the feeling that there is something more, something that cannot be rationalized, that is involved in our experience of myth."[73] It is from this multifaceted understanding of myth that he wrote apologetics essays, Narnia stories, and retold a Greek myth in *Till We Have Faces*.[74]

Since Lewis's day some apologists have argued that the archetypes that Jung and Campbell saw as being universally significant can also be found in the Gospels. The imagery of one who conquers death abounds in myths and folktales, and many today have imaginative yearnings to become like a universal hero. When apologists pick up the themes and images of the hero and the conquest of death and draw parallels to the story of Jesus's death and resurrection it can resonate deeply within a person's psyche. One can converse with neo-pagans about the Wheel of the Year myth and relate it back to the fulfillment theme in Jesus. The image of resurrection found in tarot cards is another springboard for talking about archetypes and finding their completion in Jesus's resurrection.[75] Apologists can interact with mythology as it surfaces in film, TV, novels, and in new religions as a stepping-stone to conversations about Jesus's resurrection.[76]

Myth and Metanarrative

There is one more topic related to myth that we want to discuss. It is widely accepted that we are living in a time of transition. One epoch is coming to an end, and a new epoch is emerging. The dying epoch is the age of modernity, while the emerging epoch is usually called postmodernity. In broad brushstrokes it is said that modernity is characterized by worldviews that explain reality through grand stories or metanarratives. Metanarratives purport to explain everything in terms of scientific certainty and rationality.

The metanarratives that characterize the modern age undergird belief systems in Christianity, Marxism, and modern schools of empiricist and rationalist philosophy. The pro-apartheid story of white South Africa serves as an example of a metanarrative that suited the ruling elite. The judgment of postmodern thinkers is that the metanarratives of modernity have oppressed dissenting voices. Underdog voices—the poorest social classes, ethnic and indigenous minorities, women, homosexuals—have been marginalized in the public square. So metanarratives are just ideologies masquerading as objective understandings of the world. In order to clear away the ideological fog, postmodernists employ the critical tool of deconstruction, through which one can peel away layer upon layer of ideologically-driven language to expose the illusions of those who created modern metanarratives. The end result is that metanarratives are rejected.

We agree that many modern metanarratives are destructive and disempowering. Many popular Christian writers take another step by assuming that emerging culture is rejecting all metanarratives. In the digital age baby boomers represent the last grumpy vestiges of modernity in church, state, and society. A new epoch is being reimagined by those born in the digital age—the Net generation. The current clamor for revitalizing churches is important, and there are laudable attempts being made to understand contemporary culture. We do feel, though, that a sacred cow has been erected about the end of metanarratives.

Misreading the Signs about Holistic Spirituality

Throughout this book we have provided ample illustrations of the appeal and influence of alternative holistic spiritualities. Anyone who is going to participate in urban missions today will surely encounter practitioners of these spiritualities. So, we are flummoxed when the topic is ignored or treated as a peripheral concern, or when it is claimed that nobody is now signing up for New Age 101 courses.[77] Internet booksellers like Amazon continue to sell complex books in Buddhist, gnostic, magical, and neo-pagan thought that make many pop Christian books look pathetic.[78] When Oprah interviews spirituality authors like Deepak Chopra, Marianne Williamson, and Rhonda Byrne, their book sales skyrocket. Each author has a metanarrative about how the cosmos works.[79]

In various industries such as education, health, beauty, hotel, and leisure, vocational training can expose employees to theories about how the universe works. For example, some beautician courses require trainees to study the worldview of bush spirits in order to understand what energetic forces activate the healing properties of aromatherapy products. There are various complementary healing colleges that have very high enrollments of mostly female students in all adult age brackets undertaking courses for diplomas that immerse them in metanarratives of cosmology. Parallel to the popular trends, within the elite halls of academia across Europe, North America, and Australia postgraduate studies in Gnosticism, astrology, Wicca, and New Age are surging.

Postmodern Metanarratives

John Drane remarks that these eclectic spiritual habits suggest people are much less postmodern than some interpreters would have us believe.[80] We acknowledge that Enlightenment-based metanarratives have been questioned, deconstructed, and rejected in various sectors of the academy. However, we feel that some Christians have reified (i.e., treated an abstract idea as if it is concretely real) the claim that metanarratives are passé. Holistic spiritualities and complementary healing therapies are all premised on metanarratives about ultimate reality. Astrology and Kabbalah are divinatory systems that purport to decode universal meaning. Similarly, westernized versions of reincarnation build on a metanarrative about the soul's cosmic evolution via the universal law of karma. The popular category of universal myths involves metanarrative.

Lastly, the Polish-born sociologist Zygmunt Bauman puts forward a thesis that religious fundamentalism is "a legitimate child of postmodernity, born of its joys and torments, and heir to its achievements and worries."[81] We will not debate his thesis here, but if it has credence then two points have to be faced. One is that, sociologically, fundamentalism flourishes in all major world religions: Christian, Buddhist, Hindu, Islamic, Judaic, neo-pagan, and Shinto. The second point is that every stripe of religious fundamentalism presents a metanarrative.[82] No matter whether you agree or disagree with Bauman about fundamentalism as postmodern religion, his thesis throws a cat among the pigeons. Christians are prone to taking at face value what a few interpreters have written about postmodernity, and this can be very misleading. The church would do well to reconsider the possibility that metanarratives are still thriving in the religious lives of people around the globe.

Conclusion

Ross once had an uncanny experience when he was taking a short series of Bible classes at a church on understanding and sharing the gospel. One session was on the resurrection and worldview, and the presentation brought together all the things that we have outlined in this chapter about myth, symbol, and the resurrection. The key point was equipping people on how to effectively share their faith with their friends. At the end of the session a woman asked if she could make a comment. She indicated that she was a professional tarot reader who had received a "message" that she needs to look at Jesus. She did not know where to turn but phoned a friend of hers who is a Christian. Her friend said, come with me tonight to this meeting. The woman said, "All that you are saying is like the light-switch being flicked on. I now understand the deeper meaning behind myth and Jesus's historical fulfillment." The audience applauded. Ross had a long chat with her and left her sitting with her friend as she gave her life to Christ. Myth and resurrection can meet and inspire our own personal spiritual growth, and they can speak into the lives of others.

Spiritual Audit

1. Have you settled in your faith for a mythical view of Jesus's resurrection?

2. Have you shied away from myths for fear of losing the resurrection?

3. Is your faith group capable of using myth for gospel presentation?

4. There is truth in all myths but not all myths are true. Has your faith been built up by understanding that there are God-given triggers to be found in myth, culture, and other religious stories?

5. Has your Christian faith lost its metanarrative?

10

Church History and Resurrection Thinking

By discounting the resurrection of Christ because it does not conform to our modern sensibilities, or by interpreting it as a simple metaphor divorced from actual space and time events, we have distanced ourselves from the central proclamation of Christianity, that Christ is risen indeed, which has proven throughout the ages and in many different cultural contexts to possess an inherent power far greater than philosophical systems derived from human experience alone.

Nathan D. Hieb[1]

Not too long ago the blogosphere witnessed a flurry of Christians completing an online quiz to discover "which theologian are you."[2] The quiz consists of thirty paraphrased remarks made by different theologians from church history. Participants respond to each sentence on a sliding scale from disagree to agree. The results are automatically sorted into a bar graph to indicate from participants' answers which theologian they are the closest to.

Even though it is an amusing, geeky activity, the quiz bothers us. Hardly anyone has asked a basic question: how can you honestly discover your theological affinities from a short list of out-of-context sentences? A quick quiz in truth cannot demonstrate that one's thinking is just like that of St. Anselm, Karl Barth, or Paul Tillich. The most telling point for us, though, was that the quiz completely ignored the resurrection! (We hasten to add that we are *not* asking for a parallel online quiz—"what resurrection do you believe in?")

In this chapter we will selectively survey what church history can tell us about the church's thought on the resurrection. We will start with the present and then time travel backwards era by era to the early church. This chapter also forms something of a bridge between general revelation and special revelation. Church history is littered with fallible thinking and deeds that must be judged from the standpoint of God's special revelation, which is one big reason why we are examining the Bible separately in part 3.

So choose your favorite time machine—rev up Doc Emmett Brown's DeLorean automobile, tumble through Irwin Allen's *Time Tunnel*, or dematerialize to the wheezing sounds of The Doctor's Tardis—and let us be your tour guide as we explore what theologians in different eras have thought about the resurrection.[3]

Does It Matter?

Often church history is regarded as a cure for insomnia but it does not have to become a sleeping pill. History has lessons for anyone with a discerning eye. You may agree that we can find useful things from the past but nevertheless want to say to us: "But why bother dredging up what others have thought about the resurrection? Why not just spend time *applying* the resurrection in the here and now?" While it is tempting to plow on regardless of the past, George Santayana's famous aphorism comes back to remind us: "Those who cannot remember the past are condemned to repeat it."[4] A sign of spiritual maturity is being willing to learn from the past while avoiding the mistake of romanticizing any era.

What's Been Missing

In the mid-1990s Gerald O'Collins pointed to a yawning chasm in church history studies about the resurrection:

> We still lack substantial studies of the whole story (from the New Testament to the twentieth century) of Christian belief in, preaching of, and theology about Jesus' resurrection from the dead. We also continue to lack full studies of how Jesus' resurrection was assumed and expressed by Christian liturgies through the ages—in both East and West.[5]

When O'Collins made those remarks he did so having already read Caroline Walker Bynum's study of the idea of the resurrection in late antiquity and high Middle Ages. O'Collins's basic observation remains valid up to the present time. Why this scholarly gap exists is anyone's guess. Is this another symptom of failing to emphasize Christianity's lynchpin?

In previous chapters we have referred to some aspects of church history in apologetics and art. Here we will only touch the tip of the iceberg regarding beliefs about the resurrection in church history. More needs to be written on how the resurrection has been represented in theology, apologetics, missions, ethics, pastoral care, church art, music, pageants, preaching, and liturgy, as well as on the resurrection's influence over devotional and spiritual writings.

We wish we had more space to examine thinkers like John Calvin, Augustine of Hippo, and Justin Martyr, but in this book we cannot provide a thorough survey of all the key figures in church history. We refer you instead to recent analyses of modern theologians coming from the pens of Thorwald Lorenzen and N. T. Wright.[6] They both enter into the contemporary debates about the physicality of the resurrection and the reliability of the Gospel narratives as reflected in the works of Wolfhart Pannenberg, John Dominic Crossan, Jürgen Moltmann, and Karl Barth. Our review will concentrate on a few individuals whose ideas about the resurrection are significant to the themes of this book.

Attitudes toward Resurrection in Modernity

There is a lot of positive thinking about the resurrection today as seen from authors like N. T. Wright, Gary Habermas, and Mark Driscoll. In chapter 9 we alluded to the negative conclusions of modern thinkers like David Strauss and Rudolf Bultmann. While our emphasis in this chapter will generally be on positive views of the resurrection, first we present a quick survey of modern views because we feel that some influential negative players should be noted.

Bishop Spong's *Resurrection: Myth or Reality?*[7] represents the mind-set that refuses to allow for a God who performs miracles in human history. Spong's books have circulated in both postmodern spiritual circles and among those who belong to modernity.

Ross has interviewed Spong twice on radio. They found an affinity in baseball because Spong's winning team included a star-performing Australian player; however, when it came to theology and especially the resurrection, they were light-years apart! Spong told Ross that he could not fathom how in light of modern knowledge any Christian could keep on believing in legendary things like angels, or accept at face value the Gospel narratives of Jesus's resurrection.

That live-to-air radio interview happened just a few hours after our Community of Hope team wrapped up four days of outreach at a Mind-Body-Spirit festival. Ross aptly put it to Spong that thousands of non-Christians had just flocked to this event where it was rather commonplace for them to accept that angels exist. What would the bishop like to say to all those people who are alienated from Christianity and yet nonetheless believe we can contact angels? Spong's antisupernatural bias led him to mock their journey.

We understand that not all are open to the supernatural, but many people share the tension of believing the extraordinary apostolic witness to Jesus's resurrection while living in an epoch secularized by skepticism. Bishop Spong lives out his skepticism by reinterpreting Easter. He maintains that the Gospel narratives are shaped by a Jewish literary activity known as midrash. A midrash could involve a pastoral embellishment or imaginative paraphrase of an existing story. In retelling such stories words and actions might be attributed to an historical character. Spong sees the apostles arriving at an understanding that Jesus had conquered death, but not in a physical sense. As the story was retold it became embellished by legend, myth, and the techniques of midrash for convincing others. The apostles never saw a risen Christ but as they reflected on his life and death they came to the conclusion that the grave could not contain him.

Spong's reinterpretation reflects ideas from older debates about the Gospels that can be traced back to the seventeenth century. We will take a quick backwards look at earlier attempts at grappling with resurrection in contexts of modernist thinking.

Schleiermacher

At the start of the chapter we mentioned an online quiz. One thing that raised our eyebrows was that a few bloggers were excited that the quiz results indicated "You are like Schleiermacher." We wonder if they would still feel an affinity with him if they knew what he said about the resurrection.

Friedrich Schleiermacher (1768–1834) is regarded as the father of Protestant liberal theology.[8] He lived at a time when skepticism was rife about miracles, and the historical authenticity of the Gospels was under scrutiny. Schleiermacher addressed his theology to the educated elite who despised orthodox Christian belief. Schleiermacher rejected the idea that the apostles were somehow deceived about Jesus's resurrection, so it appears that he believed that "the resurrection took place."[9]

Nathan Hieb has recently reevaluated Schleiermacher and warns that we should not take at face value what Schleiermacher said about Jesus's resurrection and our future resurrection. There are two big problems: one concerns miracles and the other, the theological meaning of the resurrection. During Schleiermacher's lifespan German theology about the resurrection and afterlife was reshaped by dissenting secular views that rejected miracles altogether.[10] His understanding of the natural world led him to retreat from affirming miracles as supernatural acts. The best he could do was to say that the apostles were not deceived with respect to the resurrection.

Of greater concern is the theological angle Schleiermacher took. Hieb points out that despite an "affirmation of the historicity of Christ's resurrection . . . Schleiermacher proceeds to empty the resurrection of redemptive significance."[11] In the "logic" of his theology neither Jesus's resurrection nor the general resurrection has any real connection to redemption. Hieb observes that if "Christ's suffering and death do not relate to redemption other than as illustrations of self-offering, then it follows that the historical claims regarding Christ's resurrection from the dead also have no direct bearing on the redeemed life of the believer."[12]

Deism and Modern Apologetics

William Lane Craig examines a major controversy about the resurrection that erupted in Europe and North America in the late seventeenth and eighteenth centuries.[13] The protagonists were known as deists because they were neither atheists nor orthodox theists. They happily believed through natural theology that God existed but held he did not act in history. Therefore they were skeptical about two broad issues: biblical miracles—particularly Jesus's resurrection—and claims that special revelation is found in both Jesus and the Bible.

During this time period, people were exploring new frontiers that led to the discipline of modern critical history. They were asking questions about the authorship and authenticity of the Bible, and there was a strong skeptical mood reemerging in philosophy. Probably the best-known skeptic of the day was David Hume (1711–1776), who came to fame by arguing that if you heard a report of a miraculous event like a resurrection you should ask whether it is more likely that the person reporting the marvel was mistaken or deceived, or that the event really happened. Hume reasoned that we have a firm and unalterable experience of the world that rules out miracles as implausible and impossible. Although he was not a deist, Hume's argument against miracles became part of the fabric of the controversy, and his position continues to be echoed today.[14]

The controversy initially involved clergymen taking opposing sides but soon spilled over to include intellectuals outside the church. Some notable deists included George Washington, Thomas Jefferson, Thomas Paine, Thomas Woolston, and Peter Annet. Christian apologists who responded included Bishop Joseph Butler, John Locke, Thomas Sherlock, Gilbert West, and William Paley.[15] This controversy partly stimulated the emergence of an apologetic defense shaped by metaphors of moot trials where lawyers for opposing sides contested the evidences for Jesus's resurrection.[16]

The deist controversy throws much light on the course of subsequent Christian thinking—conservative, liberal, and radical—about the resurrection. We are living in the shadows of that protracted controversy.

Martin Luther

We normally associate the Protestant Reformation of the sixteenth century with justification by faith. It is easy to forget that Reformers such as John Calvin and Huldrych Zwingli preached on the resurrection. We may even misjudge them. While it is understood that Calvin had a strong sense of Jesus's resurrection and its implications, some feel that he underemphasized the body for the general resurrection. However that impression may reflect the prejudices of later observers rather than what Calvin actually said.[17]

On the Lutheran side, David Hollaz (1647–1713) wrote about the general resurrection and Philipp Melanchthon preached on resurrection and justification. Melanchthon explored Christ's high priestly role of intercession in his theology of resurrection.[18] The deists later debated the topic that Melanchthon made a prescient comment about: "The apostles are witnesses to Christ, His birth, crucifixion, and resurrection. These are historical writings."[19] He even scribbled on his copy of Homer's works: "Buried together with the Lifegiver, let there be resurrection."[20] It would be fascinating to delve into what all these Reformers thought but space constraints compel us to set them aside. We will focus on Martin Luther, because he was the father of the Reformation and many see him as cross-focused.

"Lutheran preoccupation with the cross which plays down the Easter events has become a commonplace" is an oft-repeated claim.[21] It is commonly believed that Luther was a theologian of the cross and that Lutherans underemphasize the resurrection. That the doctrine of justification by grace through faith represented the heartbeat of Luther's understanding of salvation goes without saying. Luther, it is believed, was Christocentric from start to finish and emphasized Christ alone, grace alone, faith alone, and Scripture alone.

We accept that Luther was Christocentric, but we disagree with the characterization that he was just cross-centered, as our earlier references to Luther's remarks about the centrality of the resurrection in preaching and in church music indicate. In fact, the few mentions we made about Luther's views on the resurrection barely scratch the surface, and we believe his teaching on the resurrection needs to be rehabilitated today. Fred Meuser describes Luther's passion as a preacher in these terms: "To Luther, preaching Christ meant, above all, focusing on his death and resurrection."[22] Meuser notes that all the atonement themes surface in many of Luther's sermons but then says:

> Luther preached often on death and probably just as often on the resurrection. The resurrection was a melody of his sermons even when it was not the theme. In 1532/33 he preached seventeen sermons in a row on 1 Corinthians 15. During the Easter season he could hardly tear himself away from the resurrection theme.[23]

As regards this series of sermons on 1 Corinthians 15 Gerhard Sauter says that "here the Reformer develops his theological understanding of the resurrection in a more comprehensive and multi-faceted way than anywhere else."[24] Luther made many observations about both Christ's resurrection and the resurrection of the dead (see the summary list in chapter 11 in our discussion on 1 Corinthians 15). This is just one of his crucial observations:

> Paul stakes everything on the basic factor with which he began, namely, that Christ arose from the dead. This is the chief article of the Christian doctrine. No one who at all claims to be a Christian or a preacher of the Gospel may deny that.[25]

As regards Luther's Easter season sermons on the resurrection, they shed light on both his theology and apologetic.[26] In the mid-1520s he delivered a sermon on Mark 16:1–8 and sought to reconcile time measurements of three days duration—from the Sabbath to Sunday morning—with what appears to be chronologically a mere two nights and a day for Jesus's body being buried. He then shifted attention to the fruits and benefits of the resurrection by alluding to Romans 4:25. He commented that it was "not sufficient to know and believe that Christ has died" and not enough to know that Jesus has risen from the dead because "this would profit me nothing." For Luther knowing the facts of Easter was not enough:

> When I come to understand the fact that all the works God does in Christ are done for me, nay, they are bestowed upon and given to me, the effect of his resurrection being that I also will arise and live with him; that will cause me to rejoice.[27]

We discover Luther's resurrection views at numerous other points in his theology. In his lectures on the book of Genesis Luther exposited the theme of the resurrection.[28] His theology of the real presence of Christ in the Eucharist depends on understanding that the resurrected Lord is omnipresent.[29] There is also potential fertile ground in exploring how he related the resurrection theologically to the Day of Atonement in the Old Testament.

In the past three decades Finnish Lutheran scholars have reexamined Luther's teaching about becoming a "little Christ" to one's neighbor. The Finnish scholars have argued that what Luther saw as the outcome of our union with Christ through his resurrection and our resurrection has strong affinities with Eastern Orthodoxy's stance about the final goal of our resurrection.[30] We will examine the Eastern Orthodox position below.

On several occasions in his writings, Luther nominated the resurrection as *the* article of faith.[31] According to Jos Vercruysse explicit mention of the phrase "theology of the cross" only occurs five times in Luther's writings on the Psalms, and his strongest emphasis on that theme is evident in his Heidelberg Disputation.[32] Yet, Vercruysse says, "For Luther a theology of resurrection is the intrinsic complement of a theology of the cross."[33] We must let Luther be Luther and not reimagine him into something that he was not. However, it is clear that he did not relegate the resurrection to the sidelines. Perhaps we have overlooked Luther's theology of the resurrection by seeing him as just a theologian of the cross. David Scaer maintains that Luther saw Jesus's resurrection "as the linchpin of Christianity."[34]

Latin Church of the Middle Ages

In the high Middle Ages belief in both Jesus's resurrection and the general resurrection featured strongly in both theological confession and pastoral concerns.[35] Attitudes about Christ's resurrection and the general resurrection were partly shaped by stark experiences of mortality. People understood their identity through the physical body, and the general resurrection of the body was important because it was part of the doctrine of salvation. Here are a few brief examples of the diverse thinking of the era: Ademar of Chabannes (ca. 989–1034) was a monk who preached about both the resurrection of Jesus and of humanity as part of a defense of the faith against contemporary heretics.[36] Achard of St. Victor (ca. 1100–1172) preached an Easter sermon centered on Romans 7:22–25 in which he taught that "the resurrection is nothing other than our own redemption: it prefigures our future resurrection and the restoration of all things."[37] The twelfth-century writer Bernard of Clairvaux held to a holistic understanding of humans that emphasized the "psychosomatic unity" of the body rather than a body-soul dualism.[38]

St. Anselm

While the resurrection was not central in his classic book on atonement, St. Anselm did comment on the general resurrection:

> From this the future resurrection of the dead is clearly proved. For if man is to be perfectly restored, the restoration should make him such as he would have been had he never sinned. . . . Therefore, as man, had he not sinned, was to have been transferred with the same body to an immortal state, so when he shall be restored, it must properly be with his own body as he lived in this world.[39]

In his deeply moving "Prayer before Receiving the Body and Blood of Christ" Anselm asked for forgiveness and then affirmed:

> Then at the Resurrection you will refashion
> The body of my humiliation
> According to the body of your glory,
> As you promised by your apostle,
> And I shall rejoice in you for ever
> To your glory.[40]

We could learn much from St. Anselm's prayer life when celebrating the Lord's Supper, especially as it is meant to "function as a means of fellowship with the risen Lord" and foreshadows the heavenly banquet.[41]

Thomas Aquinas

If you are ever asked to name a medieval churchman chances are it will be Thomas Aquinas (1225–1274). He towers above all the Latin medieval theologians, and it is hard to overestimate just how extensive his influence has been on both Roman Catholic and Protestant thought.[42] Over the years a consensus view has built up that while Aquinas believed in the resurrection it was not central to his thinking; however, this view is open to question. The rereading of Aquinas's books by Roman Catholic theologians such as David Stanley has inspired their emphasis on the role of Jesus's resurrection in redemption.[43] Other thinkers have pointed to "the pervasive character of the resurrection" in Aquinas's writings.[44]

Aquinas emphasized the unity of the cross and resurrection by viewing them as a seamless work of God's actions. At the cross Jesus humbly obeyed God the Father, and the resurrection was God's vindication, exaltation, and reward for Jesus having accepted such a humbling event. Aquinas insisted that Jesus's resurrection was physical and not noncorporeal:

> St. Paul believed in a bodily resurrection . . . to deny this, and to affirm a purely spiritual resurrection is against the Christian Faith.[45]

Women and the Resurrection

Women in the medieval and Renaissance eras wrote works of spiritual devotion that expressed love for God by knowing Christ's suffering through the human body.[46] Carolyn Bynum indicates that what is conceptually standing behind this corpus of literature is the idea of the resurrection of the body.[47] However, women had other things to say about the resurrection. Hildegard of Bingen (1098–1179) was the abbess of a Benedictine convent who had visionary experiences concerning biblical revelation. She spent ten years writing *Scivias* (*Know-the-Ways*), which comprised a description of her visions, commentary on their meaning, and thirty-six painted images representing what she had seen. In it she explained that Jesus spent three days in the grave to confirm the three persons of the Godhead and that the Father resurrected him: "and through a great blessing the way to truth was now revealed to humankind, who had been led out of death into life."[48]

You may not have heard of Christine de Pizan (1363–1434), but she was Europe's first professional female writer. She composed hundreds of ballads and poems in French, including "The Tale of Joan of Arc." She also wrote a letter in the form of a sermon called "The Epistle of the Prison of Human Life," which connected Christ's resurrection to the hope of our resurrection. She wrote it for the women who had lost loved ones at the Battle of Agincourt (1415). She consoled her readers by describing the gift of the incorruptible resurrected body for those who die in Christ. While she emphasized that those who are resurrected will know, see, and worship the holy Trinity, she also described family reunions in heaven. Her message reassured women that they would be reunited with their dead husbands and sons.[49]

From time to time various theologians pondered whether women would be resurrected, and if so would they resemble males or be genderless. This springs from reading Jesus's rebuke of the Sadducees where he said that in heaven men and women do not marry and are like the angels.[50] The question of sexual differentiation in the resurrection surfaced as an issue from early church fathers in the second century. In colonial America Puritan theology seemed to emphasize a masculine shape to heaven as can be seen in remarks in the periodical the *British Apollo*: "Is there now, or will there be at the resurrection, any females in Heaven? . . . Since there seems to be no need of them."[51] In that cultural and doctrinal milieu came the Salem witch trials of 1692 where fourteen women were hanged for the crime of witchcraft.

Resurrection in Eastern Orthodoxy

Some Christians have the impression that Roman Catholic and Protestant churches strongly emphasize the crucifixion while the Eastern Orthodox churches have a more balanced view of the cross and resurrection. Timothy Ware pours cold water on this:

> The resurrection . . . fills the whole life of the Orthodox church. . . . Yet it would be wrong to think of Orthodoxy simply as the cult of Christ's divine glory, of His Transfiguration and Resurrection, and nothing more. . . . Representations of the Crucifixion are no less prominent in Orthodox than in non-Orthodox churches, while the veneration of the Cross is more developed in Byzantine than in Latin worship.[52]

Ware reminds us that historically the church at its best has been both/and regarding cross and resurrection. For those outside Eastern Orthodoxy he states: "One must therefore reject as misleading the common assertion that the east concentrates on the Risen Christ, the west on Christ crucified."[53]

In chapter 3 we noted how Gregory Palamas bore witness to the resurrection among Muslims. Before Palamas many other Eastern Orthodox monks, theologians, and church fathers expounded theologies of resurrection. One of the distinctive theological emphases that Eastern Orthodoxy has contributed to our understanding of resurrection is what is called "theosis" or deification. Theosis refers to the final goal of redeemed humanity being corporate partakers in the divine life. The idea sprang from reflecting on various New Testament passages such as 2 Peter 1:4, "Thus he has given us, through these things, his precious and very great promises, so that through them you may escape from the corruption that is in the world because of lust, and may become participants of the divine nature."

Maximus the Confessor (ca. 580–662) is the primary voice about theosis.[54] He understood that through the creation human beings bear the *imago Dei* and that Jesus's high priestly prayer (John 17:21) indicates that we will be in union with the triune God. Since Jesus rose from the dead those who are united to him start participating in the effects of theosis here and now, but full "deification" occurs in the resurrection from the dead. When our mortal bodies receive immortality they will be like Christ's resurrected body, and that involves partaking of his glory. The doctrine of our deification does not involve either pantheism (all is God) or polytheism (there are many gods). Both positions are rejected by Eastern Orthodoxy. When we talked about Gregory Palamas's apophatic theology we pointed out that the distinction is made between God's essence and energies. In theosis union with God means union with God's energies and not with God's essence. Humans will remain distinct from God.

Mystic Monks in Dialogue with Muslims

Christian Arab theologians were the earliest apologists to address Muslims, and they put the resurrection on the dialogue agenda.[55]

Theodore Abū Qurrah

During the eighth and early ninth century Theodore Abū Qurrah (ca. 750–825) flourished as an Arabic-speaking bishop in Haran, which is the same place where Abraham and his family once lived (Gen. 11:31; 27:43; 28:10). When Abū Qurrah was alive Haran was under Islamic rule and he composed books addressing Muslim thought. He argued in his book *On Discerning the True Religion* that among many reasoned proofs that demonstrate the truth of Christianity a very strong case can be made by appealing to biblical miracles. Miracles might justify the claims of religions like Judaism, Christianity, and Islam. Abū Qurrah wanted to show that Christ performed greater miracles than anyone else, and so to underscore the point he contrasted those performed by Moses and Christ, emphasizing that Jesus died and rose again.[56] He also considered the significance of the general resurrection of the dead.[57]

'Ammār al-Basrî

'Ammār al-Basrî (ca. 800–850) was a theologian and apologist in the Assyrian Church of the East (Nestorian). He wrote two works in response to questions that arose from Christians encountering Muslim apologists: *The Book of Proof* and *The Book of Questions and Answers*. 'Ammār al-Basrî examined three principal topics: the incarnation, the integrity of the Gospels, and the resurrection. He found that it was important to explain to Muslims why the incarnation of Christ was necessary and to reply to claims that the Gospel accounts were untrustworthy.[58] 'Ammār al-Basrî saw Muslims' belief in a general resurrection of humanity as a valuable entry point for talking about Jesus's death and resurrection. If one is already open to the general resurrection, he believed, then it should be feasible to consider the case for Jesus's resurrection as the firstfruits.

Celtic Saints and Resurrection

The beginning of the Celtic churches is popularly linked to St. Patrick in the fourth century.[59] He confessed that Jesus conquered death and that "beyond any doubt on that day we shall rise again."[60] Adomnán (ca. 628–704) talked about the resurrection in his biography of St. Columba, the founder of the monastery at Iona. Adomnán briefly recounts how St. Columba prayed for a dead child of a Pictish family who was revived and then compared this miracle to those in the ministries of Elijah, Elisha, Peter, Paul, and John.[61] Adomnán also wrote *The Holy Places*, in which he tried to resolve discrepancies in the Gospel accounts of Jesus's burial and resurrection.[62]

On the Miracles of Holy Scripture (*De mirabilibus Sacrae Scripturae*) is an anonymous Irish apologetic, exegetical, and monastic text. It is ascribed to an Irish thinker with the pseudonym Augustinus Hibernicus (or Augustine Eriugena), and later medieval readers mistakenly thought that St. Augustine of Hippo had written it. The book is dated with considerable certainty to AD 655. The writer's position is later echoed in C. S. Lewis's book on miracles. The argument is that all miracles are in harmony with the creation and that therefore the resurrection "fits" into the natural order of things. God always used the existing properties of the creation to produce a marvel. Miracles, therefore, do not contradict the natural order but involve God using the stuff of nature to work a wonder. There is a rational basis in the creation for miracles, including the resurrection.

Augustinus Hibernicus took the view that Jesus was clearly seen in a material yet glorified body by the apostles who witnessed his appearances after the crucifixion. He differentiated Jesus's resurrection body from those of Jairus's daughter, Lazarus, and Eutychus, who were resuscitated from the dead. He argued that they had only been resuscitated back in their mortal material form. Lazarus (and others) had experienced something like death (*similitudo mortis*) but which was not a permanent kind of death because we are appointed to die once and then face judgment. Lazarus came back from the grave in the "likeness of resurrection" (*similitudo resurrectionis*) but not as a partaker "of true resurrection" (*ipsa resurrectio*).[63] The true resurrection of humanity is reserved for the end of days, which is why Lazarus only underwent resuscitation.

Resurrection and Heresy

The word *heresy* may conjure unpleasant images of conflict. But as Harold O. J. Brown explains, heresies served an important function in pushing the Christian church to develop correct doctrine:

With all possible tolerance of and respect for those who are attracted to what we call "heresy," it is important to recognize that the very life of Christianity in general as well as the salvation of individual Christians depends on at least a substantial measure of right doctrine, and where right doctrine exists, contrary views must be heresies.[64]

In the early church fathers' writings we find statements of the Rule of Faith and baptismal-liturgical confessions that summarize Christian teachings. Ignatius of Antioch (AD 107), Irenaeus (AD 180), and Tertullian (AD 200) each state in outline form what has been handed on by the apostles. In the early confessions of faith known as the Apostles' Creed, Nicene Creed, and Athanasian Creed belief in Christ's resurrection and in the resurrection of the flesh are heralded.[65] First- and second-century heresies are what compelled Christians to work on matters of self-definition in theology, which led to the writing of these creeds, and that meant the resurrection was proclaimed and defended.[66]

Docetism

In the late first century and early second century there were internal doctrinal challenges concerning the humanity of Jesus. One debate was prompted by Docetist teachers who insisted that Jesus was not truly human and argued that there was only a symbolic nonphysical resurrection. Docetists viewed matter and spirit as opposites that cannot coexist, and saw the physical body as inferior to the spirit. Kevin Madigan and Jon Levenson comment:

> Docetic Christians usually assumed that the heavenly Christ merely inhabited or used the body of the man Jesus, or that his flesh was simply an optical illusion. In either case, they could not imagine that a heavenly emissary could truly have united himself to flesh.[67]

Both Ignatius of Antioch and Polycarp were second-century martyrs who replied to the Docetists by arguing that the apostles bore witness to a material, physical resurrection. Ignatius of Antioch wrote to the church at Tralles in Asia Minor: "He was also verily raised up again from the dead, for His Father raised him; and in Jesus Christ will His Father similarly raise us who believe in Him."[68] Ignatius understood the implications for the resurrection if we deny Jesus's true humanity. The bodily resurrection of Jesus is the basis on which we will be similarly raised from the dead. If Jesus's resurrection was not bodily in form, and if he was not truly human, then our hope of resurrection is void.[69] Ignatius taught there is continuity in identity between our earthly body and our future resurrected body.

Polycarp (ca. 70–155) was Bishop of Smyrna and had known the apostle John. Polycarp wrote to the church at Philippi emphasizing Jesus's bodily resurrection.[70] He was tackling "the rejection of a real resurrection by Doce-tists and gnostics, who, of course, refused to believe that material flesh could live on the eternal plane."[71]

Gnosticism

In different periods of church history there have been gnostic teachers. The fortunes of gnosticism, though, have ebbed and flowed in history as various gnostic groups have emerged, flourished, and then decayed or disappeared altogether. Gnosticism is an ancient view that has been reimagined by many people today who find selective aspects of it very attractive.[72] Glancing back at the early church may help us to understand both the ancient and modern versions of gnosticism. The term *gnostic* comes from the Greek word for knowledge and refers to a dualistic worldview that understood the created world as an inferior plane like a prison for fallen spirits that must be escaped for the higher realm of spirit.[73] Gnosticism was not a unified movement; rather there were various early schools of thought inspired by teachers like Basilides, Carpocrates, and Valentinus. In the Middle Ages the Cathars and Bogomils represented another form of gnosticism. Gnostic groups in early church history were elitist as they only taught a closed circle of membership. Some groups were ascetic and did not regard women very highly, while others had libertine attitudes towards sexual behavior.

Anyone who takes urban mission seriously today must become conversant with the new hybrid gnosticism, as well as its ancient fountainhead. The basic problem is that gnosticism denies the spiritual significance of the body. New gnostic ideas flourish on the Internet where websites provide English transla-tions of ancient gnostic texts.[74] Gnostic thought also appears in popular culture through Hollywood films like *The Matrix*; *Stigmata*, which drew positive attention to the gnostic *Gospel of Thomas*;[75] and *The Da Vinci Code*, which has characters who interact with gnostic ideas.

EARLY GNOSTIC TEXTS ON RESURRECTION

There are many sayings attributed to Jesus in gnostic texts, some of which are paralleled in the canonical Gospels, like an alternative version of the par-able of the sower that is found in *The Gospel of Thomas*.[76] The early church, however, rejected *The Gospel of Thomas* and other gnostic works.[77] Here are three snippets from early gnostic texts, two of which are about the resurrection:

1. The *Gospel of Philip* states, "Those who say they will die first and then rise are in error. If they do not receive the resurrection while they live, when they die they will receive nothing."[78] The *Gospel of Philip* has no room for a future bodily resurrection from the dead but reinterprets it as a mere metaphor for baptism.

2. *The Treatise on the Resurrection* propounded the view that the body (or flesh) of this realm will be discarded, and that our destiny involves escaping the creation.[79] As regards the resurrection it is "imagined as a present experience, a 'disclosure,' or moment of enlightenment" that only an elite few could experience, so the message of the *Treatise* is "there was emphatically no future, bodily dimension involved."[80]

3. In *The Gospel of Thomas* Jesus teaches that he will guide Mary and make her male, "for every female who makes herself male will enter the domain of heaven."[81]

Irenaeus and Tertullian

Two theologians who defended the resurrection in response to the gnostics were Irenaeus and Tertullian. Irenaeus flourished in the late second century as the Bishop of Lyons in Gaul but as a child was acquainted with Polycarp. Irenaeus wrote *Against Heresies*, in which he defended both Jesus's bodily resurrection and ours against the Valentinians. He argued that Jesus's resurrection was a fulfillment of Jesus' own prophecy regarding the destruction of the temple (John 2:19) and the sign of Jonah (Matt. 12:40). It also fulfills the Passover because Jesus is the sacrificial lamb who rises victorious from the grave. Irenaeus cited Paul's Epistles to show that the whole person in body and soul will be saved and transformed. The resurrection ensures that both death and Satan are defeated and that there will be a final divine judgment. It was an event in history. The general resurrection is taught in John's Apocalypse and by the prophets Isaiah and Ezekiel.[82]

Understandably, Irenaeus had no sympathy for gnostic teachings, and *Against Heresies* had the rhetorical goal of persuading readers to repudiate gnosticism. J. K. S. Reid says that Irenaeus's rhetorical work placed him "in the first rank of apologists" and that he grasped "the essential historicity of the Christian faith" as "a theological principle of supreme importance" and used that principle to expose "the essential weakness of the Gnostic versions of Christianity."[83]

Tertullian was a theologian and apologist in North Africa at the turn of the third century.[84] In his many writings he challenged pagan philosophy, the Docetists, gnostics, and Marcionites, and in a specific book defended the doctrine of the resurrection of the flesh.[85] He rejected Plato's idea that humans have an immortal preexistent soul. Instead he held to a view known as Traducianism: each individual receives their soul (which is ultimately created by God) in the womb from their parents. He held that our physical body and soul, which separate at death, are reunited in the general resurrection.

Reflections on Gnosticism

A resurrection way of life must be capable of confronting the grueling realities of a broken world, and Jesus's death and resurrection do just that. The bodily resurrection of the dead is gender-inclusive: both women and men are raised holistically. The cosmic effect of the resurrection culminates in a new earth and a new heaven. Any workable spiritual truth must be accessible and include the body, women, and creation. From our standpoint we can ask: If the ancient gnostics had really been "on the money" then perhaps their message would have triumphed socially and theologically long before the Emperor Constantine granted official recognition to orthodox Christianity.[86]

Souls and Bodies

Throughout church history there has been debate over the soul and body as it relates to the resurrection. If you survey biblical commentaries discussing the resurrection you will discover that opinions differ over the meaning of the Greek word *sōma* (translated as body) that is used in 1 Corinthians 15.[87] Robert Gundry in his technical study of the word has shown how some theologians interpret Paul's use of the word *sōma* in a holistic sense (the whole person encompassing body and soul), while others understand it in a dualistic sense (where body and soul are separate aspects of humans).[88] More recently, Joel Green and Nancey Murphy have tried to reimagine a holistic view that finds affinities between Scripture and contemporary understandings of personhood, the soul, and eschatology.[89]

People's beliefs about souls and bodies have led to various dogmas that concentrate on what occurs between the time we die and the judgment at the general resurrection. These include teachings about purgatory, soul-sleep, and the eternal destiny of the unrighteous: Are they punished forever or annihilated? These matters all relate back to doctrines of salvation, divine judgment, and the resurrection of the dead.[90] We will not explore those debates here, but we will describe the early church debates about the separation of the soul from the body and how that relates to the general resurrection.

There is a different kind of debate that has also been of concern to scholars in modern times, one that centers specifically on the nature of Jesus's resurrected body. A quarrel broke out among North American evangelicals in the late 1980s and early 1990s over the meaning of *sōma* as related to Jesus's resurrection.[91] It centered on what Paul meant by the "spiritual body" in 1 Corinthians 15. In *Raised Immortal* Murray Harris placed great emphasis on the transformative qualities of Jesus's resurrection body: the spiritual body is an immortal glorified body fit for eternity. The capacities that Jesus manifested—like appearing/disappearing on the Emmaus road and in the upper room—had marked differences from his preresurrection body. Harris accented the discontinuities between the pre- and postresurrection qualities of Jesus's body.[92]

Norman Geisler was disturbed by Harris's book and thought he was denying the physicality and materiality of Jesus's resurrection body. Geisler felt there were uncanny parallels between Harris's position on a spiritual body and that of Jehovah's Witnesses. Geisler insisted on emphasizing the reanimation, identity, and continuity of Jesus's pre- and postresurrection body.[93] Harris replied to Geisler in *From Grave to Glory*, followed by a flurry of essays from supporters of both men.[94] Eventually the controversy died down but Geisler still disagrees with Harris.[95] The benefit of this controversy is that it reminds us that both perspectives need to be held in tension to avoid unbalanced views on the resurrection body.

Immortal Souls versus Resurrected Bodies

Let us now turn the discussion over to the early church debates on souls and bodies. Theologians do not live in a cultural vacuum. The early church faced the same challenge that we do today—to let Scripture govern their theology while they simultaneously expressed themselves in their culture. Our mortal body, the soul, and spiritual body in the general resurrection are topics the early church discussed a lot. The intellectual milieu was dominated by Hellenistic categories of thought, especially Plato's philosophy.[96] J. N. D. Kelly outlines Plato's stance on the soul:

> In his view the soul is an immaterial entity, immortal by nature; it exists prior to the body in which it is immured, and is destined to go on existing after the latter's extinction. . . . Soul for him was the supreme directive, organizing principle, and he believed in a World-Soul animating the material universe.[97]

Notice that in Plato's thought the human soul preexisted its incarnation on earth and was by its very nature already immortal. The concept of a preexisting immortal human soul is not found in Scripture. The doctrine of the creation disavows it. And because the resurrection includes the transformation of our flesh, theologians like Tertullian did not accept the Greek belief of the natural soul being immortal and living forever in a disembodied state. Jaroslav Pelikan remarks that it was a topic that drew early criticism from theologians and apologists:

> It was not only the story of the resurrection of Christ that drew the fire of pagan critics as a fable or the report of a hysterical woman, but the significance attached to the resurrection by Christian theology. Nowhere is that significance more unequivocally expressed than in the polemic of some Christian theologians against the pagan doctrine of the immortal soul.[98]

Athenagoras and Origen

Although a school of theologians doubted Plato, there were others like Athenagoras, Origen, and Gregory of Nyssa who were influenced by him. Athenagoras in the late second century wrote *De Resurrectione Mortuorum* (*On the*

Resurrection of the Dead) using the categories of Middle Platonic philosophy. He argued that alongside the doctrine of creation there had to be a doctrine of resurrection in order for God to fulfill the divine plan. He rebutted Platonic philosophical objections to the resurrection but then attempted to prove the resurrection through Platonist categories of thought. In his view the soul already possessed immortality but the body did not. The resurrection was needed so that at the end of time the immortal soul could be reunited with a body made immortal. His biblical exegesis on the soul was shaped by Platonist ideas.[99]

In third-century Egypt the theologian Origen (ca. 185–254) wrote extensively on the resurrection in four different works, but only fragmentary pieces have survived. In *Contra Celsum* (*Against Celsus*) he defended Christ's resurrection against the criticisms of the pagan Platonist philosopher Celsus. He showed great erudition in both his capacity to analyze the weaknesses of Celsus's arguments and in his efforts to demonstrate the truth of Christianity using Platonic thought.[100]

However, Origen developed some eccentric views about the soul and the resurrection. We have found that aspects of Origen's views are still embraced by some church leaders even today. We noted in chapter 7 that he adopted the Platonist idea of the soul preexisting in heaven. Origen reasoned that preexisting souls became neglectful of their adoration of God and thus fell away so that God created the world in which fallen souls could incarnate as humans and eventually be redeemed through Christ's death and resurrection. Origen's view on the preexistence of the soul was rejected by the Council of Constantinople (553). According to a later critic, Methodius of Olympus, Origen taught that the literal resurrection of the physical body was believed in by unlearned church-goers but that the doctrine had a deeper allegorical meaning.[101] Origen did not see the resurrection of the dead involving the present physical body but held to the resurrection of a spiritual body based on his reading of the seed analogy in 1 Corinthians 15. Origen also held to an eschatological universal salvation that allowed for the possible repentance of Satan.[102]

Origen generated deep feelings of loyalty and antipathy among his admirers and detractors. He was admired by the church historian Eusebius of Caesarea (ca. 265–339) and Gregory Thaumaturgus (ca. 213–270) but drew the ire of Jerome (ca. 345–419) and Epiphanius the Bishop of Salamis (ca. 315–403). In the fourth century the Eastern Orthodox father Gregory of Nyssa (ca. 330–395) developed a biblical-philosophical synthesis of the resurrection of the body and immortal soul, and also shared Origen's stance on universal salvation.[103] These three theologians synthesized the Platonic notion of an immortal soul with the resurrection of the body, and Pelikan notes their legacy: "The idea of the immortal and rational soul is part of the Greek inheritance in Christian doctrine."[104]

What we learn from all this is that faulty theology about ideas connected to the resurrection can find a home among even the most astute followers of Christ. Origen was trying to grapple with apologetic issues of his day in relation to

Platonic thought, and for all his creative genius in contextualization he crossed the line into speculative and unhelpful theology. This is the ever-present problem for those of us who are committed to contextualization.

Theological Images

We have just explored how the early church was embroiled in controversies connected with the resurrection. However, the early church's story also includes positive emphases about the resurrection. The early church fathers used some very helpful images and themes in explaining the theology of resurrection. We will illustrate matters by pointing to four examples.

Nature Images

In 1 Corinthians 15:36–38 Paul referred to the resurrection body by using the metaphor of seeds buried in soil from which new life springs. One of the earliest writers outside the New Testament to use seed imagery was Clement of Rome. He wrote to the church in Corinth and reminded them that the seed shrivels and decays but "the power of the Lord's providence raises it from decay."[105] He emphasized that Jesus was the firstfruits of the resurrection and that the natural world is bursting with analogies.[106] Clement understood that the general resurrection encompassed humanity and the creation:

> The metaphors for resurrection in this early literature are naturalistic images that stress return or repetition: the cycle of the seasons, the flowering of trees and shrubs, the coming of dawn after darkness, the fertility of seeds. . . . The point of the metaphors is to emphasize God's power and the goodness of the creation. If the Lord can bring spring after winter . . . he can bring back men and women who sleep in the grave.[107]

Fulfillment of Passover

In both John's Gospel and Paul's first Epistle to the Corinthians Jesus is likened to the sacrificial lamb of the Passover meal (John 19:36; cf. Exod. 12:46; 1 Cor. 5:7). The early church fathers picked up the Greek word for Passover (*Pascha*, hence the Paschal feast) and emphasized a fulfillment theme: Jesus fulfilled the Passover by both the cross and resurrection. In his death he was like the sacrificial lamb and his rising from the dead brought salvation just like God's leading Israel into salvation in the Exodus from their deathlike state of enslavement in Egypt. Those who interpreted Jesus's death and resurrection via the Passover theme include Irenaeus, Clement of Alexandria, Eusebius of Caesarea, Gregory of Nazianzus, Tertullian, Lactantius, Athanasius, and Augustine of Hippo.[108]

Some Christians in the eastern part of the Roman Empire advocated the Passover theme but took it a step further. Melito was a second-century bishop of Sardis who believed that Easter should be celebrated on the day of Passover. In his understanding the cross and resurrection was a unified and single event. Instead of holding services on Good Friday and Easter Sunday, Melito's congregation held a vigil on the day of Passover until midnight and then celebrated the resurrection in their liturgy.[109]

Victory over Death and Satan

The early church emphasized Christ as the victor (*Christus Victor*) over death and Satan. God as the author of life sent his champion Christ to defeat death. At the back of this image there stands a strong theme carried throughout the Hebrew Scriptures concerning the resurrection: Yahweh the God of Israel is both the Creator of life and the victorious divine warrior over all cosmic foes including death. Jesus wielded divine power over the destructive forces in creation and in the lives of people. Donald Guthrie sums up the victory theme:

> The resurrection of Christ is viewed as the supreme display of divine power. It is the act by which the ceaseless round of death and corruption in human life has been checked. God has provided a way out of death into life, by raising his own Son from death to life.[110]

Resurrection and Christology

If you were to immerse yourself in the writings of the early theologians you would discover that there was more to be learned than just what we have discussed above about controversies over heresy, the topics of body and soul, and theological themes. In a nutshell what they concluded about the resurrection reflected who they understood Jesus Christ to be. Some of the theological points they emphasized are:

- Jesus's resurrection fulfills what was a biblically prophesied event.
- Without the bodily resurrection of Jesus there would be no salvation.
- The resurrection is corporeal: it involves reuniting the body and soul, which are transformed, glorified, and made immortal.
- Jesus's resurrection signals the end of the reign of death, and because Jesus is the firstfruits humankind is assured of being resurrected.
- Jesus's life did not end with his hideous humiliation and suffering because in the resurrection he is victorious and defeats the greatest cosmic enemies: sin, death, and Satan.
- The resurrection signals the exaltation of Jesus Christ as he is enthroned and glorified.
- The resurrection ensures that there is a last judgment.[111]

Conclusion

We argue repeatedly in this book that the resurrection is the lynchpin of Christianity. As our survey in this chapter shows, throughout the history of the church, Christians have emphasized the resurrection's centrality to varying degrees. Studies on church history have not always focused on this point enough, but hopefully a number of the figures we have highlighted in this chapter can help prod us in the right direction. In the late nineteenth century Brooke Westcott made an incisive observation, which captures the essence of what we have surveyed:

> The message of the Resurrection sums up in one fact the teaching of the Gospel. It is the one central link between the seen and the unseen. We cannot allow our thoughts to be vague or undecided upon it with impunity. We must place it in the very front of our confession, with all that it includes, or we must be prepared to lay aside the Christian name. Even in its ethical aspect Christianity does not offer a system of morality, but a universal principle of morality which springs out of the Resurrection. The elements of dogma and morality are indeed inseparably united in the Resurrection of Christ; for the same fact which reveals the glory of the Lord, reveals at the same time the destiny of man and the permanence of all that goes to make up the fullness of life. If the Resurrection be not true, the basis of Christian morality, no less than the basis of Christian theology, is gone. The issue cannot be stated too broadly. We are not Christians unless we are clear in our confession on this point. To preach the fact of Resurrection was the first function of the Evangelists; to embody the doctrine of the Resurrection is the great office of the Church; to learn the meaning of the Resurrection is the task of not one age only, but of all.[112]

Spiritual Audit

1. What is your understanding of Paul's teaching about the spiritual body and general resurrection?

2. Can you trace your theological pedigree and find out which theologian's thoughts have shaped your understanding of Jesus's resurrection and the general resurrection?

3. Why do you think work on the resurrection in church history has been piecemeal?

4. Apart from a quiz, in what meaningful ways can you help your church understand its theological heritage on the resurrection?

PART THREE

BACK
TO THE BIBLE

As the principle of death took its rise in one person and passed on in succession through the whole of human kind, in like manner the principle of the Resurrection-life extends from one person to the whole of humanity. . . . This, then, is the mystery of God's plan with regard to His death and His resurrection from the dead.

Gregory of Nyssa[1]

11

The New Testament

The concern of the primitive Christian preaching was not with the continued existence of Jesus after death in a bodiless abstraction of soul, but with witnessing to the resurrection as a new reality embracing also bodily existence.

Walter Künneth[1]

To eliminate the bodily resurrection of Christ from the Christian message is to damage all of New Testament theology.

Bernard Ramm[2]

"The resurrection is the first article of the Christian faith and the demonstration of all the rest," Paul Beasley-Murray boldly declares.[3] We should not be surprised, then, that throughout the New Testament, "the affirmation of Jesus as Lord . . . arose from the resurrection."[4] The emphasis on the resurrection as the chief article of faith and the proclamation of Jesus as Lord is most evident in the book of Acts. It is the story of the early church living in the power of the risen Christ's Spirit. We drew attention to this in chapter 1 with figure 1.1 on the centrality of the resurrection in Acts. Did Peter and Paul get it wrong? Did the early church get it wrong? Did they change their minds? Is Acts passé? Or does the proclamation of the early church clearly show that the resurrection is to be Christianity's lynchpin?

Acts

We can learn a great deal by reading through Acts chapters 1 and 2 and meditating on the question, what is the central theme? The book begins with Jesus presenting himself alive and giving instruction to the disciples that focuses on the new day that the resurrection brings with the outpouring of his Spirit and his promised eventual return. The first chapter of Acts also includes the disciples' tough decision about who would replace Judas Iscariot. The one selected had to have been a follower throughout Jesus's ministry and a witness of the resurrection.

The first sermon delivered at Pentecost refers to the crucifixion as part of God's plan, but Peter "has no developed theology of the cross" here.[5] However, as Beasley-Murray remarks:

> On the day of Pentecost Peter was concerned above all to witness to the fact that God had raised Jesus to life (2:32). What was true then must be true of our witness today. When we speak to non-Christians about Jesus, we must be sure to speak about his resurrection. For the resurrection is the great miracle of the Christian faith; it is the heart of the gospel. Without the resurrection of Jesus his life and death have no meaning.[6]

The climax of the sermon is 2:32–36 where Peter declares that God raised Jesus up and that therefore he is exalted at the right hand of God and can pour out the Spirit. Peter's climactic point is about the fruit of the resurrection and the certainty it brings that the crucified Jesus is both Lord and Messiah. We will outline here the thumbprints of a theology of the resurrection.

This first sermon in Acts provides a pattern for what follows in further speeches about the centrality of Jesus's resurrection. The resurrection is established by the twofold method of fulfilled prophecy and the eyewitness testimony of the apostles. Peter draws on David's Psalm 16:8–11 as one proof: "For you will not abandon my soul to Hades, or let your Holy One experience corruption" (Acts 2:27). Peter is clearly stating that the psalmist who was praising God for his own protection from death was also foreshadowing the one to come who would be raised to glory.

We would do well to reflect in our day on whether this twofold method of presenting the resurrection appears in contemporary proclamation and teaching. How many sermons have you heard that take up both the eyewitnesses and the background Old Testament passages to support the validity of the Easter miracle?

Allison Trites says that this important twofold testimony is fresh evidence that serves to re-open the trial of Jesus. By way of rhetorical persuasion Acts shows that the trial and execution of Christ was not just a controversy but the necessary gateway to his vindication in the resurrection. Trites points out that the twofold testimony is no accident, as it intentionally meets the Old Testament stipulation that there be twofold witnesses (Deut. 19:15).[7]

Acts 17

Acts 17 is often regarded as the primary example of the church in mission. So let us explore how well this passage corresponds with Peter's preaching in the first sermon and the first days of the early church.

> Then Paul stood in front of the Areopagus and said, "Athenians, I see how extremely religious you are in every way. For as I went through the city and looked carefully at the objects of your worship, I found among them an altar with the inscription, 'To an unknown god.' What therefore you worship as unknown, this I proclaim to you. The God who made the world and everything in it, he who is Lord of heaven and earth, does not live in shrines made by human hands, nor is he served by human hands, as though he needed anything, since he himself gives to all mortals life and breath and all things. From one ancestor he made all nations to inhabit the whole earth, and he allotted the times of their existence and the boundaries of the places where they would live, so that they would search for God and perhaps grope for him and find him—though indeed he is not far from each one of us. For 'In him we live and move and have our being'; as even some of your own poets have said, 'For we too are his offspring.' Since we are God's offspring, we ought not to think that the deity is like gold, or silver, or stone, an image formed by the art and imagination of mortals. While God has overlooked the times of human ignorance, now he commands all people everywhere to repent, because he has fixed a day on which he will have the world judged in righteousness by a man whom he has appointed, and of this he has given assurance to all by raising him from the dead."
>
> When they heard of the resurrection of the dead, some scoffed but others said, "We will hear you again about this." (17:22–32)

There are three things to be gleaned from the Areopagus speech about the resurrection:

1. The speech culminates with Jesus's resurrection from the dead.
2. It also refers to the general resurrection of the dead.
3. It provides a creative illustration of how one may introduce the resurrection in proclamation with a biblically illiterate audience.

First, Paul clearly announces Jesus's resurrection from the dead. Although this is a condensed version of Paul's sermon, Luke concludes with both the fact of the resurrection and a theological point about the resurrection—that Jesus is coming as the judge. The speech makes no mention of the cross although clearly it is implied by the emphasis on Jesus's resurrection from the dead. In the prelude to the speech we discover that Paul had already been to the synagogue to speak to Jews and God-fearers about Jesus and then turned attention to the marketplace, where he also spoke about Jesus and the resurrection (v. 18). This aroused the curiosity of the Athenians and they invited him to deliver a formal speech.

Paul's mention of the general resurrection of the dead may not seem immediately apparent. Readers often assume that those who scoffed at Paul's speech must have been bemused by the reference to Jesus's personal resurrection from the dead, but as Dag Øistein Endsjø notes, via their myths the Greeks were already accustomed to the idea of a deity coming back from the dead. Endsjø argues that Paul's listeners were more likely scoffing at the idea that all human beings could experience a resurrection. One piece of pre-Christian evidence to sustain this understanding is a remark attributed to the god Apollo when the Areopagus council itself was established: "Once a man dies and the earth drinks his blood, there is no resurrection."[8] It seems that the reference to "the resurrection of the dead" (v. 32) is a clue that Paul spoke about both Jesus rising from the dead and about the general resurrection of humanity. The fact that Paul said Jesus will be judging the world lends further weight to this. A theological point about eschatology emerges here: humanity will be raised from the dead to face the resurrected Jesus in judgment.[9]

The final point we draw from this passage relates to our discussion in chapter 3. We learn from Acts 17 how Paul talked to two different audiences—first, to those who were familiar with the Old Testament. When Paul went to the synagogue (17:17), he argued with Jews and God-fearers about Jesus. Although this passage does not specifically mention the Scripture, we do know from previous episodes that when Paul entered the synagogue he used the Law and the Prophets to demonstrate that Christ is the resurrected Messiah (Acts 13). As in the Pentecost sermon he said that Jesus's resurrection is the fulfillment of prophecy and that there were witnesses (13:29–35). Paul emphasized that "he whom God raised up experienced no corruption," and this points out that the theology of the cross is inextricably woven up in the theology of the resurrection (13:37).

The second group Paul approached were gentiles who had not read the Bible. He addressed them by starting with what was universally common in human experiences in natural theology. He corrected their misperceptions that God was contained in a temple and in idols. The framework Paul presented involved finding common ground via general revelation and providing a context that permitted him to declare the Christ-event. He made a link to their culture by citing appropriate passages from the Greek poets to affirm the creation and our relationship to the divine.

Paul followed the biblical plotline when preaching to Jews, and the same plotline comes through natural theology and shaped his interaction with those who did not know the Bible. Paul's speech used the framework of the creation (17:24–27), then made allusions to the Stoic philosophers (v. 28), and finally led into the resurrection of Christ (v. 31) and the general resurrection (v. 32). He took his audience from what they already knew in their own culture and connected them to the resurrection. Some Athenians who listened to Paul were skeptics, while others were open to what he said about resurrection (vv. 32, 34).[10]

ACTS 17: ATTRACTIONAL VERSUS MISSIONAL

How are we to proclaim good news and make disciples? Today the debate about methods for evangelism divides into two perspectives: Some insist that believers are missionaries who will make disciples by proclaiming good news in the community. Others place great emphasis on attracting non-Christians to hear the gospel preached from the pulpit.

Acts 17 provides illustrations of both approaches as Paul proclaims the resurrection. Traditional church gatherings generally attract individuals or families who hover around the church's fringes and have some cultural attachment to it but lack a living faith. The model that emphasizes attracting people is illustrated by Paul's approach in the synagogue. The listeners heard that Jesus had risen through the twofold witness of fulfilled prophecy (those in the synagogue were assumed to be familiar with the Old Testament) and reliable eyewitnesses.

The missional approach, though, is essential for interacting with the majority of people today who live outside the church culture. Paul models through his actions how he interacted with those who did not know the biblical plotline and had no association with a local church. He did not advertise to the gentiles that they could attend the synagogue to hear a sermon series, but instead engaged in dialogue with them by seeking points of contact with the culture. He went into the marketplace, and he quoted their literature. He offers us a transferable model for how we may do likewise today. We should understand our culture by discovering those elements in it that are highly esteemed and recognizing its primary stories. Throughout this book we have given plenty of examples of points of contact specifically connected to the resurrection.

Perhaps the starkest contrast between Paul's time and ours is that he was provoked and deeply distressed to see that Athens was a city filled with idols (17:16). How quiescent we are today when facing a different set of "idols" in the city! Our debates over attraction versus mission consume much of the church's energies, but we lack Paul's distress over idols and deemphasize the theology of the resurrection.

Other Speeches in Acts

All the other sermons and speeches in Acts have references to the resurrection, and the vast majority mention the cross if not the atonement (3:12–26; 4:8–12; 5:29–32; 7:52–56; 10:34–43; 13:16–41; 17:2–3; 24:10–25; 26:2–29). The sermons have a theology of the resurrection that is often linked to the vindication of Jesus at Calvary. In light of Acts it is staggering that today we focus on the cross often to the exclusion of the resurrection. A colleague suggested that our preaching has focused on a human-centered view of the gospel, that we are drawn to songs and teaching of the cross because of our need for forgiveness. However a God-centered macrocosm highlights the need for forgiveness by placing the cross onto a wider tapestry of God's creative action.

Theology of Resurrection Sound Bites in Acts

The book of Acts presents twelve theological foundations for the resurrection concerning the nature of Christ, personal transformation and empowerment, and mission:

- Fulfillment of prophecy (2:29–32)
- Vindication of deity claims (4:8–12; 13:30–37)
- Victor over death (Acts 9:36–41; 20:9–12)
- Universal judgment (17:31)
- Promised messianic kingship/author of life (2:34–36; 3:13; 10:36)
- Conversion and transformation (9:1–31)
- Forgiveness of sin/salvation in the resurrected one (4:8–12; 10:34–43; 13:38)
- General resurrection of the dead (Acts 17:32; 23:6–9; 24:15, 21); Paul in these passages seeks to divide and conquer between the Sadducees (who denied any resurrection) and Pharisees, and so says he is on trial for the resurrection of the dead.
- Empowerment and healing (lame man, Acts 3:6; Aeneas, 9:32–35)
- Human dignity of all (Acts 10:34–35, 42–43)
- Bestowal of the Spirit (2:31–33)
- Mission of the church (1:8; 10:39–42)

Is It Primitive?

At the start of the chapter we cited Walter Künneth's remarks that refer to the "primitive Christian preaching." Some people seem to think that the speeches of Acts are of a lower order in theology.[11] This came home to us recently when a senior minister of a church rang and expressed his concern that our seminary students are basing their evangelistic messages on the "primitive" preaching rather than on the higher order of material found in the Epistles. His point was that we should disregard this resurrection emphasis and refocus solely on the cross. The notion of Acts being "primitive" is sometimes a misunderstanding. Acts does *not* contain all doctrinal matters; for instance, the incarnation is scarcely mentioned. What Acts does do, though, is show us the basic "primitive" message on which we enter into faith, which must then through discipleship be built upon. It is in the Epistles that Paul and the other apostles build upon the foundation of the resurrection message to explain the cross and atonement, the incarnation, and so on.

C. H. Dodd brings clarity to this when he points out that the Acts sermons represent the "first word" to the Jewish and gentile seekers, and the Epistles the "second word" to a believing church.[12] What we have indicated throughout this book is that in many ways today's churches have tended to hurry over the basic element of the resurrection in the quest to reach the "meat" of theology. However, it is clear from Paul, for example, that the "meat" makes little sense unless one clearly has the central foundation of the resurrection.

How do we know what is the lynchpin of any worldview? Is it by listening to what people write some two thousand years afterwards, or by listening to those who were closest to the original source, in this case Jesus? We challenge anybody to read Acts and not find the resurrection at the heart of its message.

Rhetorical Gospels

One of the defining characteristics of the canonical Gospels and Acts is that these books have a rhetorical quality to them. That is, these books are composed with a strong emphasis on persuading readers to reach a conviction about Jesus and embrace the transforming way of life that comes from being his follower. Contemporary scholars have noted that the rhetorical element is most evident in the Gospels and Acts, where the story of Jesus centers on the resurrection.

In Luke-Acts the material is formally addressed to Theophilus (Luke 1:1–4; Acts 1:1), who may very well have been a Roman official involved in assessing the charges laid against Paul in his trial in Rome. Whether Theophilus played that role or not, it is evident that much of the material presented is slanted towards persuading readers. Beyond the general rhetorical quality of Luke-Acts's genre we also see characters like Paul who are familiar with rhetoric. In chapters 24–26 Paul not only appeals to Roman rules of evidence (24:19–20) but his two speeches before the Roman authorities are clearly based on Roman legal/rhetorical custom. They contain four or five standard components with the defense answering accusations.[13]

Others have noted that John's Gospel carries forward its message in what rhetorically invokes the imagery of a legal trial. Andrew Lincoln says that the fourth Gospel "is a narrative that asserts the truth about God, Christ, and life is to be seen in terms of the metaphor of a cosmic lawsuit, and it displays this assertion by making its discourse and plot have Jesus on trial, a trial in which the other characters (and, by extension the readers) have to come to a verdict and are invited to become witnesses."[14] As we have seen, the original witnesses testify to the resurrection, taking us a step beyond merely showing a good man dying for a cause on a cross.

In a general sense the style of the four Gospels reflects the style of the biography genre.[15] We will not enter into debates here about the actual authorship of the Gospels; but it is worth noting that these books are most likely written by nonprofessional writers who were acquainted with and involved with eyewitness informants. This literary engagement is the stuff of rhetoric.[16] Historian Edwin Judge observes that "what they presented was news and evidence, and a burning conviction of its authenticity, that has no parallel in ancient literature except perhaps in the law courts and in the popular concern with portents."[17]

Richard Bauckham takes a slightly different line and says that at least "the ancient historians knew that first hand insider testimony gave access to truth that could not be had otherwise. Although not uncritical, they were willing to trust their eyewitness/informants for the sake of the unique access that they gave to the truth of the events. In this respect, we can see that the Gospels are much closer to the methods and aims of ancient historiography than they are to typical modern historiography."[18]

What differentiates the Gospels from the literature of the day is that the Gospels devote considerable attention to the passion narrative. The stories tell us what Jesus has gone through on our behalf in his arrest, trial, and execution. However, the Gospels do not end with Jesus's funeral. As with any good story the climactic events are reached but are then followed by the denouement, where everything is explained and resolved. In a Sherlock Holmes story it is not just the unmasking of the culprit but the final explanation that makes sense of all the clues that pointed to the culprit. The Gospels do indeed take us through the pathos of Jesus's suffering and death, but their denouement is the resurrection. In Acts this is the heartbeat of the sermons and speeches: the proclamation is about the denouement to the Jesus story—it is the resurrection that explains it all.

Ben Witherington insists that as readers we must go through the whole Gospel narrative, and we should not merely be struck by isolated elements in parables or speeches. The parables, speeches, and other incidents in Jesus's story lead us deliberately to the climax of the story and are filled with persuasive elements.[19] Readers are supposed to reach the end of the story and be persuaded by the resurrected one. Clifton Black reinforces the matter: "Judged, therefore, by the standards of classical oratory, Hellenistic Jewish and early Christian sermons exhibit highly nuanced and sophisticated forms of proof."[20]

Four Gospels

We regularly invite students to read the accounts of Jesus's resurrected appearances on the first day of the week in the four Gospels. It does not take very long to do. We ask students to see what the different accounts record and to take note of what look like gaps, omissions, or discrepancies. This is a critical exercise for a few reasons—one, because students need to explore the resurrection, and two, because skeptics like Dan Barker take up the differences in the accounts of Easter Sunday as reasons for discrediting Christianity. Students are often astonished to discover the great variations between the four Gospels' narratives on the first day of the week appearances. This opens up the opportunity for them to explore the question of harmonization.

John

We have chosen to start our Gospel survey with John because it contains the fullest narrative on the first-day resurrection appearances and because of John's strong emphasis on being a witness. We will not discuss the authorship, priority, or dating of the canonical Gospels. John 21:24 notes that the author speaks as one who is testifying to the Christ-story and knows that it is true. As Allison Trites and others point out, the Gospel concludes its case with the apostles and characters being witnesses: "like witnesses to the fact in Greek and Hebrew courts of law, they can give first-hand information on some disputed matter; in their case, they can attest to both the words and works of Jesus."[21]

John tells his story in his own way and puts the spotlight on various players such as Mary Magdalene and Thomas. He offers the most extensive report on what happened on the first Easter Sunday, presenting it in five steps:

1. Women to the tomb (20:1)—only Mary Magdalene is named but she reports to the disciples in the plural "we."
2. Women to the disciples (20:2).
3. Disciples to the tomb (20:3–10)—Peter and John run to the tomb.
4. Mary Magdalene returns to the tomb (20:11–17, and in Matthew the other women).
5. Mary Magdalene returns to the disciples (20:18, and in Matthew the other women).

Mark's Gospel has step 1 which points to step 2 (16:1–8). Matthew (28:1–10) has steps 1 and 2 (vv. 1–8) and steps 4 to 5 (vv. 9–10). Luke (24) has steps 1–3. John Wenham suggests that at step 4 Jesus first appears to Mary Magdalene and then to the other women, as Mary's encounter is the most detailed. As people go to and from the tomb there is rush and confusion, and the Gospels record a variety of different encounters taking place with speeches from angels and then Jesus. Wenham's *Easter Enigma* is one of the finest treatments on the issue of harmonizing the diverse accounts.[22] The accounts have variations that one would expect of truthful witnesses, with some featuring some key characters and others referring to other evidence.

They do not feel the need to tell the whole Johannine account. Each selects different elements to emphasize.

John's narrative is not confined to the first Easter Sunday, but includes the later encounter between Thomas and Jesus, and another encounter when some of the disciples were fishing. What is also unfolding in John's Gospel is a theology of the resurrection that extends beyond the events of the tomb and the witnesses' encounters.

The best starting point on the theology of the resurrection is in chapter 1. Derek Tidball points out that chapters 1 and 20 of the Gospel of John are strongly related to each other. In the first chapter themes surface about the incarnate Christ, and these themes find their completion in the resurrection narrative of chapter 20. We can compare the prologue of John's Gospel with the first chapter of Genesis. Both start with the emphasis on the "beginning." The Gospel's first chapter starts with a creation theme as the Logos/Word is described as the agent of creation. The first act of the creation in Genesis was to dispel the darkness and permit light to shine. In a similar way, the light shines in the testimony of the Gospel's prologue (1:4–5).

In John 20 when Mary visits the tomb she does it before sunrise, and the light of the resurrected Christ dispels the darkness. Mary goes to the tomb on the first day of the week, just as creation began on the first day. The mention of "first day" is not simply a time-marker but carries theological significance: Jesus re-creates all things by coming back to life on the first day of the week. The resurrection theology in John 20 is about a new creation, and it is a deliberate choice of words to refer to the event occurring on the "first day." In other settings Jesus's predicted death and resurrection are referred to as occurring on the third day. (We discussed another aspect of the creation theme and theological significance of Mary meeting Jesus in the garden in chapter 2.)

In John 1 Jesus is described as both life and life giver—"in him was life" (1:4)—and the theme of death being overcome by resurrection is implicit throughout John 20. The chapter finishes by stating that those who believe in the miraculous signs will have life in his name (20:31).

There are several other parallels between John 1 and John 20. One theme is that of recognition and rejection. The prologue introduces the point that the Word is not received by everyone and in fact is rejected by some. The resurrection narrative shows those who do not immediately recognize Jesus. Another parallel shows that resurrection is about incarnate mission: In John 1 John the Baptist is a man sent by God, while in John 20 Jesus in like manner sends out the disciples. John 1:12 proclaims the right to become God's children and John 20 reads as a family passage in which God is described by Jesus as "my father" and "your father" (v. 17). In John 1:14 there is a sense of seeing his glory, while in 20:28 Thomas sees the glorified risen Jesus. In John 1 the Holy Spirit is on the one who has come into the world, while in

John 20:17 Jesus is the one who breathes the Holy Spirit upon the disciples. Tidball sums up these parallels:

> In resonance with John 1, then, the resurrection narrative of John 20 presents the resurrection as the beginning of a new creation, the channel of eternal life, the dawning of irrepressible light, the ultimate pointer to recognizing God's messiah, the confirmation of the bestowal of sonship, the affirmation that the word was indeed made flesh, the ultimate basis for a perception that leads to belief, the pledge of Christ's continuing presence, the key to imparting of the Spirit, the testimony that seekers find and an invitation to turn to Christ, who has first turned to us.[23]

John Stott makes the helpful point that Jesus came into the world with a twofold promise, to forgive sins and to pour out the Spirit. That purpose is set out in John 1 where John the Baptist tells us the Lamb of God will take away the sin of the world and will baptize with the Holy Spirit (1:29–34). It is in the resurrection that both these promises are fulfilled.

Besides the bookend chapters, John's "new day" is pressed in chapter 2 where Jesus prophesies, "Destroy this temple, and in three days I will raise it up" (2:19). Just like in Acts, the twofold witness of Jesus's prophecy of resurrection and the witness to the resurrection is emphasized. Chapter 5 begins with the healing of a man who had been paralyzed for thirty-five years and culminates in Jesus's decree that he will raise up his followers on the last day (5:24–29). When Jesus explains in chapter 6 that he is the bread of life he goes on to say that those who see and believe in him will be resurrected on the last day (6:39–40). This alludes to Jesus being the firstfruits of the harvest that is to come.

John 11 is the Lazarus narrative, which carries forward the theme that Jesus is the resurrection and the life. While Lazarus's sister Martha's faith is in the general resurrection on the last day, Jesus introduces the miracle of raising of her brother by declaring himself to be both the resurrection and the life. He is the firstfruits. Lazarus is revivified from the dead. This miracle does not confer immortality on his body, but the revivification of Lazarus is clearly a tangible sign that Jesus is the life giver and that he is, like Yahweh, able to defeat the power of death. The miracle is not of the same order as what will happen to Jesus after his execution but foreshadows the climax of the book.

John's Gospel begins with the prologue and climaxes in the resurrection and at the halfway mark of the story is the bold declaration that Jesus is the resurrection and the life. Chapter 21 concludes with additional resurrection appearances and has the pastoral call to feed the sheep and the call to mission, "follow me." It connects the resurrection message to the here and now.

We sense that the richness of the theology of the resurrection in John's Gospel is unintentionally lost in the way we sometimes preach, study the

Bible, and evangelize. We just focus on sections or parts of the story week-by-week without taking time to read the entire account and reflect on how it all holds together.

Synoptic Gospels: Mark

Of the Synoptic Gospels most scholars see Mark as the first one written, on which Matthew and Luke rely. Mark is understandably popular for our generation because of its emphasis on discipleship. Jesus's followers must commit themselves to the way of the cross: "If any want to become my followers, let them deny themselves and take up their cross and follow me" (8:34).

The call to take up one's cross comes in the key passage in Mark's Gospel—the axle on which the book turns. The shift in the narrative focuses on the sufferings that Christ will endure and follows shortly after Peter is rebuked as being in Satan's hands for denying the necessity of Christ's sufferings. Most sermons delivered about this passage fix quite rightly on the need for followers to take up the cross. However, what is often omitted is that Jesus clearly speaks about both suffering at the hands of the authorities and rising again on the third day (8:31). This critical passage is immediately followed by the transfiguration, which prefigures Jesus's resurrection and contains God's assuring message of vindication. The implication is that discipleship cannot be separated from the resurrection.

Jesus continues to speak about both his death and resurrection (9:30–32; 10:32–34), situating the call to discipleship within this framework. The resurrection is so linked to who Jesus is and what he does that the radical call to discipleship does not stop at suffering. His call to us is not about inviting people to follow and merely live a life framed by a somber event or message. Rather, Jesus knows that the suffering and humiliation he and his followers will undergo will be vindicated, and that vindication of suffering comes via the resurrection.

Michael Bird points out that the rhetorical nature of Mark is evident in parallels discerned between a Roman triumphal procession and the narrative of the passion of Christ. Jesus acts in ways that combine both the triumph and defeat of such processions. On one hand, Jesus's march into Jerusalem echoes the procession of the victorious generals, processions that typically celebrated conquering kings or professed adoration for the emperor (11:8–11). On the other hand, the tone changes with Jesus's death march following his trial and condemnation by Pilate. The death march of Jesus echoes the Roman processions that include the sacrificial victim, the weapon of execution, and a placard naming the one who is conquered and humiliated.[24] Like the vanquished captives who were paraded by the troops, Jesus's death march echoes the somberness of being humiliated. The rhetorical irony is that the death march of Jesus inevitably leads to his vindication and triumph in the resurrection. As we have seen from the words of Jesus, his humiliating death march on its own will not make sense unless the resurrection occurs.

While the resurrection is predicted and foreshadowed throughout Mark, it consists of just eight verses in the book (16:1–8). These brief verses point to the resurrection and provide vindication that the call to discipleship is warranted. Mark's resurrection narrative, just like John's, plays on the richness of the first day of the week (Mark 16:2). It is the day that God began his work of creation and the day for reordering the new creation. It was chosen from early times as the day that the church worships.

Within the space of nine verses Mark intentionally (15:40–16:1) gives us the unbroken chain of the testimony of the women who witnessed Jesus's death, burial, and resurrection. In this account we find an unmistakable message about women in the context of discipleship. They were the "habitual followers of Jesus," and Mark mentions women "more than any other Gospel."[25] It is the women alone who testify to the three events. Jewish historian Pinchas Lapide notes that because women were generally not considered credible witnesses in that culture, the testimony of women to Jesus's resurrection actually gives it a ring of truth, as one would scarcely invent a story where women are portrayed as the primary witnesses.[26]

Mark finishes his Gospel with the same emotional drama found elsewhere in his text where people experience fear and amazement at what happens around Jesus. His stilling the storm produces fear (4:41) and the raising of Jairus's daughter produces amazement (5:42). The resurrection in Mark brings an emotional response of confusion, wonder, and awe at the immensity of what has occurred.

Synoptic Gospels: Matthew

There are four unique elements in Matthew with respect to the resurrection. To begin with, the cosmic nature of the death and resurrection of Jesus is strong in Matthew. This is intimated in 27:51–54 where at the point of his death there is an earthquake, rocks are split, and deceased saints arise from their graves. This continues after the resurrection, as the resurrected saints are said to enter Jerusalem and appear to many after Jesus's resurrection (27:53). Another earthquake occurs when an angel opens the tomb (28:2). The second earthquake has consequences that mirror the first earthquake: Roman soldiers experience fear and become like dead men upon seeing the angel move the tombstone. Matthew's Gospel begins with a cosmic sign—the Bethlehem Star that guides the "pagan" Magi to find the newborn child. The death-resurrection narrative likewise picks up the cosmic sign of the earthquakes. At the macro level the creation bears witness to the birth, death, and resurrection of Jesus.

The two earthquakes carry spiritual implications. In the first earthquake the temple veil is torn (27:51), signifying that we are forgiven and have direct access to God. In the second earthquake the angel announces the good news of resurrection and women disciples are the first witnesses. In Jesus's culture this is a statement that no matter who you are, male or female, you can encounter the risen Lord. The two earthquakes also point to the resurrection of the dead. In the first there is a literal rising of the dead who after Jesus's resurrection enter Jerusalem. Jesus's own rising confirms his conquest of death and opens the way for our general resurrection. Matthew's account seems to indicate that the whole earth is involved in the resurrection.

Another element unique to Matthew's story is that it deals with the allegation that the disciples stole the corpse (28:11–15). The guards are hostile witnesses in that they experience the earthquake, see the angel appear and the women, and possibly see the tomb vacant. They report to the chief priests and are bribed to say, "His disciples came by night and stole him away while we were asleep" (28:13). The empty tomb story was known at the time Matthew wrote. He rebutted the claim that the disciples had removed Jesus's body. (See the apologetic we set out in chapter 3 about who had a motive to steal the corpse.)

The third factor we want to mention with regard to Matthew's Gospel is fulfilled prophecy. One of the Old Testament motifs concerns the raising up of Israel out of death in the Passover and Exodus. The nation is brought to life as God leads them out of slavery (slavery was a metaphorical experience of death). The opening of Matthew narrates the exile of Jesus to Egypt as a child and, after Herod's death, his return to Palestine. Matthew uses a passage from Hosea to say that Jesus has fulfilled a prophecy: "Out of Egypt have I called my son" (Matt. 2:15; see Hos. 11:1). There is an indirect fulfillment of resurrection here too because just as Israel was raised up to life by deliverance from Egypt, so Jesus comes out of Egypt. In his life and ministry Jesus recapitulates Israel's experiences, which includes coming out of the bondage of death by resurrection.

Another fulfilled prophecy concerns the messianic kingship of Jesus. This prophecy relates to Daniel's vision of the exalted one, "To him was given dominion and glory and kingship, that all peoples, nations, and languages should serve him" (Dan. 7:14). This is fulfilled in the resurrection when the risen Jesus delivers the Great Commission and states that "All authority in heaven and earth has been given to me" (Matt. 28:18).

Matthew's Gospel also shows that the resurrection is directly related to sending out the eleven disciples into the world (Matt. 28:16–20). This pericope begins with the disciples, who were Jews, worshiping Jesus, though some at first doubt. The resurrection calls them to mission and affirms the continuous presence of Jesus with them. The closing words of Matthew's Gospel provide a bookend to the story. Although the bulk of the Gospel has a strong Jewish flavor, Matthew opens with the gentile astrologers coming to the birth of Jesus and closes with the Great Commission to reach every nation.

For Matthew the resurrection is cosmic and points to the new community of life by deliverance from death. The essential point of his Gospel narrative is summed up in Jesus's words: "An evil and adulterous generation asks for a sign, but no sign will be given to it except the sign of Jonah" (Matt. 16:4; see also 12:39–42). The resurrection is this sign of Jonah, and it is central to the story of Jesus presented in the Gospel of Matthew.

Synoptic Gospels: Luke

The priority of the resurrection for Luke has been disclosed above in our discussion of the speeches in Acts. At the start of his Gospel Luke sets out his methodology: he is carrying out an investigation to provide an orderly narrative based on what eyewitnesses have seen. While there is debate around William Ramsey's assertion that Luke was a "first-rank" historian who "should be placed among the very greatest historians," there is no doubt that he set out with diligence as a responsible scribe to collect the account of the first witnesses.[27] For us a good summation of Luke's ethos is found in the observations of Alexandru Neagoe, who states that Luke is not merely a historian or a theologian or an evangelist; he is primarily an apologist whose tool is not philosophy but history and theology as he narrates the events and their significance.[28]

Luke's resurrection account finishes with the eyewitnesses joyously worshiping Jesus (24:52–53). For Luke if there is no resurrection then there is no obedience, following, or glorifying of Christ. We point out in the next chapter that Luke is committed to showing that Jesus's resurrection is not random but is a fulfillment of the Old Testament Scriptures: "everything written about me in the law of Moses, the prophets, and the psalms must be fulfilled" (24:44). Luke is making it clear that this is not mythology but is God's gospel according to the Scriptures.

Luke has the same type of pointers to the resurrection as the other Gospels, like Jairus's daughter being raised (8:40–56), and the foretelling of Jesus's resurrection (9:21–22) followed by his transfiguration. A delightful account unique to Luke is the walk to Emmaus by two disciples who do not immediately recognize Jesus when he joins them (24:13–35). This passage highlights that some disciples do not immediately recognize the risen Jesus, but it is followed by an account of his appearance to other disciples who do recognize him (24:36–43). The mysterious aspect of nonrecognition/recognition does not belie the physicality or material quality to the resurrected body of Jesus. However, a clear transformation of his body has taken place, as shown by his new capacity to appear or disappear suddenly. In the latter appearance he invites the disciples to touch him so as to dispel doubts that he is corporeal.

In supplying this particular account Luke provides a needed explanation that Jesus was not a ghost or spirit. In the Roman world ghost stories were not uncommon. This episode, however, does not allow an audience familiar with ghost stories to misunderstand the nature of the resurrection or to think this event involved an apparition. The disciples pose the question, is he a ghost? and Luke answers this apologetic question for the gentile/Roman world by making it clear there is tactile contact.[29]

The Emmaus account carries over an important spiritual point: the eyes of the two disciples had to be opened for them to recognize him (24:31). In closing the Gospel Luke sums up that with Jesus's ascension the disciples are gripped by the boundless joy that comes from the resurrection. As they return to Jerusalem Luke's theology of the resurrection emphasizes their worship of God, their empowered lives, and their readiness to serve and to bear witness (Luke 24:50–53).

Four Gospels' Theology of Resurrection Sound Bites

In the four Gospels we have identified twenty-two theological foundations for the resurrection concerning the nature of Christ, personal transformation and empowerment, and mission:

- Fulfillment of prophecy and Scripture (John 2:19; Luke 24:27, 44–46)
- Worship as deity (John 20:28; Matt. 28:17; Luke 24:52–53)
- Messianic kingship (Matt. 28:18)
- Verification of kingship (John 20:28)
- Cosmic dimension of Jesus's reign (Matt. 27:51–54; 28:2)
- Eschatology (John 21:20–23)
- Corporeal/physical resurrection (Luke 24:39–41; Matt. 28:9; John 20:17–21:14)
- Sign of Jesus as the Son of Man (Matt. 12:38–41; 16:4; Luke 11:29–32)
- Defeat of death: the empty tomb (John 20:11–28; Mark 16:6; Matt. 28:6; Luke 24:3)
- First day of the week: new creation (John 20:1; Mark 16:2; Matt. 28:1; Luke 24:1)
- Forgiveness of sin (John 20:23; Thomas forgiven of doubt, Peter's restoration)
- Receipt of the Holy Spirit for living (John 20:22)
- Hope—even for doubters (John 20:28–29)
- Pastoral care ("Feed my sheep," John 21:17)
- Eternal life (John 20:30–31)
- Bestowal of sonship (John 20:31)

- Continuing presence (John 20:21; Matt. 28:18–20)
- Empowered costly discipleship (John 21:15–19)
- Mission (Matt. 28:18–20; Luke 24:47–48; John 20:21; 21:1–14, massive catch of fish points to mission)
- Apologetic refutation of rumors (Matt. 28:11–15)
- Apologetic answer showing Jesus was not a Roman ghost/apparition (Luke 24:39–41)
- Grace for understanding (Luke 24:31)

Paul

In addition to Acts and the Gospels, the rest of the New Testament takes up other themes about the resurrection. I. Howard Marshall puts it like this:

> The raising of Jesus by God the Father is seen to be an essential part of the saving act and is not simply a way of proclaiming to humanity that the price of sin has been paid. If Christ had not been raised, we would still be in our sins. This way of understanding the significance of the resurrection for Paul corresponds to the reality expressed in a somewhat different imagery in Hebrews, 1 Peter, and Luke-Acts. Moreover, it explains how it is that on occasions the New Testament writers can depict the resurrection and exaltation of Jesus as the saving event without explicit reference to the death of Jesus.[30]

1 Corinthians 15

J. B. Phillips nominated 1 Corinthians 15 as the Bible's indispensable chapter, and Beasley-Murray says that not a funeral service passes without the use of some parts of this chapter.[31] Clearly for understanding the resurrection in Paul this is the key passage. We argued above that the message of 1 Corinthians 15 both is true and works in life. Paul's pivotal words are that without the resurrection our preaching and faith are useless. Cross-centered people tend to think Paul is using hyperbole here, but to think that is to totally misunderstand him. He is deadly serious: if there was no resurrection then the game is over!

In the creedal statement in verses 3–5 the witnesses for the resurrection are listed. Then Paul adds to this that there were five hundred other witnesses, as well as James and lastly himself (15:6–8). Jesus's appearances, however, are not always understood by scholars as being corporeal. There is a strategic debate in contemporary critical scholarship as to whether Paul even knew about the empty tomb. Some suggest that his understanding of resurrection did not involve corporeal and physically material resurrection, but was rather a "spiritual body" form of resurrection. The argument is elaborated by saying that the 1 Corinthians passage predates the Gospel accounts and there is no explicit mention of the empty tomb. Some argue that the empty tomb account is a late embellished tradition used to fortify the case for resurrection.

The luminous appearance of Jesus to Paul on the Damascus road is understood to be a visionary, spiritual appearance that differed significantly from the kinds of appearances that the other disciples experienced. As the visionary appearance to Paul was of a spiritual nature, we need not accept that there was an actual physical body and an empty tomb. There are two questions at issue here: (1) Was there an empty tomb? and (2) Was the appearance of Jesus to Paul radically different than the appearances to the other disciples?

As regards the empty tomb, in the creedal statement in 15:4 "he was buried" is followed immediately by "he was raised." To say that the tomb was not empty is an argument from silence: it is implied in these verses. Paul's speech in Acts 13:29–30 also indicates that he knew about the empty tomb. In this passage Paul says that they took Jesus down from the tree and laid him in the tomb, and that God raised him from the dead. Paul elsewhere uses the terminology that we were entombed or buried with Christ (Rom. 6:4; Col. 2:12). Paul is telling the same basic story as the other disciples even though he has not used the jargon on the tomb that some critics seem to expect of him.

With respect to the resurrection appearances of Jesus, Paul uses the same verb, "he was seen," for himself as he does for the other apostles. In other words he claims to have experienced the same kind of appearance as those who came before him. Gerd Lüdemann argues that because Paul had a spiritual and visionary experience, so too did the others.[32] The question is whether the New Testament is offering us multiple resurrection modes for Jesus: the Gospels refer to a transformed yet material body, Paul saw a nonphysical spiritual body, John's Apocalypse indicates visionary appearances, and the second advent may suggest yet another kind of resurrected Jesus. Is this really what the New Testament is driving at? Has Jesus undergone a metamorphosis at each of these different junctures? The answer to this is no.

There is assuredly a mystery to the resurrection, but it is clearly physical and glorified, and there is constancy with each of these occasions. Jesus has not changed bodies several times. There is both continuity and discontinuity between the pre- and post-resurrection body. Robert Gundry points out, "Whether seen on earth or in heaven, Jesus remains as physical after resurrection as he was before resurrection . . . a vision does not imply nonphysicality."[33] Clearly Paul saw his encounter of the risen Christ as being in line with that of the apostles. Like them, Jesus "appeared" to him (compare Acts 13:31 to 1 Cor. 15:8). He includes himself in the witness list as an eyewitness of the resurrected Christ. Sir Norman Anderson, who was an Anglican lawyer and professor at the University of London, stressed that Paul's encounter "was just as real and 'objective' as that of the other apostles, not that theirs were as 'visionary' as his."[34]

Throughout this book we have discussed that 1 Corinthians 15:17–24 is central to the argument that the resurrection is the lynchpin of Christianity.

This passage shows that the forgiveness of sin, hope for eternal life, the holistic model for our own eternal existence, eschatology, Jesus's handing of the kingdom over to God the Father after every authority and power has been subjected to him, and the resurrection of the dead are all wrapped up in the resurrection. In the latter part of the chapter Paul goes on to address the implications of the resurrection for us, including the nature of our resurrected bodies. Paul wants us to understand that since Jesus is the firstfruits of the resurrection, so too we will be resurrected.

Paul mentions in passing people being baptized by proxy on behalf of the dead (15:29–34). He does not endorse this practice but mentions it in order to emphasize his point—that there would be no point in even showing any mark of respect for the dead by such a custom if Jesus were not resurrected. If there is no resurrection of the dead, Paul argues, then why bother living the costly Christian life of discipleship? Why bother living at risk or leading a moral life? Unless the resurrection has happened there is no point to the Christian way.

Paul describes the nature of the resurrection body (15:35–49) using a variety of analogies like that of the seed that is sown in the ground and rises up as new grain. Paul notes that while our present body is mortal and will perish, the future body is imperishable. It is from the present body that the future transformed body emerges. The only example we have of a resurrected body is that of Jesus. The empty tomb indicates that the pre-resurrection body is no more; it has been changed and transformed. Jesus is the firstfruits of this transformation, and Paul argues that we will be like him.

When Paul remarks in 15:50 that "flesh and blood cannot inherit the kingdom," he is reminding his readers that the present body is fallen and not fit for eternity: it must be transformed. The spiritual body he speaks of is one that *is* fit for eternity—no longer carnal and subject to sin, death, and infirmity. Paul maintains, though, that there is still a connection between who we are now and who we become. Our physical body will be changed into this imperishable body. The dead will be raised. It is because Jesus is the firstfruits that our hope for resurrection is assured. Perhaps the most oft-quoted verse at funerals is this: "Where, O death, is your victory? Where, O death, is your sting?" (15:55). Paul's emphasis on the transformation of our bodies in the resurrection is repeated in other Epistles (Phil. 3:21; 2 Cor. 4:13–5:4).

In chapter 10 we discussed Luther's position on the resurrection and noted his series of sermons on 1 Corinthians 15.[35] The main truths that Luther drew from this passage are summarized as follows:

- "Paul stakes everything on the basic factor with which he began, namely, that Christ arose from the dead. This is the chief article of the Christian doctrine. No one who at all claims to be a Christian or a preacher of the Gospel may deny that."[36]

- The Roman authorities in Jesus's day denied the resurrection and such denial is ultimately the work of the devil. In Luther's day there were unnamed church leaders and intellectuals who he alleged did not believe in the resurrection: "if three could be found who believed this article, we should say that these were many."[37]
- Paul's list of the apostolic witnesses resembled a legal case.
- The resurrection is scripturally based and God convinces us that it is true because the Word of God proclaims Jesus's resurrection.
- Everything is linked together like links in a chain from the resurrection. Every Christian must confess Christ's resurrection, otherwise everything else to do with Christ will be repudiated.
- Jesus arose victoriously so that he could rescue us from sin, death, and hell.
- Jesus's resurrection has corporate significance because he is the firstfruits and Christians are already united in the risen Christ.
- The general resurrection of the dead is declared by God and the apostles in the Word of God. Since God exists and cannot lie, the general resurrection has to be true.
- As Christ has risen we are already sharing in the resurrection's benefits here and now, and these will be consummated in the general resurrection.

Theology of Resurrection in Paul

We align ourselves with those who emphasize that the resurrection is an integral part of salvation. The problem besetting the church is that the resurrection-focus of the gospel has been obscured. We need to build on the critical work of recent scholars like Richard Gaffin, Michael Bird, I. Howard Marshall, J. R. Daniel Kirk, and N. T. Wright. In this regard we appreciate what some are doing to show the resurrection truths of Scripture that have been neglected.

At the cross Christ was both our substitute and our representative. The church has strongly emphasized him as our substitute, but we must move on to the resurrection: because Christ has been raised we may share in his lordship. He is our representative.[38] We must go even one step further. In order to build a holistic theology we must refocus on the resurrection as the lynchpin of Christianity. At the bare minimum this involves a both/and understanding of the cross and resurrection. The themes found in Paul's writings dovetail with the resurrection zones we discussed in chapter 2 and can be correlated to various theological themes found in the Gospels and Acts.

FORGIVENESS/JUSTIFICATION

N. T. Wright remarks, "Romans is suffused with resurrection. Squeeze this letter at any point, and resurrection spills out; hold it up to the light, and you can see Easter sparkling all the way through."[39] Daniel Kirk also detects a resurrection melody in Romans that leads him to argue that it is the key theme that unlocks the entire epistle.[40]

One of the key verses is Romans 4:25 where Paul states that Jesus "was raised for our justification." Jeffrey Anderson says about this verse that "you do not understand Easter if you do not understand justification. Our justification and his resurrection are bound up in such a way that Paul can meaningfully draw a causal relationship."[41] Back in chapter 1, we referred to Stott's and Denny's emphasis on justification as what happens at the cross with Jesus's death for the sin of the world. Although they add that the resurrection says "yes" to the cross, they hold that the vindication of Christ is really centered on the cross. We maintain that this verse says something more about the resurrection and justification than just the vindication of Christ. The resurrection and cross are two parts of the same saving event. *The work of salvation involves both cross and resurrection.* Jesus's death *is* sufficient to atone for the forgiveness of sin *but* in order to make it once and for all there must also be a resurrection. The Old Testament sacrifices of animals, while atoning, had to be repeated over and over. The sacrificed animals were never resurrected! The force of Paul's point in 1 Corinthians 15 is that unless Jesus has been raised we are still in our sins. He is letting us know that theologically the resurrection is crucial to end the atoning treadmill. God's verdict at the cross has been carried out with Jesus dying, but the completion to the enactment of justification comes in his resurrection.[42] Justification is a two-sided coin.

Christ has been raised so that we may be united with him. He is our representative. If there was no resurrection of Jesus then there would be no effective benefit to his justifying death both now and on judgment day. It is also because of the resurrection that Jesus can declare on judgment day that we are indeed united with him.

Melanchthon drew attention to what he saw as the importance of judgment arising out of reflections on Romans 4:25. The accuser is constantly seeking to bring judgment against us, but Christ has been raised as our advocate and declares to our own souls and to the devil that "I am their representative."[43]

When we understand the above, it is easier to appreciate what sanctification involves in growing in Christ. Our participation in the resurrection of Christ is the door that opens to enable sanctification to occur in our lives. I. Howard Marshall sums up: "It is thus union with the Christ who died and rose for us that is the basis for our final salvation."[44]

DISCIPLESHIP

Luther's understanding of links in a chain is very helpful in understanding that if the resurrection link is removed everything else we know about Jesus collapses. Put another way, everything extends from the resurrection and everything is connected to the resurrection. The resurrection helps us to look backward to the cross and forward to the new life as a new creation. It is because of this that the apostle Paul can declare in Romans 10:9, "if you confess with your lips that Jesus is Lord and believe in your heart that God raised him from the dead, you will be saved." People often struggle with this verse because it doesn't mention the cross. However, when you take a clear-cut look at the whole of Romans the only word that can possibly embrace everything that Paul is saying is *resurrection*. We are not merely saved from sin. The message is about being raised to a new hope and a new life by the power of the Spirit. The whole of creation is to be transformed because of the resurrection. A full view of salvation recognizes that we are a new creation experiencing a new world order (2 Cor. 5:17–20).

In his practical life-oriented commentary on Ephesians called *Practice Resurrection* Eugene Peterson emphasizes the importance of resurrection:

> Ephesians is a resurrection document. It trains us in understanding ourselves as saints, not saints in the sense of haloed exceptions to garden-variety Christians, but simply Christians who realize that Jesus' resurrection places us in a position to live robustly in the world of The Holy, growing up in Christ, practicing resurrection.[45]

Although he is speaking specifically about Ephesians, one could justly say that his point covers all of what Paul wrote.

The first port of call in discipleship throughout the New Testament is the great commandment to love the Lord your God and your neighbor as yourself (Luke 10:25–27). Paul is of the same mind in Romans 13:8–10. In Romans 12–15 he shows us what this looks like. For example in Romans 12 we are to love God by being holy and being living sacrifices, and we are to love our neighbor by sharing with those in need, by forgiving, by using our gifts, and by being persons of integrity. For Paul this all flows from what has been argued in the previous eleven chapters. Only in the risen Christ can we robustly live this life. He teaches in Romans 7 that we have died to the law and we serve in the new way of the Spirit. Likewise in Romans 8 the law is not lived in us through flagellating ourselves but in reliance on the Spirit of the risen Christ. For Paul the phrases "spirit of God" and "Spirit of Christ" are interchangeable. Although the persons of the Holy Spirit and Christ are separate the experience is the same (Rom. 8:9). The resurrection is the guarantee of the pouring out of the Spirit of Christ on us.

Today many Christians see the need to pick up the social justice message found in the prophets (Isa. 58). However there is a tendency to forget that first of all we must be anchored in the power of the risen Christ. Without that we are impotent to act and to live. In Colossians 3:1 Paul says that "we have been raised with Christ," and he is now seated with God. He goes on to state what kind of life we are called to. We are not called to be merely heavenly minded but we are called into practical discipleship by putting to death impurity, lust, greed, anger, malice, and lying, and by putting on the new self.

Displaying the fruit of the Spirit (Gal. 5:22–26) and acting justly are connected to loving God and loving neighbor. In fact Paul's instruction on the fruit of the Spirit is immediately preceded by the entire law, summed up in a single command, "love your neighbor as yourself" (5:14). We are baptized into Christ (Rom. 6:3–4), clothed in him (Gal. 3:27; Rom. 13:14), and raised up with him (Col. 3:1). This teaching applies to the entire community, as Paul's analogy of the body indicates (1 Cor. 12:12; Rom. 12:1).

Discipleship is also directly connected to living and speaking ethically. We canvassed in chapter 2 the centrality of the resurrection to our epistemology of ethics. We argued there that the resurrection shows God's concern for the whole person and the whole creation. For Paul, to live ethically is to live the way of the risen Christ (Rom. 13:13–14).

Resurrection-centered discipleship also encompasses mission and building hope in believers. In Romans, in his opening salutations, Paul focuses on Jesus being a descendant from David who "was declared to be the Son of God with power . . . by resurrection from the dead." It is by this resurrection that we received grace and apostleship so that good news can be proclaimed in all nations (1:4–6). As we have seen, Acts makes it clear that Paul's entire call to mission stems directly from his encounter with the resurrected Christ, which then becomes central to his preaching (9:1–19; 26:12–23). Paul says that Jesus appeared to him specifically to appoint him to testify before the nations (26:16–18).

Living through the risen Christ enables us to love our neighbor and to exercise our spiritual gifts. It also moves toward a robust definition of discipleship. Paul makes it clear we cannot be separated from the love of Christ no matter what distress or trial comes our way. In fact in him "we are conquerors." It was Jesus who died, who was raised, and who also intercedes for us (Rom. 8:34–37).[46]

Eschatology

We have already discussed the general resurrection of the dead. In Philippians Paul makes the point that Christ will transform our bodies so that we will be like him (3:21). Throughout this book we have argued that resurrection holistically empowers believers not merely to the future life but also in the present life. The vision of the resurrected body not only speaks about God's love and care for the whole person; it also impacts our response to God in the way we live in the here and now. N. T. Wright makes this point (relying on Paul's themes in the early chapters of 1 Corinthians, Romans 6, and Colossians 3):

> What you do with your body in the present matters . . . because God raised the Lord and will also raise us by his power. Glorify God in your body because one

day God will glorify the body itself. What is to be true in the future must begin to be true in the present, or it will be called into question whether you are really on track in the first place.[47]

There is also a connection between our resurrection and the transformation of this present creation into the world that is to come. Paul refers to our groaning in the body as parallel to the groaning of the creation that is waiting for our transformation. This connection between the future of the cosmos and us centers on Christ as the firstfruits of the resurrection (Rom. 8:18–23). In 1 Corinthians 15 Paul's discourse clearly joins the resurrection of Jesus to ours and connects with the general resurrection the events of the end times (15:20–28).

Those who are resurrected will live in a renewed and fulfilled creation. The future prospect of transformation in bodily resurrection must relate to a practical sense of God's care for the world in the here and now. God will not let go of this world because he plans its renewal. The Bible paints a picture of interconnectedness—an interpenetration of heaven and earth that is yet to come. There is the visionary portrayal of this in Revelation 21, where John sees the holy city, the New Jerusalem, coming down out of heaven to earth. The images in the vision are reminiscent of those in the opening verses of Genesis: rivers, trees, and light. The passage evokes the regaining of the lost paradise. We should therefore connect with our planet and care for it, both in our environmental stewardship and in generally working for a better world. As Jesus taught, the kingdom that is to come is already mirrored in those who join with him now.

Our current cultural concerns about the degradation of the earth come into sharp focus here. The pie-in-the-sky mentality about being in heaven and having no connection to this earth almost nullifies our witness to others about Christ, who is the Creator (John 1:1–3; Col. 1:15–17). Christians who absent themselves from the cultural debates about earth stewardship and animal protection portray Christianity as having nothing worthwhile to say or contribute to current concerns about our planet.

The New Age concept of GAIA represents one approach to finding the interconnectedness of all life. GAIA is taken from the name of the ancient Greek goddess of the earth. According to this concept, the whole earth is not merely a delicate, finely tuned, and holistically linked ecosphere; it is also another form of consciousness—one that is divine. The turn in alternative spiritualities to a nature-based spirituality speaks volumes back to the church, pointing to one of our many "unpaid bills." Religious studies scholar Bron Taylor bears witness to a wide cultural movement that he dubs "dark green religion" that encapsulates an earth-centered focus for both the sacred and for living ethically.[48]

For us the coming kingdom means we do as God mandated us to: act as guardians and trustees who care for the earth now and enjoy what goodness remains in the broken creation. It is the resurrected Christ who will regenerate the whole cosmos and us.

This resurrection connection to the last things also relates to the more traditional sense of hope in eternal life and the certainty Paul trumpets that when Christ returns we will be victorious (1 Thess. 4:13–18).

NEW COMMUNITY

For Paul the coming of Jesus does more than just save people from sin. The life and teaching of Jesus establishes a new order. The new order and new day that Christ's resurrection brings about expresses itself in a new community. As we elaborated in chapter 2, there is no longer any division between people groups and no nonperson status; the resurrection reverses dysfunctional relationships from the fall (Gal. 3:27–28; Col. 3:10–11). Colossians 1:15–20 is an early hymn of the church that proclaims Christ as the Creator and reconciler who holds all things together. Most significantly with regards to the new community he is the head of the body, the "firstborn from among the dead." Although the word *resurrection* is not found here the clear implication from "firstborn" is that the resurrected Christ is the source, the fountainhead, and the preeminent one over the church.[49] Without a resurrection there can be no new creation. The church was born out of both the cross and the resurrection. The resurrection is the trigger, source, life, and gifting that gives birth and sustaining power to the formation of the new community.

LORDSHIP AND JUDGE

The Colossians hymn just noted also sees Christ as having first place in everything (see also Rom. 1:4; 14:9; 2 Cor. 5:14–15). One of the best expressions of Christ's lordship is found in Ephesians 1:19–23, where his lordship puts him in the role of judge. Another early hymn in Philippians 2:5–11 focuses on his incarnation and death in the first part, and then on his risen and exalted state in the second part. He is not just Lord but before him every knee will bow (Rom. 14:11).

In summary we believe that Paul holds the cross and resurrection as an inseparable unity. Yet Paul sees the resurrection as the great central redemptive fact (Rom. 1:4; 2 Cor. 4:13–14; Rom. 10:8–9) that is directly concerned with our justification and takes us into a new eon of discipleship that is global and cosmic. We object to seeing the resurrection as the icing on the cake for the cross. Beasley-Murray captures the gist of Paul: "The resurrection of Jesus is not to be likened to a single rabbit God pulls out of the hat to demonstrate that Jesus is his Son. Rather, it is the basis for all Christian hope."[50]

Other Passages

We have canvassed some of the major portions of the New Testament that concentrate on the resurrection: the speeches in Acts, the Synoptic Gospels,

John, and the corpus of Paul's writings. In chapter 2 we referred to Peter's teaching that because of the resurrection we are a new creation, that we are part of an eternal resurrection hope, and that we are therefore to live a life of holiness (1 Pet. 1:3–9). Peter further speaks of being an eyewitness to Christ's majesty at the transfiguration, that luminous event of Christ's glorification that points us on to the resurrection (2 Pet. 1:16–18).

In John's Apocalypse there is at the beginning the vision of the risen Lord among the seven lampstands (Rev. 1:9–18). In this vision the risen Lord is seen as the triumphant divine one who is called "the first and the last" (Rev. 1:17–18), a title that belongs only to God (Isa. 44:6). He speaks to John, saying, "I am the first and the last, and the living one; I was dead, and see, I am alive forever and ever." The resurrection here points to Jesus's deity, lordship, and judgment over all things because he holds the keys to death and Hades (1:18). From this commencement point of the vision of the resurrected one comes the unfolding portrait of the one robed in white (1:13–20), the triumphant sacrificial lamb (5:6–10), the one who is exalted and enthroned (chapter 4), the one who satisfies our thirst (21:6; 22:17), and who brings to consummation all the purposes of God in transforming the creation and resurrecting us to live forever (chapters 21–22).

Conclusion

Over the months taken in writing this book we have had stimulating chats with many Christians who have expressed keen interest in recapturing the both/and of Jesus's death and resurrection. The general agreement has been that the theology of the resurrection is missing from church life and mission. We have found it intriguing though that many of our conversation partners have essentially said, "Great, let's make sure we truly affirm the both/and and not make one primary." We started this book by looking at how John Stott has decided to make the cross primary while still seeking a both/and. After looking at what has been unpacked in this chapter about the theology of resurrection, we are not willing to take the soft option. If there was no theology of the resurrection the New Testament would dramatically shrink in size. It would just deliver us a manifesto of interesting precepts about leading a good life.

Jesus is not like a burnt-out, collapsed star. With a collapsed star you end up with a black hole in space: no light comes from it, no light penetrates it. Without the event of the resurrection and the accompanying theology about it, Christianity and the New Testament would shrink like a collapsed star. It would be a dense, invisible faith. You wouldn't be able to see it with the naked eye. That is clearly not the message that the New Testament hands on to us. For Christianity to be a workable faith with a viable spiritual life there has to be a risen Jesus, and that resurrection has to be the lynchpin that ties everything together.

Eugene Peterson nails it:

And face it—if there's no resurrection for Christ, everything we've told you is smoke and mirrors, and everything you've staked your life on is smoke and mirrors. (1 Cor. 15:14 Message)

Spiritual Audit

1. Do you model how you share your faith based on the sermons in Acts?

2. Are you like the despondent disciples in the Gospels after Jesus's death, bereft of hope? What difference does the resurrection make to your discipleship?

3. Is your Christian community resonating with Luther's words that unless Christ is risen there can be no justification?

4. Do you seek to live the Christian life through the power of the risen Christ or has the practice been to live this out by simply being obedient (Romans 12)?

5. If you have a New Testament full of holes it will be because you are reading what's left of it because the resurrection has been cut out and ignored. Would you try to hold on to your Bible, prayer, and attitudes if Christ has not been raised?

12

The Hebrew Scriptures

That those three great moments—the binding of Isaac, the giving of the Torah, and the resurrection of the dead—came to be interfused is itself powerful evidence for the centrality of the resurrection in the Judaism that the rabbis bequeathed later generations of Jews. To the rabbis, resurrection without the restoration of Israel, including its renewed adherence to the Torah, was incomprehensible. And without the expectation of resurrection, the restoration of Israel would be something less than what the rabbis thought the Torah had always intended it to be—the ultimate victory of the God of life.

Jon D. Levenson[1]

People of the ancient Near East held a variety of beliefs about the afterlife. Some looked to an embodied immortality. The mummifying of Egypt's pharaohs indicates they thought their bodies were needed in the afterlife. There were myths of agricultural gods dying in winter and reviving in spring. As an *idea* resurrection popped up in various guises in Near East cultures, but it is uncertain whether any believed in immortality for all of humanity through resurrection. What is clear is that the idea of resurrection in Mesopotamia, Canaan, and Egypt was light-years away from the later events and theology of the Gospels.

Jesus's earliest disciples were Jews and heirs of the traditions handed down by the prophets, priests, and patriarchs of Israel. How did ancient Israel understand death and the afterlife? As different characters in the Hebrew Bible often faced calamities how could they have any death-refusing hope and how could it take hold in the thinking of ancient Israel? Is there really a covert theme about death-refusing hope embedded in the Hebrew Bible? How could such a hopeful theme gradually develop into a belief in bodily resurrection of the dead?

At a first glance the Hebrew Bible does not seem to have many passages that explicitly declare belief in bodily resurrection. The principal passages that convey the *concept* of a resurrection are Job 19:23–29; Isaiah 26:19; Ezekiel 37:1–14; and Daniel 12:2. Daniel is explicit: "Many of those who sleep in the dust of the earth shall awake, some to everlasting life, and some to shame and everlasting contempt" (12:2). There are also three stories of individuals who were "resurrected" (1 Kings 17:17–22; 2 Kings 4:18–37; 2 Kings 13:20–21). So there was some understanding in ancient Israel that Yahweh (the God of Israel) could bring people back to life. The apostles probably had these passages in mind concerning the general resurrection. However, what passages could they refer to that pointed directly to the resurrection of Jesus?

Jesus and the Old Testament

Before we plunge into the Old Testament, it is helpful to recall some things that Jesus said. On the road to Emmaus two followers of Jesus were talking about all that had happened when a stranger joined them. The stranger asked them what they were talking about. They were astonished that somebody who must have been in Jerusalem could be ignorant of the news about Jesus! They explained that Jesus had been executed but they were puzzled because some women had visited his grave only to find it empty. The women reported a vision of angels who announced that Jesus had risen from the dead. The stranger who was with the travelers was actually Jesus, but they had not recognized him. He gave them a gentle rebuke, reminding them that these things had been foretold: "Then beginning with Moses and all the prophets, he interpreted to them the things about himself in all the scriptures" (Luke 24:27).

Shortly after this incident Jesus appeared to the disciples in the upper room in Jerusalem. After showing them his crucifixion scars and dispelling the misnomer that he was a disembodied ghost, Jesus then said: " 'everything written about me in the law of Moses, the prophets, and the psalms must be fulfilled.' Then he opened their minds to understand the scriptures" (Luke 24:44–45).

The Hebrew Bible is classically divided into three parts: Law (Torah), Prophets, and Writings (e.g., Psalms). In the above passages Jesus taught his disciples that the Hebrew Bible pointed to him and long ago predicted his death and resurrection from the dead. The writers of the New Testament came to understand that Jesus's resurrection was foretold in the Hebrew Bible (1 Cor. 15:3–5).

Most contemporary scholars insist that there is precious little said about the resurrection of the dead and about a resurrected messiah in the Hebrew Bible.[2] We would argue, however, that what Jesus said should be our guiding framework.[3] His words stand in tension with the views of scholars who cannot see much about the resurrection in the Hebrew Bible. As we will show in this chapter, numerous Jewish and Christian thinkers have reviewed and challenged this scholarly consensus.

We will first outline the consensus view and then explore the new scholarly outlook. We see the Hebrew Bible bursting at the seams with important building blocks that relate to the resurrection of the dead. We believe Jesus drew on these building blocks when he explained that he is the firstfruits of those who are yet to be resurrected. In the previous chapter we saw that the apostles in their speeches in Acts refer to specific Hebrew prophecies about his resurrection. Their understanding flowed out from what Jesus had taught them, and when we turn to the Hebrew Bible we must look at it with eyes wide open.

God's power over life and death, God's role as the cosmic warrior dispelling chaos, and the theology of creation are all important Old Testament themes that relate to the resurrection. Another contributing element comes from understanding how individual characters in the nation viewed life and had expectations about God fulfilling his promises concerning life and death. All of these building blocks culminate in those passages that positively declare that there will be a resurrection of the dead.

Hebrew Bible and Death-Refusing Hope

Much of the Hebrew Bible is centered in the blessings, covenantal promises, and revelatory acts of God in the creation and through the lives of families, tribes, and the nation of Israel. An initial glance can easily give the impression that with so much emphasis on blessings and renewed covenants and the rise, fall, and restoration of Israel there is very little said about the resurrection. Even in the four passages that mention resurrection there are variations in emphasis: some refer metaphorically to the nation being resurrected from exile, while others point to resurrection from the grave.

These resurrection passages fit into a much deeper matrix. In order to understand why the resurrection blossomed in Israel's faith in later times we must consider the experiential knowledge of various characters in the Old Testament. Their experiences correlate to a rich set of themes on life and death. We see different characters expressing a death-refusing hope as they place their trust in some extraordinary God-given promises.

Covert Themes and Receptive Characters

There are many subtle themes in the Old Testament, and in order to spot these covert themes readers must keep their eyes wide open. This way of reading applies to our exploration of stories, characters, and themes about life, death, and resurrection. We must penetrate the surface of the texts and look for literary devices that subtly convey a message.

One method of literary emphasis used by some of the writers of the Hebrew Scriptures is repetition. In a particular book the same theme or point may be reiterated in the actions and lives of different characters (e.g., the character studies of the judges point to their failings and repeatedly convey the covert message to "be careful about your leaders"). There may also be significant and contrasting characters within the same story (like the contrast between

King Saul's defects and David's abilities). A message may be covertly conveyed by way of juxtaposition (e.g., the genealogies in Genesis present the people of the rejected line—those who are not the direct ancestors of Israel's twelve tribes—first enjoying material success, followed by the promised line—those patriarchal ancestors of Israel through whom divine blessings are promised—being crippled by incredible difficulties). A character's speech may be structured around repetition, contrast, and juxtaposition.

The experiences of some characters highlight the great tension they felt between lived reality and God's promises. While that theme is not explicitly stated it is a strong pattern that is very evident in the stories of the patriarchs where circumstances are juxtaposed and contrasted. God promised to make Abraham the father of a great nation (Gen. 12:2), and to give him the land of Canaan (12:7). This promise stands in stark contrast to Abraham's immediate experience: the land was already occupied by other people (12:6), it was subject to a great famine (12:10), and Sarah was infertile (11:30). Isaac and Jacob faced the same difficulties: the land was occupied by others and they had spouses who were infertile. What they were experiencing completely contradicted God's promises, but within this tension their faith nonetheless gradually develops. We see their dysfunctional behavior, vulnerability, and receptivity to God, and their hope in the promises of God grows.

Death in Hebraic Thought

The Old Testament is not explicit about the theme of death-refusing hope, but a pattern can be discerned about this covert theme. Through the experiences of its leading characters much is said about God's gift of life and his power over death. Today, we think of death primarily as the termination of biological life. When we open the book of Genesis and read chapters 2–3 we also see that death carries a spiritual connotation: it is something that arises from the severing of relationships between humans, God, and the remainder of the creation (Gen. 2:17; 3:3–4). However, this is hardly the last word about death.

Death in the Hebrew Bible was not defined as the cessation of embodied life, nor was it understood to be merely the "spiritual death" of being without God. One could be alive and yet be dead because death had qualitative aspects to it. Thus one who was suffering from misfortune might be experiencing a kind of living death. Johannes Pedersen observed:

> Life and death are not two sharply distinguished spheres, because they do not mean existence or nonexistence. Life is something which one possesses in a higher or lower degree. If afflicted by misfortune, illness or something else which checks the soul, then one has only little life, but all the more death. He who is ill or otherwise in distress may say that he is dead, and when he recovers, he is pulled out of death.[4]

A prominent example we will explore later on is found in the problem of infertility and the loss of progeny. Characters like Sarah, Rebekah, Rachel, Abraham, Isaac, Jacob, Naomi, Hannah, and Job found themselves subjected to calamitous and frustrating experiences that robbed them of the joy of life. So the term *death* is nuanced in ways that go beyond our modern way of understanding calamity and disease.

Death, understood in this symbolic sense, is mentioned several times in the Old Testament in relation to experiences that exposed human mortality and frailty. Whatever robs people of the richness and joy of living is a symbolic and metaphorical form of death and dying (Deut. 30:15; Ps. 13:3–4). Death could also be portrayed as an agent or power holding sway (Job 18:13; Jer. 9:21).[5] It could also refer to a place of existence after biological life ends (Job 38:17).[6] These different nuances of death reflect subtle beliefs about life and the afterlife.

Characters experiencing deathlike situations feel the tension between living reality and God's promises. They find themselves in deathlike circumstances but are receptive to God's mysterious actions to bring life out of death. Through their stories the Hebraic mind was primed to embrace the resurrection as the ultimate refusal of death.

Modern Consensus

For a long time modern biblical scholarship has taken the view that the resurrection is not a central dogma in the Hebrew Bible. The consensus view is summarized in the following paragraphs. The concept of the resurrection of the dead, according to this view, does not exist in the Torah or in preexilic sources. The Hebrew Bible is very strongly this-worldly in its vision of life and death. John Barclay Burns gives voice to this outlook: "The Old Testament is concerned with this world and not with the world of the dead, whom Yahweh did not remember any more."[7] Death is an integral part of the creation and those who die depart to a nether region called Sheol. Sheol is not a place of good or evil but is "simply the final assembly-point of all humanity."[8] The dead remain in Sheol with no prospects of ever returning to life again.[9]

The consensus view argues that belief in the resurrection develops later in Israel's history in the period known as the Second Temple era (from 538 BC–AD 70), and comes via exposure to Zoroastrian beliefs about resurrection. The hope of resurrection offered persecuted martyrs compensation for their loss of life in the present world. As a doctrine it found a small place in ancient rabbinic thought.[10]

What modern-day scholars have largely come to accept is that there is a major difference between the preexilic outlooks (Israel's national history from the exodus until Jerusalem fell to the Babylonians in 586 BC) and postexilic outlooks (history after 538 BC) on death and the afterlife. The preexilic view sees death as the end of life on earth. The postexilic view develops as Israel is exposed to (a) ideas about resurrection, (b) Greco-Persian beliefs on retribution concerning the fate of good and wicked people, and (c) Greek concepts of immortality. The expectation that the dead will be resurrected is isolated to the canonical book of Daniel. It then developed in later noncanonical books like 2 Maccabees.[11]

Book of Daniel and Zoroaster

In the early 1960s Theodore Gaster said that belief in resurrection probably emerged in Israelite thought during the Hellenistic age (334–63 BC).[12] The reasons why scholars propose a late date are interwoven with opinions about when the genre of apocalyptic literature emerged.[13] It is generally understood that, because it contains many visions and uses symbolic language, the book of Daniel is an apocalyptic text. Mid-to-late twentieth century opinions were divided over the dating of the book of Daniel. Most feel it was written when the Maccabees revolted (167–160 BC) against the Seleucid empire, but others favor an earlier time when the Persian Empire existed (550–330 BC).[14] No matter what date one settles on for the book of Daniel, the prevailing view is that the resurrection of the dead is unknown in preexilic times and emerges very late in Israel's history.

Leaving the date of the book of Daniel aside, the other critically contentious point is that the idea of resurrection enters Jewish thought from external sources. Some scholars have mused over the possible foreshadowing of the resurrection in the Canaanite (or Ugaritic) myth about Mot. Mot was the Canaanite god of death who was dismembered and later resuscitated.[15] Others have looked further afield and insist that Israel was strongly influenced by Persian (Iranian) religious ideas (Zoroastrian) sometime during the exilic and postexilic eras. Among the raft of Old Testament doctrines that it is claimed were inspired or influenced by Persian sources are Satan, angelology, resurrection and last judgment, heaven and hell, creation, and purity.[16] John Bright says that "the notions of rewards and punishment after death may derive in part from Iranian religion, where such beliefs were current." He adds that "the idea of a resurrection begins to appear sporadically and tentatively in later Biblical literature, and by the second century was a well-established belief."[17]

Bernhard Lang has argued that Ezekiel's exilic metaphor of the resurrected dead bones (Ezek. 37:1–14) involves borrowing from Zoroastrian practices. Lang is persuaded that the visionary imagery of the dead bones in the valley is inspired by the Zoroastrian practice in which human corpses are not buried but exposed to the natural elements.[18] Although scholars acknowledge that both the Bible and Judaism have developed distinct resurrection theologies, the basic suggestion remains that the concept of resurrection originated from sources external to Israel. We will discuss this point later on.

Figurative Resurrection

Scholars in the above consensus stream of thought argue that passages such as Job 19:23–29; Isaiah 26:19; and Ezekiel 37:1–14 contain figurative or metaphorical images for the resurrection. In the case of Job scholars disagree about what is meant when he said, "For I know that my Redeemer lives, and that at the last he will stand upon the earth; and after my skin has been thus destroyed, then in my flesh I shall see God" (19:25–26). In Job's world it was commonly thought that bad things happened to bad persons. As Job was righteous and blameless he could not fathom why he was suffering, so he was expecting some kind of vindication over the calamities that he experienced. Scholars say on the basis of other parts of the book that Job, at best, hoped his blamelessness would be recorded for posterity. He was not expecting resurrection because his afterlife destiny was the shadowy place called Sheol. We will reexamine this passage later on.

Again it is often said that Isaiah's words of comfort, "Your dead shall live, their corpses shall rise . . . the earth will give birth to those long dead" (26:19), merely uses a metaphor of resurrection that is solely concerned with Israel's national restoration. The consensus view points out that this passage does not have any explicit belief in the idea of individual bodily resurrection, but the prophet's words may contain a hint of it.

Likewise, Ezekiel has a grand vision that happened when Israel was enslaved by Babylon. Yahweh shows the prophet a valley full of dry dead bones and poses this question, "Mortal, can these bones live?" (Ezek. 37:3). Yahweh promises to put new flesh on these dead bones, and out of the dead valley a multitude will come to life. Since the vision refers to the house of Israel (37:11) there is a strong metaphor of Israel as a nation being resurrected and restored to the land promised to Abraham.

In contrast to these supposed figurative notions of resurrection, Daniel expresses an explicit hope about individual resurrection from the dead. John L. McKenzie says that Daniel 12:2 refers to the resurrection of the dead and that it is "the only clear allusion to this belief in the entire Hebrew Old Testament, although it is very probable that the belief is reflected in Isaiah 26:19."[19]

A Fresh Look

The judgments of late-twentieth-century scholars almost look like the final word. However, just like the macro-micro images in the Oxfam photograph mentioned in chapter 1, there may be more than meets the eye. There are subtle signposts to the resurrection in the Hebrew Bible that are often overlooked or relegated to the periphery.

Recent discussions from the Harvard University Jewish scholar Jon Levenson indicate that a fresh look at the resurrection is indeed needed. His book *Resurrection and the Restoration of Israel* represents the culmination of earlier work and is addressed to both scholars and to members of Reformed and Conservative Judaism. He believes that scholars need to rethink their stances about the resurrection in the Hebrew Bible. He also finds there are contemporary Jewish believers whose beliefs about immortality are at odds with both biblical and classical rabbinic teaching. Our case does not slavishly follow everything that Levenson argues; indeed we will augment some aspects of his work with insights gleaned from other Jewish and Christian scholars such as Anthony Petterson, Ben Ollenburger, and Leonard Greenspoon.

Levenson maintains against the modern consensus view that the resurrection was not an innovative doctrine that suddenly emerged in the late Second Temple era. He believes that modern-day assumptions about individualism, identity, and death, and contemporary skepticism about the miraculous have converged. The convergence of these attitudes has become a major impediment in properly understanding the world of the Hebrew Bible. He argues that our modern assumptions have been imposed on the biblical material. Levenson does not claim that the oldest sections of the Hebrew Bible present any belief of individual bodily resurrection. However he detects important building blocks that have been ignored.

When we look at the assumptions about identity, life, and death that we find in the Torah, Prophets, and Writings, we can come to understand how it is that Yahweh will give life to the dead. Yahweh miraculously intervened to redeem his people from Egypt at the birth of the nation, and throughout the rest of Israel's biblical history he continued to rescue and preserve his people. Levenson sees a strong promissory element in everything that Yahweh says— and for those promises to be truly meaningful, this had to involve restoring people to life. Ancient Israel was confident that Yahweh would redeem the world, so over time their thinking was directed towards the resurrection. Put another way, resurrection is not a tangential, isolated belief but is deeply rooted in preexisting biblical ideas about life.

Building Blocks for Resurrection

The concept of resurrection is supported and anticipated by the convergence of multiple themes and symbols in the Old Testament, such as: Yahweh the divine warrior defeating chaos and death; Yahweh as the God of life; Yahweh's promises to give life to his people; and the Scriptures' view of human identity. Levenson dubs these biblical themes and symbols the "antipodes" (i.e., opposites) to death. These antipodean symbols and themes contribute to the gradual development of thoughts about resurrection. The great conviction in Israel was that "God would yet again prove faithful to his promises of life for his people and that he had the stupendous might it would take to do so."[20]

Yahweh the Divine Warrior

At the macro level of the Hebrew Bible Yahweh appears as the divine warrior: "The Lord is a warrior" (Exod. 15:3).[21] Modern-day readers might misconstrue this imagery as if it favors religious violence or enshrines macho prowess. The divine warrior is *not* an iconic counterpart to Arnold Schwarzenegger's Terminator.[22] The warrior image is of Yahweh being righteously supreme over everything and everyone (Ps. 97) so that both humans and creation flourish. It becomes a macro theme in Israel's national life as Yahweh acts mightily throughout history (Ps. 24).

The divine warrior theme permeates the Psalter, which begins by contrasting the righteous and wicked and emphasizes Yahweh's watchfulness as the righteous flourish like trees (Ps. 1). There is a strong ethical aspect because the warrior theme emphasizes "the enthronement of God in righteousness and justice," and the warrior subdues the wicked and reverses the desiccation of nature.[23] The Davidic kings were supposed to imitate Yahweh's protective care for the weak (Ps. 72). Yahweh as warrior is Israel's true king who leads the nation and quells the wicked and overthrows injustices (Josh. 23:3, 10; Judg. 5:4–20). The warrior theme continues in passages like 2 Samuel 22; Isaiah 24:19–23; Zechariah 9; and Haggai 2.

Yahweh also overcomes the foe death: "he will swallow up death forever" (Isa. 25:7). When Yahweh wields power on desiccated land, nature reacts in joy and is resurrected into new life (Isa. 35:1–2, 7; Jer. 17:5–8). Isaiah sees that such power brings healing to humans: "the eyes of the blind shall be opened, and the ears of the deaf unstopped; then the lame shall leap like a deer, and the tongue of the speechless sing for joy" (Isa. 35:5–6). Both the barren land and human infirmities are experiences akin to death; but Yahweh's power nullifies them and restores life. As the Hebraic mind reflected on this overarching theme we find all kinds of pleas for Yahweh to rescue the pleader and to restore health and fullness (Pss. 31; 88; 143). This understanding that Yahweh can devour death and restore life theologically primed the Hebraic mind for resurrection.

You will recall from chapter 9 that there were myths of dying-and-rising gods found in some ancient Near Eastern cultures. Leonard Greenspoon makes some helpful observations on the differences between Yahweh the divine warrior who can devour death and the gods of the ancient Near East. He says, "It does not follow that a belief in a dying-and-rising god and knowledge of related myths . . . necessarily lead to the conception of the resurrection of the dead found in the Hebrew Bible."[24] One major difference is that the gods of Mesopotamia, Canaan, and Egypt were compelled by nature's seasonal cycle to die, whereas Yahweh is in control of nature's cycles. Greenspoon says, "We do not see how the belief in a deity . . . who is constrained periodically to suffer death could possibly lead to an understanding of God who Himself has power over death and specifically the power to awaken the bodies of His dead believers."[25] A subsidiary point is that the "average believer" in those ancient Near East cultures had no clear prospects for personal resurrection because the myths only related to dying-and-rising gods and their nation's kings.

Yahweh Gives Life

A complementary theme to the divine warrior that also serves as a building block for the Hebrew understanding of resurrection is the belief in Yahweh as the Creator and sustainer of life. Yahweh's supremacy over the cosmos as the Creator is expressed in images concerning the original creation as well as in prophetic images of a new creation. These images form antipodes to suffering, decay, and death. The theme of God as life giver fits into creation theology because it is God's creative work that brings forth the cosmos and life. Our colleague Anthony Petterson draws attention to the theology of the creation because it undergirds the hope of resurrection by emphasizing the vitality and sustaining of all life. In his discussion of passages about bringing life to a dead womb Petterson states, "Yahweh's promise to bring life from the dead is closely tied to who he is as Creator . . . creation theology provides the grounds for a resurrection hope."[26] God as the author of life has the power to restore life to those who die.

It is God's sustaining promise in the midst of human calamities to bring about a fulfilled and renewed creation. The lives of the characters in the Hebrew Bible often involve experiences of dysfunction, disease, dying, and death. Yet these same characters also encounter the life-giving God who restores, renews, revives, and re-creates. These characters come to know about experiences of "dying" and "rising," and the way is paved thematically for Israel's faith in the resurrection to blossom. The Hebraic mind was immersed in potent imagery about dying and rising to new life.

A Communal Sense of Selfhood

Our modern notions of an individualistic self are alien to the Hebraic mind. The self in ancient Israel had an identity rooted in familial, tribal, and ethnic notions—it was a group-oriented concept.[27] The people of Israel responded to God at a communal or corporate level. This communal sense of identity enabled the tribes, family units, and individuals to make better sense of who they were in relation to each other, to God, and to strangers. In ancient Israel there was a responding self that was both individual and communal and whose identity and purpose was about being chosen by Yahweh to enjoy and experience life. Here is just one example: Jacob (later renamed Israel) was both an individual man and an entire nation: "He went down into Egypt and lived there as an alien, few in number; and there he became a great nation, mighty and populous" (Deut. 26:5). He was the ancestor and progenitor of a nation, and he enacted in his biography the subsequent story of his descendants.[28] In other words, in the Hebraic mind there was no sharp distinction between a given individual and his descendants.

God made a covenantal promise to the individual patriarchs Abraham, Isaac, and Jacob, but none of them lived to see it happen. The covenantal promise was only fulfilled in the lives of those who bore the identity and name of these individual ancestors. Levenson underscores the point that in the ancient Hebrew mind-set, the lives of progenitors and generations of subsequent descendants were interwoven. Abraham, Isaac, and Jacob after their respective deaths are understood as sharing and enjoying the fulfilled promise via their people:

> Abraham, Isaac and Jacob continue to exist after they have died, not, it should be underscored, as disembodied spirits but as the people whose fathers they will always be. That death represents an absolute terminus, as it does to the modern mind, is not a foregone conclusion in biblical thought.[29]

Family ties to kinsfolk extended beyond living relatives to include ancestors. There was a strong web of ties in oaths and customs that bound the living to their familial ancestors in expressions of united kinship. One hint of these ties is evident in Jacob's twilight-of-life request that Joseph bury him in the plot that Abraham had purchased (Gen. 47:29–31; 49:29–32). Another kind of faithful mutuality in familial relations between the living and the dead is found in the duty that brothers had towards a widowed sister-in-law (Deut. 25:5–6). Other customs were associated with restoring the name of a deceased person to property that was his rightful inheritance (Ruth 4:5–12). Today we are not accustomed to thinking about these connections between living and deceased relatives.

Infertility: Yahweh Brings Life Out of Death

A recurrent theme in the Hebrew Bible is how Yahweh brings life from death by defeating infertility. Levenson notes that "infertility and the loss of children serve as the functional equivalent of death."[30] Petterson remarks that "if barrenness is death, then the promise of descendants in Genesis 12:1–3 is nothing less than life from death."[31] The problem of infertility is stark as we can see in Rachel's complaint: "Give me children, or I shall die" (Gen. 30:1). A family line was essentially dead when infertility occurred. In the patriarchal narratives infertility looms large for Abraham and Sarah, for Isaac and Rebekah, and for Jacob and Rachel. The perpetuation of a family line is also threatened in the book of Ruth for Naomi and in the case of Job, with the deaths of his children. So God's gift of the child Isaac to Abraham and Sarah, of the twins Jacob and Esau to Isaac and Rebekah, of Joseph to Jacob and Rachel, of the son born to Ruth and Boaz, and of the renewed progeny of Job restores these respective families to life. Petterson connects the hope for progeny in the face of infertility to creation theology: "The same God who created life from the dust is able to bring life from a dead womb."[32]

The gift of the child Samuel to Hannah, who had been infertile, serves as another example (1 Sam. 1:2, 5–6, 19–20). Hannah represents a particularized hope of life being raised out of a dead womb. Her song of praise contains the line that Yahweh "kills and brings to life; he brings down to Sheol and raises up" (1 Sam. 2:6). Fifty years ago Robert Martin-Achard took the view that while Hannah's song of praise does indicate Yahweh's power to intervene victoriously, it does not foreshadow or prefigure resurrection.[33] However, R. P. Gordon observes "while it is true that resurrection is not a central dogma of the Old Testament, there is much more chance of establishing its true place in Israelite thinking if texts such as this are not silenced by scholarly presupposition before they have had the opportunity to speak."[34] Levenson sees both Hannah's song (1 Sam. 2:6) and Moses's song (Deut. 32:39) as texts that unequivocally affirm that Yahweh is sovereign over both death and Sheol. Petterson takes the matter further and remarks that "with Hannah, there is another instance of a particularization of the resurrection hope in terms of a barren womb being brought to life. . . . [T]his hope is grounded in creation; it is because Yahweh has set the world on its pillars that he is able to do these things."[35]

A literal bodily resurrection does not appear in any of these passages concerning infertility and threatened family lines. Nevertheless these texts lay the foundation for the expression of eschatology: at the end of time the dead will be resurrected. The seedbed for an analogy of resurrection is embedded in the theme of infertility (symbolic death) and fertility restored (symbolic resurrection). The gift of fertility and the restoration of lost (even deceased) offspring demonstrate that in ancient Israel there was a very strong faith in Yahweh's power over death. These passages affirm that Yahweh brings forth new life where a functional form of death blights a family unit. They also show that Yahweh has the power to fulfill his promises. Acts of deliverance, healing, and restoration bring individuals back from the dead and into the fullness of life once more. So fertility and the birth of a child represent another antipode to death.

Back from the Dead

A different example of Yahweh bringing forth life out of death is illustrated in the prophetic ministries of Elijah and Elisha. Both of these prophets meet women whose family circumstances provide opportunities for God to act in a miraculous way. When the northern kingdom of Israel was dominated by Baal worship, Elijah declared judgment via a drought. The land in effect became dead (1 Kings 17:1). In an ironic twist Elijah sheltered in the household of a pagan widow in Zarephath. The woman's son fell ill and died, but Elijah prayed and the child was revivified, and her family line was restored (1 Kings 17:17–24). The irony is that this pagan woman recognized Elijah as God's messenger while almost all of Israel ignored him.

Elisha encountered a different family: a Shunammite woman whose son died. Elisha prayed, touched the child, and he was revivified from the dead (2 Kings 4:32–35). After Elisha's death and burial another corpse was interred in his tomb. When the dead man's corpse came into contact with Elisha's bones he was revived (2 Kings 13:21). These three miraculous events illustrate that Yahweh brings life even to the dead, and as a result families experience restoration to life with the return of the dead loved one.

However, these are not cases of actual resurrections that bestow unending life: the three persons revived here later on die. They are technically revivifications or resuscitations of the dead. The New Testament presents similar cases: Jairus's daughter (Mark 5:21–24, 35–42), the widow of Nain's son (Luke 7:11–16), Lazarus (John 11:1–44), Dorcas (Acts 9:36–41), and Eutychus (Acts 20:9–12). As we have already explained, Jesus's resurrection is different from these revivifications. Likewise, the general resurrection of humanity involves more than being resuscitated from the dead.

Nevertheless these stories about Elijah and Elisha show that those who lived in preexilic times were open to the possibility of bodily resurrection. Levenson remarks:

> The resurrection that the miracle-working prophet Elisha performs is not, of course, the general resurrection that Judaism later expected at the end-time, but it does demonstrate a firm faith in God's power over death, a key point in the later expectation that is often mistakenly thought to be an innovation in the late sources.[36]

In the Elijah-Elisha stories (1 Kings 17:17–24; 2 Kings 4:32–35) the miracles reverse the death of beloved sons and restore family lines to health.

Parallel to these miracles is the action of Yahweh averting death and restoring family lines in the pivotal stories of two beloved sons: Isaac, who faced death by sacrifice (Gen. 22:7–18), and Ishmael, who faced death by lack of food and water (Gen. 21:8–20). In Isaac's case Abraham faces the excruciating tension between the promise of progeny and the deadly outcome of losing his son. He trusts Yahweh to fulfill his promise about progeny to the point of hoping for resurrection (Heb. 11:17–19). In Ishmael's story Yahweh rescues both mother and son from starvation and dehydration. Yahweh instructs Hagar to "lift up" her son (Gen. 21:18). Elisha instructs the Shunammite woman to lift up her son (2 Kings 4:36). Madigan and Levenson suggest that for the Hebraic mind this imagery of lifting up these sons from death or deathlike circumstances symbolized the idea of resurrection from the dead.[37]

Other signals of Hebraic death-refusing hope are found in the enigmatic fates of the prophet Elijah and Enoch. The stories of these two characters (2 Kings 2:1–12; Gen. 5:24) strongly imply that their respective lives on earth did not end with death.[38] Neither Elijah's fiery chariot ride into the sky—which reminds us of divine warrior imagery of Yahweh riding across the heavens (Ps. 18:10)—nor the translation of Enoch from the earth involves a resurrection. In connection with Enoch's fate Petterson remarks, "while this suggests that there is another world, and that humans can be taken there by God, it does not offer a hope that those who have died will necessarily be raised to life."[39] Both cases, however, provide preexilic hints that life with God continues beyond this world and that a few individuals were transferred from this world to be with God.

Job as Resurrection Story

The book of Job can easily conjure up in our memories the images of his great suffering. Much of the book is taken up with extensive debate between Job and his friends. It wrestles with the riddle about why horrible things happen to seemingly good individuals. Job is flummoxed by his experiences because he insists that he is blameless before God, while his friends claim that he must have done something really bad. We can easily be overwhelmed by the pathos of these debates and by God's astonishing reply to Job about the wisdom and complexity of the creation (Job 38–41).

As we mentioned above, many scholars think that for Job there is little hope of an afterlife except perhaps to exist in the gloomy netherworld of Sheol. They believe that the meaning of Job 19:23–29 is obscure and that nobody can be confident that it makes any allusion to a hope for resurrection. However, we need to reconsider this in light of death-refusing hope in the face of personal calamities.

The calamities that befall Job clearly involve the absence of the fullness of life. Job's material losses, the deaths of his children, and his decrepit health locate him among the dying and dead. He bemoans his lot as being worse than death itself (Job 3), and his sense of life's frailty already places him alongside those in the shadowy realm of Sheol (7:7–10). However, he does not perish, and as the story unfolds he is eventually delivered from being counted among those in Sheol.

At the conclusion of Job's story God restores him to health, vitality, and material prosperity. He has seven sons and three daughters and lives to witness four successive generations of kin (42:10–17). The overarching themes of loss and blessed restoration in Job parallel the patriarchs' experiences of infertility (symbolic death) and the gift of life in children (symbolic resurrection).

When Job eventually dies (42:17) it is peaceful and blessed. This "happy ending" allows us to rethink what he said: "after my skin has been thus destroyed, then in my flesh I shall see God" (19:26). When Job sought vindication his ultimate expectation was that this would happen face-to-face with God. Francis Andersen remarks on this verse, "The hope of resurrection lies at the very heart of Job's faith."[40] His hope for vindication points in an eschatological direction. In weighing these items up Petterson goes so far as to say that "Job is basically a resurrection story."[41]

Birth and Exile of the Nation

The birth of Israel as a nation is graphically narrated in the Passover and exodus from Egypt. The theme of death pervades the Passover as judgment is brought down on Egypt's firstborn. Just as the patriarchs were called to trust God, so the enslaved tribes of Israel were called to trust that Yahweh would deliver them. William Dumbrell has pointed out that Moses's song (Exod. 15:1–18) is grounded in the theme of the creation.[42] In this song we find that Yahweh has brought the nation to life out of an experience that was shrouded in oppression and death. Petterson argues that a resurrection hope is embedded in God's deliverance of the people from slavery. It is a national "resurrection." He then directs attention to Deuteronomy 32:39: "See now that I, even I, am he; there is no god besides me. I kill and I make alive; I wound and I heal; and no one can deliver from my hand." According to Petterson the resurrection hope expressed here is a "hope in Yahweh as the one who can bring life from the dead."[43]

When exile looms the prophet Hosea describes Israel's circumstances in terms of death, plagues, and Sheol (Hos. 13:14). By way of contrast the prophet invites the nation to "return to the LORD" (6:1) so that they may be revived and raised up to live once again (6:2). Levenson sees this text as a stepping-stone towards embracing the belief in bodily resurrection. Petterson points out that the verbs used in this passage for being revived, raised, and living are exactly the same as those used by Isaiah (26:14, 19).[44] As we will see below the passage in Isaiah expresses a clear hope for resurrection from the dead.

Restoration and Resurrection of Israel

Petterson believes that the Hebrew Bible depicts *both* the resurrection of the nation *and* the resurrection of individuals in a manner that shows *both* intimate connections between the two themes *and* independence for the two themes. When we read Ezekiel's vision (37:1–14), resurrection imagery acts as a metaphor for the nation's restoration.[45] The critical questions, though, are, where did this metaphor arise from? and, how would the exilic community have recognized and understood it? The modern consensus view looks to Persian sources, but Levenson, Greenspoon, and Petterson see another answer to this question. Ezekiel's metaphor is grounded in the preexilic understanding of Yahweh bringing life out of death. In chapter 7 we noted that the earliest source mentioning Zoroastrian belief in bodily resurrection is in 380 BC. While Ezekiel could have appealed to something that readers in exile might have seen in Babylon, his pictorial imagery does not resemble a Zoroastrian cemetery.[46]

According to Levenson, the restoration of Israel as a nation is thematically rooted in what we have surveyed above. The power of Yahweh to overcome infertility and Elijah, and Elisha's reviving of the dead are thematic building blocks. These building blocks connect to the metaphors used by later prophets like Isaiah and Ezekiel about Israel's postexilic fate. The nation had a corporate experience of birth (exodus), death (exile), and resurrection.[47]

The exilic messages from Isaiah evoke images of Israel as a bereaved widow who has lost her children. The consolation offered draws on the metaphors of "the return of the lost sons and daughters" (see Isa. 43:6), "the patriarchal promise of progeny" (Isa. 44:1–5; 48:17–19), the comforted barren woman (Isa. 49:14–26), and the hope of the abandoned woman (Isa. 54:4–6).[48] Once again Yahweh overcomes death by restoring Israel's lost children so that corporate and national wholeness is experienced again. The nation's exile and its subsequent restoration are symbolized in metaphors of loss and resurrection. Other passages that provide credible support for the idea of resurrection are found in Isaiah 52:13–53:12 and 66:22–24.

Besides the imagery of the bereaved widow other hopes concerning resurrection are expressed by Isaiah. It is in Isaiah 26 that the vocabulary of resurrection is clearly used. The chapter opens with a song of praise about trusting in Yahweh's everlasting salvation and peace. In verse 14 those overlords who have reigned over the people are declared the "dead" who "do not live." They are null and void and removed from this world, and they will not even be remembered. These mortal rulers are nothing compared to Yahweh.

The destiny of Yahweh's people stands in stark contrast to those of the obliterated overlords: "Your dead shall live, their corpses shall rise. O dwellers in the dust, awake and sing for joy! For your dew is a radiant dew, and the earth will give birth to those long dead" (26:19). Petterson points out that this verse clearly depicts the dead returning to life: there is a rising up of dead bodies; those who are in the dust will awaken; and the earth gives birth to those in the grave. He comments:

> This verse affirms that those who are Yahweh's possession will not suffer death as their ultimate end. They will be resurrected to partake in the festivities of Yahweh's final triumph on the day he comes to judge.[49]

Ben Ollenburger also sees hints at resurrection in the national restoration achieved here and says, "The promise of resurrection is based on an event that is announced with solemn warning in 26:19–20."[50] In his reading of chapters

24–27 Ollenburger says that Isaiah "is constrained to speak of resurrection and of the end of death's ultimately futile but still terrible reign" because in the future all of Yahweh's rivals are vanquished.[51]

In Ezekiel 37:1–14 the prophet's vision of the valley of dead bones concerns the nation's restoration from exile and involves a re-creation and rebirth. Yahweh will breathe life into the dead bones (vv. 5–6, 10). The imagery is of people coming out of tombs with new flesh. As verses 11–14 disclose, the imagery concerns the dead nation of Israel that will emerge from its exilic tomb into new life. The vocabulary used to express this hope for being raised to life again is identical to that used in Hannah's song (1 Sam. 2:6). The act of raising the nation to life is a resurrection of the community and the jargon used speaks of a new creation. Petterson observes that the term used for Yahweh breathing life into the bones is one and the same with the verbs concerning the breath of life in Genesis 2:7. He therefore links the theology of creation to the nation's resurrection.

The exilic themes of Isaiah's bereaved woman are different from Ezekiel's vision, yet both of them are concerned with the nation's resurrection. Levenson comments on Ezekiel's vision:

> In this symbolic representation of national recovery, restoration comes about not through miraculous fertility or the return of lost children but, significantly, through the resurrection of dead and despondent Israel from their graves, to return to the land God has indefeasibly promised them.[52]

The messages of Isaiah and Ezekiel open up a fresh vista for appreciating the direction that Hebraic thought took concerning eschatology. The Hebrew Bible speaks of *both* the nation's resurrection from exile *and* the anticipated hope of the physical resurrection of the dead at the end of time.[53]

Being Asleep/Being Awake

Death is sometimes described as being asleep (Ps. 13:3; Job 14:12), while resurrection involves waking up (2 Kings 4:31). John Sawyer has examined the vocabulary associated with the resurrection of the dead and found five distinct groups of words, mostly verbs concerning "to live," "to wake up," "to stand up," "to come back," and "to sprout forth."[54] The individuals who are raised from the dead by Elijah and Elisha were described as asleep and then they both wake up and stand up (1 Kings 17; 2 Kings 4). While not all Hebrew texts correlate death to sleep, the way in which the word "sleep" is used in Daniel 12:2 also occurs in Jeremiah 51:39, where Yahweh will cause Babylon's doom and make them "sleep a perpetual sleep and never wake." Here sleep is a metaphor for death.

The clearest confession of belief in the bodily resurrection of the dead is found in Daniel 12:2, "Many of those who sleep in the dust of the earth shall awake, some to everlasting life, and some to shame and everlasting contempt." This passage comes immediately after a set of visions concerning God's kingdom being established at the climax of human history. The vocabulary used to refer to the dead as being asleep and waking up from the dust has its direct parallel in Isaiah 26:19: "Your dead shall live, their corpses shall rise. O dwellers in the dust, awake and sing for joy!"

The book of Daniel provides a very explicit understanding that there will be a general resurrection of the dead at the end of time. This passage envisages eternal reward for the righteous and eternal punishment for those who have opposed God. It influenced later writers of apocryphal books (e.g., 2 Maccabees 7) that express the hope that God will give life back to the dead.[55] Daniel 12 is one building block that supports the New Testament's teaching on the general resurrection and last judgment.

Another example worth noting is in 1 Kings 18 where Elijah clashed with the prophets of Baal on Mt. Carmel. This incident was immediately preceded by the resurrection story of the son of the widow of Zarephath (1 Kings 17). Many scholars insist that Baal the Canaanite god was a dying-and-rising deity. In chapter 9 we noted the divergent opinions of Mark Smith and Tryggve Mettinger about Baal's resurrection. If Baal was a dying-and-rising deity, the clash between Elijah and Baal's prophets has some added spice. Greenspoon suggests that the vocabulary of sleeping and waking is very relevant in this clash. Elijah mocks the prophets of Baal when their prayers are unanswered: "Cry aloud! Surely he is a god; either he is meditating, or he has wandered away, or he is on a journey, or perhaps he is asleep and must be awakened" (1 Kings 18:27). If Elijah understood that Baal was a dying-and-rising god, then his mocking words take on added significance. Greenspoon amplifies the spirit of the encounter:

> Don't you see, the prophet asks, that this "no god," on whose rising all of nature is supposed to depend, is locked, as it were, in the nether-world, unable to awaken=resurrect himself? . . . Choose for you must, between a pagan deity utterly devoid of power, whose adherents yet claim him as warrior and source of fertility, and the God of Israel, who demonstrated before the eyes of all that His vitalizing power as Divine Warrior truly does extend from the provision of fertility throughout the earth to the re-awakening of His dead that is the only authentic resurrection for which one can hope.[56]

Here the Hebrew Bible bears witness to Yahweh's power being greater than that of death or of an empty fertility god who cannot answer a prayer. Yahweh's power is so great that he can raise the dead, while the Canaanite god that dies and rises again each season is impotent. Baal cannot raise the dead, and worship of Baal leads to a spiritual cul-de-sac. Worship of Yahweh opens up the pathway to life in the here and now and that finally leads to an authentic resurrection of the dead.

Conclusion

In this chapter we have surveyed afresh the Hebrew Bible on the resurrection. The survey shows that there are many thematic building blocks pointing to Yahweh's power over death and promises to give life to his people. The building blocks confirm the covert theme of a death-refusing hope that finds its mature form in confessing the resurrection of the dead. These are the building blocks that find completion in the revelation of Jesus who dies and rises again from the dead, and as the firstfruits is the promise that we too shall rise again from the dead. Jesus likely used these building blocks when he instructed his disciples on how the Hebrew Bible pointed to him and his death and resurrection, and when he explained the implications of these events for his followers.

As we wrap up our foray into understanding the resurrection we want to draw your attention to some words from Winston Churchill. He delivered a speech in November 1942 to celebrate Field Marshal Montgomery's decisive victory over Erwin Rommel in the battle of El Alamein. It signaled the beginning of the rollback of the Nazi forces in North Africa. Churchill made a wonderful remark that we feel is something that could be understood in a new context by anyone who believes in Jesus's resurrection and the general resurrection. We suggest that these words may be triumphantly affirmed as part of a eulogy: "Now this is not the end. It is not even the beginning of the end. But it is, perhaps, the end of the beginning."[57]

Spiritual Audit

1. When you picture yourself on the Emmaus road what do you think Jesus means by his words that all the Hebrew Scriptures are summed in him?

2. What are death-defining moments from your life that you seek resurrection from?

3. What part of the consensus view on beliefs about the afterlife in the Hebrew Bible has shaped or held sway over you and your group in its understanding of the Bible?

4. What does the communal sense of resurrection mean for your spiritual life and practice?

5. How is the resurrection the end of the beginning for your life?

PART FOUR

RESURRECTION HORIZONS

And it is resurrection which explains why Jesus is the coming judge. It isn't anything so trivial as that the resurrection demonstrates Jesus' divinity, or even his human superiority, and thus qualifies him for this particular tricky task. Rather, it is that with the resurrection of Jesus God's new world has begun; in other words, his being raised from the dead is the start, the paradigm case, the foundation, the beginning, of that great setting-right which God will do for the whole cosmos at the end. The risen body of Jesus is the one bit of the physical universe that has already been "set right." Jesus is therefore the one through whom everything else will be "set right."

N. T. Wright[1]

13

Resurrection Theses for the Third Millennium

We have traversed a lot of material about the resurrection in this book. We began by alluding to Luther's famous ninety-five theses, and although we do not presume to put ourselves on the same level as Luther, in the spirit of his call for church renewal and reform we conclude this book with our "theses."

1. The resurrection is the lynchpin of Christianity. No other dogma provides the glue that holds faith, life, and practice altogether.
2. The church must recover a balanced understanding of both the cross and the resurrection.
3. The resurrection does not exist just to validate the cross.
4. The resurrection defense is about the truth of the Easter event, but the traditional defense must extend into showing its relevance to all areas of life.
5. Without the resurrection of Christ there can be no future resurrection of the dead.
6. Christian hope without the resurrection of the dead is an everlasting pie-in-the-sky existence.
7. Resurrection is holistic and therefore more empowering than reincarnation.
8. To deny the resurrection of Jesus is to deny the resurrection of the dead and to deny hope.
9. The resurrection is not a New Testament "surprise." It is found in the Law, Prophets, and Writings of the Old Testament.

10. The risen Jesus gives confidence about the authenticity of the Bible; he affirms the Old Testament and the Spirit guiding the writers of the New Testament.

11. The answer to the question, what does God look like? can be found in the resurrection of Jesus.

12. The resurrection confirms the hope that Jesus is indeed coming again.

13. The first Easter showed that the women were the most faithful followers of Jesus through his death, burial, and resurrection. They are rewarded with the first-day-of-the-week appearances.

14. The resurrection brings divine meaning to the total agony and suffering of Christ on the cross.

15. Without the resurrection the call to mission in Acts would be empty nonsense.

16. Mission that focuses only on the death of Christ is not the good news.

17. It is the resurrected Christ who empowers, guides, and gives strength to the church in mission.

18. The resurrection is not hidden from humankind. We are without excuse. It is found in both special revelation and the modes of general revelation in nature, culture, and history.

19. Those who proclaim the resurrection of Christ and the resurrection of the dead should expect to be mocked and rejected in parts of the church and by scoffers in the marketplace.

20. The resurrection speaks to the post-Christendom seeker, the modernist follower, and those who are both/and in worldview.

21. Jesus's resurrection is the lynchpin and the glue of every authentic evangelistic utterance.

22. Jesus's resurrection is about evangelizing and ministering to whole people; it is not about rescuing disembodied souls to float on ethereal clouds in heaven.

23. Jesus's resurrection and the resurrection of the dead show that we must care for the whole person.

24. When the resurrection is upheld as the lynchpin, the binary view of evangelism versus social justice evaporates.

25. Looking for Aslan and Gandalf in myth and fairy tale can help point us toward the fulfillment of resurrection in Jesus.

26. Preaching that does not at least make the cross and resurrection equal is counter to the true gospel.

27. The resurrection brings us to our knees before the one who is both judge and king.

28. The resurrection is countercultural because it goes against the grain and transforms our way of life. It overturns all idolatrous and disempowering paradigms.

29. Jesus's resurrection is the critical sign of the coming kingdom.

30. Without the resurrection that brings divine judgment there will be no justice, leaving all the atrocities of history unanswered.

31. Ethics needs the fulcrum of the resurrection: it validates the message and shows the cosmic dimension of God's ethical concern for the world, for the environment, and for us.

32. The resurrection of Jesus and the resurrection of the dead do not involve planet earth ending up in a cosmic dustbin. The resurrection, to the contrary, shows that there is to be *both* a new heaven *and* a new earth that are our eternal home.

33. The resurrection of Jesus means that God loves all creation.

34. The resurrection is radical discipleship as it claims to empower, equip, and strengthen us to love our neighbor as ourselves. It is about living by the Great Commandment and the Great Commission.

35. Radical discipleship is taking up my cross and following the risen Christ.

36. The way of Jesus is only complete by way of there being a resurrection.

37. The resurrection asks: If you claim to be a resurrectionist would there be enough evidence to convict you?

38. Anyone who believes in the resurrected Christ will, like doubting Thomas, confess of Jesus, "My Lord and my God."

39. The resurrection declares that God cares for the whole of me.

40. The resurrection is as essential for the justification of the sinner as is the cross.

41. Jesus's resurrection is God's divine yes: I am forgiven.

42. When life falls apart and God seems utterly remote, the resurrection makes it clear that God is indeed with us.

43. It is because of the resurrection of Jesus that we can truly have a powerful prayer life that connects us to the one who has already walked in our journey.

44. In the resurrection of Christ I can become an effective self.

45. The resurrection of Christ must lead to a transformed personality.

46. The resurrection of Christ enables me to operate within a godly framework of a boundless self.

47. The resurrection shows Jesus as the firstborn of a new community that commenced on the first day of the week.

48. A dead, nonresurrected Messiah is as useful to the church as was Samson after his haircut.

49. If the church truly believes in the resurrection, why then are there only Stations of the Cross? This anomaly is true of much of both the evangelical and Roman Catholic worlds.

50. The resurrection declares there is neither Jew nor Greek and neither male or female, and there are no class distinctions.

51. Jesus's resurrection speaks against all nonperson abuse and, in particular, sexual abuse in the church.

52. The resurrection of Christ calls the whole church to repent.
53. In different eras the resurrection has been the heartbeat for the church's theology and mission. To our great shame the resurrection's importance and influence in church history has become a forgotten truth.
54. Wholehearted worship is a passionate way of resurrection living.
55. The resurrection is true and it works!

Notes

Part One The Resurrection Grid

1. George Beasley-Murray, *Preaching the Gospel from the Gospels* (London: Lutterworth, 1956), 46.

Chapter 1 The Resurrection Is the Lynchpin

1. The original bibliographical source for this quote in Campanella's writings is uncertain. It is partly cited by Gordon Moyes, "All the Names of Jesus: Study 14: Lamb," GordonMoyes.com, March 26, 2010, http://www.gordonmoyes.com/2010/03/26/all-the-names-of-jesus-study-14-lamb/. Moyes may have derived the quote from the sermons of Arthur John Gossip (1873–1954), who served as Professor of Christian Ethics and Practical Theology at the University of Glasgow. Part of the above quote is reproduced unreferenced in Joseph Maurus [Ferrero], *A Source Book of Inspiration* (1987; repr., Mumbai: Better Yourself Books, 2006), 172; and in Paul Beasley-Murray, *The Message of the Resurrection* (Leicester, UK: Inter-Varsity, 2000), 256.

2. Figure 1.1 was prepared by Mark Barry for publication in *SALT* magazine to show the gospel elements in Acts. The tabulated figures are based on a survey of Acts 2, 3, 4, 10, 13, 17, and 26, where major speeches or sermons were delivered by the apostles. One speech that was omitted from the survey is Stephen's speech in Acts 7.

3. Walter R. Martin, *Essential Christianity*, rev. ed. (Santa Ana, CA: Vision, 1975), 59.

4. This is very different from the stance of Bishop Azariah, the first native Indian bishop of the Church of South India. The bishop was once asked: "If you were in a village where they had never heard of Christ, what would you preach upon?" He replied, "The resurrection." See Beasley-Murray, *Message of the Resurrection*, 258.

5. John Warwick Montgomery, *In Defense of Martin Luther* (Milwaukee: Northwestern, 1970), 38.

6. Mark L. Y. Chan, "The Gospel and the Achievement of the Cross," *ERT* 33 (2009): 31.

7. Martin Luther, *LW* 30:12–13.

8. Martin Luther, *Sermons of Martin Luther*, ed. J. N. Lenker, trans. J. N. Lenker et al. (1905; repr., Grand Rapids: Baker, 1989), 3:14.

9. Philip H. Pfatteicher and Carlos Messerli, *Manual on the Liturgy, Lutheran Book of Worship* (Minneapolis: Augsburg, 1979), 14.

10. N. T. Wright, *Surprised by Hope: Rethinking Heaven, the Resurrection, and the Mission of the Church* (New York: HarperOne, 2008).

11. John R. W. Stott, *The Cross of Christ* (Downers Grove, IL: InterVarsity, 2006).

12. Steve Chalke and Alan Mann, *The Lost Message of Jesus* (Grand Rapids: Zondervan, 2003), advocate reappraising the atonement. Partisans exchange opinions in Derek Tidball, David Hilborn, and Justin Thacker, eds., *The Atonement Debate* (Grand Rapids: Zondervan, 2008).

13. John R. W. Stott, *Basic Christianity*, 2nd ed. (Leicester, UK: Inter-Varsity, 1979), 51.

14. Stott, *Cross of Christ*, 13.

15. Ibid., 17.

16. Ibid., 233, 234.

17. R. Albert Mohler, "Creating the Bridge: An Interview with John R. W. Stott," Preaching. com, accessed May 26, 2010, http://www.preaching.com/resources/preaching-online/11567090/page-4/.

18. John R. W. Stott, *Evangelical Truth* (Downers Grove, IL: InterVarsity, 1999), 85.

19. James Denny, *The Death of Christ* (1911; repr., Minneapolis: Klock & Klock, 1982), 56–57.

20. Stott, *Cross of Christ*, 232–33.

21. Ibid., 233.

22. Michael F. Bird, "Justified by Christ's Resurrection: A Neglected Aspect of Paul's Doctrine of Justification," *SBET* 22 (2004): 74.

23. Chan, "Gospel," 31.

24. Christopher J. H. Wright, "According to the Scriptures: The Whole Gospel in Biblical Revelation," *ERT* 33 (2009): 4–18; J. Kwabena Asamoah-Gyadu, "Signs, Wonders and Ministry: The Gospel in the Power of the Spirit," *ERT* 33 (2009): 32–46; Jon Bonk, "The Gospel and Ethics," *ERT* 33 (2009): 47–61.

25. Christopher J. H. Wright, "Whole Gospel, Whole Church, Whole World," *Christianity Today*, October 2009, 32.

26. "The Cape Town Commitment: A Confession of Faith and a Call to Action," Lausanne. org, accessed May 9, 2011, http://www.lausanne.org/documents/CapeTownCommitment.pdf. Expanded references to the resurrection see Part 1, 4 A, clauses 4 and 5, and 8 B.

27. David W. Bebbington, *Evangelicalism in Modern Britain: A History from the 1730s to the 1980s* (London: Unwin Hyman, 1989), 2–17.

28. George A. Rawlyk and Mark A. Noll, eds., *Amazing Grace: Evangelicalism in Australia, Britain, Canada, and the United States* (Grand Rapids: Baker, 1993). Australian Baptists in the major state of NSW are called to affirm what is known as the 1979 Statement of Faith. It has thirteen major paragraphs, not one of which discusses the resurrection of Jesus. The resurrection is only referred to in one line under the paragraph entitled "Christ's Atonement." We are sure this statement of faith is not unique in this regard.

29. Gerald O'Collins, "Thomas Aquinas and Christ's Resurrection," *TS* 31 (1970): 514; Anthony J. Kelly, *The Resurrection Effect: Transforming Christian Life and Thought* (Maryknoll, NY: Orbis, 2008), ix–x, italics original.

30. George M. Marsden, introduction to *Evangelicalism and Modern America*, ed. George Marsden (Grand Rapids: Eerdmans, 1984), ix–x.

31. This point is raised by Kelly, *Resurrection Effect*, 6–7.

32. David J. Bosch, *Transforming Mission: Paradigm Shifts in Theology of Mission* (Maryknoll, NY: Orbis, 1991), 515.

33. Ibid.

34. Wright, *Surprised by Hope*, 265.

35. Ibid., 264.

36. Timothy C. Tennant, *Christianity at the Religious Roundtable: Evangelicalism in Conversation with Hinduism, Buddhism, and Islam* (Grand Rapids: Baker, 2002), 190. Tennant refers to the resurrection for Buddhists (113) and Muslims (193), but not in the Hindu encounter.

37. William M. Thompson, "The Risen Christ, Transcultural Consciousness, and the Encounter of the World Religions," *TS* 37 (1976): 381–409; Kelly, *Resurrection Effect*, 168–72.

38. Michael Nazir-Ali, *Mission and Dialogue: Proclaiming the Gospel Afresh in Every Age* (London: SPCK, 1995), 11, 12.

39. Leo D. Lefebure, *The Buddha and the Christ: Explorations in Buddhist and Christian Dialogue* (Maryknoll, NY: Orbis, 1993), 52–53.

40. Ahmed Deedat (1918–2005) was a popular Muslim apologist; see David Westerlund, "Ahmed Deedat's Theology of Religion: Apologetics through Polemics," *JRA* 33 (2003): 263–78.

41. The Jehovah's Witnesses' position is argued in *You Can Live Forever in Paradise on Earth*, rev. ed. (New York: Watchtower Bible & Tract Society, 1989). Christian rebuttals include Walter R. Martin and Norman H. Klann, *Jehovah of the Watchtower*, rev. ed. (Minneapolis: Bethany, 1974), 69–70; John Francis Coffey, *The Gospel according to Jehovah's Witnesses* (Melbourne: Polding, 1979), 65–75.

42. Mark Albrecht, *Reincarnation: A Christian Appraisal* (Downers Grove, IL: InterVarsity, 1982); Ross Clifford and Philip Johnson, *Jesus and the Gods of the New Age* (Colorado Springs: Victor, 2003).

43. Tullian Tchividjian, interviewed in Collin Hansen, "Out of Step and Fine With It," *Christianity Today*, May 2009, 31.

44. Beth Felker Jones, *Marks of His Wounds: Gender Politics and Bodily Resurrection* (Oxford: Oxford University Press, 2007), 113.

45. Beasley-Murray, *Message of the Resurrection*, 17.

46. Richard Swinburne, *The Resurrection of God Incarnate* (Oxford: Clarendon, 2003).

47. N. T. Wright, *The Resurrection of the Son of God* (Minneapolis: Fortress, 2003).

48. See Wright, *Surprised by Hope*; N. T. Wright, *The Challenge of Easter* (Downers Grove, IL: InterVarsity, 2010).

49. I. Howard Marshall, "Raised for Our Justification: The Saving Significance of the Resurrection of Christ," in *Tough-Minded Christianity: Honoring the Legacy of John Warwick Montgomery*, ed. William Dembski and Thomas Schirrmacher (Nashville: B & H Academic, 2008), 244.

50. Richard B. Gaffin, "Redemption and Resurrection: An Exercise in Biblical-Systematic Theology," *Them* 27 (2002): 16–31.

51. Ibid., 18.

52. Ibid., 19.

53. Kelly, *Resurrection Effect*, ix.

54. Richard N. Longenecker, ed., *Life in the Face of Death: The Resurrection Message of the New Testament* (Grand Rapids: Eerdmans, 1998).

55. Steven T. Davis, Daniel Kendall, and Gerald O'Collins , eds., *The Resurrection: An Interdisciplinary Symposium on the Resurrection of Jesus* (Oxford: Oxford University Press, 1997).

56. François-Xavier Durrwell, *The Resurrection: A Biblical Study*, trans. Rosemary Sheed (London: Sheed & Ward, 1960); Walter Künneth, *The Theology of the Resurrection*, trans. James W. Leitch (London: SCM, 1965); Wolfhart Pannenberg, *Jesus: God and Man*, trans. Lewis L. Wilkens and Duane A. Priebe (Philadelphia: Westminster, 1968).

57. Sam Allberry, *Lifted: Experiencing the Resurrection Life* (Nottingham: Inter-Varsity, 2010), theologically reflects the influence of Sydney Anglican evangelicals such as Phillip Jensen, Michael Jensen, John Dickson, and John Woodhouse.

58. Mark Driscoll and Gerry Breshears, *Vintage Jesus* (Wheaton: Crossway, 2007), 127–46; Mark Driscoll and Gerry Breshears, *Doctrine: What Christians Should Believe* (Wheaton: Crossway, 2010), 279–303.

59. Driscoll and Breshears, *Doctrine*, 280–83.

60. Ibid., 303.

61. Adrian Warnock, *Raised with Christ: How the Resurrection Changes Everything* (Wheaton: Crossway, 2010), 13.

62. Also see Warnock's webcast interview with Driscoll on the importance of the resurrection: Warnock, "Interview—Mark Driscoll on the Resurrection," adrianwarnock.com, March 30, 2010, http://adrianwarnock.com/2010/03/interview-mark-driscoll-on-the-resurrection/.

63. The undocumented quote of Stott appears in Driscoll and Breshears, *Vintage Jesus*, 130–31; and Warnock, *Raised with Christ*, 19, who obtained his quote secondhand from Driscoll and Breshears. The original source is John R. W. Stott, *Christ the Controversialist: A Study in Some Essentials of Evangelical Religion* (Downers Grove, IL: InterVarsity, 1970), 61.

64. Stott, *Christ the Controversialist*, 49–64.

65. Ibid., 118; see also 119–20, 131–32.

66. Jon D. Levenson, *Resurrection and the Restoration of Israel: The Ultimate Victory of the God of Life* (New Haven: Yale University Press, 2006).

67. Ross Clifford and Philip Johnson, *Riding the Rollercoaster: How the Risen Christ Empowers Life* (Sydney: Strand, 1998).

68. Simon Smart, *A Spectator's Guide to World Views* (Sydney: Blue Bottle, 2007).

69. James W. Sire, *The Universe Next Door*, 4th ed. (Downers Grove, IL: InterVarsity, 2004).

70. James K. A. Smith, *Desiring the Kingdom: Worship, Worldview, and Cultural Formation* (Grand Rapids: Baker, 2009); James A. Herrick, *Scientific Mythologies: How Science and Science Fiction Forge New Religious Beliefs* (Downers Grove, IL: InterVarsity, 2008).

71. James D. G. Dunn, *Jesus, Paul and the Law: Studies in Mark and Galatians* (Louisville: Westminster John Knox, 1990); E. P. Sanders, *Paul and Palestinian Judaism* (London: SCM, 1977); N. T. Wright, *Paul: Fresh Perspectives* (London: SPCK, 2005); N. T. Wright, *Justification: God's Plan and Paul's Vision* (London: SPCK, 2009).

72. Bernardino Bonansea, *Tommaso Campanella: Renaissance Pioneer of Modern Thought* (Washington, DC: Catholic University of America Press, 1969).

73. "The Resurrection," Sonnet XXI in *The Sonnets of Michael Angelo Buonarroti and Tommaso Campanella*, trans. John Addington Symonds, originally published in 1878, available online at *The Project Gutenberg Ebook of Sonnets*, accessed November 26, 2003, http://www.gutenberg.org/files/10314/10314-8.txt.

74. Mal, "The Bagong Barrio," *Towards Ascension* 26 (May–June 1997): 24–29.

75. Anne Rice, *Called Out of Darkness: A Spiritual Confession* (New York: Anchor, 2010), 163–64.

Chapter 2 The Resurrection Effect: *Yours, Mine, and Ours*

1. Paul N. Tarazi, "Effective Preaching Today," in *God's Living Word: Orthodox and Evangelical Essays on Preaching*, ed. Theodore G. Stylianopoulos (Brookline, MA: Holy Cross Orthodox, 1983), 48.

2. J. R. Daniel Kirk, "A Resurrection That Matters," *Christianity Today*, April 2010, 37.

3. The Ministry Training Strategy unit in the Anglican Diocese of Sydney is bucking that trend: "The resurrection is at the centre of the theology of the New Testament, or at least as central as the crucifixion." See "Children of the Resurrection," Ministry Training Strategy Discussion Paper 2.02, *Ministry Training Strategy* website, accessed May 26, 2010, http://www.mts.com.au/. We emphasize the value of an apologetic for Jesus's resurrection in a way that this paper does not.

4. Gary R. Habermas, "Jesus' Resurrection and Contemporary Criticism: An Apologetic (Part II)," *CTR* 4 (1990): 382–83.

5. Gary R. Habermas and Antony Flew, *Did the Resurrection Happen? A Conversation with Gary Habermas and Antony Flew*, ed. David Baggett (Downers Grove, IL: InterVarsity, 2009), 34–35.

6. Dietrich Bonhoeffer, *The Cost of Discipleship*, trans. R. H. Fuller (New York: Macmillan, 1949), 7.

7. M. Scott Peck, *Further Along the Road Less Travelled* (New York: Simon & Schuster, 1993), 157.

8. Kirk, "Resurrection," 38.

9. George H. Morling, undated unpublished class lecture, held in the Baptist Archives at Morling College, Sydney. Morling influenced Ruth Bell Graham; see her "Introduction" in G. H. Morling, *The Quest for Serenity* (Dallas: Word, 1979).

10. Joni Eareckson Tada, *Heaven: Your Real Home* (Grand Rapids: Zondervan, 1995), 53.

11. We will show you in chapters 5 and 7 that our culture today plays host to a raft of other lesser and weaker worldviews concerning the afterlife. None of them can hold a candle to the resurrection, though.

12. R. C. Sproul, John H. Gerstner, and Arthur Lindsley, *Classical Apologetics* (Grand Rapids: Zondervan, 1984), 282.

13. Ross Clifford and Philip Johnson, *Riding the Rollercoaster: How the Risen Christ Empowers Life* (Sydney: Strand, 1998), 6–7.

14. The photograph became the basis for a painting that won the Blake Prize for religious art in Australia. When people see this painting on display and hear the story behind it, it leaves its mark on them. For more details about the story, the photo, and the Blake Prize painting of "The Preacher," see "George Gittoes b. 1949," Art Equity, http://www.artequity.com.au/newsletter/Exhibitions/Exhibitions%202006/GeorgeGittoesThePreacher.htm.

15. Jeannine K. Brown, "Creation's Renewal in the Gospel of John," *CBQ* 72 (2010): 275–90.

16. Anthony A. Hoekema, *The Bible and the Future* (Exeter: Paternoster, 1979), 287.

17. Allison A. Trites, *The New Testament Concept of Witness* (Cambridge: Cambridge University Press, 1977).

18. Antony Flew, *God and Philosophy* (London: Hutchinson, 1966). A second edition of this book was published by Prometheus in 2005 with a revised introduction that briefly explained his deist outlook.

19. Antony Flew and Roy Abraham Varghese, *There Is a God: How the World's Most Notorious Atheist Changed His Mind* (New York: HarperCollins, 2007).

20. William Schweiker, "The Varieties and Revisions of Atheism," *Zygon* 40 (2005): 267–76.

21. Deism is discussed in chapter 10.

22. Gary R. Habermas and Antony G. N. Flew, *Did Jesus Rise from the Dead? The Resurrection Debate*, ed. Terry L. Miethe (San Francisco: Harper & Row, 1985), 3.

23. "The Self-Revelation of God in Human History: A Dialogue on Jesus with N. T. Wright," in Flew and Varghese, *There Is a God*, 185–213.

24. Also consider Ludwig Wittgenstein's remarks about Jesus's resurrection that are reproduced at the start of chapter 6.

25. Peter H. Davids, *The First Epistle of Peter*, NICNT (Grand Rapids: Eerdmans, 1990), 19.

26. George Wolfgang Forell, *History of Christian Ethics*, vol. 1, *From the New Testament to Augustine* (Minneapolis: Augsburg, 1979).

27. N. T. Wright, *The Resurrection of the Son of God* (Minneapolis: Fortress, 2003), 484.

28. Stanley Samuel Harakas, "Resurrection and Ethics in Chrysostom," *ExAud* 9 (1993): 77–95.

29. Edwyn C. Hoskyns and Francis N. Davey, *Crucifixion-Resurrection: The Pattern of Theology and Ethics of the New Testament*, ed. Gordon S. Wakefield (London: SPCK, 1981).

30. Brian V. Johnstone, "Transformation Ethics: The Moral Implications of the Resurrection," in *The Resurrection: An Interdisciplinary Symposium on the Resurrection*, ed. Steven Davis et al. (Oxford: Oxford University Press, 1997), 339–60.

31. Thorwald Lorenzen, *Resurrection Discipleship Justice* (Macon, GA: Smyth & Helwys, 2003); Keith Dyer and David Neville, eds., *Resurrection and Responsibility: Essays on Theology, Scripture and Ethics in Honor of Thorwald Lorenzen* (Eugene, OR: Wipf & Stock, 2009).

32. Chris Sugden, "Death, Injustice, Resurrection and Transformation," *Transformation* 22 (2005): 67–71.

33. Ludwig Wittgenstein, *Tractatus Logico-Philosophicus*, 6.421, available online at Project Gutenberg, accessed July 17, 2010, http://www.gutenberg.org/files/5740/5740-h/5740-h.htm.

34. Jean-Jacques Rousseau, *The Social Contract*, trans. Maurice Cranston (Harmondsworth, England: Penguin, 1968), 84.

35. Oliver O'Donovan, *Resurrection and Moral Order: An Outline for Evangelical Ethics*, 2nd ed. (Leicester: Apollos; Grand Rapids: Eerdmans, 1994).

36. W. Clyde Tilley, "World-Affirmation and the Resurrection of Jesus Christ: A Review Article," *Perspectives in Religious Studies* 15 (1988): 165–76; Stephen N. Williams, "Outline for Ethics: A Response to Oliver O'Donovan," *Them* (NS) 13 (1988): 86–91.

37. Raymond C. van Leeuwen, "Christ's Resurrection and the Creation's Vindication," in *The Environment and the Christian: What Can We Learn from the New Testament?*, ed. Calvin B. DeWitt (Grand Rapids: Baker, 1991), 57–71; Roger E. Olson, "Resurrection, Cosmic Liberation, and Christian Earth Keeping," *ExAud* 9 (1993): 123–32; Keith Innes, "Towards an Ecological Eschatology: Continuity and Discontinuity," *EvQ* 81 (2009): 126–44.

38. See John W. Olley, "Animals in Heaven and Earth Attitudes in Ezekiel," *Colloquium* 33 (2001): 47–57; Ruth Pollard and Philip Johnson, "Animals Matter to God," *Sacred Tribes Journal* 2, no. 2 (2005): 57–125, available online at http://www.sacredtribesjournal.org/images/Articles/Vol_2/Animals_Matter_to_God.pdf.

39. After visiting the traditional site of Simon the Tanner's house where Peter spoke, the Norwegian artist Victor Sparre called this verse the world's first universal declaration of human rights. See Victor Sparre, *The Flame in the Darkness: The Russian Human Rights Struggle*, trans. A. McKay and D. McKay (London: Grosvenor, 1979), 127–28.

40. Carol Penner, "Sexual Assault, Resurrection and the Healing Community," *Consensus* 28, no. 2 (2002): 49–60.

41. Kirk, "Resurrection," 39.

42. Cornelius A. Buller, "Healing Hope: Physical Healing and Resurrection Hope in a Postmodern Context," *JPTh* 10 (2002): 74–92.

43. Ibid., 85.

44. Robert Sorensen, "The Resurrection and Pastoral Care: Some Theological and Psychological Issues," *Di* 19 (1980): 11–16.

45. Daniel J. Louw, "The HIV Pandemic from the Perspective of a *Theologia Resurrectionis*: Resurrection Hope as a Pastoral Critique on the Punishment and Stigma Paradigm," *JTSA* 126 (2006): 100–114.

46. Glenn D. Weaver, "Senile Dementia and a Resurrection Theology," *ThTo* 42 (1986): 452.

47. Patricia J. Lull, "Telling the Truth: Introducing Death and Resurrection to the Young," *WW* 11 (1991): 42. See also Elaine Champagne, "Living and Dying: A Window on (Christian) Children's Spirituality," *IJCS* 13 (2008): 253–63.

48. Rob Moll, "A Culture of Resurrection," *Christianity Today*, June 2010, 34–36.

Chapter 3 Cynics, Post-Christendom Seekers, and Resurrection

1. James Orr, *The Resurrection of Jesus* (London: Hodder & Stoughton, 1909), 288.

2. Ion Bria, "Dynamics of Resurrection in the Church's Tradition and Mission," *IRM* 92 (2003): 258.

3. The word *postmodern* describes the broad processes of cultural change as we leave behind the modern era and emerge into a new era. Post-Christendom is not synonymous with postmodernism but is a cultural reality of our postmodern times. "Post-Christendom" means that Christianity is no longer the culturally dominant expression of belief in Australia, Europe, and North America. "Post-Christendom seeker" refers to people who are exploring spiritual pathways beyond Christianity who have either (a) grown up with no church affiliations or (b) have lapsed in church participation and no longer believe in its message.

4. Kenneth D. Boa and Robert M. Bowman, *Faith Has Its Reasons: An Integrative Approach to Defending Christianity* (Colorado Springs: NavPress, 2001), 21.

5. Avery Dulles, *A History of Apologetics*, rev. ed. (San Francisco: Ignatius, 2005).

6. See Leslie J. Francis, *Faith and Psychology: Personality, Religion and the Individual* (London: Darton, Longman & Todd, 2005); and Leslie J. Francis, "Personality Theory and Empirical Theology," *JET* 15 (2001): 37–53.

7. Andrew Village and Leslie J. Francis, "The Relationship of Psychological Type Preferences to Biblical Interpretation," *JET* 18 (2005): 75.

8. Leslie J. Francis, Charlotte L. Craig, and Gill Hall, "Psychological Type and Attitude Towards Celtic Christianity among Committed Churchgoers: An Empirical Study," *JCR* 23 (2008): 183.

9. Besides the publications in notes 6–8 also see Leslie J. Francis, "Personality Type and Communicating the Gospel," *Modern Believing* 42 (2001): 32–46; Leslie J. Francis and Mandy Robbins, "Psychological Types of Male Evangelical Church Leaders," *JBV* 23 (2002): 217–20; Mandy Robbins, James Hair, and Leslie J. Francis, "Personality and Attraction to the Charismatic Movement: A Study Among Anglican Clergy," *JBV* 20 (1999): 239–46.

10. Tommy H. Poling and J. Frank Kennedy, *The Hare Krishna Character Type: A Study of the Sensate Personality* (Lewiston, NY: Mellen, 1986).

11. J. E. Kennedy, "Personality and Motivations to Believe, Misbelieve and Disbelieve in Paranormal Phenomena," *JPara* 69 (2005): 263–92; Leslie J. Francis and Emyr Williams, "Contacting the Spirits of the Dead: Paranormal Belief and the Teenage Worldview," *JRCE* 18 (2009): 20–35.

12. William K. Kay and Leslie J. Francis, "The Young British Atheist: A Socio-psychological Profile," *JET* 8 (1995): 5–26.

13. On critical drawbacks see Rachel Atkinson, "Alternative Worship: Post-Modern or Post-Mission Church?" *Anvil* 23 (2005): 259–73.

14. Remarks by Brad Cecil of the group Axxess (Texas) in Eddie Gibbs and Ryan K. Bolger, *Emerging Churches: Creating Christian Community in Postmodern Cultures* (Grand Rapids: Baker, 2005), 125.

15. Richard Dawkins, *The God Delusion* (London: Bantam, 2006).

16. Terry C. Muck, "After Selfhood: Constructing the Religious Self in a Post-Self Age," *JETS* 41 (1998): 107. On the subject of "self" in relation to Christian missions see Terry C. Muck, "From Identity Replacement to Identity Construction: Dynamic Identity, Christian Conversion, and Missiological Praxis," in *Perspectives on Post-Christendom Spiritualities: Reflections on New Religious Movements and Western Spiritualities*, ed. Michael T. Cooper (Macquarie Park, NSW: Morling Press, 2010), 197–222.

17. Ogden Nash, *I Wouldn't Have Missed It: Selected Poems of Ogden Nash* (Boston: Little, Brown, 1975).

18. Douglas E. Chismar and John S. Brent, "The Empathic Apologist: Pastoral Counseling Insights into Christian Apologetics," *CurTM* 10 (1983): 93.

19. Ibid.

20. Rupert Till, "The Nine O'Clock Service: Mixing Club Culture and Postmodern Christianity," *CulRel* 7 (2006): 93–110; Ronald M. Enroth, *Churches That Abuse* (Grand Rapids: Zondervan, 1992).

21. Peter Rollins, *How (Not) to Speak of God* (London: SPCK, 2006), 35–37. Ironically, he favorably quotes G. K. Chesterton's *Orthodoxy* xv and Blaise Pascal's *Pensées* 90 but both works are classic apologetics texts that use "word and wonder" arguments that Rollins urges us to abandon.

22. Rollins, *How (Not) to Speak of God*, 40, 41.

23. Ibid., 42.

24. Gary R. Habermas, "The Personal Testimony of the Holy Spirit to the Believer and Christian Apologetics," *JCA* 1 (1997): 49–64; John Warwick Montgomery, "The Holy Spirit and the Defense of the Faith," *BibSac* 154 (1997): 387–95.

25. John W. Mauck, *Paul on Trial: The Book of Acts as a Defense of Christianity* (Nashville: Nelson, 2001); Ross Clifford, *John Warwick Montgomery's Legal Apologetic: An Apologetic for All Seasons* (Bonn: Kultur und Wissenschaft, 2004).

26. Rollins, *How (Not) to Speak of God*, 36.

27. On the misuse of 1 Corinthians 2:1–5 see D. A. Carson, *Exegetical Fallacies* (Grand Rapids: Baker, 1984), 134; Alister McGrath, *Bridge Building* (Leicester, UK: Inter-Varsity, 1992), 49, 231–33.

28. Harold A. Netland, "Toward Contextualized Apologetics," *Miss* 16 (1988): 289–303; Dean Flemming, "Contextualizing the Gospel in Athens: Paul's Areopagus Address as a Paradigm for Missionary Communication," *Miss* 30 (2002): 199–214.

29. Rollins, *How (Not) to Speak of God*, 36.

30. Attempts to reconfigure apologetics today include John G. Stackhouse, *Humble Apologetics: Defending the Faith Today* (New York: Oxford University Press, 2002); Joseph D. Wooddell, "Jonathan Edwards, Beauty, and Apologetics," *CTR* (NS) 5 (2007): 81–95. The "Truth and the Christian Imagination Series" of books by Alister E. McGrath, such as *Resurrection* (Minneapolis: Fortress, 2008), also point to different apologetics horizons.

31. John Meyendorff, *Byzantine Theology: Historical Trends and Doctrinal Themes* (London: Mowbrays, 1975), 11–14.

32. John Meyendorff, *A Study of Gregory Palamas* (London: Faith Press, 1962), 115.

33. Emmanuel Cazabonne, "Gregory Palamas (1296–1359): Monk, Theologian and Pastor," *CSQ* 37 (2003): 324.

34. Ibid., 325.

35. Daniel J. Sahas, "Gregory Palamas (1296–1360) on Islam," *MusW* 73 (1983): 1–21.

36. See Daniel J. Sahas, "Captivity and Dialogue: Gregory Palamas (1296–1360) and the Muslims," *GOTR* 25 (1980): 409–36.

37. Ibid., 416.

38. Ibid., 427.

39. Ibid., 421.

40. James Cameron is the producer and director of films such as *Titanic, The Terminator,* and *True Lies.* For evaluation of Cameron's documentary see René A. López, "Does *The Jesus Family Tomb* Disprove His Physical Resurrection?" *BibSac* 165 (2008): 425–46.

41. Si Johnston's remarks in Gibbs and Bolger, *Emerging Churches*, 126. Missiologists regard apologetics as an essential tool; on this see Harold A. Netland, *Encountering Religious Pluralism: The Challenge to Christian Faith and Mission* (Downers Grove, IL: InterVarsity, 2001); Paul J. Griffiths, *An Apology for Apologetics: A Study in the Logic of Interreligious Dialogue* (Maryknoll, NY: Orbis, 1991).

42. Gibbs and Bolger, *Emerging Churches*, 126.

43. Paul Elie, *The Life You Save May Be Your Own: An American Pilgrimage* (New York: Farrar, Straus & Giroux, 2003), 472.

44. John Drane, Ross Clifford, and Philip Johnson, *Beyond Prediction: The Tarot and Your Spirituality* (Oxford: Lion, 2001).

45. Ruth Pollard, "Jesus among the Alternative Healers: Sacred Oils, Aromatherapists, and the Gospel," in *Encountering New Religious Movements*, ed. Irving Hexham, Stephen Rost, and John W. Morehead (Grand Rapids: Kregel, 2004), 261–78.

46. Philip Johnson and Gus diZerega, *Beyond the Burning Times: A Pagan and Christian in Dialogue* (Oxford: Lion, 2008), 122–29.

47. John Smulo, Bill Stewart, and Steven Hallam, "Symbolically Foreshadowed: The Gospel and the Wheel of the Year," *STJ* 2, no. 2 (2005): 35–56, available online at http://www.sacredtribesjournal.org/images/Articles/Vol_2/Wheel_of_the_Year.pdf.

48. Ross Clifford, *Leading Lawyers' Case for the Resurrection* (Edmonton: Canadian Institute for Law, Theology and Public Policy, 1996).

49. Gary R. Habermas, "The Core Resurrection Data: The Minimal Facts Approach," in *Tough-Minded Christianity: Honoring the Legacy of John Warwick Montgomery*, ed. William Dembski and Thomas Schirrmacher (Nashville: B & H Academic, 2008), 387–405.

50. N. T. Wright, *The Resurrection of the Son of God* (Minneapolis: Fortress, 2003), 7–8; N. T. Wright, "Resurrecting Old Arguments: Responding to Four Essays," *JSHJ* 3 (2005): 209–31.

51. Simon Greenleaf, *The Testimony of the Evangelists* (Grand Rapids: Baker, 1984), 28.

52. John Warwick Montgomery, *Human Rights and Human Dignity* (Grand Rapids: Zondervan, 1986), 141.

53. Gerd Thiessen, *Sociality, Reality and the Early Christians* (Minneapolis: Fortress, 1992), 64–66.

54. Richard Swinburne, *The Existence of God* (Oxford: Clarendon, 1979), 207.

55. Walter Chandler, *The Trial of Jesus from a Lawyer's Standpoint* (1925; repr., Norcross, GA: Harrison, 1976), 25–34.

56. M. Scott Peck, *Further Along the Road Less Travelled* (New York: Simon & Schuster, 1993), 160–61.

57. Barbara Thiering, *Jesus the Man: A New Interpretation from the Dead Sea Scrolls* (Sydney: Doubleday, 1992), 114–25.

58. David Friedrich Strauss, *The Life of Jesus for the People*, trans. Marian Evans, 2nd ed. (London: William & Norgate, 1879), 412.

59. Pinchas Lapide, *The Resurrection of Jesus: A Jewish Perspective* (Minneapolis: Augsburg, 1983), 97–99.

60. Paul Gwynne, "The Fate of Jesus' Body: Another Decade of Debate," *Colloq* 32 (2008): 8.

61. Raymond E. Brown, *The Death of the Messiah: A Commentary on the Passion Narratives in the Four Gospels*, Anchor Bible Reference Library (New York: Doubleday, 1994), 2:1240.

62. See Clifford, *Leading Lawyers' Case for the Resurrection*, 98–108.

63. J. N. D. Anderson, *The Evidence for the Resurrection* (London: Inter-Varsity, 1966), 20.

64. Philip Johnson, "Neil's Spiritual U-Turn," in *Australian Stories for the Heart*, compiled by David Dixon and Rachel Dixon (Sydney: Strand, 2002), 110–15.

65. Ross Clifford and Philip Johnson, *Jesus and the Gods of the New Age* (Colorado Springs: Victor, 2003), 217–48.

66. Ross Clifford, "Reframing a Traditional Apologetic to Reach New Spirituality Seekers," in *Encountering New Religious Movements*, ed. Hexham, Rost, and Morehead (Grand Rapids: Kregel, 2004), 193–208.

Part Two Thumbprints of the Resurrection in Culture

1. Anthony J. Kelly, *The Resurrection Effect: Transforming Christian Life and Thought* (Maryknoll, NY: Orbis, 2008), 7.

Chapter 4 The Resurrection in Popular and High Culture

1. Linda Marie Delloff, "The Resurrection: Link between Faith and Art," *CurTM* 18 (1991): 97.

2. Edgar Krentz, "Images of the Resurrection in the New Testament," *CurTM* 18 (1991): 108.

3. A fanciful account about how John Drane "discovered" the tarot's potential value in mission is told by John Noble in "Talking to John Noble about the Charismatic Movement and the Future," *Jesus Army Magazine*, accessed May 26, 2010, http://www.jesus.org.uk/ja/mag_talkingto_noble.shtml.

4. John Drane, Ross Clifford, and Philip Johnson, *Beyond Prediction: The Tarot and Your Spirituality* (Oxford: Lion, 2001).

5. See their resurrection paintings at "Resurrection Paintings," *Bible-Art*, accessed May 26, 2010, http://www.bible-art.info/Resurrection.

6. Rita Nakashima Brock, "Communities of the Cross: Christa and the Communal Nature of Redemption," *FemTh* 14 (2005): 110.

7. Jaroslav Pelikan, *Jesus Through the Centuries: His Place in the History of Culture* (New Haven: Yale University Press, 1985), 99–100.

8. Adrian Warnock, *Raised with Christ: How the Resurrection Changes Everything* (Wheaton: Crossway, 2010), 29.

9. The "Alexamenos graffito" is held in the Palatine Museum in Rome. A photograph of it can be viewed at http://penelope.uchicago.edu/~grout/encyclopaedia_romana/gladiators/graffito.html.

10. Anatole Frolow, "The Veneration of the Relic of the True Cross at the End of the Sixth and the Beginning of the Seventh Centuries," *SVSQ* 2 (1958): 13–30.

11. Brock, "Communities," 115–16; Karen Louise Jolly et al., eds., *Cross and Culture in Anglo-Saxon England: Studies in Honor of George Hardin Brown* (Morgantown: West Virginia University Press, 2008).

12. Brock, "Communities," 119.

13. Ibid., 111.

14. Leslie W. Barnard, "Early Christian Art as Apologetics," *JRH* 10 (1978): 20–31.

15. Walter Oetting, *The Church of the Catacombs* (St. Louis: Concordia, 1964), 27; W. H. C. Frend, *The Archaeology of Early Christianity: A History* (Minneapolis: Fortress, 1996), 198–99.

16. James Stevenson, *The Catacombs: Rediscovered Monuments of Early Christianity* (London: Thames & Hudson, 1978), 95.

17. Brock, "Communities," 112, 113.

18. Andrée Hayum, *The Isenheim Altarpiece: God's Medicine and the Painter's Vision* (Princeton: Princeton University Press, 1990).

19. Peter L. Berger, *A Rumor of Angels* (New York: Doubleday, 1969), 78.

20. See Robert D. Hawkins, "'*O felix culpa . . .*': Death and Resurrection in Church Music," *WW* 11 (1991): 30.

21. Dr. Harold Taylor served as a missionary in Papua New Guinea and was lecturer in missiology at the Bible College of Victoria.

22. Hawkins, "'*O felix culpa,*'" 32.

23. Charles Seeger, "On the Moods of Music-Logic," *JAMusSoc* 13 (1960): 224–61.

24. Mark P. Bangert, "The Image of the Resurrection in Music," *CurTM* 18 (1991): 116.

25. Dom Matthew Britt, ed., *The Hymns of the Breviary and Missal* (New York: Benziger, 1948), 8–9.

26. Bishop Kallistos Ware, *The Orthodox Way* (Crestwood, NY: St. Vladimir's Seminary Press, 1990), 111.

27. Bangert, "Image," 116.

28. Ibid., 119.

29. Leon Russell, "Roll Away the Stone," on *Leon Russell*, Shelter Records, 1970. See Russell's website: http://www.leonrussellrecords.com/.

30. John Robb, *The Stone Roses and the Resurrection of British Pop* (London: Ebury, 2001).

31. Lenny Kravitz, "The Resurrection," lyrics by Craig David Ross and Lenny Kravitz, on *Circus*, Virgin Records America, 1995. See Kravitz's website: http://www.lennykravitz.com/.

32. Alfred H. Ackley (1887–1960). Lyrics found at "I Serve a Risen Savior," Hymnal.net, accessed May 26, 2010, http://www.hymnal.net/hymn.php/h/503.

33. Charles Wesley (1707–1788). Lyrics found at "Christ the Lord Is Risen Today," Cyberhymnal.org, accessed May 26, 2010, http://www.cyberhymnal.org/htm/c/t/ctlrisen.htm.

34. Hawkins, "*'O felix culpa,'*" 30.

35. N. T. Wright, *Surprised by Hope: Rethinking Heaven, the Resurrection, and the Mission of the Church* (New York: HarperOne, 2008), 20–23, 256.

36. Martin Luther, "Preface to the Burial Hymns," in *LW* 53:326.

37. Francis C. Rossow, "Echoes of the Gospel-Event in Literature and Elsewhere," *CoJ* 9 (1983): 50–58.

38. See Don Richardson, *Eternity in Their Hearts* (Ventura, CA: Regal, 1981); David Marshall, *True Son of Heaven: How Jesus Fulfills the Chinese Culture* (Seattle: Kuai Mu, 2002).

39. *The Day the Earth Stood Still* (Twentieth Century Fox, 1951). On Klaatu-Christ comparisons see Melvin E. Matthews, *1950s Science Fiction Films and 9/11: Hostile Aliens, Hollywood and Today's News* (New York: Algora, 2007), 54.

40. On Superman's death and resurrection see Dan Jurgens et al., *The Death of Superman* (New York: DC Comics, 1992); Dan Jurgens et al., *World Without a Superman* (New York: DC Comics, 1993); Dan Jurgens et al., *The Return of Superman* (New York: DC Comics, 1993).

41. *The Matrix* (Warner Bros, 1999). See William Irwin, ed., *The Matrix and Philosophy: Welcome to the Desert of the Real* (Peru, IL: Open Court, 2002).

42. On discontinuities between Jesus and Neo see Ben Witherington, "Neo-Orthodoxy: Tales of the Reluctant Messiah, Or, 'Your Own Personal Jesus,' " in *More Matrix and Philosophy: Revolutions and Reloaded Decoded*, ed. William Irwin (Peru, IL: Open Court, 2005), 165–74.

43. *Matrix Reloaded* (Warner Bros, 2003).

44. Jeffery Wittung and Daniel Bramer, "From Superman to Brahman: The Religious Shift of the Matrix Mythology," *Journal of Religion and Film* 10, no. 2 (October 2006), available online at http://www.unomaha.edu/jrf/Vol10No2/WittungBramer_Matrix.htm.

45. Andy Murray, "The Talons of Robert Holmes," in *Time and Relative Dissertations in Space: Critical Perspectives on Doctor Who*, ed. David Butler (Manchester: Manchester University Press, 2007), 230. The Time Lord's Matrix was introduced in 1977 in "The Deadly Assassin" and starred Tom Baker as the Doctor.

46. The three episodes from *The Simpsons* include "Sideshow Bob's Last Gleaming" (broadcast November 26, 1995), "Mayored to the Mob" (broadcast December 20, 1998), and "Treehouse of Horror X" (broadcast October 31, 1999). "Paging Doctor Who" is a remark made in a crime-story about time-experiments in the *CSI New York* episode "Time's Up" (broadcast on October 17, 2007).

47. Thomas Bertonneau and Kim Paffenroth, *The Truth Is Out There: Christian Faith and the Classics of TV Science Fiction* (Grand Rapids: Brazos, 2006), 31–59. On the series' significance see James Chapman, *Inside the Tardis: The Worlds of Doctor Who* (London: Tauris, 2006).

48. Barry Letts interviewed in Jonathan Wynne-Jones, "The Church Is Ailing—Send for Dr. Who," *Telegraph*, May 4, 2008, available online at http://www.telegraph.co.uk/news/newstopics/howaboutthat/1925338/The-church-is-ailing—-send-for-Dr-Who.html.

49. David Rafer, "Mythic Identity in Doctor Who," in Butler, ed., *Time and Relative Dissertations*, 125.

50. Michael Hand, "Regeneration and Resurrection," in *Doctor Who and Philosophy: Bigger on the Inside*, ed. Courtland Lewis and Paula Smithka (Chicago: Open Court, 2010), 213–23.

51. The television movie that carried the title *Doctor Who* was a joint production of the BBC, Universal Television, and the Fox Network, and starred Paul McGann.

52. Sean Stewart, *Resurrection Man* (New York: ACE, 1995); *Resurrection Man* (New York: DC Comics, 1997–1999).

53. "The Parting of the Ways," *Doctor Who*, BBC Wales Series 1, 2005; "Utopia," *Doctor Who*, BBC Wales Series 3, 2007.

54. "Regeneration," broadcast on April 3, 2010, Network Ten (Australia).

55. J. K. Rowling, *Harry Potter and the Deathly Hallows* (London: Bloomsbury, 2007).

56. Greg Garrett, *One Fine Potion: The Literary Magic of Harry Potter* (Waco, TX: Baylor University Press, 2010).

57. *Captain Scarlet and the Mysterons*, created by Gerry and Sylvia Anderson (Century 21, September 1967–May 1968); Chris Bentley, *The Complete Book of "Captain Scarlet"* (London: Carlton, 2001).

58. Paul G. Hiebert, *Anthropological Reflections on Missiological Issues* (Grand Rapids: Baker, 1994), 203–15.

59. *Alien Resurrection* (Twentieth Century Fox, 1997).

60. W. W. Jacobs, "The Monkey's Paw," in *Great Short Stories of Detection, Mystery and Horror*, ed. Dorothy L. Sayers (London: Gollancz, 1959), 2:206–16, available online at http://www.americanliterature.com/Jacobs/SS/TheMonkeysPaw.html.

61. Two other resurrected enemies include the renegade Time Lord Morbius and the Daleks. In a story ("The Brain of Morbius") reminiscent of Frankenstein, Morbius was executed, but a mad surgeon named Solon preserved the brain. The Doctor (Tom Baker) rebukes Solon saying that he is "resurrecting evil." The Daleks experience "resurrection" in "The Resurrection of the Daleks," *Doctor Who*, BBC Season 21, 1984. See Fiona Moore and Alan Stevens, "The Human Factor: Daleks, the 'Evil Human' and Faustian Legend in *Doctor Who*," in Butler, ed., *Time and Relative Dissertations*, 138–58.

62. Both "The Sound of Drums" and "The Last of the Time Lords" were broadcast in *Doctor Who*, BBC Wales Series 3, 2007.

63. Some Christians struggle with the earthiness of some of his stories. Updike was raised a Lutheran but in later life joined his second wife in attending an Episcopalian church. See Benedicta Cipolla, "John Updike on Religion," *Religion & Ethics* newsweekly 812, PBS.org, November 19, 2004, http://www.pbs.org/wnet/religionandethics/week812/exclusive.html.

64. John Updike, "Remarks Upon Receiving the Campion Medal," in *John Updike and Religion: The Sense of the Sacred and Notions of Grace*, ed. James Yerkes (Grand Rapids: Eerdmans, 1999), 4–5.

65. John Updike, "Seven Stanzas at Easter," in *Telephone Poles and Other Poems* (New York: Knopf, 1961), 72.

66. J. Todd Billings, "John Updike as Theologian of Culture: *Roger's Version* and the Possibility of Embodied Redemption," *ChrLit* 52 (2003): 203–13.

67. Michael Frost, *Seeing God in the Ordinary: A Theology of the Everyday* (Peabody, MA: Hendrickson, 2000).

68. Gordon V. Boudreau, "Herman Melville, Immortality, St. Paul, and Resurrection: From Rose-bud to Billy Budd," *ChrLit* 52 (2003): 343–64; Matthew G. Condon, "The Cost of Redemption in Conrad's *Lord Jim*," *LitTh* 12 (1998): 135–48.

69. Fyodor Dostoevsky, *Crime and Punishment*, trans. Constance Garnett (New York: Bantam, 1981), 471; Francis C. Rossow, "The Gospel Pattern of Death and Resurrection in Fyodor Dostoevsky's *Crime and Punishment*," *CoJ* 34 (2008): 38–48.

70. David Patterson, "The Theological Dimensions of Tolstoy's Resurrection," *ChrLit* 40 (1991): 123–36.

71. Andrew Sanders, *Charles Dickens, Resurrectionist* (New York: Palgrave Macmillan, 1982).

72. Kevin Rulo, "A Tale of Two Mimeses: Dickens's *A Tale of Two Cities* and René Girard," *ChrLit* 59 (2009): 20.

73. Ibid., 20.

74. On Dickens's religious views see Janet L. Larson, *Dickens and the Broken Scripture* (Athens: University of Georgia Press, 1985).

75. Elizabeth Stuart Phelps, *The Gates Ajar*, ed. Helen Sootin Smith (1870; repr., Cambridge, MA: Belknap Press of Harvard, 1964).

76. Ibid., 79.

77. Sean Benson, "The Resurrection of the Dead in *The Winter's Tale* and *The Tempest*," *Ren* 61 (2008): 4; Sean Benson, "Materialist Criticism and Cordelia's Quasi-Resurrection in *King Lear*," *RelArts* 11 (2007): 436–53.

78. Benson, "Resurrection," 3.

79. Ibid., 21.

80. Will Self, *How the Dead Live* (New York: Grove, 2000).

81. *Wit* (HBO Films, 2001).

82. Michael Baigent et al., *The Holy Blood and The Holy Grail* (London: Jonathan Cape, 1982).

83. Fiona Horne, *Life's a Witch!* (Sydney: Random House, 2000), 3.

84. Anatha Wolfkeepe, "Jesus Is One of Us," *Witchcraft* 12 (1999): 42.

85. Timothy Freke and Peter Gandy, *The Jesus Mysteries* (London: Thorsons, 1999). For critical discussion see Ross Clifford and Philip Johnson, *Jesus and the Gods of the New Age* (Colorado Springs: Victor, 2003), 40–55, 149–69.

86. Chris Seay and Greg Garrett, *The Gospel Reloaded: Exploring Spirituality and Faith in The Matrix* (Colorado Springs: Piñon, 2003). This book only analyzed the first two films through a Christian paradigm. Very few Christians have discussed the Hindu cosmology in *Matrix Revolutions* and nine animated short stories, *The Animatrix*, that connect the plotline between the first and second films.

87. Jin Kyu Park, " 'Creating My Own Cultural and Spiritual Bubble': Case of Cultural Consumption by Spiritual Seeker Anime Fans," *CulRel* 6 (2005): 399.

88. Ibid., 402, italics original.

Chapter 5 Cultural Expressions of Death-Refusing Hope

1. Jacque Lynn Foltyn, "Dead Famous and Dead Sexy: Popular Culture, Forensics, and the Rise of the Corpse," *Mort* 13 (2008): 170.

2. Elisabeth Kübler-Ross, *On Death and Dying* (London: Tavistock, 1970), is the classic text in this regard but her afterlife beliefs were New Age. See Ross Clifford and Philip Johnson, *Jesus and the Gods of the New Age* (Colorado Springs: Victor, 2003), 157–75.

3. Peter L. Berger, "Secularization Falsified," *First Things*, no. 180 (February 2008): 23–27.

4. Peter L. Berger, *A Rumor of Angels* (New York: Doubleday, 1969), x.

5. Ibid., 81.

6. Christopher T. Burris and Keehan Bailey, "What Lies Beyond: Theory and Measurement of Afterdeath Beliefs," *IJPsyRel* 19 (2009): 173–86.

7. See William Crockett, ed., *Four Views on Hell* (Grand Rapids: Zondervan, 1992); Robert A. Morey, *Death and the Afterlife* (Minneapolis: Bethany, 1984), 199–222.

8. Burris and Bailey, "What Lies Beyond," 182.

9. Naomi Wolf, *The Beauty Myth: How Images of Beauty Are Used Against Women* (New York: Morrow, 1991).

10. Caroline Walker Bynum, *The Resurrection of the Body in Western Christianity 200–1336* (New York: Columbia University Press, 1995), 15.

11. We discuss the undead in chapter 7.

12. See Bill Ellis, *Aliens, Ghosts, and Cults: Legends We Live* (Jackson: University Press of Mississippi, 2001).

13. *Randall and Hopkirk (Deceased)*, ITC Entertainment, broadcast from 1969–1970 in England and released in the USA as *My Partner the Ghost*. A series remake was done in 2000–2001 by Working Title Films for the BBC. *The Ghost and Mrs. Muir* was an American TV series broadcast from 1968–70 and based on the film *The Ghost and Mrs. Muir* (Twentieth Century Fox, 1947).

14. *Blithe Spirit*, based on a play by Noël Coward (United Artists, 1945); *The Time of Their Lives* (Universal Pictures, 1946); *Heaven Can Wait* (Twentieth Century Fox, 1943). The latter film should not be confused with *Heaven Can Wait* (Paramount, 1978), which was a remake of

Here Comes Mr. Jordan (Columbia, 1941) and has a plot implying the reincarnation of the lead character's soul due to a premature death.

15. *The X-Files* (1993–2002) was created by Chris Carter and featured two FBI agents investigating unexplained phenomena. Fox Mulder (played by David Duchovny) was the "true believer" and Dr. Dana Scully (played by Gillian Anderson) was the medically-trained skeptical scientist. The TV series also spawned two motion pictures: *The X-Files: Fight the Future* (Twentieth Century Fox, 1998) and *The X-Files: I Want to Believe* (Twentieth Century Fox, 2008). *Afterlife* (ITV, 2005–2006) featured the psychic medium Alison Mundy (played by Lesley Sharp) and the skeptic Dr. Robert Bridge (played by Andrew Lincoln).

16. *The Sixth Sense* (Hollywood Pictures, 1999); *The Others* (Dimension Films, 2001).

17. The co-executive producer of the *Ghost Whisperer* series (2005) is the American medium James van Praagh. The lead character of *Medium* (2005) is based on the real-life American-born medium Allison DuBois.

18. Swedenborg is discussed in chapter 7.

19. *Dead Like Me* (Showtime Network, 2003–2004) starred Ellen Muth as Georgie, who died but was assigned by "God" the job of working in a team of grim reapers collecting souls from accidents, suicides, and homicides and escorting them to the afterlife.

20. In *On a Clear Day You Can See Forever* (Paramount, 1970) the lead character, Daisy Gamble, exhibits extrasensory perception (ESP) and under hypnosis discloses her past life as an eighteenth-century woman named Melinda. *Kundun* (Touchstone Pictures, 1997) is based on the life of the Dalai Lama. *Reincarnation* (Toho, 2005) is a Japanese horror film directed by Takashi Shimizu. Other films mentioned include *Little Buddha* (Miramax, 1994) and *Dead Again* (Paramount Pictures, 1991).

21. The third film in the trilogy, *Matrix Revolutions*, gave explicit affirmation to the concept of karma. Karma provides the moral framework within which reincarnation is comprehended. Karma will be further discussed in chapter 7.

22. *What Dreams May Come* (PolyGram Filmed Entertainment, 1998).

23. *Robocop* (Orion Pictures, 1987).

24. *Freejack* (HBO; distributed by Warner Bros, 1992).

25. *Vanilla Sky* (Paramount, 2001).

26. For further discussion see Sara L. Knox, "Death, Afterlife, and the Eschatology of Consciousness: Themes in Contemporary Cinema," *Mort* 11 (2006): 233–52.

27. More than sixty years ago the novelist Evelyn Waugh took a sardonic look at American commercial funeral service providers who sanitize and even eroticize our images of the dead. See Evelyn Waugh, *The Loved One: An Anglo-American Tragedy* (Boston: Little, Brown, 1948).

28. *Gattaca* (Columbia, 1997); *Minority Report* (Twentieth Century Fox, 2002).

29. Noreen Herzfeld, "Cybernetic Immortality versus Christian Resurrection," in *Resurrection: Theological and Scientific Assessments*, ed. Ted Peters, Robert John Russell, and Michael Welker (Grand Rapids: Eerdmans, 2002), 194.

30. Ibid., 198.

31. Ibid., 199.

32. Margaret Atwood, *Oryx and Crake: A Novel* (New York: Doubleday, 2004).

33. William Bogard, "Empire of the Living Dead," *Mort* 13 (2008): 197.

34. Ibid., 193.

35. Paul Virilio, *The Information Bomb*, trans. Chris Turner (New York: Verso, 2000), 93–106.

36. Foltyn, "Dead Famous," 162.

37. Ibid.

38. Ibid., 170.

39. Ibid.

40. *Flatliners* (Columbia, 1990).

41. "Bart Gets Hit by a Car," *The Simpsons*, season 2, episode 10 (Gracie Films, in association with Twentieth Century Fox). See also Samuel F. (Skip) Parvin and Mark I. Pinsky, *The Gospel According to the Simpsons*, 2nd ed. (Louisville: Westminster John Knox, 2007).

42. *The Sopranos* (HBO, Brad Grey Television, and Chase Films, 1999–2007). See also Chris Seay, *The Gospel According to Tony Soprano* (New York: Tarcher/Putnam, 2002).

43. "From Where to Eternity," *The Sopranos*, season 2, episode 22.

44. The story of Tony Soprano's NDE is told in "Join the Club" and "Mayham," season 6, episodes 67 and 68. It is in "Kaisha," season 6, episode 77, that Soprano divulges what happened.

45. Maurice Rawlings, *Beyond Death's Door* (New York: Bantam, 1979); Maurice Rawlings, *To Hell and Back* (Nashville: Nelson, 1993).

46. Carol Zaleski, *Otherworld Journeys* (New York: Oxford University Press, 1987).

47. Carol Zaleski, *Life of the World to Come: Near Death Experience and Christian Hope* (New York: Oxford University Press, 1996).

48. J. Gordon Melton, ed., "Kennedy Worshippers," in *Encyclopedia of American Religions*, 6th ed. (Detroit: Gale Research, 1999), 1026.

49. John Drane, *Cultural Change and Biblical Faith* (Carlisle: Paternoster, 2000), 78–103.

50. Madeleine Rigby, "Graceland: A Sacred Place in a Secular World?," in *The End of Religions? Religion in an Age of Globalisation*, ed. Carole M. Cusack and Peter Oldmeadow (Sydney: University of Sydney, 2001), 155.

51. John Updike, "Jesus and Elvis," in *Americana and Other Poems* (New York: Knopf, 2001), 92.

52. John McTavish, "'Jesus and Elvis' and John Updike's Poetry," *ThTo* 63 (2007): 441.

53. Clifford and Johnson, *Jesus and the Gods of the New Age*, 157–97, 217–48.

Chapter 6 Signs of the Resurrection in General Revelation

1. Ludwig Wittgenstein, *Culture and Values*, trans. P. Winch (Oxford: Blackwell, 1980), 33. Wittgenstein (1889–1951), who was a Jewish atheist, spearheaded the twentieth-century school of analytical philosophy. He apparently never converted to faith in Jesus but these diarized remarks show he thought deeply about the resurrection.

2. On Clement of Rome's apologia see chapter 10.

3. Joseph Butler, *The Analogy of Religion* (London: Bell & Daldy, 1871), 81–88.

4. C. S. Lewis, *Miracles: A Preliminary Study* (Glasgow: Fount, 1978), 136–67.

5. See Marina Smyth, "The Body, Death, and Resurrection: Perspectives of an Early Irish Theologian," *Spec* 83 (2008): 531–71.

6. P. H. Brazier, "C. S. Lewis and Christological Prefigurement," *HeyJ* 48 (2007): 742–75.

7. C. S. Lewis, "Myth Became Fact," in *God in the Dock: Essays on Theology and Ethics* (Grand Rapids: Eerdmans, 1970), 63–67.

8. Leon McKenzie, *Pagan Resurrection Myths and the Resurrection of Jesus: A Christian Perspective* (Charlottesville, VA: Bookwrights, 1997).

9. E. W. Bullinger, *The Witness of the Stars* (1893; repr., Grand Rapids: Kregel, 1967). Others in this camp include Joseph A. Seiss, *The Gospel in the Stars* (1882; repr., Grand Rapids: Kregel, 1972); Frances Rolleston, *Mazzaroth* (1865; repr., York Beach: Weiser, 2001).

10. Bullinger, *Witness of the Stars*, 82.

11. Seiss, *Gospel in the Stars*, 69, 70.

12. Rita Nakashima Brock, "Communities of the Cross: Christa and the Communal Nature of Redemption," *FemTh* 14 (2005): 112.

13. See her website, http://www.archeociel.com/Accueil_eng.htm, and also the website of The International Society for Archaeoastronomy & Astronomy in Culture, http://www.archaeoastronomy.org/.

14. For different views see Robert S. Ellwood, *The Politics of Myth: A Study of C. G. Jung, Mircea Eliade, and Joseph Campbell* (Albany: State University of New York Press, 1999); Douglas Allen, *Myth and Religion in Mircea Eliade* (London: Routledge, 2002).

15. Steven M. Wasserstrom, *Religion After Religion: Gershom Scholem, Mircea Eliade and Henry Corbin at Eranos* (Princeton: Princeton University Press, 1999).

16. Mircea Eliade, *The Myth of the Eternal Return or, Cosmos and History*, trans. Willard R. Trask (Princeton: Princeton University Press, 1971); Mircea Eliade, *Myths, Dreams and Mysteries*, trans. Philip Mairet (New York: Harper & Row, 1975).

17. William F. Albright, *Yahweh and the Gods of Canaan* (London: Athlone, 1968), 98–99.

18. On Butler see Avery Dulles, *A History of Apologetics*, rev. ed. (San Francisco: Ignatius, 2005), 140–43; James Rurak, "Butler's *Analogy*: A Still Interesting Synthesis of Reason and Revelation," *AThR* 62 (1980): 365–81.

19. Bullinger's position is rejected in Charles Strohmer, "Is There a Christian Zodiac, a Gospel in the Stars?" *CRJ* 22, no. 4 (2003): 22–25, 40–44.

20. Philip Johnson, Simeon Payne, and Peter Wilson, "Toward a Contextualized Astrological Apologetic, with a Case Study for Booth Ministry Outreach," *Miss* 36 (2008): 193–96.

21. Also refer to Nicholas Wolterstorff, "The Migration of the Theistic Arguments: From Natural Theology to Evidentialist Apologetics," in *Rationality, Religious Belief and Moral Commitment: New Essays in the Philosophy of Religion*, ed. Robert Audi and William J. Wainwright (Ithaca, NY: Cornell University Press, 1986), 38–81.

22. Julius Wellhausen, *Prolegomena to the History of Israel*, trans. J. Sutherland Black and Allan Menzies (Edinburgh: A & C Black, 1885).

23. Stephen Karcher, *The Illustrated Encyclopedia of Divination* (Shaftesbury, Dorset: Element, 1997).

24. For further discussion see Frederick H. Cryer, *Divination in Ancient Israel and Its Near Eastern Environment: A Socio-Historical Investigation* (Sheffield: Sheffield Academic Press, 1994).

25. Ben Witherington, *Jesus the Seer: The Progress of Prophecy* (Peabody, MA: Hendrickson, 1999).

26. Classical apologists insist on the apologetic case beginning with the existence of God because unless a theistic universe is established a case for miracles or resurrection will not make sense. See William Lane Craig, "Classical Apologetics," in *Five Views on Apologetics*, ed. Steven B. Cowan (Grand Rapids: Zondervan, 2000), 25–55.

27. "Yes . . . But" refers to the presuppositionalists who comprise a theologically conservative modern-day school of thought within the broader Calvinist/Reformed tradition and who believe that we must begin with a commitment to the Christian worldview; otherwise our sin blocks out the true reading of the signs. Lesslie Newbigin was not aligned with the theological positions of Henry and Van Til, even though his background was in the Church of Scotland and later with the United Reformed Church in England. Newbigin rejected the distinction between facts and values, and also the idea of neutrality in knowledge, and these are points where his thinking had some parallels to the positions adopted by Henry and Van Til.

28. John Calvin, *Institutes of the Christian Religion*, 1.3.1–1.4.1. Some may dispute this. For further discussion see Kenneth D. Boa and Robert M. Bowman, *Faith Has Its Reasons: An Integrative Approach to Defending Christianity* (Colorado Springs: NavPress, 2001).

29. Boa and Bowman, *Faith Has Its Reasons*, 139–334.

Chapter 7 Other Religions, the Undead, and Resurrection

1. Pinchas Lapide, *The Resurrection of Jesus: A Jewish Perspective* (Minneapolis: Augsburg, 1983), 131.

2. Paul G. Hiebert, R. Daniel Shaw, and Tite Tiénou, *Understanding Folk Religion: A Christian Response to Popular Beliefs and Practices* (Grand Rapids: Baker, 1999).

3. Lynne Hume, "Liminal Beings and the Undead: Vampires in the 21st Century," in *Popular Spiritualities*, ed. Lynne Hume and Kathleen McPhillips (Aldershot, England: Ashgate, 2006), 3–16. David Keyworth, "The Socio-Religious Beliefs and Nature of the Contemporary Vampire Subculture," *JCR* 17 (2002): 355–70.

4. Keyworth, "Socio-Religious Beliefs," 365.

5. Emyr Williams, Mandy Robbins, and Laura Picton, "Adolescent Television Viewing and Belief in Vampires," *JBV* 27 (2006): 227–29.

6. Christian authors who do recognize the key moral questions include Paul Leggett, *Terence Fisher: Horror, Myth and Religion* (Jefferson, NC: McFarland, 2002); Kim Paffenroth, *Gospel of the Living Dead: George Romero's Visions of Hell on Earth* (Waco: Baylor University Press, 2006). See Paffenroth's blog *Gospel of the Living Dead*, http://gotld.blogspot.com/.

7. Adele Olivia Gladwell and James Havoc, *Blood and Roses: The Vampire in 19th Century Literature* (London: Creation, 1992); J. Gordon Melton, *The Vampire Book: The Encyclopedia of the Undead* (Detroit: Visible Ink, 1994).

8. The vampire Angel appeared as a character in the first three seasons of the television series *Buffy the Vampire Slayer*, and then in a spin-off series *Angel*. Angel represents a vampire in search of redemption and who acts to protect humanity. *Buffy the Vampire Slayer* (1997–2003) and *Angel* (1999–2003) were produced by Mutant Enemy Productions. The 1999 film *Blade* (New Line Cinema) starring Wesley Snipes portrays a saviorlike being with two natures—half-human/half-vampire—who protects humanity. Stephenie Meyer's Edward Cullen takes a nonvampire spouse Isabella Swan and guards her and their daughter from other vampires.

9. Beth Felker Jones, *Touched by a Vampire: Discovering the Hidden Messages in the Twilight Saga* (Colorado Springs: Multnomah, 2009).

10. Tracey Bateman, *Thirsty: A Novel* (Colorado Springs: Waterbrook, 2009); Eric Wilson has produced a trilogy: *Field of Blood* (Nashville: Nelson, 2008); *Haunt of Jackals* (Nashville: Nelson, 2009); and *Valley of Bones* (Nashville: Nelson, 2010).

11. Anne Rice, *Interview with the Vampire* (New York: Knopf, 1976). The story was adapted into the film *Interview with the Vampire* (Geffen Pictures, 1994).

12. Nina Auerbach, *Our Vampire, Ourselves* (Chicago: University of Chicago Press, 1995); Laurence A. Rickels, *The Vampire Lectures* (Minneapolis: University of Minnesota Press, 1999).

13. See Anne Rice, *Called Out of Darkness: A Spiritual Confession* (New York: Anchor, 2010), 206, 220, 240.

14. Eirena Evans, "There's Power in the Blood," *Christianity Today*, February 2010, 38.

15. Tina Pippin, "Of Gods and Demons: Blood Sacrifice and Eternal Life in Dracula and the Apocalypse of John," in *Screening Scripture*, ed. George Aichele and Richard Walsh (Harrisburg, PA: Trinity, 2002), 24–41.

16. Zoroaster's dates range anywhere between 1200–600 BC. See Edwin M. Yamauchi, *Persia and the Bible* (Grand Rapids: Baker, 1990), 413–15.

17. James Barr, "The Question of Religious Influence: The Case of Zoroastrianism, Judaism and Christianity," *JAAR* 53 (1985): 201–35; John Hinnells, "Zoroastrian Saviour Imagery and Its Influence on the New Testament," *Numen* 16 (1969): 161–85.

18. Yamauchi, *Persia and the Bible*, 456–62.

19. Stan Guthrie, "Thus Spake Jesus: Former Zoroastrian Overcomes Opposition to Seek Other Parsees," *EMQ* 35 (1999): 344–48.

20. Yvonne Yazbeck Haddad and Jane I. Smith, *The Islamic Understanding of Death and Resurrection* (Albany: State University of New York Press, 1981).

21. See Badru D. Kateregga and David W. Shenk, *Islam and Christianity: A Muslim and a Christian in Dialogue* (Grand Rapids: Eerdmans, 1981), 140.

22. The Ahmadiyya view is argued in A. Faber-Kaiser, *Jesus Died in India* (London: Abacus, 1978), and evaluated in Ross Clifford and Philip Johnson, *Jesus and the Gods of the New Age* (Colorado Springs: Victor, 2003), 224–27.

23. See Kenneth Cragg, *Jesus and the Muslim: An Exploration* (Oxford: Oneworld, 1999), 166–88.

24. See Mark N. Swanson, "Resurrection Debates: Qur'anic Discourse and Arabic Christian Apology," *Di* 48 (2009): 248–56; Maurice Bucaille, *The Bible, The Qur'an and Science: The Holy Scriptures Examined in the Light of Modern Knowledge*, trans. A. D. Pannell and M. Bucaille (Delhi: Taj, 1993).

25. William S. Hatcher and J. Douglas Martin, *The Bahá'i Faith: The Emerging Global Religion* (San Francisco: Harper & Row, 1985), 103–15.

26. Jacob Neusner, "Judaism," in *Our Religions*, ed. Arvind Sharma (San Francisco: Harper Collins, 1993), 293–355.

27. Gershom Scholem, *Origins of the Kabbalah*, trans. R. J. Zwi Werblowsky (Philadelphia: Jewish Publication Society; Princeton: Princeton University Press, 1987).

28. Ninian Smart, *The Religious Experience of Mankind* (Glasgow: Fount, 1980), 390–91.

29. Jon D. Levenson, *Resurrection and the Restoration of Israel: The Ultimate Victory of the God of Life* (New Haven: Yale University Press, 2006), 1–22; Alan F. Segal, "Life after Death: The Social Sources," in *The Resurrection: An Interdisciplinary Symposium*, ed. Steven T. Davis, Daniel Kendall, and Gerald O'Collins (Oxford: Oxford University Press, 1997), 90–125.

30. Peter G. Bolt, "What Were the Sadducees Reading? An Enquiry into the Literary Background of Mark 12:18–23," *TynBul* 45 (1994): 369–94.

31. Lapide, *Resurrection of Jesus*, 151.

32. Swami Bhaktipada, *Christ and Krishna: The Path of Pure Devotion* (Moundsville, WV: Bhaktipada Books, 1985), 64–65.

33. Wendy Doniger O'Flaherty, ed., *Karma and Rebirth in Classical Indian Traditions* (Delhi: Motilal Banarsidass, 1983).

34. Richard Fox Young, *Resistant Hinduism: Sanskrit Sources on Anti-Christian Apologetics in Early Nineteenth-Century India* (Vienna: De Nobili Research Library, 1981).

35. Peter Harvey, *An Introduction to Buddhism: Teachings, History and Practices* (Cambridge: Cambridge University Press, 1990).

36. Dalai Lama, *The Good Heart* (London: Rider, 1996), 117–21.

37. Ibid., 147, 148, and the italics are Father Laurence's.

38. Thich Nhat Hanh, *Living Buddha, Living Christ* (London: Rider, 1995), 132.

39. Tucker N. Callaway, *Zen Way Jesus Way* (Rutland, VT: Tuttle, 1976), 205.

40. A. L. De Silva, *Beyond Belief: A Buddhist Critique of Fundamentalist Christianity* (Sydney: Three Gem, 1994), 50, available online at http://www.buddhanet.net/pdf_file/beyond-belief02.pdf.

41. Ibid., 51.

42. See Rita M. Gross and Terry C. Muck, eds., *Buddhists Talk about Jesus, Christians Talk about Buddha* (New York: Continuum, 2000).

43. Anna Seidel, "Post-Mortem Immortality, or: The Taoist Resurrection of the Body," in *Gilgul: Essays on the Transformation, Revolution and Permanence in the History of Religions*, ed. Shaul Shaked, D. Shulman, and G. G. Stroumsa (Leiden: Brill, 1987), 223–37.

44. Donald Harper, "Resurrection in Warring States Popular Religion," *Taoist Resources* 5, no. 2 (December 1994): 13–28.

45. Margaret Stutley, *Shamanism: An Introduction* (London: Routledge, 2003).

46. Ibid., 104.

47. Mircea Eliade, *Shamanism: Archaic Techniques of Ecstasy*, trans. Willard R. Trask (Princeton: Princeton University Press, 1964), 33, 38, 45, 55, 64, 76.

48. Nevill Drury, *The Elements of Shamanism* (Shaftesbury, Dorset: Element, 1989).

49. Christadelphian views are proclaimed in Alan Hayward, *God's Truth: A Scientist Shows Why It Makes Sense to Believe the Bible* (London: Marshall, Morgan & Scott, 1973). For evaluation see Philip Johnson, "Reaching the Christadelphians," in *Encountering New Religious*

Movements, ed. Irving Hexham, Stephen Rost, and John W. Morehead (Grand Rapids: Kregel, 2004), 175–92.

50. See *You Can Live Forever in Paradise on Earth*, rev. ed. (New York: Watchtower Bible & Tract Society, 1989), 7–15, 76–89, 120–26, and 155–83. On Jehovah's Witnesses see Andrew Holden, *Jehovah's Witnesses: Portrait of a Contemporary Religious Movement* (London: Routledge, 2002); Robert M. Bowman, *Understanding Jehovah's Witnesses: Why They Read the Bible the Way They Do* (Grand Rapids: Baker, 1991).

51. A helpful introduction is Douglas J. Davies, *An Introduction to Mormonism* (Cambridge: Cambridge University Press, 2003). Excellent responses include David L. Rowe, *I Love Mormons* (Grand Rapids: Baker, 2005); John L. Bracht, *Mormonism: Magnificent Illusion* (Macquarie Park, NSW: Morling, 2010); John L. Bracht, *Man of Holiness: The Mormon Search for a Personal God* (n. p.: Sacred Tribes Press, 2010), http://www.sacredtribespress.com/.

52. John A. Saliba, *Understanding New Religious Movements*, 2nd ed. (Walnut Creek, CA: Alta Mira, 2003), 2–7, 203–39; Philip Johnson, *Apologetics, Mission, and New Religious Movements: A Holistic Approach* (n.p.: Sacred Tribes Press, 2010) http://www.sacredtribes press.com/.

53. Walter R. Martin, *The Christian and the Cults* (Grand Rapids: Zondervan, 1956), 118–33.

54. Walter R. Martin, *The Kingdom of the Cults*, ed. Ravi Zacharias, rev. ed. (Bloomington, MN: Bethany, 2003), 163–64, 175–77.

55. Unitarian opinion can be accessed in George C. Anastos, "The Purpose of the Resurrection," *UUC* 51–52 (1996–1997): 264–66.

56. See Martin, *Kingdom of the Cults*, 333–49.

57. J. K. Van Baalen, *The Chaos of Cults*, 4th ed. (Grand Rapids: Eerdmans, 1962), 390–98.

58. James Redfield, "Ninth Insight: The Emerging Culture," CelestineVision.com, accessed July 3, 2010, http://www.celestinevision.com.

59. See Paul Badham, "Religious and Near-Death Experience in Relation to Belief in a Future Life," *Mort* 2 (1997): 7–21.

60. Janet Oppenheim, *The Other World: Spiritualism and Psychical Research in England, 1850–1914* (Cambridge: Cambridge University Press, 1985).

61. Jesse C. F. Grumbine, *The Resurrection Demonstrated by Spiritualism* (Boston: Order of the White Rose, 1911).

62. Joscelyn Godwin, *The Theosophical Enlightenment* (Albany: State University of New York Press, 1994).

63. Janet Farrar and Stewart Farrar, *Eight Sabbats for Witches, and Rites for Birth, Marriage, and Death* (London: R. Hale, 1981); Philip Johnson and John Smulo, "Reaching Wiccan and Mother Goddess Devotees," in *Encountering New Religious Movements*, 209–25.

64. Raël, *Intelligent Design: Message from the Designers* (n.p.: Nova Distribution, 2005), http://rael.org/download.php?view.1; Susan J. Palmer, *Aliens Adored: Raël's UFO Religion* (New Brunswick, NJ: Rutgers University Press, 2004).

65. Clifford and Johnson, *Jesus and the Gods of the New Age*, 227–28; Richard Fox Young, "Magic and Morality in Modern Japanese Exorcistic Technologies: A Study of Mahikari," *JJRelStud* 17 (1990): 29–49.

66. Gary R. Habermas, "Resurrection Claims in Non-Christian Religions," *RelS* 25 (1989): 167–77.

67. Noel Langley, *Edgar Cayce on Reincarnation* (New York: Warner, 1967), 173.

68. Origen, *Commentary on Matthew*, 13.1, in ANF 10, ed. Alexander Roberts and James Donaldson (Grand Rapids: Eerdmans, 1979), 474.

69. Joseph Wilson Trigg, *Origen: The Bible and Philosophy in the Third-Century Church* (London: SCM, 1983).

70. Due to the sensitive circumstances the names are withheld.

71. Michael Graham, *From Guru to God: The Experience of Ultimate Truth* (Melbourne: Michael Graham, 2007).

72. Cyril J. Davey, *The Story of Sadhu Sundar Singh* (Chicago: Moody, 1963), reissued as *Sadhu Sundar Singh* (Bromley, England: STL, 1980); Phyllis Thompson, *Sadhu Sundar Singh* (Carlisle, UK: OM, 1992).

73. Thompson, *Sadhu Sundar Singh*, 26.

74. Davey's account makes no reference to Jesus showing his scars or saying the words reported in Thompson's account. See Davey, *Story of Sadhu Sundar Singh*, 31–33.

75. Signe Toksvig, *Emanuel Swedenborg: Scientist and Mystic* (London: Faber, 1948); John L. Brooke, *The Refiner's Fire: The Making of Mormon Cosmology 1644–1844* (Cambridge: Cambridge University Press, 1994); Mary Ann Meyers, "Death in Swedenborgian and Mormon Eschatology," *DiJMTh* 19 (1981): 58–64.

76. Letter from Singh to the Swedenborgian pastor John Goddard, May 30, 1928. See Eric J. Sharpe, *The Riddle of Sadhu Sundar Singh* (New Delhi: Intercultural Publications, 2004), 153.

77. Sharpe, *Riddle of Sadhu Sundar Singh*, 153.

78. Martin, *Kingdom of the Cults*, 629–41; Van Baalen, *Chaos of Cults*, 177–87.

Chapter 8 Understandings of Selfhood and the Resurrection

1. Beth Felker Jones, *Marks of His Wounds: Gender Politics and Bodily Resurrection* (Oxford: Oxford University Press, 2007), 114.

2. Thomas Streeter, "The Romantic Self and the Politics of Internet Commercialization," *CulSt* 17 (2003): 650.

3. David L. Kimbrough, *Taking Up Serpents: Snake Handlers of Eastern Kentucky* (Chapel Hill: University of North Carolina Press, 1995).

4. Linda Woodhead, "Theology and the Fragmentation of the Self," *IJSysTh* 1 (1999): 53–72.

5. Ibid., 59–60.

6. Ibid., 60.

7. Ibid., 60–62.

8. Uta Ranke-Heinemann, *Putting Away Childish Things: The Virgin Birth, the Empty Tomb, and Other Fairy Tales You Don't Need to Believe to Have a Living Faith*, trans. Peter Heinegg (San Francisco: HarperSanFrancisco, 1994).

9. The pro–mind control view is represented in Michael D. Langone, ed., *Recovery from Cults* (New York: Norton, 1993). For evaluation see Massimo Introvigne, "Anti-Cult and Counter-Cult Movements in Italy," in *Anti-Cult Movements in Cross-Cultural Perspective*, ed. Anson D. Shupe and David G. Bromley (New York: Garland, 1994), 171–219.

10. Woodhead, "Theology," 63.

11. Paul Heelas, *The New Age Movement: The Celebration of the Self and the Sacralization of Modernity* (Oxford: Blackwell, 1996), 161.

12. On holistic spiritual practices see Jon P. Bloch, *New Spirituality, Self, and Belonging: How New Agers and Neo-Pagans Talk about Themselves* (Westport, CT: Praeger, 1998); Daren Kemp, *New Age: A Guide* (Edinburgh: Edinburgh University Press, 2004).

13. Paul H. Ray and Sherry Ruth Anderson, *The Cultural Creatives: How 50 Million People Are Changing the World* (New York: Harmony, 2000). See also http://www.culturalcreatives.org/.

14. Streeter, "Romantic Self," 651–53.

15. Woodhead, "Theology," 64.

16. Ibid., 64–65.

17. Barrie Dolnick, *The Executive Mystic* (New York: HarperBusiness, 1998); Anthony Robbins, *Awaken the Giant Within* (New York: Simon & Schuster, 1991); Nevill Drury, *The Elements of Human Potential* (Shaftesbury, Dorset: Element, 1989).

18. Eeva Sointu and Linda Woodhead, "Spirituality, Gender and Expressive Selfhood," *JSSR* 47 (2008): 259–76.

19. Charles Taylor, *Sources of the Self* (Cambridge, MA: Harvard University Press, 1989).

20. Charles Taylor, "The Politics of Recognition," in *Multiculturalism, Examining the Politics of Recognition*, ed. A. Gutmann (Princeton: Princeton University Press, 1994), 31; Charles Taylor, *The Ethics of Authenticity* (Cambridge, MA: Harvard University Press, 1991).

21. Charles Taylor, *Varieties of Religion Today: William James Revisited* (Cambridge, MA: Harvard University Press, 2002), 89, 107.

22. Sointu and Woodhead, "Spirituality," 260.

23. Ibid., 265, italics original.

24. Jones, *Marks of His Wounds*.

25. Sointu and Woodhead, "Spirituality," 266.

26. Ibid., 267.

27. Ibid.

28. Ibid., 272, 273.

29. Ibid., 273.

30. Terry C. Muck, "After Selfhood: Constructing the Religious Self in a Post-Self Age," *JETS* 41 (1998): 107–22.

31. Kevin J. Madigan and Jon D. Levenson, *Resurrection: The Power of God for Christians and Jews* (New Haven: Yale University Press, 2008), 69–80.

32. See Philip Johnson and Gus diZerega, *Beyond the Burning Times: A Pagan and Christian in Dialogue* (Oxford: Lion, 2008), 60–61, 131.

33. Jin Kyu Park, " 'Creating My Own Cultural and Spiritual Bubble': Case of Cultural Consumption by Spiritual Seeker Anime Fans," *CulRel* 6 (2005): 393–94.

34. Pokémon is a contraction of "Pocket Monsters," while Digimon is a contraction of "Digital Monsters." The official website for Pokémon is http://www.pokemon.com/.

35. Park, "Creating," 394.

36. Ibid., 400.

37. Ibid., 401.

38. Ibid., 409.

39. For a sociological interpretation of this behavior see Douglas E. Cowan, *Bearing False Witness? An Introduction to the Christian Countercult* (Westport, CT: Praeger, 2003).

40. These tendencies surface in Phil Phillips, *Turmoil in the Toybox* (Lancaster, PA: Starburst, 1986).

41. Bill Ellis, *Lucifer Ascending: The Occult in Folklore and Popular Culture* (Lexington: University Press of Kentucky, 2004).

42. Lorne L. Dawson and Douglas E. Cowan, ed., *Religion Online: Finding Faith on the Internet* (New York: Routledge, 2004).

43. Douglas E. Cowan, *Cyberhenge: Modern Pagans on the Internet* (New York: Routledge, 2005).

44. Adam Possamai, *Religion and Popular Culture: A Hyper-Real Testament* (Brussels: P.I.E.-Peter Lang, 2005).

45. Ibid., 101–2; Wendy Parkins, "Oprah Winfrey's Change Your Life TV and the Spiritual Everyday," *Continuum: Journal of Media and Cultural Studies* 15 (2001): 145–57.

46. Possamai, *Religion and Popular Culture*, 90–93.

47. Les Daniels, *Batman: The Complete History* (San Francisco: Chronicle, 1999).

48. Les Daniels, *Superman: The Complete History, the Life and Times of the Man of Steel* (San Francisco: Chronicle, 1998).

49. Les Daniels, *Wonder Woman: The Life and Times of the Amazon Princess: The Complete Story* (San Francisco: Chronicle, 2000).

50. J. E. Kennedy, "Personality and Motivations to Believe, Misbelieve and Disbelieve in Paranormal Phenomena," *JPara* 69 (2005): 263–92.

51. Nevill Drury, *The History of Magic in the Modern Age: A Quest for Personal Transformation* (London: Constable, 2000).

52. Carole M. Cusack, *Invented Religions: Faith, Fiction, Imagination* (Aldershot, England: Ashgate, 2010).

53. Possamai, *Religion and Popular Culture*, 98–99.

54. Ibid., 161.

55. Streeter, "Romantic Self," 651.

56. Christian apologists Raymond Lull, Wilhelm Shickhard, Blaise Pascal, and Charles Babbage were influential in the prehistory of computers. See John Warwick Montgomery, "Computer Origins and the Defense of the Faith," *PSCF* 56 (2004): 189–203.

57. Streeter, "Romantic Self," 649.

58. Ibid., 649–50, italics original.

59. Ibid., 652.

60. See the Open Source Theology project, http://www.opensourcetheology.net/.

61. Andrew Keen, *The Cult of the Amateur: How Today's Internet Is Killing Our Culture* (New York: Doubleday, 2007), 16.

62. Tom Zeller, "Link by Link: The Internet Black Hole That Is North Korea," *New York Times*, October 23, 2006.

63. Wagner James Au, "New World Editorial: Only Mass Adoption of Second Life Will Best Address All SL's Major Challenges," New World Notes, October 14, 2009, http://nwn.blogs.com/nwn/2009/10/sl-needs-growth.html.

64. "Down the Rabbit Hole," *CSI: New York*, season 4, episode 76. See also Bill Carter, "Fictional Characters Get Virtual Lives, Too," *New York Times*, October 4, 2007, http://www.nytimes.com/2007/10/04/arts/television/04CSI.html.

65. Wagner James Au, *The Making of Second Life: Notes from the New World* (New York: HarperCollins, 2008).

66. Ibid., 15.

67. Ibid.

68. Ibid., 20.

69. For example see "You Only Live Twice," from the investigative journalism show *Four Corners*, available online at http://www.abc.net.au/4corners/special_eds/20070319/.

70. On alienation in urban societies see Robert D. Putnam, *Bowling Alone: The Collapse and Revival of American Community* (New York: Simon & Schuster, 2000).

71. On Burning Life see http://burninglife.secondlife.com/.

72. Christopher Partridge, "The Spiritual and the Revolutionary: Alternative Spirituality, British Free Festivals, and the Emergence of Rave Culture," *CulRel* 7 (2006): 41–60; Scott Hutson, "The Rave: Spiritual Healing in Modern Western Subcultures," *AnthQ* 73 (2000): 35–49.

73. The official website for Burning Man in Nevada is http://www.burningman.com/. The first Australian festival of Burning Man was held from June 5–8, 2009, http://www.burningmanaustralia.com/. Also see Robert V. Kozinets and John F. Sherry, "Dancing on Common Ground: Exploring the Sacred at Burning Man," in *Rave Culture and Religion*, ed. Graham St. John (London: Routledge, 2004), 287–303.

74. John W. Morehead, "Burning Man in Alternative Interpretive Analysis," *STJ* 4, no. 1 (2009): 19–41, available online at http://www.sacredtribesjournal.org/htdocs/images/Articles/Vol_4/Morehead_Burning_Man.pdf.

75. Meg Twycross, "The Theatricality of Medieval English Plays," in *The Cambridge Companion to Medieval English Theatre*, ed. Richard Beadle (Cambridge: Cambridge University Press, 1994), 37–84; Carla Dauven-van Knippenberg, "Dramatic Celebration of the Easter Festival," in *Christian Feast and Festival: The Dynamics of Western Liturgy and Culture*, ed. Louis van Tongeren et al. (Leuven: Peeters, 2001), 405–22.

76. Stella Sai-Chun Lau, "Churched Ibiza: Evangelical Christianity and Club Culture," *CulRel* 7 (2006): 77–92.

77. Streeter, "Romantic Self," 650.

Chapter 9 Myth, Resurrection, and the Human Psyche

1. C. S. Lewis, *God in the Dock: Essays on Theology and Ethics* (Grand Rapids: Eerdmans, 1970), 66, 67.

2. J. R. R. Tolkien, "On Fairy-Stories," in *Essays Presented to Charles Williams*, ed. C. S. Lewis (1948; repr., Grand Rapids: Eerdmans, 1981), 83–84.

3. Margery Hourihan, *Deconstructing the Hero: Literary Theory and Children's Literature* (London: Routledge, 1997), 1.

4. Jürgen Kleist and Bruce A. Butterfield, eds., *Mythology: From Ancient to Post-Modern* (New York: Lang, 1992).

5. Christopher Vogler, *The Writer's Journey: Mythic Structure for Storytellers* (Studio City, CA: Michael Wiese, 1998).

6. Joseph Campbell with Bill Moyers, *The Power of Myth* (New York: Doubleday, 1988).

7. Irving Hexham and Karla Poewe, *New Religions as Global Cultures: Making the Human Sacred* (Boulder: Westview, 1997), 81, italics original.

8. Ibid., 84–96.

9. Mark Levon Byrne, *Myths of Manhood: The Hero in Jungian Literature*, Sydney Studies in Religion 3 (Sydney: RLA, 2001), 1.

10. Geoffrey S. Kirk, *Myth: Its Meaning and Functions in Ancient and Other Cultures* (Cambridge: Cambridge University Press, 1970).

11. Carolina López-Ruiz, *When the Gods Were Born: Greek Cosmogonies and the Near East* (Cambridge, MA: Harvard University Press, 2010).

12. Ross Clifford and Philip Johnson, *Jesus and the Gods of the New Age* (Colorado Springs: Victor, 2003), 71–86, 217–48.

13. A useful anthology of early European views of myth is Burton Feldman and Robert D. Richardson, *The Rise of Modern Mythology 1680–1860* (Bloomington: Indiana University Press, 2000). On the rise of mythography see Eric J. Sharpe, *Comparative Religion: A History*, rev. ed. (LaSalle, IL: Open Court, 1986), 40–96.

14. John Goldingay, *Approaches to Old Testament Interpretation*, rev. ed. (Downers Grove, IL: InterVarsity, 1990); Stephen Neill and Tom Wright, *The Interpretation of the New Testament, 1861–1986*, rev. ed. (Oxford: Oxford University Press, 1988).

15. Tore Tybjerg, "Wilhelm Mannhardt—A Pioneer in the Study of Rituals," in *Problem of Ritual*, ed. Tore Ahlbäck (Stockholm: Almqvist & Wicksell, 1993), 27–37; Lourens Peter van den Bosch, *Friedrich Max Müller: A Life Devoted to the Humanities* (Leiden: Brill, 2002).

16. The solar theory originated with Charles-François Dupuis (1742–1809) but Mannhardt and Müller amplified it.

17. Richard Noll, *The Jung Cult: Origins of a Charismatic Movement* (London: Fontana, 1996), 75–108.

18. Robert Ackerman, *J. G. Frazer: His Life and Work* (Cambridge: Cambridge University Press, 1987).

19. See Sharpe, *Comparative Religion*, 87; C. J. Wright, "The Legacy of Sir James Frazer," *Modern Churchman* 44 (1954): 54–56.

20. Edwin M. Yamauchi, "Tammuz and the Bible," *JBL* 84 (1965): 283–90.

21. Edwin M. Yamauchi, *Persia and the Bible* (Grand Rapids: Baker, 1990), 493–521.

22. Nicholas Perrin, "On Raising Osiris in 1 Corinthians 15," *TynBul* 58 (2007): 117–28.

23. Giovanni Casadio, "The Failing Male God: Emasculation, Death and Other Accidents in the Ancient Mediterranean World," *Numen* 50 (2003): 231–68.

24. Sharpe, *Comparative Religion*, 88–94.

25. John W. Parrish, "It's All in the Definition: The Problem with 'Dying and Rising Gods,'" *CSSRB* 35 (2006): 71–75.

26. Mark S. Smith, *The Origins of Biblical Monotheism* (Oxford: Oxford University Press, 2001).

27. Jonathan Z. Smith, *Drudgery Divine: On the Comparison of Early Christianities and the Religions of Late Antiquity* (Chicago: University of Chicago Press, 1990).

28. Tryggve N. D. Mettinger, *The Riddle of Resurrection: "Dying and Rising" Gods in the Ancient Near East* (Stockholm: Almqvist & Wicksell, 2001).

29. Allan Sun, "Chasing One's Tail: Some Reflections on the Methodologies of Mircea Eliade and Jonathan Z. Smith," in *On a Panegyrical Note: Studies in Honour of Garry W. Trompf*, ed. Victoria Barker and Frances Di Lauro, Studies in Religion 6 (Sydney: University of Sydney, 2007), 189–204.

30. Samuel Sandmel, "Parallelomania," *JBL* 81 (1962): 1–13.

31. Paul W. Barnett, *Jesus and the Logic of History* (Leicester: Apollos, 1997).

32. Robert Ackerman, *The Myth and Ritual School: J. G. Frazer and the Cambridge Ritualists* (New York: Garland, 1991).

33. S. H. Hooke, *Middle Eastern Mythology* (Harmondsworth, England: Penguin, 1963).

34. Ronald E. Clements, *A Century of Old Testament Study*, rev. ed. (Cambridge: Lutterworth, 1992), 95–121.

35. Colin Brown, *Jesus in European Protestant Thought 1778–1860* (Grand Rapids: Baker, 1988), 183–204.

36. Hans Werner Bartsch, ed., *Kerygma and Myth: A Theological Debate*, trans. Reginald H. Fuller (New York: Harper & Row, 1961), is a succinct introduction to Bultmann. For critical evaluation see James D. G. Dunn, "Demythologizing: The Problem of Myth in the New Testament," in *New Testament Interpretation: Essays of Principles and Methods*, ed. I. Howard Marshall (Exeter: Paternoster, 1987), 285–307.

37. Robert M. Price, *Deconstructing Jesus* (Amherst, NY: Prometheus, 2000), 88.

38. Ibid.

39. Edwin M. Yamauchi, *Pre-Christian Gnosticism: A Survey of the Proposed Evidences*, rev. ed. (Grand Rapids: Baker, 1983); Yamauchi, *Persia and the Bible*, 493–521; Ronald H. Nash, *Christianity and the Hellenistic World* (Grand Rapids: Zondervan, 1984).

40. Perrin, "Osiris," 127–28.

41. J. W. Drane, "Some Ideas of Resurrection in the New Testament Period," *TynBul* 24 (1973): 108, 109.

42. See chapter 6.

43. Humphrey Carpenter, *The Inklings: C. S. Lewis, J. R. R. Tolkien, Charles Williams and Their Friends* (London: Allen & Unwin, 1978), 32; A. N. Wilson, *C. S. Lewis: A Biography* (London: Collins, 1990), 117–19.

44. P. H. Brazier, "C. S. Lewis and Christological Prefigurement," *HeyJ* 48 (2007): 765, 770.

45. Carl Gustav Jung, *Memories, Dreams, Reflections*, ed. Aniela Jaffé, trans. Richard and Clara Winston (New York: Vintage, 1962).

46. Robert A. Segal, "Jung and Gnosticism," *Religion* 17 (1987): 301–36.

47. Joseph Campbell and Richard Roberts, *Tarot Revelations* (San Anselmo, CA: Vernal Equinox, 1987), 253–54.

48. Start with Ellwood, *The Politics of Myth*, 127–69.

49. Such as Australia and Germany; see Byrne, *Myths of Manhood*, 164.

50. Robin Morgan, *The Demon Lover: On the Sexuality of Terrorism* (New York: Norton, 1989).

51. Christine Downing, "Masks of the Goddess: A Feminist Response," in *Paths to the Power of Myth: Joseph Campbell and the Study of Religion*, ed. Daniel C. Noel (New York: Crossroad, 1990), 97–107.

52. Clarissa Pinkola Estés, *Women Who Run with the Wolves: Contacting the Power of the Wild Woman* (London: Rider, 1992), is a Jungian attempt to find positive feminine symbols in mythology.

53. George Miller, "The Apocalypse and the Pig: or the Hazards of Storytelling," *The Sydney Papers* 8, no. 4 (1996): 39–49.

54. Allen Chinen, *Beyond the Hero: Classic Stories of Men in Search of a Soul* (New York: Tarcher/Putnam, 1993).

55. Byrne, *Myths of Manhood*, 177.

56. Harold Schechter and Jonna Gormely Semeiks, "Joseph Campbell and the 'Vanilla-Coated Temple,'" in *The Uses of Comparative Mythology: Essays on the Work of Joseph Campbell*, ed. Kenneth L. Golden (New York: Garland, 1992), 179–92.

57. Adrian Warnock, *Raised with Christ: How the Resurrection Changes Everything* (Wheaton: Crossway, 2010), 156.

58. Byrne, *Myths of Manhood*, 177.

59. F. F. Bruce, *Paul: Apostle of the Heart Set Free*, rev. ed. (Exeter: Paternoster, 1980), 242.

60. On the strengths and limitations of Jung see Stanton L. Jones and Richard E. Butman, *Modern Psychotherapies: A Comprehensive Christian Appraisal* (Downers Grove, IL: InterVarsity, 1991), 119–42.

61. Richard J. Clifton, "The Hebrew Scriptures and the Theology of Creation," *TS* 46 (1985): 507–23.

62. On the *imago Dei* start with Gordon J. Wenham, *Genesis 1–15*, WBC 1 (Waco: Word, 1987), 29–34; William Dumbrell, "Genesis 2:1–3: Biblical Theology of Creation Covenant," *ERT* 35 (2001): 219–30.

63. On the Spirit of God in creation generally start with Wilf Hildebrandt, *An Old Testament Theology of the Spirit of God* (Peabody, MA: Hendrickson, 1995); R. C. Sproul, *The Mystery of the Holy Spirit* (Wheaton: Tyndale, 1990), 75–90.

64. R. C. Sproul, *If There Is a God, Why Are There Atheists?* (Minneapolis: Bethany, 1978), 56–80.

65. Royce Gordon Gruenler, "Jesus as Author of the Evangelium: J. R. R. Tolkien and the Spell of the Great Story," in *New Approaches to Jesus and the Gospels: A Phenomenological and Exegetical Study of Synoptic Christology* (Grand Rapids: Baker, 1982), 204–20.

66. Philip Johnson, "Apologetics and Myths: Signs of Salvation in Postmodernity," *LTJ* 32 (1998): 62–72.

67. C. S. Lewis, *Surprised by Joy* (Glasgow: Fount, 1977), 19–20.

68. On Euhemerus see Ken Dowden, *The Uses of Greek Mythology* (London: Routledge, 1998), 50–51.

69. Roger Lancelyn Green and Walter Hooper, *C. S. Lewis: A Biography* (Glasgow: Collins, 1974), 48–49.

70. Ibid., 116–18.

71. C. S. Lewis, "Psycho-Analysis and Literary Criticism," in *Selected Literary Essays*, ed. Walter Hooper (Cambridge: Cambridge University Press, 1969), 286–300; C. S. Lewis, *An Experiment in Criticism* (Cambridge: Cambridge University Press, 1961).

72. Lewis, *Experiment in Criticism*, 40–49.

73. David Rafer, "Mythic Identity in Doctor Who," in *Time and Relative Dissertations in Space*, ed. David Butler (Manchester: Manchester University Press, 2007), 129.

74. C. S. Lewis, *Till We Have Faces* (Glasgow: Fount, 1978). See Chad Walsh, *The Literary Legacy of C. S. Lewis* (New York: Harcourt Brace Jovanovich, 1979), 196–99, 243–45.

75. John Drane, Ross Clifford, and Philip Johnson, *Beyond Prediction: The Tarot and Your Spirituality* (Oxford: Lion, 2001), 29–37.

76. See John Warwick Montgomery, ed., *Myth, Allegory and Gospel* (Minneapolis: Bethany, 1974).

77. Steve Taylor, *The Out of Bounds Church?* (Grand Rapids: Zondervan, 2005), 27. An exception is in the outreach of *Sanctus1*; see Ben Edson, "An Exploration into the Missiology of the Emerging Church in the UK through the Narrative of *Sanctus1*," *IJSCC* 6 (2006): 24–37.

78. On the depth of New Age books versus the shallowness of popular Christian literature see Irving Hexham, "The Evangelical Response to the New Age," in *Perspectives on the New Age*, ed. James R. Lewis and J. Gordon Melton (Albany: State University of New York Press, 1992), 161–63.

79. On Oprah's impact generally see Wendy Parkins, "Oprah Winfrey's Change Your Life TV and the Spiritual Everyday," *Continuum: Journal of Media and Cultural Studies* 15 (2001): 145–57.

80. John Drane, *Do Christians Know How to Be Spiritual? The Rise of the New Spirituality and the Mission of the Church* (London: Darton, Longman & Todd, 2005), 24–26.

81. Zygmunt Bauman, "Postmodern Religion?" in *Religion, Modernity and Postmodernity*, ed. Paul Heelas et al. (Oxford: Blackwell, 1998), 74.

82. Christopher H. Partridge, ed., *Fundamentalisms* (Carlisle: Paternoster, 2001).

Chapter 10 Church History and Resurrection Thinking

1. Nathan D. Hieb, "The Precarious Status of Resurrection in Friedrich Schleiermacher's *Glaubenslehre*," *IJSysTh* 9 (2007): 414.

2. The quiz is available at http://quizfarm.com/quizzes/new/svensvensven/which-theologian -are-you/.

3. Doc Brown's DeLorean automobile was featured in the *Back to the Future* films. The *Time Tunnel* was the 1966–1967 TV series created by Irwin Allen. The Tardis is Doctor Who's time travel capsule.

4. George Santayana, *The Life of Reason or The Phases of Human Progress* (London: Archibald Constable, 1906), 284. Available online at http://www.archive.org/stream/thelifeofreasono 00santuoft#page/284/.

5. Gerald O'Collins, "The Resurrection: The State of the Questions," in *The Resurrection: An Interdisciplinary Symposium on the Resurrection*, ed. Stephen T. Davis, Daniel Kendall, and Gerald O'Collins (Oxford: Oxford University Press, 1997), 20.

6. Thorwald Lorenzen, *Resurrection Discipleship Justice* (Macon, GA: Smyth & Helwys, 2003); N. T. Wright, *The Resurrection of the Son of God* (Minneapolis: Fortress, 2003).

7. John Shelby Spong, *Resurrection: Myth or Reality?* (San Francisco: HarperSanFrancisco, 1994).

8. C. W. Christian, *Friedrich Schleiermacher* (Waco: Word, 1979), 12.

9. Ibid., 128.

10. Todd Weir, "The Secular Beyond: Free Religious Dissent and Debates over the Afterlife in Nineteenth-Century Germany," *CH* 77 (2008): 629–58.

11. Hieb, "Precarious Status," 399.

12. Ibid., 402.

13. William Lane Craig, *The Historical Argument for the Resurrection of Jesus during the Deist Controversy* (Lewiston, NY: Edwin Mellen, 1985).

14. Francis J. Beckwith, *David Hume's Argument Against Miracles: A Critical Analysis* (Lanham, MD: University Press of America, 1989).

15. Hans Joachim Hillerbrand, "Historicity of Miracles: The Early Eighteenth-Century Debate among Woolston, Annet, Sherlock and West," *SR* 3 (1973): 132–51.

16. Ross Clifford, *John Warwick Montgomery's Legal Apologetic: An Apologetic for All Seasons* (Bonn: Kultur und Wissenschaft, 2004), 19–56.

17. See Thomas J. Davis, "Not 'Hidden and Far Off': the Bodily Aspect of Salvation and Its Implications for Understanding the Body in Calvin's Theology," *CTJ* 29 (1994): 406–18.

18. David R. Maxwell, "The Resurrection of Christ: Its Importance in the History of the Church," *CoJ* 34 (2008): 34.

19. "Preface of Philipp Melanchthon to His Theological Topics," in Martin Chemnitz, *Loci Theologici* 1, trans. J. A. O. Preus (St. Louis: Concordia, 1989), 35.

20. Sachiko Kusukawa, *The Transformation of Natural Philosophy: The Case of Philip Melanchthon* (Cambridge: Cambridge University Press, 1995), 197.

21. Gerald O'Collins, "Thomas Aquinas and Christ's Resurrection," *TS* 31 (1970): 513.

22. Fred W. Meuser, "Luther as Preacher of the Word of God," in *The Cambridge Companion to Martin Luther*, ed. Donald K. McKim (Cambridge: Cambridge University Press, 2003), 139.

23. Ibid., 145.

24. Gerhard Sauter, "Luther on the Resurrection: The Proclamation of the Risen One as the Promise of Our Everlasting Life with God," *LQ* 15 (2001): 195. See also Anthony C. Thiselton, "Luther and Barth on 1 Cor. 15: Six Theses for Theology in Relation to Recent Interpretation," in *The Bible, the Reformation and the Church*, ed. W. P. Stephens (Sheffield: Sheffield Academic Press, 1995), 258–89.

25. Martin Luther, *LW*, 28:94.

26. Marguerite Shuster, "The Preaching of the Resurrection of Christ in Augustine, Luther, Barth, and Thielicke," in *The Resurrection: An Interdisciplinary Symposium on the Resurrection*, ed. Stephen T. Davis, Daniel Kendall, and Gerald O'Collins (Oxford: Oxford University Press, 1997), 308–38.

27. Martin Luther, "A Sermon on Christ's Resurrection: Mark 16:1–8," available online at *Our Redeemer Lutheran Church* website, accessed April 11, 2011, http://www.orlutheran.com/html/mlsem16l.html.

28. Paul T. McCain, "Luther on the Resurrection: Genesis Lectures, 1535–1546," *Logia* 13 (2004): 35–40.

29. P. David Pahl, "A Bodily Influence in the Sacrament, in the Fathers, in Luther, in Modern Lutheranism," in *Theologia Crucis: Studies in Honour of Hermann Sasse*, ed. Henry Paul Hamann (Adelaide: Lutheran, 1975), 61–69.

30. Carl E. Braaten and Robert W. Jenson, eds., *Union with Christ: The New Finnish Interpretation of Luther* (Grand Rapids: Eerdmans, 1998); Jonathan Linman, "Martin Luther: 'Little Christs' for the World; Faith and Sacraments as a Means to Theosis," in *Partakers of the Divine Nature: The History and Development of Deification in the Christian Traditions*, ed. Michael J. Christensen and Jeffery A. Wittung (Grand Rapids: Baker, 2008), 189–99.

31. Luther was a prolific writer who said many things at different times. He also once emphasized John 1:29 as the chief article of faith, and on another occasion nominated the second article of the creed.

32. Jos E. Vercruysse, "Luther's Theology of the Cross at the Time of the Heidelberg Disputation," *Greg* 57 (1976): 523–48; Marit Trelstad, "The Way of Salvation in Luther's Theology: A Feminist Evaluation," *Di* 45 (2006): 236–45.

33. Vercruysse, "Luther's Theology of the Cross," 539.

34. David P. Scaer, "Luther's Concept of the Resurrection in His Commentary on 1 Corinthians 15," *CTQ* 47 (1983): 209.

35. Caroline Walker Bynum, "Bodily Miracles and the Resurrection of the Body in the High Middle Ages," in *Belief in History: Innovative Approaches to European and American Religion*, ed. Thomas Kselman (Notre Dame, IN: University of Notre Dame Press, 1991), 68–106.

36. Michael Frassetto, "Resurrection of the Body: Eleventh-Century Evidence from the Sermons of Ademar of Chabannes," *JRH* 26 (2002): 235–49.

37. Timothy F. Merrill, "Achard of Saint Victor and the Medieval Exegetical Tradition: Rom 7:22–25 in a Sermon on the Feast of the Resurrection," *WTJ* 48 (1986): 48.

38. Caroline Walker Bynum, *The Resurrection of the Body in Western Christianity 200–1336* (New York: Columbia University Press, 1995), 13.

39. St. Anselm, *Cur Deus Homo* 2.3, in *St. Anselm: The Basic Writings*, trans. S. W. Deane (LaSalle, IL: Open Court, 1962), 241.

40. *The Prayers and Meditations of St. Anselm with the Proslogion*, trans. Sister Benedicta Ward (London: Penguin, 1973), 101.

41. I. Howard Marshall, *Last Supper and Lord's Supper* (Exeter: Paternoster, 1980), 150.

42. James Weisheipl, *Friar Thomas D'Aquino: His Life, Thought, and Works* (Washington DC: Catholic University of America Press, 1983); Norman L. Geisler, *Thomas Aquinas: An Evangelical Appraisal* (Grand Rapids: Baker, 1991).

43. David Michael Stanley, *Christ's Resurrection in Pauline Soteriology* (Graz, Austria: Akademische Druck-und Verlagsanstalt, 1963).

44. Anthony J. Kelly, *The Resurrection Effect: Transforming Christian Life and Thought* (Maryknoll, NY: Orbis, 2008), 175. See also O'Collins, "Thomas Aquinas," 512–22; Pim Valenkenberg, *Reading John with St. Thomas Aquinas* (Washington, DC: Catholic University of America Press, 2005), 277–89.

45. *Summa Contra Gentiles* 3.79, in Thomas Gilby, *St. Thomas Aquinas: Theological Texts* (Durham, NC: Labyrinth, 1982), 662.

46. Anke E. Passenier, "The Suffering Body and the Freedom of the Soul: Medieval Women's Ways of Union with God," in *Begin with the Body: Corporeality, Religion and Gender*, ed. Jonneke Bekkenkamp and Maaike de Haardt (Louvain: Peeters, 1998), 264–87.

47. Bynum, *Resurrection of the Body*, 157–62, 334–40.

48. *Scivias*, in *Hildegard of Bingen: Selected Writing*, ed. Mark Atherton (London: Penguin, 2001), 19.

49. Josette A. Wisman, "The Resurrection According to Christine De Pizan," *RelArts* 4 (2000): 337–58.

50. See Caroline Vander Stichele, "Like Angels in Heaven: Corporeality, Resurrection, and Gender in Mark 12:18–27," in *Begin with the Body*, ed. Bekkenkamp and de Haardt, 215–32.

51. For discussion of this quote see Eve LaPlante, *Salem Witch Judge* (New York: Harper-One, 2007), 241–58.

52. Timothy Ware, *The Orthodox Church* (Harmondsworth, England: Penguin, 1984), 231.

53. Ibid., 232.

54. Adam G. Cooper, *The Body in St. Maximus the Confessor: Holy Flesh, Wholly Deified* (Oxford: Oxford University Press, 2005).

55. Samir Khalil Samir and Jørgen S. Nielsen, eds., *Christian Arabic Apologetics during the Abbasid Period (750–1258)* (Leiden: Brill, 1994); Steven J. McMichael, "The Death, Resurrection and Ascension of Jesus in Medieval Christian Anti-Muslim Religious Polemics," *ICMR* 21 (2010): 157–73.

56. John C. Lamoreaux, *Theodore Abū Qurrah* (Provo, UT: Brigham Young University Press, 2005), 29, 43, 46, 116–17, and 138–39.

57. Ibid., 55–57.

58. Mark N. Swanson, "Resurrection Debates: Qur'anic Discourse and Arabic Christian Apology," *Di* 48 (2009): 248–56.

59. John T. McNeill, *The Celtic Churches: A History AD 200 to 1200* (Chicago: University of Chicago Press, 1974).

60. Brian De Breffny, *In the Steps of St. Patrick* (London: Thames & Hudson, 1982), 163.

61. Adomnán, *Life of St. Columba*, book 2, 32, trans. Richard Sharpe (London: Penguin, 1995), 180.

62. Thomas O'Loughlin, *Celtic Theology: Humanity, World and God in Early Irish Writings* (London: Continuum, 2000), 80.

63. Marina Smyth, "The Body, Death and Resurrection: Perspectives of an Early Irish Theologian," *Spec* 83 (2008): 560.

64. Harold O. J. Brown, *Heresies: The Image of Christ in the Mirror of Heresy and Orthodoxy from the Apostles to the Present* (Garden City, NY: Doubleday, 1984), 21, 22.

65. See Philip Schaff, ed., *The Creeds of Christendom*, vol. 2, *The Greek and Latin Creeds*, 6th ed. (Grand Rapids: Baker, 1983), 11–20, 45–61, and 66–70.

66. J. N. D. Kelly, *Early Christian Creeds*, 3rd ed. (London: Continuum, 2006); J. G. Davies, "Factors Leading to the Emergence of Belief in the Resurrection of the Flesh," *JTS* (NS) 23 (1972): 448–55.

67. Kevin J. Madigan and Jon D. Levenson, *Resurrection: The Power of God for Christians and Jews* (New Haven: Yale University Press, 2008), 222.

68. *The Epistle to the Trallians*, 9, in *Early Christian Writings: The Apostolic Fathers*, trans. Maxwell Staniforth, revised by Andrew Louth (London: Penguin, 1987), 80.

69. W. H. C. Frend, *The Early Church: From the Beginnings to 461*, 3rd ed. (London: SCM, 1991), 36–41.

70. *The Epistle of Polycarp to the Philippians*, 1.4, 2.9, 2.13, 9.9, in ANF 1, ed. Alexander Robertson and James Donaldson (Grand Rapids: Eerdmans, 1979).

71. J. N. D. Kelly, *Early Christian Doctrines*, 5th ed. (New York: Harper & Row, 1978), 463.

72. John Drane, *Cultural Change and Biblical Faith* (Carlisle: Paternoster, 2000), 36–56.

73. On ancient gnosticism see Bentley Layton, *The Rediscovery of Gnosticism*, 2 vols. (Leiden: Brill, 1980–1981); Charles W. Hedrick and Robert Hodgson, *Nag Hammadi, Gnosticism and Early Christianity* (Peabody, MA: Hendrickson, 1986).

74. Such as the Gnostic Society Library, http://www.gnosis.org/library/gs.htm.

75. *Stigmata* (MGM/UA, 1999).

76. Craig L. Blomberg, "Tradition and Redaction in the Parables of the Gospel of Thomas," in *Gospel Perspectives 5: The Jesus Tradition Outside the Gospels*, ed. David Wenham (Sheffield: JSOT Press, 1984), 177–205.

77. There is a complex field of study that seeks to understand why the early church rejected gnostic texts. See Craig A. Evans, *Noncanonical Writings and New Testament Interpretation* (Peabody, MA: Hendrickson, 1992); Bruce M. Metzger, *The Canon of the New Testament: Its Origin, Development, and Significance* (Oxford: Clarendon, 1987).

78. *Gospel of Philip* 73:1–3, in *The Nag Hammadi Library in English*, ed. James M. Robinson, 3rd rev. ed. (San Francisco: HarperSanFrancisco, 1990), 153.

79. The *Treatise* is also known as the *Epistle to Rheginos*. See *Nag Hammadi Library in English*, 51–57.

80. Madigan and Levenson, *Resurrection*, 223.

81. *The Gospel of Thomas*, 114, in *The Five Gospels: The Search for the Authentic Words of Jesus*, ed. Robert W. Funk et al. (New York: Macmillan, 1993), 532.

82. Irenaeus, *Against Heresies 5*, in ANF 1, ed. Robertson and Donaldson, 526–67. On Irenaeus's apologetic against gnosticism see Terrance L. Tiessen, "Gnosticism as Heresy: The Response of Irenaeus," *Did* 18 (2007): 31–48; W. H. C. Frend, *The Rise of Christianity* (Philadelphia: Fortress, 1984), 244–50.

83. J. K. S. Reid, *Christian Apologetics* (Grand Rapids: Eerdmans, 1970), 56.

84. Timothy D. Barnes, *Tertullian: A Historical and Literary Study* (Oxford: Clarendon, 1971); Mark S. Burrows, "Christianity in the Roman Forum: Tertullian and the Apologetic Use of History," *VC* 42 (1988): 209–35.

85. Ernest Evans, *Tertullian's Treatise on the Resurrection* (London: SPCK, 1960).

86. For sociological explanations on why ancient gnosticism declined see Henry Alan Green, "Suggested Sociological Themes in the Study of Gnosticism," *VC* 31 (1977): 169–80.

87. See Manfred Kwiran, *The Resurrection of the Dead: Exegesis of 1 Cor 15 in German Protestant Theology from F. C. Baur to W. Künneth* (Basel: Frederich Reinhardt, 1972).

88. Robert H. Gundry, *Sōma in Biblical Theology* (Cambridge: Cambridge University Press, 1976).

89. Joel B. Green, "Eschatology and the Nature of Humans: A Reconsideration of Pertinent Biblical Evidence," *SciCB* 14 (2002): 33–50; Nancey Murphy, "Physicalism without Reductionism:

Toward a Scientifically, Philosophically and Theologically Sound Portrait of Human Nature," *Zygon* 34 (1999): 551–71.

90. Brian Edgar, "Biblical Anthropology and the Intermediate State," *EvQ* 74 (2002): 27–45, 109–21; Joseph Ratzinger, *Eschatology: Death, and Eternal Life*, ed. A. Nichols, trans. M. Waldstein (Washington, DC: Catholic University of America Press, 1988).

91. Timothy C. Morgan, "The Mother of All Muddles," *Christianity Today*, April 5, 1993, 62–66.

92. Murray J. Harris, *Raised Immortal: Resurrection and Immortality in the New Testament* (Grand Rapids: Eerdmans, 1985).

93. Norman L. Geisler, *The Battle for the Resurrection* (Nashville: Nelson, 1989).

94. Murray J. Harris, *From Grave to Glory: Resurrection in the New Testament. Including a Reply to Dr Norman L. Geisler* (Grand Rapids: Zondervan, 1990).

95. Norman L. Geisler and Ron Rhodes, *Conviction without Compromise* (Eugene, OR: Harvest, 2008), 116.

96. Peter G. Bolt, "Life, Death and the Afterlife in the Greco-Roman World," in *Life in the Face of Death: The Resurrection Message of the New Testament*, ed. Richard N. Longenecker (Grand Rapids: Eerdmans, 1998), 51–79.

97. Kelly, *Early Christian Doctrines*, 16.

98. Jaroslav Pelikan, *The Christian Tradition: A History of the Development of Doctrine* vol. 1, *The Emergence of the Catholic Tradition (100–600)* (Chicago: University of Chicago Press, 1971), 1, 30.

99. Leslie Kline, "The *De Resurrectione Mortuorum* of Athenagoras," *ResQ* 11 (1968): 249–61.

100. Henry Chadwick, "Origen, Celsus, and the Resurrection of the Body," *HTR* 41 (1948): 83–102.

101. See Lawrence R. Hennessey, "Origen of Alexandria: The Fate of the Soul and the Body after Death," *SecCent* 8 (1991): 163–78.

102. See Ilaria L. E. Ramelli, "Christian Soteriology and Christian Platonism: Origen, Gregory of Nyssa and the Biblical and Philosophical Basis of the Doctrine of *Apokatastasis*," *VC* 61 (2007): 313–56.

103. John L. Drury, "Gregory of Nyssa's Dialogue with Macrina: The Compatibility of Resurrection of the Body and Immortality of the Soul," *ThTo* 65 (2005): 210–22.

104. Pelikan, *Christian Tradition*, 51.

105. *The First Epistle of Clement to the Corinthians* 24, in *Early Christian Writings*, trans. Staniforth, revised by Louth, 33.

106. Bynum, *Resurrection of the Body*, 24–26.

107. Ibid., 23.

108. Raniero Cantalamessa, *Easter in the Early Church: An Anthology of Jewish and Early Christian Texts*, trans. James M. Quigley and Joseph T. Lienhard (Collegeville, MN: Liturgical Press, 1993), 50–109.

109. Alistair Stewart-Sykes, *Melito of Sardis: On Pascha* (Crestwood, NY: St. Vladimir's Seminary Press, 2001).

110. Donald Guthrie, *New Testament Theology* (Leicester, UK: Inter-Varsity, 1981), 390.

111. Summary based on Kelly, *Early Christian Doctrines*, 459–89.

112. Brooke Foss Westcott, *The Gospel of the Resurrection: Thoughts on Its Relation to Reason and History*, 3rd ed. (London: Macmillan, 1874), 7–8.

Part Three Back to the Bible

1. Gregory of Nyssa, *The Great Catechism*, in NPNF 5, ed. Philip Schaff and Henry Wace (Grand Rapids: Eerdmans, 1979), 489.

Chapter 11 The New Testament

1. Walter Künneth, *The Theology of the Resurrection*, trans. James W. Leitch (London: SCM, 1965), 40.

2. Bernard L. Ramm, *An Evangelical Christology: Ecumenic and Historic* (Nashville: Nelson, 1985), 97.

3. Paul Beasley-Murray, *The Message of the Resurrection* (Leicester, UK: Inter-Varsity, 2000), 17.

4. Peter M. Head, "Jesus' Resurrection in Pauline Thought: A Study in the Epistle to the Romans," in *Proclaiming the Resurrection: Papers from the First Oak Hill College Annual School of Theology*, ed. Peter M. Head (Carlisle: Paternoster, 1998), 75.

5. Beasley-Murray, *Message of the Resurrection*, 173.

6. Ibid., 176.

7. Allison A. Trites, *The New Testament Concept of Witness* (Cambridge: Cambridge University Press, 1977), 133–35.

8. Aeschylus, *Eumenides*, 647–48.

9. Dag Øistein Endsjø, "Immortal Bodies, before Christ: Bodily Continuity in Ancient Greece and 1 Corinthians," *JSNT* 30 (2008): 417–36.

10. Don A. Carson, *The Gagging of God: Christianity Confronts Pluralism* (Grand Rapids: Zondervan, 1996), 501–5; F. F. Bruce, *Paul: Apostle of the Heart Set Free*, rev. ed. (Exeter: Paternoster, 1980), 235–47; Dean Flemming, "Contextualizing the Gospel in Athens: Paul's Areopagus Address as a Paradigm for Missionary Communication," *Miss* 30 (2002): 199–214.

11. See Ernst Haenchen, *The Acts of the Apostles: A Commentary*, trans. Bernard Noble and Gerald Shinn, rev. by R. McL. Wilson (Oxford: Blackwell, 1971), 528–30.

12. C. H. Dodd, *The Apostolic Preaching and Its Developments* (London: Hodder & Stoughton, 1944), 9. Dodd remains the authority in this field.

13. Bruce W. Winter, "Official Proceedings and the Forensic Speeches in Acts 24–26," in *The Book of Acts in Its First Century Setting*, vol. 1, *The Book of Acts in Its Ancient Literary Settings*, ed. B. W. Winter (Grand Rapids: Eerdmans, 1994), 333–36.

14. Andrew T. Lincoln, *Truth on Trial: The Lawsuit Motif in the Fourth Gospel* (Peabody, MA: Hendrickson, 2000), 169–70.

15. Paul W. Barnett, *Jesus and the Logic of History* (Leicester: Apollos, 1997), 159–61.

16. Richard Bauckham, *Jesus and the Eyewitnesses: The Gospels as Eyewitness Testimony* (Grand Rapids: Eerdmans, 2006); Samuel Byrskog, *Story as History—History as Story* (Tübingen: Mohr Siebeck, 2001), 65–91; Peter M. Head, "The Role of Eyewitnesses in the Formation of the Gospel Tradition," *TynBul* 52 (2001): 275–94.

17. Edwin A. Judge, unpublished inaugural lecture at Moore Theological College, 1968, cited in Peter F. Jensen, "History and the Resurrection of Jesus Christ—III," *Colloq* 3 (1970): 349–50.

18. Bauckham, *Jesus and the Eyewitnesses*, 10–11. See also Byrskog, *Story*, 26–33.

19. Ben Witherington, *New Testament Rhetoric: An Introductory Guide to the Art of Persuasion in and of the New Testament* (Eugene, OR: Cascade, 2009).

20. C. Clifton Black, *The Rhetoric of the Gospel: Theological Artistry in the Gospels and Acts* (St. Louis: Chalice, 2001), 128.

21. Trites, *New Testament Concept of Witness*, 114. See also Norman L. Geisler, "Johannine Apologetics," *BibSac* 136 (1979): 338.

22. John W. Wenham, *Easter Enigma*, rev. ed (Grand Rapids: Baker, 1992).

23. Derek Tidball, "Completing the Circle: The Resurrection according to John," *EvRT* 30 (2006): 182.

24. Michael Bird, " 'Jesus Is the Christ': Messianic Apologetics in the Gospel of Mark," *RTR* 64 (2005): 8–9.

25. Claudia Setzer, "Excellent Women: Female Witness to the Resurrection," *JBL* 116 (1997): 264, 266.

26. Pinchas Lapide, *The Resurrection of Jesus: A Jewish Perspective* (Minneapolis: Augsburg, 1983), 97–99.

27. William M. Ramsey, *The Bearing of Recent Discovery on the Trustworthiness of the New Testament* (repr., Grand Rapids: Baker, 1953), 221.

28. Alexandru Neagoe, *The Trial of the Gospel: An Apologetic Reading of Luke's Trial Narratives* (Cambridge: Cambridge University Press, 2002), 223–25.

29. Deborah Thompson Prince, "The 'Ghost' of Jesus: Luke 24 in Light of Ancient Narratives of Post-Mortem Appearances," *JSNT* 29 (2007): 287–301.

30. I. Howard Marshall, "Raised for Our Justification: The Saving Significance of the Resurrection of Christ," in *Tough-Minded Christianity: Honoring the Legacy of John Warwick Montgomery*, ed. William Dembski and Thomas Schirrmacher (Nashville: B & H Academic, 2008), 265.

31. Beasley-Murray, *Message of the Resurrection*, 120.

32. Paul Copan and Ronald K. Tacelli, *Jesus' Resurrection: Fact or Figment? A Debate between William Lane Craig and Gerd Lüdemann* (Downers Grove, IL: InterVarsity, 2000), 57–92, 180–98.

33. Robert H. Gundry, "Trimming the Debate," in *Jesus' Resurrection: Fact or Figment?*, ed. Copan and Tacelli, 116.

34. Sir Norman Anderson, *Jesus Christ: The Witness of History* (Leicester, UK: Inter-Varsity, 1985), 135.

35. *LW* 28:94.

36. Ibid.

37. *LW* 28: 61.

38. Marshall, "Raised for Our Justification," 261–65.

39. N. T. Wright, *The Resurrection of the Son of God* (Minneapolis: Fortress, 2003), 241.

40. J. R. Daniel Kirk, *Unlocking Romans: Resurrection and the Justification of God* (Grand Rapids: Eerdmans, 2008).

41. Jeffrey Anderson, "The Holy Spirit and Justification: A Pneumatological and Trinitarian Approach to Forensic Justification," *EvRT* 32 (2008): 300.

42. See Bird, "Justified by Christ's Resurrection," 72–91; Bruce A. Lowe, "Oh διά! How is Romans 4:25 to be Understood?" *JTS* 57 (2006): 149–57.

43. See David R. Maxwell, "The Resurrection of Christ: Its Importance in the History of the Church," *CoJ* 34 (2008): 34.

44. I. Howard Marshall, *Aspects of the Atonement: Cross and Resurrection in the Reconciling of God and Humanity* (London: Paternoster, 2007), 88.

45. Eugene H. Peterson, *Practice Resurrection: A Conversation on Growing Up in Christ* (Grand Rapids: Eerdmans, 2010), 272.

46. Agatha Christie, the number-one-selling mystery writer, grasped this, as a prized possession she left by her deathbed indicates. It was Thomas à Kempis's little instruction book *The Imitation of Christ*. On the fly-leaf in her own hand were found the words of Romans 8:35–39. On her life and faith see Agatha Christie Mallowan, *Come Tell Me How You Live*, rev. ed. (New York: Dodd Mead, 1976); Janet P. Morgan, *Agatha Christie: A Biography* (London: Collins, 1984).

47. N. T. Wright, *Surprised by Hope: Rethinking Heaven, the Resurrection, and the Mission of the Church* (New York: HarperOne, 2008), 283.

48. Bron Taylor, *Dark Green Religion: Nature Spirituality and the Planetary Future* (Berkeley: University of California Press, 2010).

49. Beasley-Murray, *Message of the Resurrection*, 228–34.

50. Ibid., 169.

Chapter 12 The Hebrew Scriptures

1. Jon D. Levenson, *Resurrection and the Restoration of Israel: The Ultimate Victory of the God of Life* (New Haven: Yale University Press, 2006), 229.

2. The general consensus is that Daniel 12:2 explicitly refers to the resurrection of the dead, and it is argued that Daniel is the last Old Testament book to be written.

3. Byron Wheaton, "As It Is Written: Old Testament Foundations for Jesus' Expectation of Resurrection," *WTJ* 70 (2008): 245–53.

4. Johannes Pedersen, *Israel: Its Life and Culture* (London: Oxford University Press, 1926), 1:153.

5. See Walter Brueggemann, "Theology of Death," in *IDBSup*, 219–20; Lloyd R. Bailey, *Biblical Perspectives on Death* (Philadelphia: Fortress, 1979), 39–47.

6. Desmond Alexander, "The Old Testament View of Life after Death," *Them* (NS) 11 (1986): 41.

7. John Barclay Burns, "The Mythology of Death in the Old Testament," *SJT* 26 (1973): 340.

8. Ibid.

9. The consensus position on Sheol is open to review. See Philip S. Johnston, *Shades of Sheol: Death and Afterlife in the Old Testament* (Downers Grove, IL: InterVarsity, 2002); Kevin J. Madigan and Jon D. Levenson, *Resurrection: The Power of God for Christians and Jews* (New Haven: Yale University Press, 2008), 42–80.

10. Our summarization derives from Levenson, *Resurrection and the Restoration of Israel*, ix–x.

11. On the resurrection in the Apocrypha and Pseudepigrapha see Anthony Petterson, "Antecedents of the Christian Hope of Resurrection, Part 2: Intertestamental Literature," *RTR* 59 (2000): 53–64; Richard Bauckham, "Resurrection as Giving Back the Dead: A Traditional Image of Resurrection in the Pseudepigrapha and the Apocalypse of John," in *The Pseudepigrapha and Early Biblical Interpretation*, ed. James H. Charlesworth and Craig A. Evans, Journal for the Study of the Pseudepigrapha Supplement Series 14 (Sheffield: Sheffield Academic Press, 1993), 269–91.

12. Theodore H. Gaster, "Resurrection," in *IDB*, 39.

13. D. S. Russell, *The Method and Message of Jewish Apocalyptic* (Philadelphia: Westminster, 1964); Paul D. Hanson, *The Dawn of Apocalyptic* (Philadelphia: Fortress, 1975).

14. John Bright, *A History of Israel*, rev. ed. (London: SCM, 1972), 426–29, supports a Maccabean era date. D. J. Wiseman et al., *Notes on Some Problems in the Book of Daniel* (London: Tyndale, 1965), argue for an earlier date. For an overview see William Sanford La Sor, David Allan Hubbard, and Frederic William Bush, *Old Testament Survey: The Message, Form and Background of the Old Testament*, 2nd ed. (Grand Rapids: Eerdmans, 1996), 566–82.

15. The principal Canaanite myths are found in J. C. L. Gibson, *Canaanite Myths and Legends*, 2nd ed. (Edinburgh: T & T Clark, 1978). On Canaanite culture and Israel see Peter C. Craigie, *Ugarit and the Old Testament* (Grand Rapids: Eerdmans, 1983).

16. Shaul Shaked, "Iranian Influence on Judaism: First Century BCE to Second Century CE," in *Cambridge History of Judaism*, ed. W. D. Davies and Louis Finkelstein (New York: Cambridge University Press, 1984), 1:308–25.

17. Bright, *History of Israel*, 453.

18. Bernhard Lang, "Street Theater, Raising the Dead, and the Zoroastrian Connection in Ezekiel's Prophecy," in *Ezekiel and His Book: Textual and Literary Criticism and Their Interrelation*, ed. Johan Lust (Leuven: Leuven University Press, 1986), 297–316.

19. John L. McKenzie, *A Theology of the Old Testament* (Garden City, NY: Doubleday, 1974), 307–8.

20. Levenson, *Resurrection and the Restoration of Israel*, xiii.

21. See Leonard J. Greenspoon, "The Origin of the Idea of Resurrection," in *Traditions in Transformation: Turning Points in Biblical Faith*, ed. Baruch Halpern and Jon D. Levenson (Winona Lake, IN: Eisenbrauns, 1981), 247–321, esp. 262–81.

22. Levenson, *Resurrection and the Restoration of Israel*, 208–13.

23. Madigan and Levenson, *Resurrection*, 193.

24. Greenspoon, "Origin," 258.

25. Ibid., 259.

26. Anthony Petterson, "Antecedents of the Christian Hope of Resurrection, Part 1: The Old Testament," *RTR* 59 (2000): 4.

27. Levenson, *Resurrection and the Restoration of Israel*, 108–22.

28. Ibid., 29.

29. Ibid., 30.

30. Ibid., 119.

31. Petterson, "Antecedents," 4.

32. Ibid.

33. Robert Martin-Achard, *From Death to Life: A Study of the Development of the Resurrection in the Old Testament*, trans. John Penney Smith (Edinburgh: Oliver & Boyd, 1960), 57.

34. R. P. Gordon, *1 and 2 Samuel: A Commentary*, TOTC (Grand Rapids: Zondervan, 1986), 80.

35. Petterson, "Antecedents," 5.

36. Levenson, *Resurrection and the Restoration of Israel*, xii.

37. Madigan and Levenson, *Resurrection*, 121–31.

38. Levenson, *Resurrection and the Restoration of Israel*, 99–102.

39. Petterson, "Antecedents," 3.

40. Francis I. Andersen, *Job*, TOTC (Leicester, UK: Inter-Varsity, 1976), 194.

41. Petterson, "Antecedents," 7.

42. William J. Dumbrell, *The End of the Beginning* (Sydney: Lancer, 1985), 167–71.

43. Petterson, "Antecedents," 5.

44. Ibid., 8.

45. Another death-refusing image is the temple of God which replaces Eden as heaven on earth. It is the dwelling-place that is the antipode of death. See Madigan and Levenson, *Resurrection*, 81–106.

46. Daniel I. Block, *The Book of Ezekiel Chapters 25–48*, NICOT (Grand Rapids: Eerdmans, 1998), 383–92.

47. Joseph E. Coleson, "Israel's Life Cycle from Birth to Resurrection," in *Israel's Apostasy and Restoration: Essays in Honor of Roland K. Harrison*, ed. Avraham Gileadi (Grand Rapids: Baker, 1988), 237–50.

48. Levenson, *Resurrection and the Restoration of Israel*, 143, 144, 145, and 153.

49. Petterson, "Antecedents," 9–10.

50. Ben C. Ollenburger, "If Mortals Die, Will They Live Again? The Old Testament and Resurrection," *ExAud* 9 (1993): 39.

51. Ibid., 40.

52. Levenson, *Resurrection and the Restoration of Israel*, xii.

53. Block, *Book of Ezekiel*, 379–92.

54. John F. A. Sawyer, "Hebrew Words for the Resurrection of the Dead," *VT* 23 (1973): 218–34.

55. See Bauckham, "Resurrection," 269–91.

56. Greenspoon, "Origin," 317–18.

57. Winston Leonard Spencer Churchill, "The End of the Beginning," delivered on November 10, 1942, at the Lord Mayor's Luncheon in Mansion House, London. The speech was published in *New York Times*, November 11, 1942, available online at http://www.ibiblio.org/pha/policy/1942/421110b.html. It is also reproduced in Charles Eade, *The End of the Beginning: War Speeches by the Right Hon. Winston S. Churchill* (Boston: Little, Brown, 1943), 225.

Part Four Resurrection Horizons

1. N. T. Wright, *Acts for Everyone: Part 2 Chapters 13–28* (London: SPCK; Louisville: Westminster John Knox, 2008), 93.

Ross Clifford is the principal of Morling Theological College, which is the largest Baptist seminary in Australia. Prior to joining the Morling faculty as head of theology he was a pastor for twelve years, and before that he practiced law. He often speaks at conferences and has for thirteen years had his own top-rated Sunday night radio program, *Connections*. He is the past president of the Baptist Union of Australia. His doctorate is with the Australian College of Theology, and he also holds a postgraduate qualification with the University of Sydney. He is the author/coauthor of nine books, including *Jesus and the Gods of the New Age,* which has become a key reference book for missional models. In particular Ross is known for writing and ministering in the area of theology that connects belief to the marketplace.

Philip Johnson is a graduate of the University of Sydney (BA, BD) and Australian College of Theology (MTh), and has been a guest lecturer at Morling College for sixteen years. With Ross he cofounded the Community of Hope ministry in alternate spirituality festivals. He is a cofounding editor of *Sacred Tribes Journal* and coauthor of *Jesus and the Gods of the New Age, Riding the Rollercoaster, Beyond Prediction,* and *Beyond the Burning Times.* He is also a contributor to the *Baker Dictionary of Cults, Encountering New Religious Movements,* and *Tough-Minded Christianity,* and had peer-reviewed essays published in *Lutheran Theological Journal, Missiology,* and *Australian Religion Studies Review.*

RESURRECTION HOPE

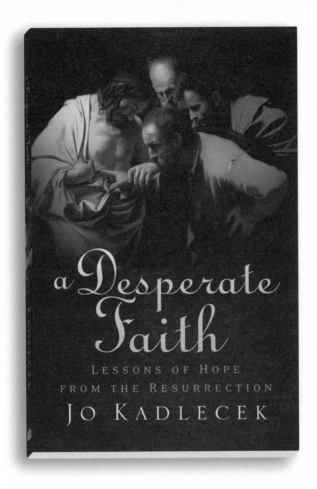

In this fascinating book of stories, Jo Kadlecek explores the time Jesus spent on earth after his resurrection from the dead. She serves as a guide through each story, revealing what happens when once desperate and fearful friends encounter the risen Lord. Their lives—and all of history—were changed for good. And she invites you to enter the story, discovering anew how every part of your life can be transformed by the unprecedented truth of the once dead, now living Jesus.

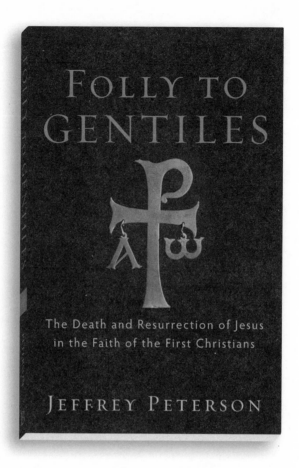

THE TINSLEY INSTITUTE
A Center for the Study of Global Mission

The Tinsley Institute was founded in 1999 by missiologist Michael Frost for the purpose of motivating, equipping, and resourcing both individual Christians and churches for evangelism, church health, and cross-cultural mission. At present our primary focus centers on the development of missional leaders who are prepared for Christian service in both the West and the Majority World, and are able to take God's Word to God's world in contextualized and effective ways.

Tinsley operates at three broad, related levels:

1. the provision of training in evangelism, contextualization and cross-cultural mission, church planting, and apologetics;

2. academic study at both graduate and postgraduate level, including research, of methods of evangelism and world mission, including reflection on and examination of postmodern, pluralistic culture, and examination of church history regarding evangelism and world mission;

3. the development of a base for resourcing existing practitioners of evangelism and mission, including the development of a specialist library, the production of resources (video, audio, web-based, etc.) for practitioners, and the publishing of research pertinent to evangelism and mission.

Past guest lecturers and trainers have included Ross Clifford, Alan Hirsch, Erwin McManus, George Barna, Chris Wright, Alan Roxburgh, Stuart Murray, William Lane Craig, and Vinoth Ramachandra, among many others.

The Tinsley Institute offers internships, seminars, conferences, and public lectures, and continues to host and broker networks of church planters, cross-cultural missionaries, and church leaders for the purpose of generating greater missional health in the church.

We have recently extended our influence to include a department of public theology, making contributions to academic and public policy debates on social and ethical issues from an evangelical perspective.

• *www.morling.nsw.edu.au/tinsley_institute* •